FUNDAMENTALS OF
SUPPLY CHAIN THEORY

FUNDAMENTALS OF SUPPLY CHAIN THEORY

Lawrence V. Snyder
Lehigh University

Zuo-Jun Max Shen
University of California, Berkeley

A JOHN WILEY & SONS, INC., PUBLICATION

Library of Congress Cataloging-in-Publication Data:

Snyder, Lawrence V., 1975–
  Fundamentals of supply chain theory / Lawrence V. Snyder, Zuo-Jun Max Shen.
    p. cm.
  Includes bibliographical references and index.
  ISBN 978-0-470-52130-4 (hardback)
1. Business logistics. I. Shen, Zuo-Jun Max, 1970– II. Title.
  HD38.5.S6256 2011
  658.701—dc22   2011012196

Printed in the United States of America.

10 9 8 7 6 5 4 3 2

To Suzanne and Matilda
–L.V.S.

To Irene, Michelle, and
Jeffrey
–Z.-J.M.S.

CONTENTS IN BRIEF

CONTENTS

LIST OF FIGURES

LIST OF TABLES

PREFACE

Goals of This Book

The field of supply chain management arose from managers' recognition that buying, selling, manufacturing, assembling, warehousing, transporting, and delivering goods—that is, the activities of a supply chain—are expensive endeavors, and that careful attention to how these activities are carried out may reduce their cost. Supply chains used to be viewed, at least by some managers, as "necessary evils." As a result, the mindset for supply chain managers revolved around reducing costs, by reducing inventory levels, taking advantage of economies of scale in shipping, optimizing network designs, reducing volatility in demands, and so on. By and large, these improvements were invisible to companies' customers, provided that they did not result in longer lead times, more frequent stockouts, or other degraded service.

By the end of the last century, however, the purpose of the supply chain had begun to change as some firms discovered that supply chains could be a source of competitive advantage, rather than simply a cost driver. For example, Dell demonstrated that, through excellent supply chain management, it could deliver computers—fully customized to the buyer's specifications—just a few days after they were ordered. In doing so, it shattered the existing paradigm for computer purchases, in which consumers could choose from only a limited number of pre-configured options. Similarly, Walmart showed that, by operating an extremely high-volume supply chain, it could land products on shelves for less money per item. As a result, Walmart offered its customers a high level of product availability and low prices, and this combination ushered the company to its place as the world's largest retailer. Amazon.com built a supply chain that is not only quick and reliable, but also feature-rich, offering users varied shipping options, convenient tracking tools, and flexible return policies. This expansive supply chain has allowed Amazon to overcome consumers' desire for instant gratification and their preference for seeing and touching products before they buy them.

Just as the *practice* of supply chain management has come into its own, so, we would argue, has the *study* of supply chain management. In the past 30 years or so, a huge number of papers have been published that introduce mathematical models for evaluating, analyzing, and optimizing supply chains. Supply chain management became one of the most popular applications of operations research (OR), and one of its greatest success stories. But recently, the mathematical study of supply chains has begun to be viewed not simply as an application area for OR tools, but rather as a methodological area, capable of standing on its own two feet, with its own tools and theory. These tools are now themselves starting to be applied, not just to supply chains, but to health care, energy, finance, the service sector, and other industries.

We wrote this book to help codify the foundations of this emerging supply chain theory and to demonstrate how recent developments build upon the classical models. Our focus is primarily on the seminal models and algorithms of supply chain theory— the building blocks that underlie much of the supply chain literature. We believe that an understanding of these models provides researchers with a sort of guidebook to the literature, as well as a toolbox to draw from when developing new models. We also discuss some more recent models that demonstrate how the classical models can be extended and applied in richer settings. These models provide graduate students and other new researchers in the field with some examples of the trajectory of research on supply chain theory—how the building blocks can be assembled to create something more complex, interesting, or useful.

Studying supply chain theory as a whole allows us the luxury of gaining some perspective on the field as a whole, a perspective that is not always evident when we immerse ourselves deeply in the literature on a particular topic. To that end, wherever possible, we have attempted to highlight the connections among supply chain models—for example, the conceptual similarities among different supply chain pooling models, the ways that inventory and location models can be combined, or the ways that inventory theory interacts with game theory to produce supply chain coordination models.

Who Should Read This Book

This book was written for anyone who is interested in mathematical approaches for studying supply chains. This includes people from a wide range of disciplines, such as industrial engineering/operations research, mathematics, management, economics, computer science, and finance. This also includes students (primarily graduate students), faculty, researchers, and practitioners of supply chain theory. And it includes scholars who are new to supply chain theory and want a gentle but rigorous introduction to it, or scholars who are well versed in the field and want a refresher or a reference for the seminal models. Finally, since you are holding this book, it most likely includes you.

One of the hallmarks—and, in our opinion, the great pleasures—of supply chain theory is that it makes use of a wide variety of the tools of operations research, mathematics, and computer science. In this book, you will find mathematical programming models (linear, integer, nonlinear, stochastic, robust), duality theory, optimization techniques (Lagrangian relaxation, column generation, dynamic programming, line search, plus optimization by calculus and finite differences), heuristics and approximations, probability, stochastic processes, game theory, simulation, and convexity theory.

To make use of this book, you need not be an expert in all of these. (We are not.) We assume that you are familiar with basic optimization theory—that you know how to formulate a linear program and its dual, that you know how branch and bound works, and that you can perform a simple line search method such as bisection search. We also assume that you understand probability distributions and know how to compute expectations of random variables and functions thereof. We assume that your calculus is in good working order, that you can compute derivatives and integrals, including ones that involve multiple variables or other derivatives or integrals. We assume you have met Markov chains before, but we don't require you to remember much about them. For just about everything else, we will start from the ground up and tell you (or remind you of) what you need to know in order to understand the topic at hand. For some topics, you will find a useful reference in Appendix C, which lists formulas for calculating expectations, loss functions, geometric series, and some tricky derivatives and integrals. Because Lagrangian relaxation plays a role in several chapters of this book, we have included a brief primer on that topic in Appendix D.

Probably the single most important prerequisite for this book is a high level of general mathematical maturity. We discuss a lot of mathematical proofs, and ask you to write your own in the homework problems. If you do not have much experience in this area, you may find the proofs to be the most challenging aspect of this book. To help you out, we have included in Appendix B a short guide to proof-writing. We hope this appendix will familiarize you with some of the basic principles of proof-writing, as well as some of the finer points of proof style and syntax. But, proof-writing is perhaps more art than science, and the appendix will only get you so far. You will learn to be a good proof-writer mainly by practicing the craft.

Organization of This Book

Our intention in writing this book was to cover a broad range of topics in supply chain theory, even if that meant that we could not cover some topics as deeply as we might have liked. Most of the material in this book is derived from earlier papers, and of course we have cited those papers carefully so that readers can delve deeper into any topics they wish. We have also cited important related references, and review articles where possible, so that readers can find more information about topics that interest them.

This book is, loosely speaking, organized into two sections. The first section (Chapters 2–9) covers *centralized* supply chain models, in which all of the decision variables are under the control of a single decision maker. Most classical supply chain models, such as those for optimizing inventories and facility locations, are centralized models. In contrast, the *decentralized* models of the second section (Chapters 10–12) involve multiple parties with independent, conflicting objectives and the autonomy to choose their decision variables to optimize those objectives. The bullwhip effect (Chapter 10) is an example of a result of this decentralization, while the models of Chapter 11 and 12 discuss strategies for mitigating the negative effects of decentralization.

The chapters of this book are as follows:

- Chapter 1 ("Introduction") gives an overview of supply chain management and defines terms that we will use throughout the book.

- Chapter 2 ("Forecasting and Demand Modeling") discusses classical forecasting methods as well as three approaches—the Bass diffusion model, leading indicators, and choice models—that have been used more recently to predict demand. We refer to these latter approaches as "demand modeling" to differentiate them from classical forecasting techniques and to emphasize the fact that they are also applied to problems outside of forecasting.

- We discuss classical single-location inventory models in Chapters 3 ("Deterministic Inventory Models") and 4 ("Stochastic Inventory Models"). For most of these models, we discuss how to formulate the objective function as well as how to optimize it—exactly or heuristically, in closed form or using algorithms—by our choice of inventory parameters. We also prove the optimality of base-stock and (s, S) policies for problems without and with (respectively) fixed costs.

- In Chapter 5 ("Multi-Echelon Inventory Models"), we discuss multi-echelon inventory models, including both stochastic-service models (including the Clark–Scarf model for serial systems and the Shang and Song approximation) and guaranteed-service models (also known as strategic safety stock placement problems).

- Chapter 6 ("Dealing with Uncertainty in Inventory Optimization") builds upon the classical inventory models by considering different types of uncertainty—in particular, supply uncertainty—and different ways to mitigate uncertainty within an inventory system other than simply holding more inventory.

- In Chapter 7 ("Facility Location Models"), we turn our attention to facility location models. We present the classical uncapacitated fixed-charge location problem (UFLP) in some detail, including its formulation as an integer programming problem and its solution by Lagrangian relaxation. We also discuss a multi-echelon location model that more accurately represents the complexity of today's supply chains.

- In Chapter 8 ("Dealing with Uncertainty in Facility Location"), we consider the ways in which uncertainty can be incorporated into facility location models. We discuss a model that incorporates inventory into the location decisions, models for stochastic and robust facility location, and a model for locating facilities under the threat of disruptions. We discuss formulations for these problems as well as solution methods (in most cases, Lagrangian relaxation).

- Chapter 9 ("Process Flexibility") discusses models for evaluating the benefit of manufacturing process flexibility and for optimizing the flexibility within manufacturing processes.

- In Chapter 10 ("The Bullwhip Effect") we discuss a phenomenon of demand variability amplification known as the bullwhip effect. The bullwhip effect can occur because of irrational or suboptimal behavior on the part of supply chain managers, but it can also occur as the result of rational, optimizing behavior. We cover mathematical models for proving that the bullwhip effect occurs as a result of the latter type.

- When supply chain partners each optimize their own objective functions, they typically arrive at solutions that are suboptimal from the point of view of the total supply chain. In Chapter 11 ("Supply Chain Contracts"), we discuss contracts that achieve coordination within a supply chain made up of individual players with differing objectives.

- Chapter 12 ("Auctions") introduces mathematical models for auctions, which are frequently used to set prices within supply chains.

- The book concludes with four appendices. Appendix A contains homework problems whose solutions use material from multiple chapters. Appendix B provides a short primer on how to write mathematical proofs. Appendix C lists helpful formulas that are used throughout the book. Appendix D gives a brief overview of Lagrangian relaxation.

The material in this book can accommodate a good deal of reordering and omission by the instructor. The only real exception is the inventory-theoretic material (Chapters 3–5), which is at the core of much of the subsequent material in the book and therefore should be covered early on, and in the order presented. However, not all of the material in the inventory chapters is used elsewhere, and much of it can be skipped if desired. A bare-bones treatment of the essential inventory topics would include Section 3.2 on the EOQ model, Section 4.3 on (r, Q) policies, and Section 4.4.2 on the newsvendor problem—and even this material could be omitted for students who are already familiar with it. In addition, the material on facility location under uncertainty (Chapter 8) relies on the chapter that precedes it. Other than these, there are no other precedence constraints regarding the sequence of material covered, and the instructor should feel free to rearrange the material according to his or her preferences, interests, and expertise, as well as those of the students.

Each of the chapters (except Chapter 1) is followed by a set of homework problems, and Appendix A presents problems that use material from multiple chapters. The problems challenge readers to understand, interpret, and extend the models and algorithms discussed in the text. Some of them involve simply applying the models and algorithms presented in the book as-is. Most of them, however, ask the reader to prove theorems, develop models, or somehow explore the material more deeply than it is covered in the chapters. Some of the problems require data sets that are too large to include in the text itself. These data sets are posted on the web site for this book at http://coral.ie.lehigh.edu/~sctheory.

That web site also contains a list of errata. If you find errors not contained on this list, please e-mail them to larry.snyder@lehigh.edu.

An instructor's manual containing full solutions to the homework problems is available to professors. Please send requests for the instructor's manual on department letterhead, by mail, fax, or e-mail, to Jackie Palmieri, Assistant Editor, John Wiley & Sons, Inc., 111 River Street, MS 8-01, Hoboken, NJ 07030, USA, (201) 748-8888 (fax), jpalmier@wiley.com.

Acknowledgments

We owe a debt of gratitude to many people for many reasons. First, we wish to thank our editor at Wiley, Susanne Steitz-Filler, as well as Melissa Yanuzzi, Jackie Palmieri, and the rest of the editorial team at Wiley, for championing the book and bringing it to fruition.

We would like to thank our professors at Northwestern University who taught us while we were graduate students there. Special thanks go to Mark Daskin and David Simchi-Levi, who served as our advisors and mentors. Many of the results in Chapter 8 are the result of our collaborations with Mark. Both Mark and David are outstanding researchers, excellent teachers, and generous, supportive advisors—not to mention accomplished textbook authors—and we would not be the professors we are without them.

We thank our colleagues at Lehigh and Berkeley, as well as our current and former Ph.D. students, especially Zümbül Atan, Gang Chen, Leon Chu, Tingting Cui, Tianhu Deng, Çağrı Latifoğlu, Shan Li, Ho-Yin Mak, Lian Qi, Ying Rong, Amanda Schmitt, Ye Xu, and Lezhou Zhan, for contributing to this book through their research collaborations (some of which are reflected in the material in this book) and the many productive discussions we have had with them about research and teaching.

This book emerged from lecture notes we developed for our graduate-level supply chain courses at Lehigh and Berkeley. Many students suffered through the early versions of these notes. Their questions, suggestions, and confused faces helped us find and correct errors and improve the exposition throughout the book. Tingting Cui, Ho-Yin Mak, Scott DeNegre, Kewen Liang, Gokhan Metan, Cory Minglegreen, Jack Oh, Jim Ostrowski, and Ye Xu, among others, made insightful comments that resulted in a better explanation, an interesting new homework problem, or an elegant solution to a homework problem.

Tolga Seyhan provided invaluable assistance with the preparation of this book, crafting many of the figures, writing the index, assembling references, and lending us his impeccable attention to detail. We also thank Pete Ferrari for helping us build BibTeX databases, Amy Hendrickson of TeXnology, Inc. for sharing her expertise in all things LaTeX, and Andrew Ross for his patient answers to questions about stochastic processes.

Finally, and most importantly, we thank our families—Suzanne, Irene, Matilda, Michelle, and Jeffrey—and our extended families for their support, love, encouragement, and guidance as we wrote this book.

CHAPTER 1

INTRODUCTION

1.1 OVERVIEW OF SUPPLY CHAIN MANAGEMENT

The term **supply chain management** is difficult to define, and its definition has changed over time as the purposes and components of supply chains have evolved. Perhaps the most authoritative definition comes from the Council of Supply Chain Management Professionals (CSCMP), who define supply chain management as follows:

> Supply chain management encompasses the planning and management of all activities involved in sourcing and procurement, conversion, and all logistics management activities. Importantly, it also includes coordination and collaboration with channel partners, which can be suppliers, intermediaries, third party service providers, and customers. In essence, supply chain management integrates supply and demand management within and across companies. (Council of Supply Chain Management Professionals (CSCMP) 2011)

In the interest of keeping things a little simpler, we offer the following definitions:

> A *supply chain* consists of the activities and infrastructure whose purpose is to move products from where they are produced to where they are consumed. *Supply chain management* is the set of practices required to perform the functions of a supply chain and to make them more efficient, less costly, and more profitable.

Fundamentals of Supply Chain Theory, First Edition. Lawrence V. Snyder, Zuo-Jun Max Shen.
© 2011 John Wiley & Sons, Inc. Published 2011 by John Wiley & Sons, Inc.

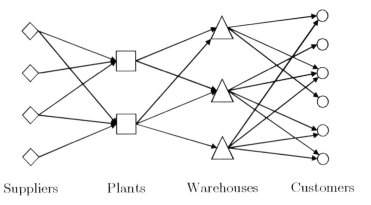

Suppliers   Plants   Warehouses   Customers

Figure 1.1   Schematic diagram of supply chain network.

Supply chain management costs firms over US$1 trillion per year in the United States alone (Council of Supply Chain Management Professionals (CSCMP) 2010), representing nearly 10% of gross domestic product (GDP). These practices include a huge range of tasks, such as forecasting, production planning, inventory management, warehouse location, supplier selection, procurement, and shipping. Mathematical models have been developed to analyze and optimize each of these practices, and these models are the primary focus of this book.

The terms "logistics" or "logistics management" are closely related to "supply chain management." In fact, we consider them to be roughly synonymous.

Supply chains are often represented graphically as a schematic *network* that illustrates the relationships between its elements. (See Figure 1.1.) Each vertical "level" of the supply chain (suppliers, plants, etc.) is called an *echelon*. A location in the network is referred to as a *stage* or *node*. The links between stages represent some type of flow—typically, the flow of goods, but sometimes the flow of information or money. The portion of the supply chain from which products originate (the left-hand portion in Figure 1.1) is referred to as *upstream*, while the demand end is referred to as *downstream*.

Actually, the phrase "supply chain" is a bit of a misnomer, since "chain" implies a linear system like the one pictured in Figure 1.2. In this system, sometimes referred to as a *serial system*, each echelon has only a single stage. But today's supply chains more closely resemble the complex network in Figure 1.1; each echelon may have dozens, hundreds, or even thousands of nodes. (Nevertheless, we will often study serial systems of the type pictured in Figure 1.2. Even more frequently, we will study single-stage systems.)

The models we study generally try to find the least-cost or greatest-profit solution that satisfies some constraints. For example, a firm might want to choose warehouse locations to minimize transportation costs, subject to the constraint that every customer must be served. Or it might want to decide how much inventory should

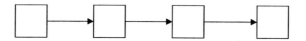

Figure 1.2   Supply "chain."

be stored at a given warehouse in order to minimize the cost of holding inventory, subject to a "service level" constraint that requires a certain percentage of customer orders to be satisfied on time. Or it might want to design a contract with its supplier to maximize its own profit, or that of the supply chain as a whole.

The ideal supply chain management model would *globally* optimize every aspect of the supply chain, but such a model is impossible both because of the difficulties in modeling some aspects of the supply chain mathematically, and because the resulting model would be too large and complex to solve. Instead, supply chain models typically focus on *local* optimization of one element of the supply chain, or on the integration of two or more aspects of the supply chain, generally in less detail.

1.2   LEVELS OF DECISION MAKING IN SUPPLY CHAIN MANAGEMENT

It is convenient to think about three levels of supply chain management decisions: strategic, tactical, and operational.

- *Strategic* aspects of the supply chain involve decisions that take effect over a long time horizon, typically years or decades. These aspects have a major impact on all functions of the firm. Examples include locations and sizes of warehouses, locations and capabilities of factories, and contracts with suppliers.

- *Tactical* aspects of the supply chain involve decisions over a moderate time horizon like months. Tactical decisions can be changed periodically but generally with some difficulty. Examples include assignments of customers to warehouses and inventory replenishment policies at warehouses.

- *Operational* aspects of the supply chain occur over short planning horizons like days or weeks, during which policies must be executed but cannot be changed. Examples include filling customer orders and routing of delivery vehicles.

The models in this book are mostly concerned with strategic and tactical decisions.

1.3   APPLICATIONS OF SUPPLY CHAIN MANAGEMENT

Although the models and algorithms in this book are most commonly applied to traditional, private-sector supply chains, many can be applied to new kinds of supply chains, and even to areas we might not think of as supply chains. Understanding the building blocks of traditional supply chains will prepare you to understand more recent applications of supply chain theory, a few of which are briefly discussed below.

"Green" Supply Chains: Companies, like individuals, are increasingly concerned about their environmental impacts, and many have begun to make their supply chains "greener." Some companies have started to look at overall supply chain carbon emissions, from the burning of fuel in truck engines to the generation of power to maintain warehouse temperatures. However, early research on supply chain emissions has tended to focus narrowly on one aspect of the supply chain at a time, ignoring the internal dynamics of the supply chain. There is a need to develop integrated supply chain models that evaluate the environmental impacts of suppliers, manufacturers, and distributors in order to make environmentally sound decisions. Some of the topics covered in this book, especially the models that integrate multiple functions of the supply chain, may help lay the groundwork for such research.

Energy: Historically, electricity grids have functioned like the ultimate just-in-time supply chains, with no (or very little) inventory and almost instantaneous delivery of goods (i.e., energy). However, the modernization of electricity grids will provide new opportunities for optimizing their design and operation. Tomorrow's grids are likely to look a lot like today's supply chains, with inventories (in the form of large-scale batteries and other storage devices), supply uncertainty (from volatile renewable generation sources such as wind and solar), demanding customer service requirements (as electricity markets continue to become deregulated and new competitors enter the marketplace), and novel pricing schemes (enabled by new communication infrastructure that can communicate pricing information in real time). In addition, classical principles of facility location will play a role in designing these grids, as will newer models for robust and resilient network design, as it becomes increasingly important to protect the grid from accidental or intentional disruptions that can affect the lives and livelihoods of millions of people. By viewing the grid as a supply chain network, we can leverage existing tools to develop a new generation of electricity systems.

Health Care: The portion of the United States gross domestic product (GDP) that is devoted to health care is roughly equal to the entire GDP of China, and health care costs continue to grow. The health care system encompasses many complex supply chains, and there are many opportunities to improve the operations of these supply chains using the tools discussed in this book. Moreover, there are "virtual" supply chains within the health care system—flows of people, expertise, money, and other resources whose behavior can be modeled using many of the same techniques. In addition, the health care system consists of a huge number of individual parties—hospitals, doctors, insurers, pharmaceutical and device companies, patients—with often conflicting objectives. Coordination models of the type covered in this book will be useful tools for ensuring that the net result of the interactions among these parties is beneficial to patients and to society as a whole.

CHAPTER 2

FORECASTING AND DEMAND MODELING

2.1 INTRODUCTION

Demand forecasting is one of the most fundamental tasks that a business must perform. It can be a significant source of competitive advantage by improving customer service levels and by reducing costs related to supply–demand mismatches. The goal of forecasting is to estimate the quantity of a product or service that consumers will purchase.

Most classical forecasting techniques involve time-series methods that require substantial historical data. Some of these methods are designed for demands that are stable over time. Others can handle demands that exhibit trends or seasonality, but even these require the trends to be stable and predictable. However, products today have shorter and shorter life cycles, in part driven by rapid technology upgrades for high-tech products. As a result, firms have much less historical data available to use for forecasting, and any trends that may be evident in historical data may be unreliable for predicting the future.

In this chapter, we first discuss some classical methods for *forecasting* demand, in Section 2.2. Then we discuss several methods that can be used to predict demands for new products or products that do not have much historical data. To distinguish these

Fundamentals of Supply Chain Theory, First Edition. Lawrence V. Snyder, Zuo-Jun Max Shen.
© 2011 John Wiley & Sons, Inc. Published 2011 by John Wiley & Sons, Inc.

methods from classical time-series-based methods, we call them *demand modeling* techniques.

The methods that we discuss in this chapter are theory-based. They all involve mathematical models with parameters that must be calibrated. In contrast, some popular methods for forecasting demand with little or no historical data, such as the *Delphi method*, rely on experts' qualitative assessments or questionnaires to develop forecasts.

Demand processes may exhibit various forms of non-stationarity over time. These include:

- *Trends*: Demand consistently increases or decreases over time.

- *Seasonality*: Demand shows peaks and valleys at consistent intervals.

- *Product life cycles*: Demand goes through phases of rapid growth, maturity, and decline.

Moreover, demands exhibit *random error*—variations that cannot be explained or predicted—and this randomness is typically superimposed on any underlying non-stationarity.

2.2 CLASSICAL DEMAND FORECASTING METHODS

Classical forecasting methods use prior demand history to generate a forecast. Some of the methods, such as moving average and (single) exponential smoothing, assume that past patterns of demand will continue into the future, that is, no trend is present. As a result, these techniques are best used for mature products with a large amount of historical data. On the other hand, regression analysis and double and triple exponential smoothing can account for a trend or other pattern in the data. We discuss each of these methods next.

In each of the models below, we use $D_1, D_2, \ldots, D_t, \ldots$ to represent the historical demand data, i.e., the realized demands in periods $1, 2, \ldots, t, \ldots$. We also use y_t to denote the forecast of period t's demand that is made in period $t - 1$.

2.2.1 Moving Average

The *moving average* method calculates the average amount of demand over a given time period and uses this average to predict the future demand. As a result, moving average forecasts work best for demand that has no trend or seasonality.

A moving average forecast of order N uses the N most recent observed demands. The forecast for the demand in period t is simply given by

$$y_t = \frac{1}{N} \sum_{i=t-N}^{t-1} D_i. \tag{2.1}$$

That is, the forecast is simply the arithmetic mean of the previous N observations. This is known as a *simple moving average forecast of order N*.

A generalization of the simple moving average forecast is the *weighted moving average*, which allows each period to carry a different weight. For instance, if more recent demand is deemed more relevant, then the forecaster can assign larger weights to recent demands than to older ones. If w_i is the weight placed on the demand in period i, then the weighted moving average forecast is given by

$$ y_t = \frac{\sum_{i=t-N}^{t-1} w_i D_i}{\sum_{i=t-N}^{t-1} w_i}. \tag{2.2} $$

Typically, the weights decrease by 1 in each period: $w_{t-1} = N$, $w_{t-2} = N - 1, \ldots,$ $w_{t-N} = 1$.

2.2.2 Exponential Smoothing

Exponential smoothing is a technique that uses a weighted moving average of past data as the basis for the forecast. It gives more weight to recent information and smaller weight to observations in the past. Single exponential smoothing assumes that the demand process is stationary. Double exponential smoothing assumes that there is a trend, while triple exponential smoothing accounts for both trends and seasonality. These methods all require user-specified parameters that determine the relative weights placed on recent and older observations when predicting the demand, trend, and seasonality. These three weights are called, respectively, the *smoothing factor*, the *trend factor*, and the *seasonality factor*. We discuss each of these three methods next.

2.2.2.1 *Single Exponential Smoothing*   Define $0 < \alpha \leq 1$ as the smoothing constant. Then we can express the current forecast as the weighted average of the previous forecast and most recently observed demand value:

$$ y_t = \alpha D_{t-1} + (1 - \alpha)y_{t-1}. \tag{2.3} $$

Note that α is the weight placed on the demand observation and $1 - \alpha$ is the weight placed on last forecast. Typically we place more weight on the previous forecast, so α is closer to 0 than to 1.
  Using (2.3), we can write

$$ y_{t-1} = \alpha D_{t-2} + (1 - \alpha)y_{t-2}, $$

so

$$ y_t = \alpha D_{t-1} + \alpha(1 - \alpha)D_{t-2} + (1 - \alpha)^2 y_{t-2}. $$

We can continue the substitution in this way and eventually obtain

$$ y_t = \sum_{i=0}^{\infty} \alpha(1 - \alpha)^i D_{t-i-1} = \sum_{i=0}^{\infty} \alpha_i D_{t-i-1}, $$

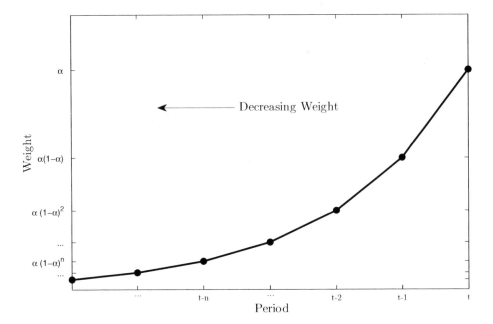

Figure 2.1   Weight distribution.

where $\alpha_i = \alpha(1 - \alpha)^i$. The single exponential smoothing forecast includes all past observations, but since $\alpha_i < \alpha_j$ for $i > j$, the weights are decreasing as we move backward in time, as illustrated in Figure 2.1. Moreover,

$$\sum_{i=0}^{\infty} \alpha_i = \sum_{i=0}^{\infty} \alpha(1 - \alpha)^i = 1$$

by (C.20) in Appendix C. These weights can be approximated with an exponential function $f(i) = \alpha e^{-\alpha i}$. This is why this method is called exponential smoothing.

2.2.2.2   *Double Exponential Smoothing*   Double exponential smoothing can be used to forecast demands with a linear trend. The forecast for the demand in period t is the sum of two separate estimates from period $t - 1$: one of the *base signal* (the value of the trend) and one of the *slope*. That is,

$$y_t = I_{t-1} + S_{t-1}, \tag{2.4}$$

where I_{t-1} is the estimate of the base signal and S_{t-1} is the estimate of the slope, both made in period $t - 1$. I_{t-1} represents our estimate of where the demand process fell in period $t - 1$; in period t, the process will be S_{t-1} units greater. The estimates of the base signal and slope are calculated as follows:

$$I_t = \alpha D_t + (1 - \alpha)(I_{t-1} + S_{t-1}) \tag{2.5}$$

$$S_t = \beta(I_t - I_{t-1}) + (1 - \beta)S_{t-1}, \tag{2.6}$$

where α is the smoothing constant and β is the trend constant. Equation (2.5) is similar to (2.3) for single exponential smoothing in the sense that α is the weight placed on most recent actual demand D_t and $1 - \alpha$ is the weight on the previous forecast. Equation (2.6) can be explained similarly: It places a weight of β on the most recent estimate of the slope (obtained by taking the difference between the two most recent base signals) and a weight of $1 - \beta$ on the previous estimate. Note that, if the trend is downward-sloping, then S_t will (usually) be negative.

This particular version of double exponential smoothing is also known as *Holt's method* (Holt 1957).

2.2.2.3 *Triple Exponential Smoothing*   Triple exponential smoothing can be used to forecast demands that exhibit both trend and seasonality. Seasonality means that the demand series has a pattern that repeats every N periods, $N \geq 3$. N consecutive periods are called a *season*. (If the demand pattern repeats every year, for example, then a season is one year. This is different from the common usage of the word "season," which would refer to a portion of the year.)

To model the seasonality, we use a parameter c_t, $1 \leq t \leq N$, to represent the ratio between the average demand in period t and the overall average. (Thus, $\sum c_t = N$.) For example, if $c_6 = 0.88$, then on average the demand in period 6 is 12% below the overall average demand. The c_t are called *seasonal factors*. We assume that the seasonal factors are unknown but that they are the same every season. The demand process can be modeled as follows:

$$D_t = (I + tS)c_t + \epsilon_t, \tag{2.7}$$

where I is the value of base signal at time 0, S is the true slope, and ϵ_t is a random error term. (See Figure 2.2.)

The forecast for period t is given by

$$y_t = (I_{t-1} + S_{t-1})c_{t-N}, \tag{2.8}$$

where I_{t-1} and S_{t-1} are the estimates of the base signal and slope in period $t - 1$ and c_{t-N} is the estimate of the seasonal factor one season ago.

The idea behind smoothing with trend and seasonality is basically to "de-trend" and "de-seasonalize" the time series by separating the base signal from the trend and seasonality effects. The method uses three smoothing parameters, α, β, and γ, in estimating the base signal, the trend, and the seasonality, respectively:

$$I_t = \alpha \frac{D_t}{c_{t-N}} + (1 - \alpha)(I_{t-1} + S_{t-1}) \tag{2.9}$$

$$S_t = \beta(I_t - I_{t-1}) + (1 - \beta)S_{t-1} \tag{2.10}$$

$$c_t = \gamma \frac{D_t}{I_t} + (1 - \gamma)c_{t-N}. \tag{2.11}$$

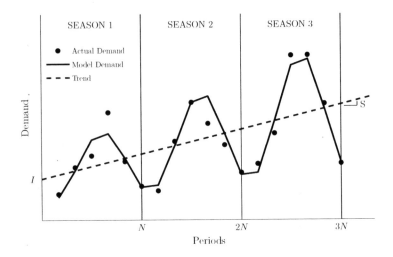

Figure 2.2   Random demands with trend and seasonality.

Equations (2.9) and (2.10) are very similar to (2.5) and (2.6) for double exponential smoothing, except that (2.9) uses the deseasonalized demand observation, D_t/c_{t-N}, instead of D_t, to average with the current forecast. In (2.11), I_t is our estimate of the base signal, so D_t/I_t is our estimate of c_t based on the most recent demand. This is averaged with our previous estimate of c_t (made N periods ago) using weighting factor γ.

This method is also sometimes known as the *Winters's method* or the *Holt–Winters method*.

2.2.3   Linear Regression

Historical data can also be used to forecast demands by determining a cause–effect relationship between some independent variables and the demand. For instance, the demand for sales of a brand of laptop computer may heavily depend on the sales price and the features. A regression model can be developed which describes this relationship. The model can then be used to forecast the demand for laptops with a given price and a given set of features.

In linear regression, the model specification assumes that the independent variable, Y, is a linear combination of the independent variables. For example, in *simple linear regression* there is one independent variable, X, and two parameters, β_0 and β_1:

$$Y = \beta_0 + \beta_1 X. \tag{2.12}$$

The objective of regression analysis is to estimate the parameters.

To build a regression model, we need historical data points—observations of both the independent variable(s) and the dependent variable. Let $(x_1, y_1), (x_2, y_2), \ldots,$

(x_n, y_n) be n paired data observations for a simple linear regression model. The goal is to find values of β_0 and β_1 so that the line defined by (2.12) gives the best fit of the data. In particular, β_0 and β_1 are chosen to minimize the sum of the squared residuals, where the residual for data point i is defined as the difference between the observed value of y_i and the predicted value of y_i obtained by substituting $X = x_i$ in (2.12). These optimal values of β_0 and β_1 can be calculated using standard formulas; see, e.g., Tamhane and Dunlop (1999).

If the demands exhibit a linear trend over time, then we can use regression analysis to forecast the demand using the time period itself (rather than, say, price or features) as the independent variable. In this case, it can be shown (see, e.g., Nahmias 2005, Appendix 2-B) that the optimal values of β_0 and β_1 are given by:

$$\beta_1 = \frac{A_{xy}}{A_{xx}} \tag{2.13}$$

$$\beta_0 = \frac{1}{n} \sum_{i=1}^{n} D_i - \frac{\beta_1(n+1)}{2}, \tag{2.14}$$

where $D_1, \ldots, D_n$ are the observed demands and

$$A_{xy} = n \sum_{i=1}^{n} i D_i - \frac{n(n+1)}{2} \sum_{i=1}^{n} D_i \tag{2.15}$$

$$A_{xx} = \frac{n^2(n+1)(2n+1)}{6} - \frac{n^2(n+1)^2}{4}. \tag{2.16}$$

2.3 DEMAND MODELING TECHNIQUES

As the pace of technology updates accelerates, companies are introducing new products faster and faster to stay competitive. There is a diffusion process associated with the demand for any new product, so companies need to plan the timing and quantity of new product releases carefully to match supply and demand as closely as possible. To do so, they need to understand the life cycles and demand dynamics of their products.

One of the authors has worked with a high-tech company in China. The company was complaining about their very inaccurate demand forecasts, which led to excess inventory valued at approximately $25 million. The author was invited to give lectures on demand forecasting and inventory management. The first day's lecture focused on the classical time-series demand forecasting techniques discussed earlier in this chapter. The reaction from the company's forecasting team was lukewarm. They were already quite familiar with these techniques and had tried hard to make them work, unsuccessfully. It turns out that classical forecasting techniques did not work well with the company's highly variable, short-life-cycle products, so the firm introduced products at the wrong times in the wrong quantities. The forecasting

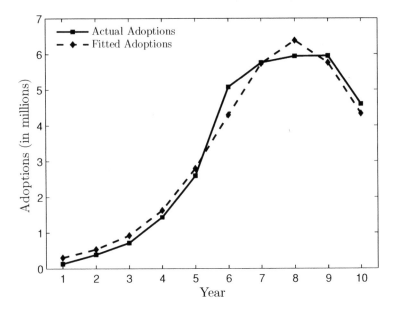

Figure 2.3   Color TVs in the 1960s: Forecasts from Bass model and actual demands. Reprinted by permission, Bass, Empirical generalizations and marketing science: A personal view, *Marketing Science*, 14(3), 1995, G6–G19. ©1995, the Institute for Operations Research and the Management Sciences (INFORMS), 7240 Parkway Drive, Suite 300, Hanover, MD 21076 USA.

team's reaction was quite different when the author discussed the Bass diffusion model, the leading-indicator method, and choice models, which are designed to account for short life cycles and other important factors. We discuss each of these methods in detail in the following sections. (As a postscript, the company reported more than a 50% increase in sales about one and a half years after they improved their forecasting techniques, partially due to the fact that money was being invested in a better mix of products.)

2.4   BASS DIFFUSION MODEL

The sales patterns of new products typically go through three phases: rapid growth, maturity, and decline. The *Bass diffusion model* (Bass 1969) is a well-known parametric approach to estimating the demand trajectory of a single new product over time. Bass's basic three-parameter model has proved to be very effective in delivering accurate forecasts and insights for a huge variety of new product introductions, regardless of pricing and advertising decisions. The model forecasts well even when limited or no historical data are available. For example, Figure 2.3 depicts demand data (forecast and actual) for the introduction of color television sets in the 1960s.

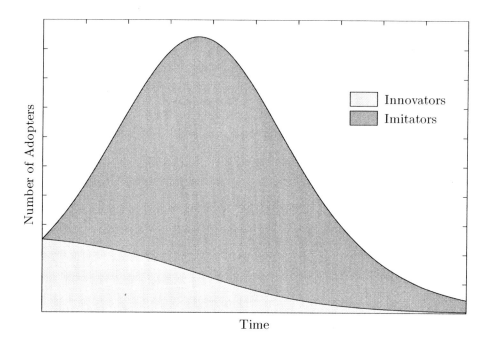

Figure 2.4   Bass diffusion curve.

The premise of the Bass model is that customers can be classified into *innovators* and *imitators*. Innovators (or *early adopters*) purchase a new product without regard to the decisions made by other individuals. Imitators, on the other hand, are influenced in the timing of their purchases by previous buyers through word-of-mouth communication. Refer to Figure 2.4 for an illustration. Whereas the number of innovators decreases over time, the number of imitators purchasing the product first increases, and then decreases. The goal of the Bass model is to characterize this behavior in an effort to forecast the demand. It mathematically characterizes the word-of-mouth interaction between those who have adopted the innovation and those who have not yet adopted it. Moreover, it attempts to predict two important dimensions of a forecast: how many customers will eventually adopt the new product, and when they will adopt. Knowing the timing of adoptions is important as it can guide the firm to smartly utilize resources in marketing the new product. Our analysis of this model is based on that of Bass (1969).

2.4.1   The Model

The Bass model assumes that $P(t)$, the probability that a given buyer makes an initial purchase at time t given that she has not yet made a purchase, is a linear function of the number of previous buyers; that is,

$$P(t) = p + \frac{q}{m}D(t), \tag{2.17}$$

where $D(t)$ is the cumulative demand by time t. Equation (2.17) suggests that two factors will influence the probability that a customer makes a purchase at time t. The first factor is the *coefficient of innovation*, denoted p, which is a constant, independent of how many other customers have adopted the innovation before time t. The second factor, $\frac{q}{m}D(t)$, measures the "contagion" effect between the innovators and the imitators and is proportional to the number of customers who have already adopted by time t. The parameters q and m represent the *coefficient of imitation* and the *market size*, respectively. We require $p < q$. In fact, usually $p \ll q$; for example, $p = 0.03$ and $q = 0.38$ have been reported as average values (Sultan et al. 1990).

We assume that the time index, t, is measured in years. Of course, any time unit is possible, but the values we report for p and q implicitly assume that t is measured in years.

Let $d(t)$ be the derivative of $D(t)$, i.e., the demand *rate* at time t. Using Bayes' rule, one can show that

$$P(t) = \frac{d(t)}{m - D(t)}. \tag{2.18}$$

Combining (2.17) and (2.18), we have

$$d(t) = \left(p + \frac{q}{m}D(t)\right)(m - D(t)). \tag{2.19}$$

Our goal is to characterize $D(t)$ so that we can understand how the demand evolves over time. To a certain extent, (2.19) does this, but (2.19) is a differential equation; it expresses $D(t)$ in terms of its derivative. Our preference would be to have a closed-form expression for $D(t)$. Fortunately, this is possible:

Theorem 2.1

$$D(t) = m\frac{1 - e^{-(p+q)t}}{1 + \frac{q}{p}e^{-(p+q)t}} \tag{2.20}$$

$$d(t) = \frac{mp(p+q)^2 e^{-(p+q)t}}{\left(p + qe^{-(p+q)t}\right)^2} \tag{2.21}$$

Proof. Omitted.   ∎

As a corollary, one can determine the time at which the demand rate peaks, and the demand rate and cumulative demand at that point:

Corollary 2.1 *The peak demand occurs at time*

$$t^* = \frac{1}{p+q}\ln\left(\frac{q}{p}\right). \tag{2.22}$$

The demand rate and cumulative demand at time t^* are given by

$$d(t^*) = \frac{m(p+q)^2}{4q} \tag{2.23}$$

$$D(t^*) = \frac{m(q-p)}{2q}. \tag{2.24}$$

Proof. Omitted; see Problem 2.8.   ∎

If p is very small, then the demand growth occurs slowly, whereas if p and q are large, sales take off rapidly and fall off quickly after reaching their maximum. Note that the formulas in Corollary 2.1 are only well defined if $q > p$, which we assumed above to be true. If, instead, $q < p$, then the innovation effects will dominate the imitation effects and the peak demand will occur immediately upon the introduction of the product and will decline thereafter. In summary, by varying the values of p and q, we can represent many different patterns of demand diffusion.

Seasonal influence factors can be incorporated into the Bass framework. Kurawarwala and Matsuo (1996) present a growth model to forecast demand for short-life-cycle products that is motivated by the Bass diffusion model. They use α_t to denote the seasonal influence parameter at time t, given as a function with a periodicity of 12 months. Their proposed seasonal growth model is characterized by the following differential equation:

$$d(t) = \left(p + \frac{q}{m}D(t)\right)(m - D(t))\alpha_t, \tag{2.25}$$

where $D(t)$ is the cumulative demand by time t ($D(0) \equiv 0$), $d(t)$ is its derivative, and m, p, and q are the scale and shape parameters, which are analogous to parameters in the Bass diffusion model. This is identical to (2.19) except for the multiplier α_t.

Integrating (2.25), we get the cumulative demand $D(t)$ as follows:

$$D(t) = m\left[\frac{1 - e^{-(p+q)\int_0^t \alpha_\tau \, d\tau}}{1 + \frac{q}{p}e^{-(p+q)\int_0^t \alpha_\tau \, d\tau}}\right] \tag{2.26}$$

When $\alpha_t = 1$ for all t, (2.26) reduces to (2.20) from Bass's original model.

2.4.2 Discrete-Time Version

A discrete-time version of the Bass model is available. In this case, d_t represents the demand in period t and D_t represents the cumulative demand up to period t. Then the discrete-time analogue of (2.19) is

$$d_t = \left(p + \frac{q}{m}D_{t-1}\right)(m - D_{t-1}), \tag{2.27}$$

where $D_0 \equiv 0$.

2.4.3   Parameter Estimation

The Bass model is heavily driven by the parameters m, p, and q. In this section, we briefly discuss how these parameters may be estimated.

Market Potential m: Because the Bass model is typically used for new products, in most cases early sales data are not available to estimate the market potential. Instead, m is typically estimated qualitatively, using judgment or intuition from management about the size of the market, market research, or the Delphi method. In some markets these estimates can be rather precise. For instance, the pharmaceutical industry is known for their accurate demand estimates, which derive from abundant data regarding the incidence of diseases and ailments (Lilien et al. 2007).

Coefficients of Innovation and Imitation, p **and** q: If historical data are available, we can estimate the parameters p and q by first finding the least-squares estimates of the parameters a, b, and c in the following linear regression model:

$$d_t = a + bD_{t-1} + c(D_{t-1})^2, \qquad t = 2, 3, \ldots.$$

Note that this model uses the discrete-time version of the Bass model (in which we observe demands d_t and calculate cumulative demands D_t) since, in practice, we observe discrete demand quantities rather than a continuous demand function. After finding a, b, and c using standard regression analysis, the parameters of the Bass model can be determined as follows:

$$m = \frac{-b - \sqrt{b^2 - 4ac}}{2c} \tag{2.28}$$

$$p = \frac{a}{m} \tag{2.29}$$

$$q = -mc \tag{2.30}$$

However, since the Bass model is mainly used to forecast demand before the product is introduced to the market, typically no sales data exist to be used in the regression model. One alternate approach is to use the coefficients estimated from the diffusion patterns of similar products. Lilien and Rangaswamy (1998) provide industry-specific data for a wide range of industries. (See Table 2.1 for some examples.)

2.4.4   Extensions

After more than 40 years, the Bass model is still actively used in demand forecasting and production planning. Sultan et al. (1990), Mahajan et al. (1995), and Bass (2004) provide broad overviews of these applications. The original model has also been extended in a number of ways. Ho et al. (2002) provide a joint analysis of demand and sales dynamics when the supply is constrained, and thus the usual word-of-mouth effects are mitigated. Their analysis generalizes the Bass model to include backorders and lost sales and describes the diffusion dynamics when the firm actively makes supply-related decisions to influence the diffusion process. Savin and

Table 2.1   Bass model parameters. Adapted with permission from Lilien and Rangaswamy, *Marketing Engineering: Computer-Assisted Marketing Analysis and Planning*, Prentice Hall, 1998, p. 201.

Product	p	q
Cable TV	0.100	0.060
Camcorder	0.044	0.304
Cellular phone	0.008	0.421
CD player	0.157	0.000
Radio	0.027	0.435
Home PC	0.121	0.281
Hybrid corn	0.000	0.797
Tractor	0.000	0.234
Ultrasound	0.000	0.534
Dishwasher	0.000	0.179
Microwave	0.002	0.357
VCR	0.025	0.603

Terwiesch (2005) describe the demand dynamics of two new products competing for a limited target market, generalizing the innovation and imitation effects in Bass's original model to account for this competition. Schmidt and Druehl (2005) explore the influence of product improvements and cost reductions on the new-product diffusion process.   Li and Shen (2008) consider the problem of extending a product line while accounting for both inventory (supply) and diffusion (demand). The model determines whether and when to introduce the line extension and the corresponding production quantities.

2.5   LEADING INDICATOR APPROACH

Product life cycles are becoming shorter and shorter, so it is difficult to obtain enough historic data to forecast demands accurately. One idea that has proven to work well in such situations is the use of *leading indicators*—products that can be used to predict the demands of other, later products because the two products share a similar demand pattern. This approach was introduced by Aytac and Wu (2010) and by Wu et al. (2006), who describe an application of the method at the semiconductor company Agere Systems.

The approach is applied in situations in which a company introduces many related products, such as multiple varieties of semiconductors, cellular phones, or grocery items. The idea is first to group the products into clusters so that all of the products within a cluster share similar attributes. There are several ways to perform this clustering. If one can identify a few demand patterns that all products follow, then it is natural simply to group products sharing the same pattern into the same cluster. For instance, after examining demand data for about 3500 products, Meixell and Wu (2001) find that the products follow six basic demand patterns (i.e., diffusion curves

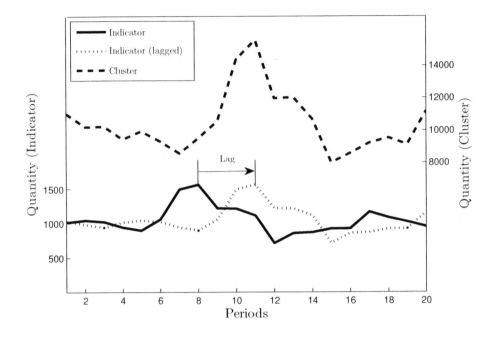

Figure 2.5   An example of a leading-indicator product.

from the Bass model in Section 2.4) and can be grouped into these patterns using statistical cluster analysis. Wu et al. (2006), on the other hand, focus on exogenously defined product characteristics, such as resources, technology group, or sales region, and group the products that have similar characteristics into the same cluster.

The goal is then to identify some potential leading-indicator products within each cluster. A product is a leading indicator if the demand pattern of this product will likely be approximately repeated later by other products in the same cluster. For example, Figure 2.5 depicts the demand for a leading indicator product (solid line) and the total demand for all of the products in the cluster (dashed line). If the leading indicator curve is shifted to the right by approximately three periods (the "lag"), the two curves share a similar structure. Therefore, the leading indicator product provides some basis for predicting the demand of the rest of the products in the cluster. Even though all of the products are on the market simultaneously, the lag provides enough time so that supply chain planning for the products in the cluster can take place based on the forecasts provided by the leading indicator. Of course, correctly identifying the leading indicator is critical.

Wu et al. (2006) suggest the following procedure to identify a leading indicator within a given cluster. Let C be the set of products, i.e., the cluster. Each product $i \in C$ will be treated as a potential leading indicator. Suppose we have historical demand data through period T. Let D_{it} be the observed demand for product i in period t and let D_t be the total demand for the entire cluster in period $t, t = 1, \ldots, T$. Then leading indicators can be identified using the following algorithm.

Algorithm 2.1 (Leading-Indicator Identification)

1. *Initialization*: Choose thresholds representing the minimum time lag (k_{min}), maximum time lag (k_{max}), and correlation (ρ_{min}). (If one product leads the rest of the products by k periods, $k_{min} \le k \le k_{max}$, and their demands have a correlation greater than ρ_{min}, the earlier product is a leading-indicator candidate.)

2. *Correlation Calculation*: For each product $i \in C$:

   (a) Set the time lag $k = k_{min}$.

   (b) Shift the demand time series for product i by k time periods. Calculate the correlation (denoted ρ_{ik}) between this shifted series and the demand time series for the set $C \setminus \{i\}$:

   $$\rho_{ik} = \frac{\sum_{t=k+1}^{T}(D_{i,t-k} - \bar{D}_i)(D_t^{-i} - \bar{D}^{-i})}{\sqrt{\sum_{t=k+1}^{T}(D_{i,t-k} - \bar{D}_i)^2 \sum_{t=k+1}^{T}(D_t^{-i} - \bar{D}^{-i})^2}},$$

   where D_{it} is the observed demand for product i in period t, $\bar{D}_i$ is its mean over the time interval $[k+1, T]$, D_t^{-i} is the total demand for all products in the cluster excluding i in period t, and $\bar{D}^{-i}$ is its mean over the time interval $[k+1, T]$. The correlation ρ_{ik} measures how well the demand of item i over the time interval $[1, T-k]$ predicts the demand of the cluster over $[k+1, T]$.

   (c) Set $k = k + 1$. If $k \le k_{max}$, go to 2(a).

3. *Identification of Leading Indicators*: For each product $i \in C$ and each time lag $k \in \{k_{min}, \ldots, k_{max}\}$, if $\rho_{ik} \ge \rho_{min}$, then label product i as a leading indicator with time lag k. If any such leading indicators were found, go to step 5. If not, continue to step 4.

4. *Reclustering*: Recluster as follows:

   (a) Using statistical cluster analysis, subdivide C into multiple clusters based on statistical patterns in the demands. The attributes used for clustering can include mean demand, shipment frequency, demand volatility, etc.

   (b) Repeat steps 2–4 for each new cluster.

5. *Termination*: Return the leading indicator(s) and corresponding cluster(s).

Once a leading indicator i with time lag k is identified as having a satisfactory correlation coefficient ρ_{ik}, we can forecast the demand for the rest of the product cluster using the demand history from the leading indicator as follows:

1. Regress the demand time series of product cluster C (excluding i) over $[k+1, T]$ against the time series of the leading indicator over $[1, T - k]$ using the model

$$D_t^{-i} = \beta_0 + \beta_1 D_{i,t-k} \qquad (2.31)$$

and determine the optimal regression parameters β_0 and β_1.

2. For a given month $t > T$ (that is, a month for which we do not have historical data but whose demand we wish to forecast), generate the forecast for the cluster, $\tilde{D}_t^{-i}$, using the time series of the leading indicator i from k periods earlier:

$$\tilde{D}_t^{-i} = \beta_0 + \beta_1 D_{i,t-k} \qquad (2.32)$$

2.6   DISCRETE CHOICE MODELS

2.6.1   Introduction to Discrete Choice

In economics, *discrete choice models* involve choices between two or more discrete alternatives. For example, a customer chooses which of several competing products to buy; a firm decides which technology to use in production; or a passenger chooses which transportation mode to travel by. The set of choices is assumed to be discrete, and the corresponding models are therefore called discrete choice models. (A related set of models, called continuous choice models, assume that the range of choices is continuous. Although these models are not the focus of our discussion, many of the concepts that we describe below are easily transferable to continuous choice models. In fact, discrete choices generally reveal less information about the choice process than continuous ones, so the econometrics of discrete choice is usually more challenging.)

The idea behind discrete choice models is to build a statistical model that predicts the choice made by an individual based on the individual's own attributes as well as the attributes of the available choices. For example, a student's choice of which college to attend is determined by factors relating to the student, including his or her career goals, scholarly interests, and financial situation, as well as factors relating to the colleges, including their reputations and locations. Choice models attempt to quantify this relationship statistically.

At first it may seem that discrete choice models mainly deal with "which"-type rather than "how many"-type decisions, unlike the other forecasting and demand modeling techniques described in this chapter. However, discrete choice models can be and have been used to forecast quantities, such as the number and duration of phone calls that households make (Train et al. 1987); the demand for electric cars (Beggs et al. 1981) and mobile telephones (Ida and Kuroda 2009); the demand for planned transportation systems, such as highways, rapid transit systems, and airline routes (Train (1978), Ramming (2001), and Garrow (2010)); and the number of vehicles a household chooses to own (McFadden 1984). Choice models estimate the probability that a person selects a particular alternative. Thus, aggregating the "which" decision across the population will give answers to the "how many" questions and can be very useful for forecasting demand.

Discrete choice models take many forms, including binary and multinomial logit, binary and multinomial probit, and conditional logit. However, there are several features that are common to all of these models. These include the way they characterize the choice set, consumer utility, and the choice probabilities. We briefly describe each of these features next. (See Train (2009) for more details about these features.)

The Choice Set: The *choice set* is the set of options that are available to the decision maker. The alternatives might represent competing products or services, or any other options or items among which the decision maker must choose. For a discrete choice model, the set of alternatives in the choice set must be *mutually exclusive, exhaustive,* and *finite.* The first two requirements mean that the set must include all possible alternatives (so that the decision maker necessarily does make a choice from within the set) and that choosing one alternative means not choosing any others (so one alternative from the set dominates all other options for the decision maker). The third requirement distinguishes discrete choice analysis from, say, linear regression analysis in which the dependent variable can (theoretically) take an infinite number of values.

Consumer Utility: Suppose there are N decision makers, each of whom must select an alternative from the choice set I. A given decision maker n would obtain a certain level of *utility* from alternative $i \in I$; this utility is denoted U_{ni}. Discrete choice models usually assume that the decision maker is a utility maximizer. That is, he will choose alternative i if and only if $U_{ni} > U_{nj}$ for all $j \in I, j \neq i$.

If we know the utility values U_{ni} for all $n \in N$ and all $i \in I$, then it will be very easy for us to calculate which alternative decision maker n will choose (and therefore to predict the demand for each alternative). However, since in most cases we do not know the utility values perfectly, we must estimate them. Let V_{ni} be our estimate of alternative i's utility for decision maker n. (The V_{ni} values are called *representative utilities.* We omit a discussion about how these might be calculated; see, for example, Train (2009).) Normally, $V_{ni} \neq U_{ni}$, and we use ϵ_{ni} to denote the random estimation error; that is,

$$U_{ni} = V_{ni} + \epsilon_{ni}. \tag{2.33}$$

Choice Probabilities: Once we have determined the V_{ni} values, we can calculate P_{ni}, the probability that decision maker n chooses alternative i, as follows:

$$
\begin{aligned}
P_{ni} &= P(U_{ni} > U_{nj} \quad \forall j \neq i) \\
&= P(V_{ni} + \epsilon_{ni} > V_{nj} + \epsilon_{nj} \quad \forall j \neq i)
\end{aligned}
\tag{2.34}
$$

The V_{ni} values are constants. To estimate the probability, then, we need to know the probability distributions of the random variables ϵ_{ni}.

Different choice models arise from different distributions of ϵ_{ni} and different methods for calculating V_{ni}. For instance, the logit model assumes that ϵ_{ni} are drawn iid from a member of the family of generalized extreme value distributions, and this gives rise to a closed-form expression for P_{ni}. (Logit is therefore the most widely used discrete choice model.) The probit model, on the other hand, assumes that ϵ_{ni} come from a multivariate normal distribution (and are therefore correlated, not iid), but the resulting P_{ni} values cannot be found in closed form and must instead be estimated using simulation.

2.6.2   The Multinomial Logit Model

Next we derive the multinomial logit model. (Refer to McFadden (1974) or Train (2009) for further details of the derivation.) "Multinomial" means that there are multiple options from which the decision maker chooses. (In contrast, binomial models assume there are only two options.) The logit model is obtained by assuming each ϵ_{ni} is independently and identically distributed from the standard Gumbel distribution, a type of generalized extreme value distribution (also known as type I extreme value). The pdf and cdf of the standard Gumbel distribution are given by

$$f(x) = e^{-x}e^{-e^{-x}} \tag{2.35}$$

$$F(x) = e^{-e^{-x}}. \tag{2.36}$$

We can rewrite the probability that decision maker n chooses alternative i (2.34) as

$$P_{ni} = P(\epsilon_{nj} < V_{ni} + \epsilon_{ni} - V_{nj} \quad \forall j \neq i). \tag{2.37}$$

Since ϵ_{nj} has a Gumbel distribution, by (2.36) the probability in the right-hand side of (2.37) can be written as

$$e^{-e^{-(\epsilon_{ni}+V_{ni}-V_{nj})}}$$

if ϵ_{ni} is given. Since the ϵ are independent, the cumulative distribution over all $j \neq i$ is the product of the individual cumulative distributions:

$$P_{ni}|\epsilon_{ni} = \prod_{j \neq i} e^{-e^{-(\epsilon_{ni}+V_{ni}-V_{nj})}}.$$

Therefore we can calculate P_{ni} by conditioning on ϵ_{ni} as follows:

$$
\begin{aligned}
P_{ni} &= \int (P_{ni}|\epsilon_{ni}) f(\epsilon_{ni}) d\epsilon_{ni} \\
&= \int (P_{ni}|\epsilon_{ni}) e^{-\epsilon_{ni}} e^{-e^{-\epsilon_{ni}}} d\epsilon_{ni} \\
&= \int \left(\prod_{j \neq i} e^{-e^{-(\epsilon_{ni}+V_{ni}-V_{nj})}} \right) e^{-\epsilon_{ni}} e^{-e^{-\epsilon_{ni}}} d\epsilon_{ni}. \tag{2.38}
\end{aligned}
$$

After some further manipulation (see Problem 2.14), we get

$$P_{ni} = \frac{e^{V_{ni}}}{\sum_j e^{V_{nj}}}. \tag{2.39}$$

Note that the probability that individual n chooses alternative i is between 0 and 1 (as is necessary for a well defined probability). As V_{ni}, the estimate of i's utility for n, increases, so does the probability that n chooses i; this probability approaches 1 as V_{ni} approaches ∞. Similarly, as V_{ni} decreases, so does the probability that n chooses i, approaching 0 in the limit.

The expected number of individuals who will choose product i, $N(i)$, is simply given by

$$N(i) = \sum_{n=1}^{N} P_{ni}. \tag{2.40}$$

Of course, we usually don't know P_{ni} for every individual n, so instead we resort to methods to estimate $N(i)$ without relying on too much data. See Koppelman (1975) for a discussion of several useful techniques for this purpose.

We refer the readers to other texts (Ben-Akiva and Lerman 1985, Train 2009) for details about this and other choice models. We next give an example of how discrete choice modeling techniques can be used to estimate demand in a supply chain management setting.

2.6.3 Example Application to Supply Chain Management

Suppose there is a retailer who sells a set I of products. The retailer is interested in estimating the probability that a given customer would be interested in purchasing product i, for $i \in I$, so that he can decide which products to offer. Suppose that the customer follows a multinomial logit choice model, as in Section 2.6.2. The retailer's estimate U_i of the customer's utility V_i for product $i \in I$ is given by

$$U_i = V_i + \epsilon_i. \tag{2.41}$$

(Equation (2.41) is identical to (2.33) except that we have dropped the index n since we are considering only a single customer.) If $i = 0$, then U_i and V_i denote the estimated and actual utility of making no purchase.

For any subset $S \subseteq I$, let $P_i(S)$ denote the probability that the customer will purchase product i, assuming that her only choices are in the set S, and let $P_i(S) = 0$ if $i \notin S$. Let $P_0(S)$ denote the probability that the customer will not purchase any product. Then, from (2.39), we have

$$P_i(S) = \begin{cases} \frac{e^{V_i}}{V_0 + \sum_j e^{V_j}}, & \text{if } i \in S \cup \{0\}, \\ 0, & \text{otherwise} \end{cases} \tag{2.42}$$

The retailer's objective is to choose which products to offer in order to maximize his expected profit. Suppose that the retailer earns a profit of π_i for each unit of product i sold. Suppose also that the retailer cannot offer more than C products. (C might represent shelf space.) Then the retailer needs to solve the following *assortment problem*:

$$\text{maximize} \quad \sum_{i \in S} \pi_i P_i(S) \tag{2.43}$$

$$\text{subject to} \quad |S| \leq C \tag{2.44}$$

$$S \subseteq I \tag{2.45}$$

(If there are multiple customers, we can just multiply the objective function by the number of customers, assuming they have identical utilities. For a discussion of handling non-homogenous customers, see Koppelman (1975).) This is a combinatorial optimization problem; the goal is to choose the subset S. This problem is not trivial to solve (though it can be solved efficiently). However, the bigger problem is that the utilities V_i, and hence the probabilities $P_i(S)$, are unknown to the retailer. One option is for the retailer to offer different assortments of products over time, estimate the utilities based on the observed demands for each assortment, and refine his assortment as his estimates improve. Rusmevichientong et al. (2010) propose such an approach. They introduce a policy that the retailer can follow to generate a sequence of assortments in order to maximize the expected profit over time. The assortment offered in a given period depends on the demands observed in the previous periods. Rusmevichientong et al. (2010) also propose a polynomial-time algorithm to solve the assortment problem itself.

PROBLEMS

2.1 **(Forecasting without Trend)** A hospital receives regular shipments of liquefied oxygen, which it converts to oxygen gas that is used for life support. The company that sells the oxygen to the hospital wishes to forecast the amount of liquefied oxygen the hospital will use tomorrow. The number of liters of liquefied oxygen used by the hospital in each of the past 30 days is reported in the file oxygen.xlsx.
   a) Using a moving average with $N = 7$, forecast tomorrow's demand.
   b) Using single exponential smoothing with $\alpha = 0.1$, forecast tomorrow's demand.

2.2 **(Forecasting with Trend)** The demand for a new brand of dog food has been steadily rising at the local PetMart pet store. The previous 26 weeks' worth of demand (number of bags) are given in the file dog-food.xlsx.
   a) Using double exponential smoothing with $\alpha = 0.2$ and $\beta = 0.1$, forecast next week's demand. Initialize your forecast by setting $I_t = D_t$ for $t = 1, 2$ and $S_2 = I_2 - I_1$.
   b) Using linear regression, forecast next week's demand.

2.3 **(Forecasting with Seasonality)** A hardware store sells potting soil, the demand for which is highly seasonal and has also exhibited a slight upward trend. The number of bags of soil sold each month for the past 40 months is reported in the file `potting-soil.xlsx`. Using triple exponential smoothing with $\alpha = 0.2$, $\beta = 0.1$, and $\gamma = 0.3$, forecast the demand for May. Initialize your forecast by setting

$$I_t = D_t$$
$$S_t = I_t - I_{t-1}$$
$$c_t = \frac{12 D_t}{\sum_{i=1}^{12} D_i}$$

for periods $t = 1, \ldots, 12$. (There are better ways to initialize this method, but this method is simpler.)

2.4 (Forecasting Using Regression) The demand for bottled water at football (aka soccer) matches is correlated to the outside temperature at the start of the match. The file `bottled-water.xlsx` reports the temperature (°C) and number of bottles of water sold for each home match played at a certain stadium for the past two seasons (19 home matches per season).

a) Using these data, build a linear regression model to relate the demand for bottled water to the match-time temperature. What are β_0 and β_1?

b) The temperatures for the next three matches are predicted to be 21.6°, 27.3°, and 26.6°, respectively. Forecast the demand for bottled water at each of these matches.

2.5 (Bass Diffusion for LPhone) HCT, an Asian manufacturer of a new 4G cell phone, the LPhone 5, is planing to enter the U.S. market, and they are in the process of signing a contract with a third-party logistics (3PL) provider in which they must specify the size of the warehouse they want to rent from the 3PL. HCT wants to forecast the total sales of the LPhone 5, as well as the time at which the LPhone 5 reaches its peak sales. After some thorough market research, HCT has estimated that $p = 0.008$, $q = 0.421$, and $m = 5.8$ million. Calculate when the peak sales will occur and how many LPhone 5 the company will have sold by that point.

2.6 (Bass Diffusion for iPeel) Banana Computer Co. plans to launch its latest consumer electronic device, the iPeel, early next year. Based on market research, it estimates that the market potential for the iPeel is 170,000 units, with coefficients of innovation and imitation of 0.07 and 0.31, respectively.

a) If the iPeel is introduced on January 1, on what date will the sales peak? What will be the demand rate on that date, and how many units will have been sold?

b) On what date will 90% of the sales have occurred?

c) Plot the demand rate and cumulative demand as a function of time.

2.7 (Bass Diffusion for Books) A new novel was published recently, and the demand for it is expected to follow a Bass diffusion process. The publisher decided to print only a limited number of copies, observe the demand for the book for 20 weeks, estimate the Bass parameters, and then undertake a second printing for the remainder of the life cycle of the book using these parameters. The demand for the book during these 20 weeks is reported in the file `novel.xlsx`. Using these data, estimate m, p, and q using the method described in Section 2.4.3.

2.8   **(Proof of Corollary 2.1)** Prove Corollary 2.1.

2.9   **(Influentials and Imitators)** Suppose that potential adopters of a given product fall into two distinct segments: *influentials* and *imitators*. Each segment has its own within-segment innovation and imitation parameters and experiences its own Bass-type contagion process. In addition, the influentials can exert a cross-segment influence on the imitators, but not vice-versa. Let θ denote the proportion of influentials in the population of eventual adopters ($0 \le \theta \le 1$), and $\bar{\theta} = 1 - \theta$ denote the proportion of imitators. Let p_i and q_i denote the within-segment innovation and imitation parameters, respectively, for $i = 1, 2$, where $i = 1$ represents influentials and $i = 2$ represents imitators. Let q_c denote the cross-segment imitation parameter.

   a) Write a formula expressing each segment's instantaneous adoption behavior, analogous to (2.19).
   b) What is special about the case in which $\theta = 0$ or $\theta = 1$?
   c) If there are no pre-release purchases (i.e., $D_1(0) = D_2(0) = 0$), write a formula expressing the cumulative adoption at time t, analogous to (2.20).

2.10   **(Demand Diffusion Across Multiple Markets)** A company plans to introduce a variety of new products to multiple vertical markets. The demands from these verticals are likely to follow different diffusion patterns. The company is interested in combining diffusion models derived from different vertical markets to help characterizing the overall market demand. However, they are not sure about whether doing so would introduce additional variances and biases into the forecast. Show that combining forecasts of different diffusion models using weights that are inversely proportional to their forecast variances yields a combined forecast variance that is smaller than the forecast variance of each individual diffusion model.

2.11   **(Leading Indicators)** A battery manufacturer produces a large number of models of lithium-ion batteries for use in computers and other electronic devices. The products are introduced at different times and follow different demand processes. The company wishes to determine whether some of the products can serve as leading indicators for the rest of the products. The file `batteries.xlsx` contains historical demand data for 25 products for the past 26 weeks.

   a) Using Algorithm 2.1 with parameters $k_{\min} = 3$, $k_{\max} = 9$, and $\rho_{\min} = 0.85$, determine all pairs (i, k) such that product i is a leading indicator with lag k. (*Note:* You should not need to recluster the products.)
   b) Using one of the (i, k) you found in part (a), forecast the demand for the rest of the cluster in periods 27 and 28.

2.12   **(Discrete Choices for Day Care)** A university is in the process of choosing a location for a new day care center for its faculty's children. The two options for the location are city A, where the university is located, or city B, a neighboring city known for larger houses but a longer commute. The university wants to estimate the number of faculty with kids who are living or will live in city A during the next 10 years. To that end, the university wishes to estimate the choice probability between the two cities for a typical family. Suppose that the utility a family obtains from living in each city depends only on the average house purchase price, the distance between the city and the campus, and the family's opinion of the convenience and quality of life of each city. The first two of these factors can be observed by the researcher, but the researcher cannot observe the third. The researcher believes that the observed part of the utility is a linear function of the observed factors; in particular, the utility of living in each city can be written as

$$U_A = -0.45PP_A - 0.23D_A + \epsilon_A$$
$$U_B = -0.45PP_B - 0.23D_B + \epsilon_B,$$

where the subscripts A and B denote city A and city B, and PP and D are the purchase price and distance. The unobserved component of the utility for each alternative, ϵ_A and ϵ_B, vary across households depending on how each household views the quality and convenience of living in each city. If these unobserved components are distributed iid with a standard Gumbel distribution, calculate the probability that a household will choose to live in city A.

2.13 (Using Discrete Choice to Forecast Movie Sales) Three new movies will be shown at a movie theater this weekend. The theater wishes to estimate the expected number of people who will come to see each movie so they can decide how many screenings to offer, how large a theater each movie should be shown in, and so on. The movie studios that produced the three movies held "sneak peak" screenings of the films and conducted post-movie interviews of the attendees. Based on these interviews, they estimated the utility of each movie based on a viewer's age range. They also estimated the utility of not seeing any movie. These estimated utilities are denoted V_{ni}, although here n refers not to an individual but to a *type* of individual (based on age range). The table below lists the V_{ni} values, as well as the number of people that are considering seeing a movie at that theater this weekend.

Movie	Age Range 16–25	26–35	36+
Prognosis Negative	0.22	0.54	0.62
Rochelle, Rochelle	0.49	0.57	0.51
Sack Lunch	0.53	0.31	0.38
No movie	0.10	0.27	0.41
Population	700	1900	1150

a) Assume that the actual utilities U_{ni} differ from the estimated utilities V_{ni} by an additive iid error term that has a standard Gumbel distribution. Using the multinomial logit model of Section 2.6.2, calculate the expected demand for each movie.

b) Now suppose the movie theater doesn't know about the multinomial logit model and assumes that P_{ni} is simply calculated using a weighted sum of the V_{ni} values; that is,

$$P_{ni} = \frac{V_{ni}}{\sum_j V_{nj}}.$$

What are the expected demands for each movie using this method?

2.14   (**Proof of** (2.39)) Prove equation (2.39).

CHAPTER 3

DETERMINISTIC INVENTORY MODELS

3.1 INTRODUCTION TO INVENTORY MODELING

3.1.1 Why Hold Inventory?

Think about some of the products you bought the last time you went to the grocery store. How much of each did you buy? Why did you choose these quantities?

Here are some possible reasons:

1. You bought a gallon of milk but only a pint of cream because you drink much more milk than cream in a week.

2. You bought a six-pack of soda, rather than a single bottle, because you don't want to have to go to the store every time you want to drink a bottle of soda.

3. You bought a "family size" box of cereal, rather than a small box, because larger boxes are more cost-effective (cheaper per ounce) than smaller ones.

4. Although you usually eat one bag of potato chips per week, you bought three bags in case your hungry friends show up unexpectedly one night this week.

5. You asked the store to special-order your favorite brand of gourmet mustard (which it doesn't normally stock), even though you already have a half jar at home, because you know it will take a few weeks before the mustard is delivered.

6. Although it would be more cost-effective and convenient to buy 12 rolls of paper towels, you only bought 3, because you don't have enough space to store 12 rolls at home.

7. You bought four boxes of pasta, even though you only eat one box per week, because they were on sale for a greatly reduced price.

8. Even though grapes were on sale, you bought one pound instead of two because you knew the second pound would spoil before you had a chance to eat them.

9. You bought a pound of butter (four sticks), even though you probably won't use more than one stick before your next trip to the store, because butter only comes in 1-pound packages.

All of these decisions affected the amount of inventory of groceries that you have in your home. Aside from the cost you paid to purchase these items, you are also paying a cost simply to hold the inventory (as opposed to buying a single item each time you need it and using it immediately). For example, if you used your credit card to make your purchase, then you are paying a little more interest by buying a six-pack of soda today rather than buying individual bottles throughout the week. If you paid cash, then you are tying up your cash in groceries rather than using it for some other purpose, such as going to the movies, or putting your money in an interest-earning savings account. You are also paying for the physical space required to store your groceries (as part of your rent or mortgage), the energy required to keep refrigerated items cold, and the insurance to protect your grocery investment if your house is burglarized or damaged in a fire.

Companies, too, would prefer not to hold any inventory, since inventory is expensive (even more than it is for you). However, most companies hold some inventory, for the same reasons that you hold inventory of your groceries:

1. Different products are purchased at different rates—the *demand rate*—and therefore require different levels of inventory.

2. There is an inconvenience, and often an expense, associated with placing an order with a supplier (analogous to your trip to the grocery store). For example, there may be an administrative cost to process the order and transmit it to the supplier, or there may be a cost to rent a truck to deliver the products. These are *fixed costs* since they are (roughly) independent of the size of the order, and they make it impractical to place an order each time a single item is needed.

3. Firms often receive *volume discounts* for placing large orders with their suppliers. Volume discounts and fixed costs are both types of *economies of scale*,

which make it more cost-effective to order in bulk; that is, to place fewer, larger orders.

4. Demand for most products is random, and often so are lead times and other supply factors, and this *uncertainty* requires firms to hold inventory to ensure that they can satisfy the demand (at least most of the time).

5. After a firm places an order, the products do not arrive until after a (typically non-zero) *lead time*. Since the firm's own customers usually don't want to wait for this lead time, especially in retail settings, the firm must place a replenishment order even when it is still holding some inventory.

6. Warehouses have only a finite amount of *storage capacity*, and this may constrain the size of the firm's order. A related type of capacity (which is less relevant for the grocery example) is *production capacity*: If demand is highly seasonal (e.g., for snowblowers) but production capacity is limited, the firm may need to produce more in off-peak times (summer) in order to meet the demand during peak times (winter).

7. Suppliers often offer sales and temporary discounts, just like retail stores do, and prices for many products (especially commodities) vary constantly. In response to both types of *price fluctuations*, firms buy large quantities when prices are low and hold goods in inventory until they're needed.

8. Some inventory is *perishable*, so firms must limit the quantity they buy to avoid being saddled with unusable inventory.

9. Many products are available only in fixed *batch sizes* such as cases or pallets, and the firm is forced to order in increments of those units.

These are all reasons that firms plan to hold inventory. In addition, firms may hold *unplanned* inventory—for example, inventory of products that have become obsolete sooner than expected.

Firms may hold inventory of goods at all stages of production—raw materials, components, work-in-process, and finished goods. The latter types of inventory are usually made by the firm, rather than ordered from a supplier, but similar issues still arise—for example, there may be a fixed cost to initiate a production run, it may be cheaper per unit to produce large batches, the processing time may be uncertain, and so on. In fact, although we tend to discuss inventory models as though the firm is buying a product from an outside supplier, most inventory models apply equally well to production systems, in which case we are deciding how much to produce, rather than how much to order, and the "ordering" costs are really production costs.

3.1.2 Classifying Inventory Models

Mathematical inventory models can be classified along a number of different dimensions:

- *Demand.* Is demand deterministic or stochastic? Does the rate stay the same all the time or does it vary over time—say, from season to season?

- *Lead time.* Is production or delivery instantaneous, or is there a positive lead time?

- *Review time.* Is inventory assessed *continuously* or *periodically*? In continuous-review models, the inventory is constantly monitored, and an order is placed whenever a certain condition is met (for example, the inventory level falls below a given value). In periodic-review models, the inventory is only checked every time period (say, every week), and an order is placed if the reorder condition is met. In periodic-review models, we usually assume that demands occur at a single instant during the period, even though they may really occur continuously throughout it.

- *Planning horizon.* *Finite-horizon* models consider a finite number of periods or time units, while *infinite-horizon* models assume the planning horizon extends forever. Although it is unrealistic to assume that the firm will continue operating the same system, under the same conditions, forever, infinite-horizon models are often more tractable than finite-horizon ones and are therefore quite common.

- *Stockout type.* If demand exceeds supply, how is the excess demand handled? Most models consider either *backorders*, in which case excess demand stays on the books until it can be satisfied from a future shipment, or *lost sales*, in which case excess demands are simply lost—the customer takes her business elsewhere. In retail settings, it is usually more accurate to assume lost sales, whereas backorders are more common in business-to-business settings.

- *Ensuring good service.* Some models ensure that not too many stockouts occur by including a penalty in the cost function for each stockout. Others include a constraint on the allowable percentage of demands that may be stocked out. The former approach often leads to more tractable models, but it can be very difficult to quantify the cost of a stockout; therefore, service-level constraints are common in practice.

- *Fixed cost.* Some inventory models include a fixed cost to place an order, while others do not. The presence and magnitude of a fixed cost determines whether the firm places many small orders or few large orders. Moreover, inventory models with fixed costs are often more difficult to analyze and solve than those without, so we often ignore the fixed cost in modeling an inventory system even if one is present in the real system.

- *Perishability.* Can inventory be held across multiple time periods, or is it perishable? Perishable items include not just foods, but also fresh flowers and medicine (which will spoil), high-tech products (which will become obsolete), and newspapers and airline tickets (which have a deadline after which they can't be sold).

Like all mathematical models, inventory models must balance two competing factors—realism and tractability. In many cases, it is more accurate to assume one thing but easier to assume the opposite. For example, many inventory models are much more mathematically tractable if we assume backorders, so we might do so even if we are modeling inventory at a retail store, for which the lost-sales assumption is more accurate. Similarly, it is often convenient to assume lead times are zero even though they rarely are in practice. If the lead time is short compared to the order cycle—for example, if the firm places monthly orders and the lead time is two days—this assumption may not hurt the model's accuracy. Modeling is as much an art as a science, and part of modeling process involves determining both the cost (in terms of realism) and the benefit (in terms of tractability) of "assuming away" a given real-life factor.

3.1.3 Costs

The goal of most inventory models is to minimize the cost (or maximize the profit) of the inventory system. Four types of costs are most common:

- *Holding cost.* This represents the cost of actually keeping the inventory on hand. Like the costs associated with storing your groceries, the holding cost includes the cost of storage space, taxes, insurance, breakage, theft, and, most significantly, opportunity cost—the money the firm could be earning if it didn't have its capital tied up in inventory. The holding cost is often expressed as a percentage of the value of the product per year. For example, the holding cost might be 25% per year. If the item costs \$100, then it costs \$1562.50 to hold 250 items for 3 months ($1562.50 = 0.25 \cdot 100 \cdot 250 \cdot (3/12) = 1750$). We will usually use h to represent the holding cost per item per unit time.

  In reality, the inventory level is not constant but fluctuates over time, as pictured in Figure 3.1. Here, the holding cost is the area under the curve times h, so we would use integration to compute it. In some of the inventory models discussed in this book, the inventory "curve" is made up of straight lines, so computing the area is easy.

- *Fixed cost.* This is the cost to place an order, independent of the size of the order. It is sometimes called the *setup cost* and we will usually denote it by K. The fixed cost accounts for the administrative cost of placing an order, the cost of using a truck to deliver the product, and so on.

- *Purchase cost.* This is the cost per unit to buy and ship the product, generally denoted by c. (It is also sometimes known as the *variable cost* or *per-unit cost*.) Therefore, the total order cost (fixed + purchase) is given by

$$\begin{cases} 0, & \text{if } x = 0 \\ K + cx, & \text{if } x > 0 \end{cases}$$

  One picky but important note: If there is a non-zero lead time, then we typically assume that the firm pays the purchase cost c when the order arrives, not when

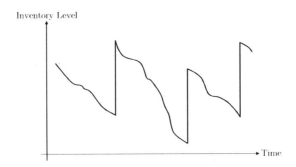

Figure 3.1   Inventory curve.

it is placed. This assumption doesn't affect the total purchase cost per year (unless we're modeling the time value of money), but it does affect the holding cost if h is a function of c: If the firm were to pay the purchase cost when the order is placed, its capital would be tied up during the lead time, but this would not be accurately reflected in the holding cost.

- *Stockout cost.* This is the cost of not having sufficient inventory to meet demand, also called the *penalty cost* or *stockout penalty*, and is denoted by p. If excess demand is backordered, the penalty cost includes bookkeeping costs, delay costs, and—most significantly—*loss of goodwill* (the potential loss of future business since the customer is unhappy). If excess demand is lost, the penalty cost also includes the lost profit from the missed sale. The penalty is generally charged per unit of unmet demand. If excess demand is backordered, the penalty may be proportional to the amount of time the backorder is on the books before it is filled, or (less commonly) it may be a one-time penalty charged when the demand is backordered.

3.1.4   Inventory Level and Inventory Position

There are several measures that we use to assess the amount of inventory in the system at any given time. *On-hand inventory* (OH) refers to the number of units that are actually available at the stocking location. *Backorders* (BO) represent demands that have occurred but have not been satisfied. Generally, it's not possible for the on-hand inventory *and* the backorders to be positive at the same time.

The *inventory level* (IL) is equal to the on-hand inventory minus backorders:

$$IL = OH - BO.$$

If $IL > 0$, we have on-hand inventory, and if $IL < 0$, we have no units on hand but we do have backorders. Therefore, we can write

$$OH = IL^{+}$$

$$BO = IL^-,$$

where $x^+ = \max\{x, 0\}$ and $x^- = |\min\{x, 0\}|$. (Be warned: Some authors use $x^- = \min\{x, 0\}$.)

It seems reasonable to think of IL as the relevant measure to consider when making ordering decisions—we look at the shelves, see how much inventory we have, and place an order if there's not enough. But IL by itself does not give us enough information to make good ordering decisions. For instance, suppose the inventory level is 5, you're expecting a demand of 50 next week, and there's a lead time of 4 weeks. How much should you order? The answer depends on how much you've already ordered—i.e., how much is "in the pipeline," ordered but not received. Such items are called *on order* (OO). Therefore, we usually make ordering decisions based on the *inventory position* (IP), which equals the inventory level plus items on order:

$$IP = OH - BO + OO.$$

The distinction between inventory level and inventory position is subtle but important. Typically, we use inventory position to make ordering decisions, but holding and backorder costs are assessed based on inventory level. If the lead time is zero, then $OO = 0$ and $IL = IP$.

3.1.5 Roadmap

In this chapter and the next two, we will explore some classical inventory models and a few of their variants. This chapter discusses deterministic models—first a continuous-review model, the economic order quantity (EOQ) model, perhaps the oldest and best-known mathematical inventory model (Section 3.2), and then a periodic-review model, the Wagner-Whitin model (Section 3.3). Then, Chapter 4 discusses stochastic models. The models in both of these chapters make inventory decisions for a single stage (location). Multi-stage models are considered in Chapter 5.

The models discussed in this chapter are sometimes known as *economic lot size models*. In fact, there is some inconsistency about how this term is used in the literature. Some authors refer to the economic order quantity model (Section 3.2) as *the* economic lot size model. Other authors refer to the Wagner-Whitin model (Section 3.3) as *the* economic lot size model. More generally, the term can be used to refer to any model in which an optimal lot size must be determined, typically under deterministic demand. To avoid confusion, we will avoid this term and instead use the names of the individual models discussed.

3.2 CONTINUOUS REVIEW: THE ECONOMIC ORDER QUANTITY MODEL

3.2.1 Problem Statement

The *economic order quantity* (EOQ) model is one of the oldest and most fundamental inventory models; it was first introduced by Harris (1913). The goal is to determine the optimal amount to order each time an order is placed to minimize the average cost per year. (We'll express everything per year, but the model could just as easily be per month or any other time period.)

We assume that demand is deterministic and constant with a rate of λ units per year. Stockouts are not allowed—we must always order enough so that demand can be met. Since demand is deterministic, this is a plausible assumption. The lead time is 0—orders are received instantaneously. There is a fixed cost K per order, a purchase cost c per unit ordered, and an inventory holding cost h per unit per year. There is no stockout penalty since stockouts are not allowed.

The inventory level[1] evolves as follows. Assume that the on-hand inventory is 0 at time 0; we place an order at time 0, and it arrives instantaneously. The inventory level then decreases at a constant rate λ until the next order is placed, and the process repeats.

Any optimal solution for the EOQ model has two important properties:

- *Zero-inventory ordering (ZIO) property.* Since the lead time is 0, it never makes sense to place an order when there is a positive amount of inventory on hand—we only place an order when the inventory level is 0.

- *Constant order sizes.* If Q is the optimal order size at time 0, it will also be the optimal order size every other time we place an order since the system looks the same every time the inventory level hits 0. Therefore, the order size is the same every time an order is placed.

(You should convince yourself that these properties are indeed optimal.) The inventory level is pictured as a function of time in Figure 3.2. T is called the *cycle length*—the amount of time between orders—and it relates to the order quantity Q and λ by the equation

$$T = \frac{Q}{\lambda}.$$

3.2.2   Cost Function

We want to find the optimal Q to minimize the average annual cost. (We say "average" annual cost since the actual cost in any given year may fluctuate a bit as the sawtooth pattern falls slightly differently across the start of each year.) Note that minimizing the annual cost is not the same as minimizing the cost per cycle; minimizing the cost per cycle would mean choosing very tiny order quantities. The key tradeoff is between fixed cost and holding cost: If we use a large Q, we'll place fewer orders and hold more inventory (small fixed cost but large holding cost), whereas if we use a small Q, we'll place more orders and hold less inventory (large fixed cost but small holding cost).

The strategy for solving the EOQ is to express the average annual cost as a function of Q, then minimize it to find the optimal Q.

---

[1]Since the lead time is 0, the inventory position is equal to the inventory level at all times.

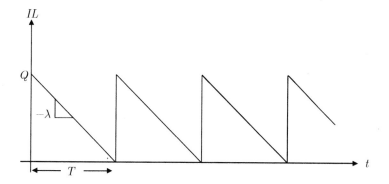

Figure 3.2   EOQ inventory curve.

Order Cost: Each order incurs a fixed cost of K. It also incurs a purchase cost of c per unit ordered, but this cost is irrelevant for the optimization problem at hand—that is, the optimal value of Q does not depend on c. (Why?) Therefore, we'll ignore the per-unit cost c in our analysis. Since the time between orders is T years, the order cost per year is

$$\frac{K}{T} = \frac{K\lambda}{Q}. \tag{3.1}$$

Holding Cost: The average inventory level in a cycle is $Q/2$, so the average amount of inventory per year is $Q/2 \cdot 1$ year $= Q/2$. (Another way to think about this is that the area of a triangle in the inventory curve in Figure 3.2 is $QT/2$, and there are $1/T$ cycles per year, so the total area under the inventory curve for one year is $QT/2 \cdot 1/T = Q/2$.) Therefore, the average annual holding cost is

$$\frac{hQ}{2}. \tag{3.2}$$

Total Cost: Combining (3.1) and (3.2), we get the total average annual cost, denoted $g(Q)$:

$$g(Q) = \frac{K\lambda}{Q} + \frac{hQ}{2}. \tag{3.3}$$

The fixed, holding, and total cost curves are plotted as a function of Q in Figure 3.3.

3.2.3   Optimal Solution

The optimal Q can be obtained by taking the derivative of $g(Q)$ and setting it to 0:

$$\frac{dg(Q)}{dQ} = -\frac{K\lambda}{Q^2} + \frac{h}{2} = 0$$

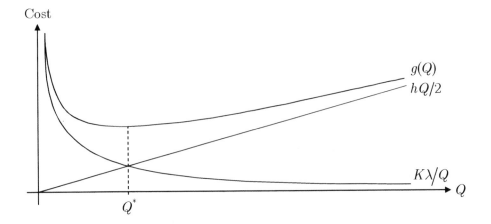

Figure 3.3   Fixed, holding, and total costs as a function of Q.

$$\Longrightarrow Q^2 = \frac{2K\lambda}{h}$$

$$\Longrightarrow Q^* = \sqrt{\frac{2K\lambda}{h}}. \tag{3.4}$$

Q^* is known as the *economic order quantity*. ("Economic" is just another word for "optimal.") We should also take a second derivative to verify that $g(Q)$ is convex (and thus the first-order condition yields a minimum, not a maximum):

$$\frac{d^2 g(Q)}{dQ^2} = \frac{2K\lambda}{Q^3} > 0,$$

as desired.

Note that in Figure 3.3, we drew the optimal order quantity Q^* at the intersection of the fixed and holding cost curves. This was not an accident. Of course, in general, it is not true that the minimum of the sum of two functions occurs where the two functions intersect, but it happens to be true for the EOQ. Why? The curves intersect when

$$\frac{K\lambda}{Q} = \frac{hQ}{2} \quad \Longrightarrow \quad \frac{K\lambda}{Q^2} = \frac{h}{2}.$$

This is exactly the condition obtained by setting the first derivative to 0. Thus, the fixed and holding costs should always be balanced. If the fixed cost $K\lambda/Q$ is greater than the holding cost $hQ/2$, then Q is not optimal; we should be ordering less frequently and holding more inventory. (And vice-versa.)

It should also be noted that, although we ignored the per-unit cost c in this analysis, c does influence Q^* indirectly if h is a function of c.

The optimal cost can be expressed as a function of the parameters by plugging the optimal Q^* into $g(Q)$:

$$g(Q^*) = \frac{K\lambda}{\sqrt{\frac{2K\lambda}{h}}} + \frac{h}{2}\sqrt{\frac{2K\lambda}{h}}$$

$$= \sqrt{\frac{K\lambda h}{2}} + \sqrt{\frac{K\lambda h}{2}}$$

$$= \sqrt{2K\lambda h}. \tag{3.5}$$

It's nice that the optimal cost has such a convenient form. This is not true for many other problems. The ability to express $g(Q^*)$ in closed form allows us to learn about structural properties of the EOQ and related models, such as the power-of-two policies discussed in Section 3.2.6, as well as to embed the EOQ into other, richer models, such as the LMRP model in Section 8.2.

The optimal EOQ solution and its cost are summarized in the next theorem, whose proof follows from arguments already made above.

Theorem 3.1 *The optimal order quantity in the EOQ model is given by*

$$Q^* = \sqrt{\frac{2K\lambda}{h}} \tag{3.6}$$

and its cost is given by

$$g(Q^*) = \sqrt{2K\lambda h}. \tag{3.7}$$

Using Theorem 3.1, we can make some statements about how the solution changes as the parameters change:

- As h increases, Q^* decreases, since larger holding cost $\implies$ it's more expensive to hold inventory $\implies$ order smaller quantities more frequently

- As K increases, Q^* increases, since it's more expensive to place orders $\implies$ we place fewer of them, with larger quantities

- As c increases, Q^* decreases if h is proportional to c (and stays the same if they are independent)

- As λ increases, Q^* increases

Obviously, if any of the costs increase, then $g(Q^*)$ will increase. If λ increases, $g(Q^*)$ will increase, as well. This does not mean that the firm prefers small demand, however. Remember that the EOQ only reflects costs, not revenues; the increased cost of large λ would be outweighed by the increased revenue.

☐ **EXAMPLE 3.1**

Joe's corner store sells 1300 candy bars per year. It costs $8 to place an order to the candy bar supplier. Each candy bar costs the store 75 cents. Holding costs are estimated to be 30% per year. What is the optimal order quantity?
We have $h = 0.3 \cdot 0.75 = 0.225$, so

$$Q^* = \sqrt{\frac{2K\lambda}{h}} = \sqrt{\frac{2 \cdot 8 \cdot 1300}{0.225}} = 304.1.$$

The optimal cycle time is

$$T^* = Q^*/\lambda = 304.1/1300 = 0.23.$$

So the store should order 304.1 candy bars every 0.23 years, or approximately 4 times per year. The optimal cost is

$$\sqrt{2K\lambda h} = \sqrt{2 \cdot 8 \cdot 1300 \cdot 0.225} = 68.41.$$

If we must order in integer quantities, then we need to round Q^* down and up and check the cost of each:

$$g(304) = \frac{8 \cdot 1300}{304} + \frac{0.225 \cdot 304}{2} = 68.4105$$

$$g(305) = \frac{8 \cdot 1300}{305} + \frac{0.225 \cdot 305}{2} = 68.4108,$$

so we should order 304.   ☐

3.2.4 Sensitivity to Q

Suppose the firm did not want to order Q^* exactly. For example, it might need to order in multiples of 10 ($Q = 10n$), or it might want to order every month ($T = 1/12$). How much more expensive is a suboptimal solution? It turns out that the answer is "not much," and that we can determine the exact percentage increase in cost using a very simple formula.

Theorem 3.2 *Suppose Q^* is the optimal order quantity in the EOQ model. Then for any $Q > 0$,*

$$\frac{g(Q)}{g(Q^*)} = \frac{1}{2}\left(\frac{Q^*}{Q} + \frac{Q}{Q^*}\right). \tag{3.8}$$

Proof.

$$\frac{g(Q)}{g(Q^*)} = \frac{\frac{K\lambda}{Q} + \frac{hQ}{2}}{\sqrt{2K\lambda h}}$$

$$= \frac{K\lambda}{Q\sqrt{2K\lambda h}} + \frac{hQ}{2\sqrt{2K\lambda h}}$$

$$= \frac{1}{Q}\sqrt{\frac{K\lambda}{2h}} + \frac{Q}{2}\sqrt{\frac{h}{2K\lambda}}$$

$$= \underbrace{\frac{1}{2Q}\sqrt{\frac{2K\lambda}{h}}}_{=Q^*} + \underbrace{\frac{Q}{2}\sqrt{\frac{h}{2K\lambda}}}_{=1/Q^*}$$

$$= \frac{1}{2}\left(\frac{Q^*}{Q} + \frac{Q}{Q^*}\right)$$

∎

The right-hand side of (3.8) grows slowly as Q deviates more from Q^*, meaning that the EOQ is not very sensitive to errors in Q. For example, if we order twice as much as we should ($Q = 2Q^*$), the error is 1.25—25% more expensive than optimal. If we order half as much ($Q = Q^*/2$), the error is also 1.25.

Theorem 3.2 ignores the per-unit cost c. If we include the annual cost $c\lambda$ in the numerator and denominator of (3.8), then the percentage increase in cost would be even smaller (and the expressions would not simplify as nicely).

☐ **EXAMPLE 3.2**

Suppose Joe's Corner Store (Example 3.1) ordered 250 candy bars per order instead of the optimal 304. How much would the cost increase as a result of this suboptimal solution?

$$\frac{g(Q)}{g(Q^*)} = \frac{1}{2}\left(\frac{304}{250} + \frac{250}{304}\right) = 1.019$$

So this solution would cost 1.9% more than the optimal solution. (You can also confirm this by calculating $g(250)$ explicitly and comparing it to $g(Q^*)$.)   ☐

3.2.5   Order Lead Times

We assumed the lead time is 0. What if the lead time was positive—say, L years? The optimal solution doesn't change—we just place our order L years before it's needed. For example, if $L = 1$ month = 1/12 years, then the order should be placed 1/12 years before the inventory level reaches 0. It's generally more convenient to express this in terms of the *reorder point* (r). When the inventory level reaches r, an order is placed. How do we compute r? Well, r should be equal to the amount of product demanded during the lead time, or

$$r = \lambda L. \tag{3.9}$$

☐ **EXAMPLE 3.3**

In Example 3.1, if $L = 1/12$, the store should place an order whenever the inventory level reaches $r = 1300 \cdot (1/12) = 108$.   ☐

3.2.6 Power-of-Two Policies

From Section 3.2.3, we know that the optimal solution to the EOQ model is $Q^* = \sqrt{2K\lambda/h}$. We also know that the order interval T is given by $T = Q/\lambda$, so the optimal order interval is $T^* = \sqrt{2K/\lambda h}$. But what if T^* is some inconvenient number? How can we place an order, for example, every $\sqrt{10}$ weeks? In this section, we discuss *power-of-two policies*, in which the order interval is required to be a power-of-two multiple of some *base period*. The base period may be any time period—week, day, work shift, etc. If the base period is a day (say), then the power-of-two restriction says that orders can be placed every 1 day, or every 2 days, or every 4 days, or every 8 days, and so on, or every 1/2 day, or every 1/4 day, and so on. Policies based on a convenient base period like days or months are more convenient to implement than those involving base periods like $\sqrt{10}$. We already know that the EOQ model is relatively insensitive to deviations from the optimal solution from Theorem 3.2. Our goal is to determine exactly how much more expensive a power-of-two policy is than the optimal policy.

Power-of-two policies have another advantage over the optimal EOQ policy: They make coordination easier at a central warehouse. If retailers each order according to their own EOQ policies, the warehouse will see a chaotic mess of order times. If, instead, each retailer follows a power-of-two policy with the same base period, the warehouse will see orders line up nicely, making its own inventory planning easier. The problem of finding optimal order intervals in this setting is one version of a problem known as the *one warehouse, multi-retailer (OWMR) problem*. The optimal policy for the OWMR problem is not known, but it has been shown that power-of-two policies are very close to optimal (Roundy 1985, Muckstadt and Roundy 1993).

3.2.6.1 *Analysis* The problem statement is exactly as in the EOQ model (see Section 3.2.1). In addition, we assume there is some base planning period T_B. The actual reorder interval chosen must be of the form

$$T = T_B 2^k \tag{3.10}$$

for some $k \in \{\ldots, -2, -1, 0, 1, 2, \ldots\}$. We need to determine (a) the best power-of-two policy, i.e., the best value of k, and (b) how far from optimal this policy is.

From the EOQ model, we know that the optimal order interval is

$$T^* = \sqrt{\frac{2K}{\lambda h}}. \tag{3.11}$$

Let $f(T)$ be the EOQ cost if an order interval of T is chosen, ignoring the per-unit cost; that is,

$$f(T) = \frac{K}{T} + \frac{h\lambda T}{2}. \tag{3.12}$$

(This follows from substituting $Q = T\lambda$ in the EOQ cost function (3.3).) One can easily verify that f is convex, so the optimal k in (3.10) is the smallest integer k

satisfying

$$f(T_B 2^k) \leq f(T_B 2^{k+1}), \tag{3.13}$$

that is,

$$\frac{K}{T_B 2^k} + \frac{h\lambda}{2} T_B 2^k \leq \frac{K}{T_B 2^{k+1}} + \frac{h\lambda}{2} T_B 2^{k+1}$$

$$\iff \frac{K}{T_B 2^{k+1}} \leq \frac{h\lambda}{2} T_B 2^k$$

$$\iff \frac{K}{h\lambda} \leq (T_B 2^k)^2$$

$$\iff \frac{1}{\sqrt{2}} T^* = \sqrt{\frac{K}{h\lambda}} \leq T_B 2^k = T. \tag{3.14}$$

Therefore, the optimal power-of-two order interval is $T = T_B 2^k$, where k is the smallest integer satisfying (3.14).

3.2.6.2 *Error Bound*

Theorem 3.3 *If T is the optimal power-of-two order interval and T^* is the optimal (not necessarily power-of-two) order interval, then*

$$\frac{f(T)}{f(T^*)} \leq \frac{3}{2\sqrt{2}} \approx 1.06.$$

In other words, the cost of the optimal power-of-two policy is no more than 6% greater than the cost of the optimal (non-power-of-two) policy. This holds for any choice of the base period T_B.

Proof. Since k is the smallest integer satisfying (3.13), we have

$$f(T_B 2^{k-1}) > f(T_B 2^k)$$

$$\iff \frac{K}{T_B 2^k} > \frac{h\lambda}{2} T_B 2^{k-1}$$

$$\iff \sqrt{\frac{4K}{h\lambda}} > T_B 2^k,$$

or

$$T < \sqrt{2} T^*. \tag{3.15}$$

Together, (3.14) and (3.15) imply that the optimal power-of-two order interval T must be in the interval $[\frac{1}{\sqrt{2}} T^*, \sqrt{2} T^*)$. Note that this is true for *any* base period T_B. Now, using (3.11) and (3.12),

$$f\left(\frac{1}{\sqrt{2}}T^*\right) = \frac{\sqrt{2K}}{T^*} + \frac{h\lambda}{2}\frac{1}{\sqrt{2}}T^*$$

$$= \frac{\sqrt{2K}}{\sqrt{\frac{2K}{\lambda h}}} + \frac{h\lambda}{2}\frac{1}{\sqrt{2}}\sqrt{\frac{2K}{\lambda h}}$$

$$= \frac{3}{2\sqrt{2}}\sqrt{2K\lambda h}$$

$$= \frac{3}{2\sqrt{2}}f(T^*).$$

Similarly,

$$f(\sqrt{2}T^*) = \frac{K}{\sqrt{2}T^*} + \frac{h\lambda}{2}\sqrt{2}T^*$$

$$= \frac{1}{\sqrt{2}}\sqrt{\frac{K\lambda h}{2}} + \frac{\sqrt{2}}{2}\sqrt{2K\lambda h}$$

$$= \frac{3}{2\sqrt{2}}\sqrt{2K\lambda h}$$

$$= \frac{3}{2\sqrt{2}}f(T^*).$$

Since f is convex and the optimal T lies somewhere between $\frac{1}{\sqrt{2}}T^*$ and $\sqrt{2}T^*$,

$$\frac{f(T)}{f(T^*)} \leq \frac{3}{2\sqrt{2}} \approx 1.06.$$

∎

Since we don't know precisely where T falls in the range $[\frac{1}{\sqrt{2}}T^*, \sqrt{2}T^*)$, this is only a worst-case bound that occurs on the endpoints of the range. If T falls somewhere in the middle of the range, the power-of-two policy may be even better than 6% above optimal. In fact, if we assume that T is uniformly distributed in the range, we get an expected bound of only 2%:

Theorem 3.4 *Assuming that the optimal power-of-two order interval T is uniformly distributed in the range $[\frac{1}{\sqrt{2}}T^*, \sqrt{2}T^*]$,*

$$\frac{E[f(T)]}{f(T^*)} \leq \frac{1}{\sqrt{2}}\left(\ln 2 + \frac{3}{4}\right) \approx 1.02. \qquad (3.16)$$

Proof. Omitted.   ∎

☐ **EXAMPLE 3.4**

Suppose Joe (owner of Joe's Corner Store, from Example 3.1) must order candy bars in power-of-two multiples of one month. What is the optimal power-of-two order interval, and what is the cost ratio versus the optimal (non-power-of-two) solution?

We have $T_B = 1/12$ years. You can confirm that

$$f\left(T_B 2^0\right) = f(0.0833) = 108.19$$
$$f\left(T_B 2^1\right) = f(0.1667) = 72.38$$
$$f\left(T_B 2^2\right) = f(0.3333) = 72.75$$

By the convexity arguments above, the optimal power-of-two order interval is $T = 0.1667$ years, or every 2 months. The cost ratio is $72.38/68.41 = 1.0580$, within the bound of 1.06.   ☐

3.2.7 The EOQ with Quantity Discounts

It is common for suppliers to offer discounts based on the quantity ordered. The larger the order, the lower the purchase cost per item. (You may have observed something similar when you shop for groceries. When you buy in bulk, you pay less per unit.) The specific structure for the discounts can take many forms, but two types are most common: *all-units discounts* and *incremental discounts*. Both discount structures use *breakpoints* to determine the purchase price. For example, the supplier may charge $1 per unit if the firm orders 0–100 units, $0.90 per unit if the firm orders 100–250 units, and $0.85 per unit if the firm orders more than 250 units. The two discount structures differ based on how the total purchase cost is determined.

We assume there are n *breakpoints*, denoted $b_1, \ldots, b_n$. For convenience, we also define $b_0 \equiv 0$ and $b_{n+1} \equiv \infty$. The interval $[b_j, b_{j+1})$ is called the *region* for breakpoint j, or simply region j for short. Each breakpoint b_j, $j = 0, \ldots, n$, is associated with a purchase price c_j. The costs are decreasing in j: $c_0 > c_1 > \ldots > c_n$. The total purchase cost, denoted $c(Q)$, is calculated in each of the discount structures as follows:

- *All-units discounts.* All units in the order incur the price determined by the breakpoint. That is, if $Q \in [b_j, b_{j+1})$, then the total purchase cost is $c(Q) = c_j Q$.

- *Incremental discounts.* The units in each region incur the purchase price for that region. That is, if $Q \in [b_j, b_{j+1})$, then the total purchase cost is

$$c(Q) = \sum_{i=0}^{j-1} c_i(b_{i+1} - b_i) + c_j(Q - b_j). \tag{3.17}$$

(Note that $c(Q)$ does not include the fixed ordering cost.)

□ EXAMPLE 3.5

Suppose that Joe's candy supplier (from Example 3.1) charges $0.75 per candy bar if Joe orders 0–400 candy bars, $0.72 each for 401–800, and $0.68 each for 800 or more. That is, $b_1 = 400$, $b_2 = 800$, $c_0 = 0.75$, $c_1 = 0.72$, and $c_2 = 0.68$. Figures 3.4(a) and 3.4(b) depict the total purchase cost, $c(Q)$, for the all-units and incremental discount structures, respectively. □

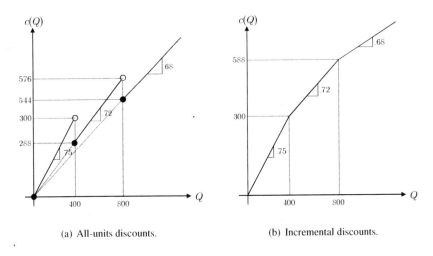

(a) All-units discounts. (b) Incremental discounts.

Figure 3.4 Total purchase cost $c(Q)$ for Example 3.5.

We will formulate models to determine the optimal order quantity under both discount structures. In both cases, the approach will amount to solving multiple EOQ problems, one for each region, and using their solutions to determine the solution to the original problem.

3.2.7.1 *All-Units Discounts*

We can no longer ignore the purchase cost as we did in (3.3). In fact, not only do we need to include the purchase cost itself, but we must also account for the fact that the holding cost typically depends on the purchase cost, as discussed in Section 3.1.3. Let i be the annual holding cost rate expressed as a percentage of the purchase cost. That is, if $i = 0.25$ and $c = 100$, then $h = 25$ per year.

Suppose we knew that the optimal order quantity lies in region j. Then we would simply need to find the Q that minimizes the EOQ cost function for region j:

$$g_j(Q) = c_j\lambda + \frac{K\lambda}{Q} + \frac{ic_jQ}{2}. \tag{3.18}$$

As j increases, c_j decreases, $g_j(Q)$ shifts down and becomes flatter, and its minimum point moves to the right; see Figure 3.5. The heavy segments of the cost curves identify the "active" cost function in each region. Our objective is to minimize $g(Q)$, the discontinuous function defined by the heavy segments.

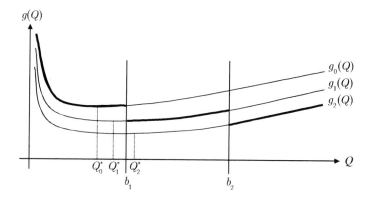

Figure 3.5   Total cost curves for all-units quantity discount structure.

The function $g_j(Q)$ has the same structure as $g(Q)$ in (3.3) except for the additional constant. Therefore, its minimizer is given by

$$Q_j^* = \sqrt{\frac{2K\lambda}{ic_j}}. \qquad (3.19)$$

Of course, if Q_j^* falls outside of region j, then if the firm orders Q_j^*, it will incur a cost other than $g_j(Q_j^*)$. Q_j^* is meaningless in this case. We say that Q_j^* is *realizable* if it lies in region j. In Figure 3.5, only Q_0^* is realizable. Does this mean that Q_0^* is necessarily the optimal solution? No: The breakpoints to the right of Q_0^* are also candidates.

The optimal order quantity always equals either the largest realizable Q_j^* or one of the (left) breakpoints to its right. (Why?)

Therefore, we can determine Q^* as follows. First, we calculate Q_j^* for each j. Suppose Q_i^* is the largest realizable Q_j^*. We then evaluate $g_j(b_j)$ for each b_j greater than Q_i^*. Finally, we evaluate the cost of the quantities identified and set Q^* to the quantity with the lowest cost.

Since Q_j^* increases as j increases, if we start in region n when we calculate Q_j^* and work backwards, we can stop as soon as we find one realizable Q_j^*; this is necessarily the largest realizable Q_j^*.

☐ **EXAMPLE 3.6**

Recall from Example 3.1 that $\lambda = 1300$, $K = 8$, and $i = 0.3$. If candy purchases follow the quantity discount structure in Example 3.5, what is Joe's optimal order quantity?

We first determine the largest realizable Q_j^* by working backwards from segment 2:

$$Q_2^* = \sqrt{\frac{2 \cdot 8 \cdot 1300}{0.3 \cdot 0.68}} = 319.3$$

$$Q_1^* = \sqrt{\frac{2 \cdot 8 \cdot 1300}{0.3 \cdot 0.72}} = 310.3$$

$$Q_0^* = \sqrt{\frac{2 \cdot 8 \cdot 1300}{0.3 \cdot 0.75}} = 304.1$$

Only Q_0^* is realizable, and it has cost

$$0.75 \cdot 1300 + \sqrt{2 \cdot 8 \cdot 1300 \cdot 0.3 \cdot 0.75} = 1043.4.$$

Next, we calculate the cost of the breakpoints to the right of Q_0^*:

$$g_1(400) = 0.72 \cdot 1300 + \frac{8 \cdot 1300}{400} + \frac{0.3 \cdot 0.72 \cdot 400}{2} = 1005.2$$

$$g_2(800) = 0.68 \cdot 1300 + \frac{8 \cdot 1300}{400} + \frac{0.3 \cdot 0.68 \cdot 400}{2} = 978.6$$

Therefore, the optimal order quantity is $Q = 800$, which incurs a purchase cost of \$0.68 and a total annual cost of \$978.60. $\square$

3.2.7.2 *Incremental Discounts*

We now turn our attention to incremental discounts. The total cost function for region j is given by

$$g_j(Q) = \frac{c(Q)}{Q}\lambda + \frac{K\lambda}{Q} + \frac{i\frac{c(Q)}{Q}Q}{2},$$

where $c(Q)$ is given by (3.17). Note that the purchase cost term is no longer a constant with respect to Q, even within a given segment: As Q increases, so does the number of "cheap" units, and the average cost per unit decreases.

We can rewrite $g_j(Q)$ as

$$\begin{aligned}
g_j(Q) = &\frac{1}{Q}\left[\sum_{i=0}^{j-1} c_i(b_{i+1} - b_i) - c_j b_j\right]\lambda + c_j\lambda + \frac{K\lambda}{Q} \\
&+ \frac{i}{2}\left[\sum_{i=0}^{j-1} c_i(b_{i+1} - b_i) - c_j b_j\right] + \frac{ic_j Q}{2} \\
= &c_j\lambda + \frac{i\bar{c}_j}{2} + \frac{(K + \bar{c}_j)\lambda}{Q} + \frac{ic_j Q}{2},
\end{aligned} \qquad (3.20)$$

where

$$\bar{c}_j = \sum_{i=0}^{j-1} c_i(b_{i+1} - b_i) - c_j b_j.$$

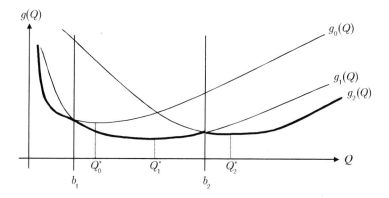

Figure 3.6   Total cost curves for incremental quantity discount structure.

The right-hand side of (3.20) is structurally identical to the EOQ cost function; therefore, its minimizer is given by

$$Q_j^* = \sqrt{\frac{2(K + \bar{c}_j)\lambda}{ic_j}} \tag{3.21}$$

with cost

$$g_j(Q_j^*) = c_j\lambda + \frac{i\bar{c}_j}{2} + \sqrt{2(K + \bar{c}_j)\lambda ic_j}. \tag{3.22}$$

Figure 3.6 plots $g_j(Q)$ for a two-breakpoint problem. As a rule, $g_j(Q)$ is always the lowest curve in region j because the functions are convex and are equal at the breakpoints. On the other hand, Q_j^* is not always realizable. (In the figure, Q_0^* is not realizable.) Our objective is to minimize $g(Q)$, the continuous, piecewise function defined by the heavy segments.

If Q_j^* is not realizable, then clearly it cannot be optimal for $g(Q)$, and moreover, its breakpoints cannot be optimal either. (Why?) Therefore, the optimal order quantity is equal to the realizable Q_j^* that has the lowest cost.

□ **EXAMPLE 3.7**

Return to Example 3.6 and suppose now that Joe faces an incremental quantity discount structure with the same breakpoints and purchase costs. What is Joe's optimal order quantity?

We first determine $\bar{c}_j$ for each j:

$$\bar{c}_0 = 0$$
$$\bar{c}_1 = 0.75 \cdot 400 - 0.72 \cdot 400 = 12$$
$$\bar{c}_2 = 0.75 \cdot 400 + 0.72 \cdot 400 - 0.68 \cdot 800 = 44$$

Next, we calculate Q_j^* for each j:

$$Q_0^* = \sqrt{\frac{2(8+0)1300}{0.3 \cdot 0.75}} = 304.1$$

$$Q_1^* = \sqrt{\frac{2(8+12)1300}{0.3 \cdot 0.72}} = 490.7$$

$$Q_2^* = \sqrt{\frac{2(8+44)1300}{0.3 \cdot 0.68}} = 814.1$$

All three solutions are realizable. Using (3.22), these solutions have the following costs:

$$g_0(Q_0^*) = 0.75 \cdot 1300 + \frac{0.3 \cdot 0}{2} + \sqrt{2(8+0)1300 \cdot 0.3 \cdot 0.75} = 1043.4$$

$$g_1(Q_1^*) = 0.72 \cdot 1300 + \frac{0.3 \cdot 12}{2} + \sqrt{2(8+12)1300 \cdot 0.3 \cdot 0.72} = 1043.8$$

$$g_2(Q_2^*) = 0.68 \cdot 1300 + \frac{0.3 \cdot 44}{2} + \sqrt{2(8+44)1300 \cdot 0.3 \cdot 0.68} = 1056.7$$

Therefore, the optimal order quantity is $Q = 304.1$, which incurs a total annual cost of \$1043.40. $\square$

3.2.7.3 Modified All-Units Discounts

All-units discounts are somewhat problematic because, for order quantities Q just to the left of breakpoint j, it is cheaper to order b_j than to order Q, even though $Q < b_j$. For example, under the cost structure in Example 3.5, it costs \$292.50 to purchase 390 units but \$288.00 to purchase 400 units. (See Figure 3.4(a).)

In practice, suppliers usually allow the buying firm to pay the lower price—\$288.00 in the example above—for order quantities that fall into this awkward zone. This is especially true for transportation costs, since all-units discounts are common in shipping, with the cost determined based on the weight shipped. If a shipment totals, say, 390 kg but it is cheaper to ship 400 kg, the firm could add 10 kg worth of bricks to the shipment, but a solution that is preferable for both the shipper and the transportation company is for the firm to "ship x, declare y"—for example, ship 390 kg, declare 400 kg.

This structure is sometimes known as the *modified all-units discount structure*. Its $c(Q)$ curve is displayed in Figure 3.7(a). The flat portions of the curve represent the regions in which the firm orders or ships one quantity but declares a greater quantity.

Sometimes there is also a minimum charge for each order or shipment, in which case there is an additional horizontal segment at the start of the $c(Q)$ curve; see Figure 3.7(b).

A special case of the modified all-units discount structure is the *carload discount structure*, in which the b_j are equally spaced and c_j is the same for all j. This structure arises from rail or truck carload shipments, in which the transportation company charges a per-unit cost c for each unit shipped, up to some maximum cost

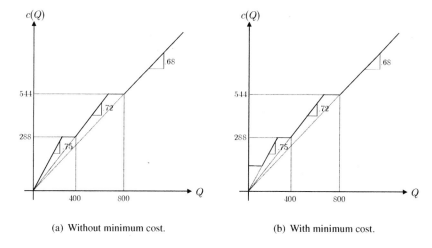

(a) Without minimum cost.   (b) With minimum cost.

Figure 3.7 Total purchase cost $c(Q)$ for modified all-units discounts structure.

for each car. Once the capacity of a car is exceeded, a new car begins, at a cost of c per unit, and so on.

Unfortunately, modified all-units discount structures are much more difficult to analyze than the discount structures discussed above. (See, for example, Chan et al. (2002).) We omit further discussion here.

3.2.8   The EOQ with Planned Backorders

We assumed in Section 3.2.1 that backorders are not allowed. In this section, we discuss a variant of the EOQ problem in which backorders are allowed. Since demand is deterministic, we have the same number of backorders in every order cycle—they are "planned" backorders. (See Figure 3.8.) We'll call this model the *EOQ with backorders* (EOQB).

Let p be the backorder penalty per item per year, and let x be the fraction of demand that is backordered. Both Q and x are decision variables. The holding cost is charged based on on-hand inventory; the average on-hand inventory is given by

$$\frac{Q(1-x)^2}{2}.$$

Similarly, the backorder cost is charged based on the number of backorders; the average backorder level is given by

$$\frac{Qx^2}{2}.$$

(Compute the area under the triangle, then divide by the length of an order cycle.) Finally, the number of orders per year is given by λ/Q, just like in the EOQ model.

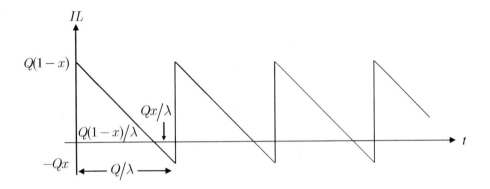

Figure 3.8   EOQB inventory curve.

Therefore, the total average cost per year in the EOQB is given by

$$g(Q, x) = \frac{hQ(1 - x)^2}{2} + \frac{pQx^2}{2} + \frac{K\lambda}{Q}. \tag{3.23}$$

Note that g is a function of both Q and x. Therefore, to minimize it, we need to take partial derivatives with respect to both variables and set them equal to 0.

$$\frac{\partial g}{\partial x} = -hQ(1 - x) + pQx = 0 \tag{3.24}$$

$$\frac{\partial g}{\partial Q} = \frac{h(1 - x)^2}{2} + \frac{px^2}{2} - \frac{K\lambda}{Q^2} = 0 \tag{3.25}$$

Let's first look at (3.24):

$$-hQ(1 - x) + pQx = 0$$
$$\Longleftrightarrow \quad h(1 - x) = px$$
$$\Longleftrightarrow \quad x^* = \frac{h}{h + p} \tag{3.26}$$

Interestingly, x^* does not depend on Q; even if we choose a suboptimal Q, the optimal x to choose is still $h/(h + p)$. At this point we could substitute $h/(h + p)$ for x in (3.25) and solve for Q, but instead we'll plug x^* into $g(Q, x)$:

$$g(Q, x) = \frac{hQ}{2} \left(\frac{p}{h + p} \right)^2 + \frac{pQ}{2} \left(\frac{h}{h + p} \right)^2 + \frac{K\lambda}{Q}$$
$$= \frac{Q}{2} \left(\frac{p^2 h + h^2 p}{(h + p)^2} \right) + \frac{K\lambda}{Q}$$
$$= \frac{hp}{h + p} \frac{Q}{2} + \frac{K\lambda}{Q}$$

This is exactly the same form as the EOQ cost function (3.3) with the holding cost h replaced by $hp/(h + p)$. In other words, the EOQB model is equivalent to the EOQ model with the holding cost h scaled by $p/(h + p)$. Therefore we can use (3.6) and (3.7) to obtain the optimal Q and the optimal cost for the EOQB, as stated in the next theorem.

Theorem 3.5 *In the EOQ model with backorders, the optimal solution and cost are given by*

$$Q^* = \sqrt{\frac{2K\lambda(h + p)}{hp}} \tag{3.27}$$

$$x^* = \frac{h}{h + p} \tag{3.28}$$

$$g(Q^*, x^*) = \sqrt{\frac{2K\lambda hp}{h + p}} \tag{3.29}$$

How do the optimal solution and cost in Theorem 3.5 compare to the analogous quantities from the EOQ model? First, comparing (3.29) and (3.7), we can see that the optimal cost is smaller in the EOQB than in the EOQ. This makes sense, since the EOQ is a special case of the EOQB in which the constraint $x = 0$ has been added. From (3.27), we can see that the optimal order quantity is greater in the EOQB than in the EOQ. This is because placing larger orders in the EOQB does not require us to carry quite as much inventory as it does in the EOQ, and therefore the extra flexibility offered by the backorder option allows us to place larger orders.

As $p \to \infty$, Q^* approaches the optimal EOQ order quantity, x^* approaches 0, and the optimal cost approaches the EOQ optimal cost.

Note also that x is strictly greater than 0, provided that h is. Therefore, it is *always* optimal to allow some backorders. To see why, suppose we set $x = 0$—then the EOQB inventory curve in Figure 3.8 collapses to the EOQ curve in Figure 3.2. Now, if we increase x slightly, we create a tiny negative triangle at the end of each cycle in Figure 3.8, incurring a tiny backorder cost. But we also reduce the height of the positive part of the inventory curve throughout the rest of the cycle, resulting in a substantial savings in holding cost.

What if we consider the same model but assume that unmet demands are lost, rather than backordered? It turns out that in this case it is optimal either to meet every demand ($x = 0$) or to meet no demands ($x = 1$)—see Problem 3.11.

□ **EXAMPLE 3.8**

Recall Example 3.1. Suppose Joe is willing to stock out occasionally and estimates that each backorder costs the store $5 in lost profit and loss of good will. What is the optimal order quantity, the optimal fill rate (fraction of demand met from stock), and the optimal cost?

$$Q^* = \sqrt{\frac{2K\lambda(h+p)}{hp}} = \sqrt{\frac{2 \cdot 8 \cdot 1300(0.225+5)}{0.225 \cdot 5}} = 310.81$$

$$x^* = \frac{h}{h+p} = 0.0431$$

$$g(Q^*, x^*) = \sqrt{\frac{2K\lambda hp}{h+p}} = \sqrt{\frac{2 \cdot 8 \cdot 1300 \cdot 0.225 \cdot 5}{0.225+5}} = 66.92$$

The cost has decreased by 2.2% versus the cost without backorders.   □

3.3 PERIODIC REVIEW: THE WAGNER-WHITIN MODEL

3.3.1 Problem Statement

We now shift our attention to a periodic-review model known as the *Wagner-Whitin model* (Wagner and Whitin 1958). Like the EOQ model, the Wagner-Whitin model assumes that the demand is deterministic, there is a fixed cost to place an order, and stockouts are not allowed. The objective is to choose order quantities to minimize the total cost. However, unlike the EOQ model, the Wagner-Whitin model allows the demand to change over time—to be different in each period.

Because of the fixed cost, it may not be optimal to place an order in every time period. However, we will show that, as in the EOQ, optimal solutions have the zero-inventory ordering (ZIO) property. Therefore, the problem boils down to deciding how many whole periods' worth of demand to order at once.

Unlike the infinite-horizon EOQ model, the Wagner-Whitin model considers a finite horizon, consisting of T periods. In each period, we must decide whether to place a replenishment order, and if so, how large an order to place. The demand in period t is given by d_t, and stockouts are not allowed. The lead time is 0. As in the EOQ model, there is a fixed cost K per order and an inventory holding cost h per unit per period. (Note that h represents the holding cost per year in the EOQ model but per period here.) One could also include a purchase cost c, but since the total number of units ordered throughout the horizon is constant (independent of the ordering pattern), it is safe to ignore this cost.

Assume that the on-hand inventory is 0 at time 0. In each time period, the following events occur, in the following order:

1. The replenishment order, if any, is placed and is received instantly.

2. Demand occurs and is satisfied from inventory.

3. Holding costs are assessed based on the on-hand inventory.

(This type of timeline is known as a *sequence of events*. It is important to specify the sequence of events clearly in periodic-review models. For example, the holding costs would be very different if events 2 and 3 were reversed.)

This model can be formulated as an integer programming (IP) problem. However, we will instead solve the model using dynamic programming (DP), which does not rely on the IP formulation, and will therefore omit the IP formulation.

3.3.2 Dynamic Programming Algorithm

The DP algorithm depends on the following result:

Theorem 3.6 *Every optimal solution to the Wagner-Whitin model has the ZIO property; that is, it is optimal to place orders only in time periods in which the initial inventory is zero.*

Proof. Suppose (for a contradiction) there is an optimal solution in which an order is placed in period t even though the inventory level at the beginning of period t, denoted I_t, is positive. The I_t units in inventory were ordered in a period before t and incurred a holding cost to be held from period $t - 1$ to t. If these items had instead been ordered in period t, then (a) the holding cost would decrease since fewer units are held in inventory, and (b) the fixed cost would stay the same since the number of orders would not change, only the size of each order. This contradicts the assumption that the original policy is optimal; hence, every optimal solution must have the ZIO property. ∎

Theorem 3.6 and its proof assume that $h > 0$; if h may equal 0, then the theorem would read "There exists an optimal solution..."

As a corollary to Theorem 3.6, each order is of a size equal to an integer number of subsequent periods; that is, in period t we either order d_t, or $d_t + d_{t+1}$, or $d_t + d_{t+1} + d_{t+2}$, and so on. The problem then boils down to deciding in which periods to order. We formulate this problem as a DP.

Let θ_t be the optimal cost in periods $t, t + 1, \ldots, T$ if we place an order in period t (and act optimally thereafter). We can define θ_t recursively in terms of θ_s for later periods s. First define $\theta_{T+1} \equiv 0$. Then:

$$\theta_t = \min_{t < s \leq T+1} \left\{ K + h \sum_{i=t}^{s-1} (i - t)d_i + \theta_s \right\}. \tag{3.30}$$

The minimization determines the next period s in which we will place an order, assuming that we order in period t. (Setting $s = T + 1$ means we never order again; the order in period t is the last order.) A given choice of s is evaluated using the expression inside the braces. The first two terms calculate the cost incurred in periods t through $s - 1$: the order cost of K, plus the holding cost for the items that will be held until future periods. (The d_t units demanded in period t will be held for 0 periods; d_{t+1} units will be held for 1 period; ...; and d_{s-1} units will be held for $s - 1 - t$ periods.) A new order will be placed in period s, and θ_s includes the cost in period s and all future periods.

The DP algorithm for the Wagner-Whitin problem is summarized in Algorithm 3.1.

Algorithm 3.1 (Wagner-Whitin Algorithm)

1. Set $\theta_{T+1} \leftarrow 0$ and $t \leftarrow T$.

2. Compute θ_t using (3.30) and set $s(t)$ equal to the s that minimizes the expression inside the braces.

3. Set $t \leftarrow t - 1$. If $t = 0$, STOP. Otherwise, go to 2.

At the conclusion of the algorithm, θ_1 equals the cost of the optimal solution. The optimal solution itself is obtained by "backtracking"—we place orders in period 1, period $s(1)$, period $s(s(1))$, and so on.

The complexity of the algorithm is $O(T^2)$ since step 2 requires $O(T)$ operations and must be performed $O(T)$ times. Faster algorithms, which run in $O(T)$ time, have been developed for this problem but will not be discussed here. (See Federgruen and Tzur (1991), Wagelmans et al. (1992).) Despite the efficiency of this algorithm, a number of heuristics have been introduced and are still popular in practice. These include Silver–Meal, part period balancing, least unit cost, and other heuristics (Silver et al. 1998). One explanation for the persistent use of these approximate methods is that they tend to be less sensitive to changes in the data, so that as demand forecasts change for several periods into the future, the current production plan doesn't change much.

The Wagner-Whitin model can equivalently be represented by a network with $T+1$ nodes in which each node represents a time period and an arc from period t to period s represents ordering in period t to satisfy the demands of periods $t, t+1, \ldots, s-1$. The cost of this arc is

$$K + h \sum_{i=t}^{s-1} (i - t) d_i.$$

Solving the Wagner-Whitin problem is equivalent to finding a shortest path through this network (which is, in turn, equivalent to solving the DP given above.) Figure 3.9 depicts the network for a 4-period problem. Note that there is one extra node, node s, called the "dummy node," that serves as a sink for arcs representing ordering from the current time period until the end of the horizon.

☐ EXAMPLE 3.9

A garden center sells bags of organic compost for vegetable gardens. Compost is heavy, and special trucks must be used to transport it, so shipping is expensive; each order therefore incurs a fixed cost of $500. The holding cost for each cubic meter of compost is $2 per week. We consider a 4-period planning horizon. The demand for compost in periods 1–4 is 90, 120, 80, and 70 cubic meters, respectively. Find the optimal order quantity in each period and the total cost.

From (3.30), we have:

$$\theta_5 = 0$$
$$\theta_4 = K + h(0 \cdot d_4) + \theta_5$$

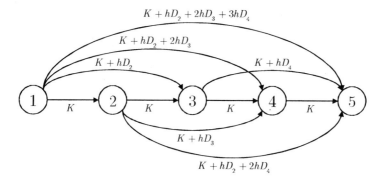

Figure 3.9   Wagner-Whitin network.

$$=500 \quad [s(4) = 5]$$
$$\theta_3 = \min\{K + h(0 \cdot d_3) + \theta_4, K + h(0 \cdot d_3 + 1 \cdot d_4) + \theta_5\}$$
$$= \min\{1000, 640\}$$
$$=640 \quad [s(3) = 5]$$
$$\theta_2 = \min\{K + h(0 \cdot d_2) + \theta_3, K + h(0 \cdot d_2 + 1 \cdot d_3) + \theta_4,$$
$$K + h(0 \cdot d_2 + 1 \cdot d_3 + 2 \cdot d_4) + \theta_5\}$$
$$= \min\{1140, 1160, 940\}$$
$$=940 \quad [s(2) = 5]$$
$$\theta_1 = \min\{K + h(0 \cdot d_1) + \theta_2, K + h(0 \cdot d_1 + 1 \cdot d_2) + \theta_3,$$
$$K + h(0 \cdot d_1 + 1 \cdot d_2 + 2 \cdot d_3) + \theta_4,$$
$$K + h(0 \cdot d_1 + 1 \cdot d_2 + 2 \cdot d_3 + 3 \cdot d_4) + \theta_5\}$$
$$= \min\{1440, 1380, 1560, 1480\}$$
$$=1380 \quad [s(1) = 3]$$

Therefore, we order in periods 1 and $s(1) = 3$; the optimal order quantities are $Q_1 = d_1 + d_2 = 110$ and $Q_3 = d_3 + d_4 = 150$ cubic meters; and the total cost is 1380.   □

3.3.3 Extensions

Many of the assumptions made in Section 3.3.1 can be relaxed without making the problem substantially harder. For example, period-specific costs (h_t, K_t, c_t) can easily be accommodated. Similarly, non-zero lead times can be handled, provided the lead time is still fixed and constant. Positive initial inventories can be handled with appropriate modifications to the cost function in period 1.

Other extensions are considerably more difficult. For example, we assumed implicitly that there were no capacity constraints—an order can be placed of any size, and any amount of inventory can be carried over. Capacitated versions of the Wagner-Whitin model turn out to be NP-hard (Florian et al. 1980). Backlogging and concave order costs (instead of linear) are considered by Zangwill (1966); the model is still polynomially solvable, but the solution approach is less tractable than the DP presented here.

PROBLEMS

3.1 **(EOQ for Steel)** An auto manufacturer uses 500 tons of steel per day. The company pays $1100 per ton of steel purchased, and each order incurs a fixed cost of $2250. The holding cost is $275 per ton of steel per year. Using the EOQ model, calculate the optimal order quantity, reorder interval, and average cost per year.

3.2 **(EOQ for MP3s)** Suppose that your favorite electronics store maintains an inventory of a certain brand and model of MP3 player. The store pays the manufacturer $165 for each MP3 player ordered. Each order incurs a fixed cost of $40 in order processing, shipping, etc. and requires a 2-week lead time. The store estimates that its cost of capital is 17% per year, and it estimates its other holding costs (warehouse space, insurance, etc.) at $1 per MP3 player per month. The demand for MP3 players is steady at 40 per week.

    a) Using the EOQ model, calculate the optimal order quantity, reorder point (r), and average cost per year.

    b) Now suppose that backorders are allowed, and that each backorder incurs a stockout penalty of $60 per stockout per year. Using the EOQ model with planned backorders, calculate the optimal order quantity, stockout percentage (x), reorder point (r), and average cost per year. How much money would the store save per year by allowing stockouts, expressed as a percentage?

3.3 **(EOQ with Non-Zero Lead Time)** Consider the EOQ model with fixed lead time $L > 0$ (Section 3.2.5). Prove that the average amount of inventory on order is equal to the lead-time demand.

3.4 **(EOQ with Batches)** Suppose that in the EOQ model we can only order batches that are an integer multiple of some number Q_B; that is, we can order a batch of size $Q_B, 2Q_B, 3Q_B$, etc.

    a) Prove that, for the optimal order quantity $Q^* = mQ_B$,

$$\sqrt{\frac{m-1}{m}} \le \frac{Q_E}{Q^*} \le \sqrt{\frac{m+1}{m}},$$

    where $Q_E = \sqrt{2K\lambda/h}$ is the optimal (non-integer-multiple) EOQ quantity.

    b) Suppose that $m \ge 2$ for Q^*. Using the result in part (a), prove that $g(Q^*) \le 1.32g(Q^e)$, where $g(\cdot)$ is the EOQ cost function.

    c) *Bonus*: Prove that $g(Q^*) \le 1.06g(Q_E)$.

3.5 **(Tightness of Power-of-2 Bound)** Prove that the bound given in Theorem 3.3 is tight by developing an instance of the problem such that

$$\frac{f(T)}{f(T^*)} = \frac{3}{2\sqrt{2}}.$$

Hint: You should be able to come up with a suitable value of T_B in terms of the problem parameters. That is, you shouldn't need to pick values for λ, h, and K; instead, you should be able to leave the values of these parameters unspecified and to express T_B in terms of the parameters to achieve the desired result.

3.6 **(Quantity Discounts for Steel)** Return to Problem 3.1 and suppose that the steel supplier offers the auto manufacturer a price of \$1,490 per ton of steel if $Q < 1200$ tons; \$1,220 per ton if $1200 \le Q < 2400$, and \$1,100 per ton if $Q \ge 2400$. The annual holding cost rate, i, is 0.25.

a) Calculate Q^* and $g(Q^*)$ for the all-units discount structure.
b) Calculate Q^* and $g(Q^*)$ for the incremental discount structure.

3.7 **(Sequence of Q_j^*)** In the EOQ model with incremental quantity discounts, prove that $Q_{j-1}^* < Q_j^*$ for all $j = 1, \ldots, n$.

3.8 **(Inventory-Related Costs in EOQ and EOQB)** Prove that the optimal average holding plus backorder cost per year in the EOQB model is less than the optimal average holding cost per year in the EOQ model. (The same is clearly true for the optimal order cost per year; therefore, both types of costs decrease when we allow backorders.)

3.9 **(Sensitivity Analysis for EOQB: Q)** Prove that a result analogous to Theorem 3.2 also describes the sensitivity of the EOQB model with respect to Q; that is, prove that, for any Q:

$$\frac{g(Q, x^*)}{g(Q^*, x^*)} = \frac{1}{2}\left(\frac{Q^*}{Q} + \frac{Q}{Q^*}\right).$$

3.10 **(Sensitivity Analysis for EOQB: x)** In this problem you will explore the EOQB model's sensitivity to x, the fraction of demand that is backordered.

a) Let $Q(x)$ be the optimal Q for a given x. Derive an expression for $g(Q(x), x)$, the cost that results from choosing an arbitrary value of x and then setting Q optimally.
b) Prove that for any $0 \le x \le 1$,

$$\frac{g(Q(x), x)}{g(Q^*, x^*)} = \sqrt{\frac{(1-x)^2 h + x^2 p}{x^* p}}.$$

c) Prove that if $h < p$, then for all x,

$$\frac{g(Q(x), x)}{g(Q^*, x^*)} \le \frac{1}{\sqrt{x^*}}.$$

3.11   (EOQ with Lost Sales) Suppose that we are allowed to stock out in the EOQ model, but instead of excess demands being backordered (as in Section 3.2.8), they are lost. Let x be the fraction of demand that is lost, and let p be the cost per lost sale. Let c be the cost to order each unit. In the standard EOQ and the EOQ with backorders, we could ignore c because each year we order exactly λ items per year on average, regardless of the order quantity Q. But if some demands are lost, we will not order items to replenish those demands; therefore, the total per-unit ordering cost per year *does depend* on the solution we choose.

- **a)** Formulate the total cost per year as a function of Q and x.
- **b)** Prove that

$$x^* = \begin{cases} 0, & \text{if } \lambda(p - c) > \sqrt{2K\lambda h} \\ 1, & \text{if } \lambda(p - c) < \sqrt{2K\lambda h} \\ \text{anything in } [0, 1], & \text{if } \lambda(p - c) = \sqrt{2K\lambda h} \end{cases}$$

- **c)** Give an interpretation of the condition $\lambda(p - c) > \sqrt{2K\lambda h}$ and explain in words why the optimal value of x^* follows the rule given in part (b).
- **d)** Part (b) implies that either we meet *every* demand or we stock out on *every* demand—x^* is never strictly between 0 and 1 (except in the special case in which $\lambda(p - c) = \sqrt{2K\lambda h}$). This is not the case in the EOQ with backorders. Explain in words why the two models give different results.

3.12   (EOQ with Nonlinear Holding Costs) We assumed that the holding cost for one item in the EOQ model equals ht, where t is the amount of time the item is in inventory. Suppose instead the holding cost for one item is given by he^{bt}, for $b > 0$.

- **a)** Write the average annual cost as a function of Q, $g(Q)$. (Your answer should not include integrals.)
- **b)** Write the first-order condition (i.e., $dg/dQ = 0$) for the function you derived in part (a).
- **c)** The first-order condition cannot be solved directly for Q—we can't write an expression like $Q^* = $ [something or other]. Instead, $g(Q)$ must be optimized numerically. Using a nonlinear programming solver, find the Q that minimizes $g(Q)$ using the following parameter values: $\lambda = 500$, $K = 100$, $h = 1$, $b = 0.5$. Report both Q^* and $g(Q^*)$.

    Note: As part (e) establishes, $g(Q)$ is quasiconvex everywhere; therefore, you may use a nonlinear solver that relies on this property.
- **d)** Prove that $g(Q)$ is convex at $Q = Q^*$.

    Hint: We know the first-order condition says $dg/dQ = 0$ at $Q = Q^*$. Write the second-order condition in such a way that you can make use of the first-order condition.
- **e)** A function f is said to be *unimodal* if there exists some point x^* such that f is increasing on the range $x \le x^*$ and decreasing on the range $x \ge x^*$. A function f is said to be *quasiconvex* if $-f$ is unimodal. Prove that $g(Q)$ is quasiconvex for all $Q > 0$.
- **f)** *Bonus*: Prove that $g(Q)$ is convex for all $Q > 0$.

3.13 **(Wagner-Whitin for Aircraft Engines)** The Pratt & Whitin Company, which manufactures aircraft engines, needs to decide how many units of a particular bolt to order in order to build engines over the next four months. Orders for engines are placed over a year in advance, so the company knows its near-term demand exactly; in particular, the number of engines to produce in the next four months will be 150, 100, 80, and 200 in months 1 through 4, respectively. Each engine requires a single bolt. Orders for bolts incur a fixed cost of $120, and bolts held in inventory incur a holding cost of $0.80 per bolt per month. Find the optimal order quantities in each period and the optimal total cost.

3.14 **(Wagner-Whitin for Sunglasses)** The file `sunglasses.xlsx` contains forecast demand (measured in cases) for sunglasses at a major retailer for each of the next 52 weeks. Each order placed to the supplier incurs a fixed cost of $1100. One case of sunglasses held in inventory for one period incurs a holding cost of $2.40. Find the optimal order quantities in each period and the optimal total cost.

3.15 **(Wagner-Whitin with Randomly Perishable Goods)** Suppose that in the Wagner-Whitin model, all of the items currently held in inventory will perish (be destroyed) with some probability q at the *end* of each time period. That is, if we order 4 periods' worth of demand in period 1, the demand for period 1 will be satisfied for sure, but the inventory consisting of the demand for periods 2–4 will perish with probability q; if it survives (with probability $1 - q$), the inventory for periods 3–4 will perish at the end of period 2 with probability q; and so on.

Obviously, we can no longer require that all demand be satisfied. We will assume that unmet demand is lost (not backordered), and that lost demands incur a penalty cost of p per unit. As in the standard Wagner-Whitin model, we will assume a holding cost of h per unit per time period and a setup cost of K per order.

1. Show how the arc costs can be computed to capture the new cost function so that the Wagner-Whitin dynamic programming algorithm can still be used. Simplify your answer as much as possible.

   Hint: The formulas in Section C.4 may come in handy.

2. Illustrate your method by finding the optimal solution for the following 4-period instance: $h = 0.2$, $K = 200$, $p = 3$, $q = 0.25$, and the demands in periods 1–4 are 200, 125, 250, 175. Indicate the optimal solution (order schedule) and the cost of that solution.

3. Do you think the optimal solution to the problem with perishability will involve *more* orders, *fewer* orders, or *the same number* of orders than the optimal solution to the normal Wagner-Whitin problem (without perishability)? Explain your answer.

CHAPTER 4

STOCHASTIC INVENTORY MODELS

4.1 PRELIMINARIES

In this chapter, we will consider inventory models in which the demand is stochastic. A key concept in this chapter will be that of a *policy*. A policy is a simple rule that provides a solution to the inventory problem. For example, consider a continuous-review model with fixed costs (like the EOQ) but with stochastic demands and a non-zero lead time. (We will examine such a model more closely in Section 4.3.) One could imagine several possible policies for this system. Here are a few:

1. Every T years, place an order for Q units.

2. Every T years, place an order of sufficient size to bring the inventory position to S.

3. Whenever the inventory position falls to r, order Q units.

4. Place an order whose size is equal to the first two digits of last night's lottery number. Then wait a number of days equal to the last two digits of the lottery number before placing another order.

Fundamentals of Supply Chain Theory, First Edition. Lawrence V. Snyder, Zuo-Jun Max Shen. **63**

Now, you probably suspect that some of these policies will perform better (in the sense of keeping costs small) than others. For example, policy 4 is probably a bad one. You probably also suspect that the performance of a policy depends on its *parameters*.[1] For example, policy 1 sounds reasonable, but only if we choose good values for T and Q.

It is often possible (and always desirable) to prove that a certain policy is *optimal* for a given problem—that no other policy (even policies that no one has thought of yet) can outperform the optimal policy, provided that we set the parameters of that policy optimally. For example, policy 3 turns out to be optimal for the model in Section 4.3: If we choose the right r and Q, we are guaranteed to incur the smallest possible expected cost.

When using policies, then, inventory optimization really has two parts: Choosing the optimal policy, and choosing the optimal parameters for that policy. Sometimes we can't solve one of these parts optimally, so we use approximate methods. For example, although it's possible to find the optimal r and Q for the model in Section 4.3, heuristics are commonly used to find approximately optimal values. Similarly, for some problems, no one even knows the form of the optimal policy, so we simply choose a policy that seems plausible.

We'll first consider continuous-review models (in Section 4.3) and then periodic-review models (in Sections 4.4 and 4.5). In both of these sections, we'll simply choose a policy to use, and focus on optimizing the policy parameters. Then, in Section 4.6, we'll prove that the policies we chose for the periodic-review models in Section 4.4 and 4.5 are, in fact, optimal. (We won't prove policy optimality for the continuous-review models in Section 4.3, but those policies, too, are optimal.)

We'll continue to use the same notation introduced in Chapter 3. All of the costs we discussed in Section 3.1.3 are in play, including fixed cost K, purchase cost c, holding cost h, and stockout cost p. We'll assume that K and c are non-negative and h and p are strictly positive. Now, however, we'll represent the demand as a random variable D with mean μ, variance σ^2, pdf $f(d)$, and cdf $F(d)$. (D will represent demands over different time intervals in different models, but we'll make this clear in each section.) We'll usually assume that D is a continuous random variable, though the models below can be modified to incorporate discrete demands instead.

Before continuing, we introduce two important concepts in stochastic inventory theory: cycle stock and safety stock. *Cycle stock* (or working inventory) is the inventory that is intended to meet the expected demand. *Safety stock* is extra inventory that's kept on hand to buffer against demand uncertainty. The target inventory level or order quantity set by most stochastic inventory problems can be decomposed into cycle and safety stock components. We'll see below that the cycle stock depends on the *mean* of the demand distribution, while the safety stock depends on the *standard deviation*.

---

[1] We don't mean the inputs to the problem, such as costs or demand parameters. Rather, we mean decision variables for the inventory optimization problem, which are often referred to as "parameters."

4.2 DEMAND PROCESSES

In real life, customers tend to arrive at a retailer at random, discrete points in time. Similarly, retailers tend to place orders to wholesalers at random, discrete times, and so on up the supply chain. One way to model these demands is using a *Poisson process*, which describes random arrivals to a system over time. If each customer may demand more than one unit, we might use a *compound Poisson process*, in which arrivals are Poisson and the number of units demanded by each customer is governed by some other probability distribution.

It will often be convenient for us to work with continuous demand distributions (rather than discrete distributions such as Poisson), most commonly the normal distribution with mean μ and variance σ^2. Sometimes the normal distribution is used as an approximation for the Poisson distribution, in which case $\mu = \sigma^2$ since the Poisson variance equals its mean. (This approximation is especially accurate when the mean is large.)

In the continuous-review case, normally distributed demands mean that the demand over any t time units is normally distributed, with a mean and standard deviation that depend on t. Although it's unusual to think of demands occurring "continuously" in this way, it's a useful way to model demands over time. In the periodic-review case, we simply assume that the demand in each time period is normally distributed.

One drawback to using the normal distribution is that any normal random variable will sometimes have negative realizations, even though the demands that we aim to model are non-negative. If the demand mean is much greater than its standard deviation, then the probability of negative demands is so small that we can simply ignore it. This suggests that the normal distribution is appropriate as a model for the demand only if $\mu \gg \sigma$—say, if $\mu > 4\sigma$. If this condition fails to hold, then it is more appropriate to use a distribution whose support does not contain negative values, such as the lognormal distribution. (If the true demands are Poisson and we are using the normal distribution to approximate it, then another justification for the condition $\mu \gg \sigma$ is that the normal approximation for the Poisson distribution is most effective when the Poisson mean, λ, is large, in which case $\lambda \gg \sqrt{\lambda}$, which is the standard deviation.)

4.3 CONTINUOUS REVIEW: (r, Q) POLICIES

4.3.1 Problem Statement

In this section, we consider a setting like the EOQ model (Section 3.2) but with stochastic demand. The mean demand per year is λ. The inventory level is monitored continuously, and orders may be placed at any time. There is a deterministic lead time L (≥ 0). Unmet demands are backordered.

If the demand has a continuous distribution, then the inventory level decreases smoothly but randomly over time, with mean rate λ, as in Figure 4.1. (Think of liquid draining out of a tank at a fluctuating rate.) This is the interpretation in Sections 4.3.2

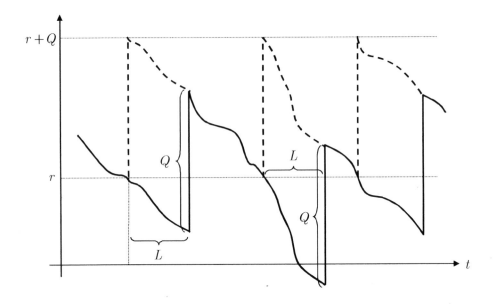

Figure 4.1   Inventory level (solid line) and inventory position (dashed line) under (r, Q) policy.

and 4.3.4. Or demands may occur at discrete points in time (as customers arrive), for example, if the demand follows a Poisson process, as in Section 4.3.4.

We'll assume the firm follows an (r, Q) *policy*: When the inventory position reaches a certain point (call it r), we place an order of size Q. L years later, the order arrives. In the intervening time, the inventory on hand may have been sufficient to meet demand, or we may have stocked out. Note that the inventory level (solid line in Figure 4.1) and inventory position (dashed line) differ from each other during lead times but coincide otherwise. An (r, Q) policy is known to be optimal for the setting described here, although we will not prove this.

Whereas the EOQ model has a single decision variable Q, an (r, Q) policy has two decision variables: Q (the order size) and r (the reorder point). Our goal is to determine the optimal r and Q to minimize the *expected cost* per year. The strategy will be first to formulate an expression for the expected cost as a function of the decision variables, then to minimize this function.

We will discuss two versions of this model. The first assumes that demands are continuously distributed (we'll use the normal distribution). We present an approximation for this model in Section 4.3.2 and another approximation, briefly, in Section 4.3.3. In Section 4.3.4, we discuss the second version of the model, which uses a discrete demand distribution (we'll use Poisson) and is an exact model.

4.3.2 Approximate Model with Continuous Distribution

This formulation assumes that the demand is continuously (normally) distributed. We will make two approximations in order to make the model tractable:

- *Simplifying Assumption 1* (SA1): We incur holding costs at a rate of $h \cdot IL$ per year, where IL is the inventory level, *whether IL is positive or negative*.

- *Simplifying Assumption 2* (SA2): The stockout cost is charged once per unit of unmet demand, not per year.

Neither assumption is particularly realistic, but we make them for mathematical convenience. SA1 is obviously untrue, but it is reasonably accurate if the expected number of stockouts is fairly small. SA2 is not as outrageous, but it is not typical, either in practice or in other inventory models. (Actually, SA1 would not be problematic at all if we didn't also assume SA2. If the stockout cost were charged per year, then we could simply replace the stockout cost p with $p + h$, thus canceling the artificial "credit" of h for negative inventory.)

4.3.2.1 Expected Cost Function   In this section, we will derive an expression for the expected cost per year as a function of the decision variables Q and r.

Holding Cost: Figure 4.2 contains a graph of the *expected* inventory over time. s is the expected on-hand inventory when the order arrives:

$$s = r - \lambda L.$$

In other words, s is the safety stock—the extra inventory held on hand to meet demand in excess of the mean.

The average inventory level is

$$s + \frac{Q}{2} = r - \lambda L + \frac{Q}{2}. \tag{4.1}$$

By SA1, the expected holding cost per year is

$$h \left(r - \lambda L + \frac{Q}{2} \right). \tag{4.2}$$

Of course, this expression is only approximate. The essence of the approximation is that we are calculating the expected holding cost as $h \cdot E[IL] = h \cdot E[IL]^+$ (assuming, as is typical, that $E[IL] > 0$), whereas it actually equals $h \cdot E[IL^+]$, and the two are not equal. The problem is more difficult without SA1 because of the nonlinearity introduced by the $[\cdot]^+$ operator. As noted above, the approximation becomes less accurate as the expected number of stockouts increases, or, equivalently, as s decreases.

Fixed Cost: The expected fixed cost per year is given by K times the expected number of orders per year. From Figure 4.2, we see that $E[T] = Q/\lambda$. Therefore,

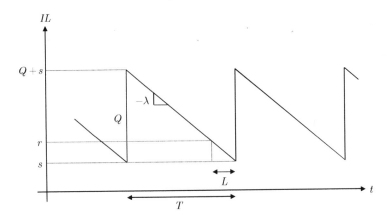

Figure 4.2   Expected inventory curve for (r, Q) policy.

the expected cost per year is

$$\frac{K\lambda}{Q}. \tag{4.3}$$

Purchase Cost: As in the EOQ, the annual purchase cost is given by $c\lambda$. Since it's independent of both Q and r, we'll ignore it in the cost calculations.

Stockout Cost: Since stockouts can only occur during lead times, the random variable of interest for computing the expected stockout cost is the *lead-time demand*, not the demand per year. Let D represent the lead-time demand; let $f(x)$ and $F(x)$ be its pdf and cdf, respectively; and let μ and σ^2 be its mean and variance, respectively. It is important to remember that D, μ, σ, etc. refer to lead-time demand, not to demand per year. Of course, the two are closely related. If the demand per year has mean λ and standard deviation τ and the lead time is L years, then the lead-time demand has mean λL and standard deviation $\tau\sqrt{L}$, assuming independence of demand across time.

The expected number of stockouts per order cycle is given by

$$\int_0^\infty (d-r)^+ f(d)dd = \int_r^\infty (d-r)f(d)dd. \tag{4.4}$$

This is known as the *loss function* and is denoted $n(r)$; see Section C.2.1 in Appendix C. The expected number of stockouts per year is $n(r)/E[T] = \lambda n(r)/Q$. By SA2, the expected stockout cost per year is simply

$$\frac{p\lambda n(r)}{Q}. \tag{4.5}$$

(The reason we make simplifying assumption SA2 is that, if the stockout cost were charged per year, then the integrand in (4.4) would contain $(x - r)^2$ in place of $(x - r)$, and this would be significantly harder to analyze.)

Total Cost: Combining (4.2), (4.3), and (4.5), we get the total expected cost per year:

$$g(r, Q) = h\left(r - \lambda L + \frac{Q}{2}\right) + \frac{K\lambda}{Q} + \frac{p\lambda n(r)}{Q}. \tag{4.6}$$

4.3.2.2 Optimal Solution
As in the EOQ model, we will optimize by setting the first derivative to 0. Since there are two decision variables, we must take partial derivatives with respect to each and set them both to 0:

$$\frac{\partial g}{\partial Q} = \frac{h}{2} - \frac{K\lambda}{Q^2} - \frac{p\lambda n(r)}{Q^2} = 0$$

$$\Longleftrightarrow \frac{1}{Q^2}[K\lambda + p\lambda n(r)] = \frac{h}{2}$$

$$\Longleftrightarrow Q^2 = \frac{2(K\lambda + p\lambda n(r))}{h}$$

or

$$Q = \sqrt{\frac{2\lambda[K + pn(r)]}{h}}. \tag{4.7}$$

And:

$$\frac{\partial g}{\partial r} = h + \frac{p\lambda n'(r)}{Q} = 0$$

$$\Longrightarrow h + \frac{p\lambda(F(r) - 1)}{Q} = 0$$

(using (C.6)), so

$$r = F^{-1}\left(1 - \frac{Qh}{p\lambda}\right) \tag{4.8}$$

Now we have two equations with two unknowns, but these equations cannot be solved in closed form. One way to solve the equations is to use the following heuristic:

Algorithm 4.1 (Iterative Heuristic for Approximate Continuous-Review Model)

1. Set Q equal to the EOQ quantity (i.e., ignore the randomness in the demand).

2. Using the current value of Q, calculate r using (4.8).

3. Using the current value of r, calculate Q using (4.7).

4. Repeat from step 2 until convergence.

This usually converges sufficiently within only a few iterations.

☐ **EXAMPLE 4.1**

Recall Joe's corner store from Example 3.1. Suppose now that the annual demand for candy bars is normally distributed with a mean of 1300 and a standard deviation of 150. Joe's customers are fiercely loyal, both to Joe and to his brand of candy, so if the store is out of stock, they are willing to wait for their candy. (That is, demands are backordered, not lost.) However, each stockout costs $0.50 in lost profit and $7.00 in loss of goodwill. The lead time is $L = 1/12$ year. What are the optimal r and Q?

We have $K = 8$, $h = 0.225$, and $p = 7.5$. The lead-time demand has parameters $\mu = 1300/12 = 108.3$, and $\sigma = 150/\sqrt{12} = 43.3$.

Using Algorithm 4.1, we first set Q equal to the EOQ quantity, which we know from Example 3.1 to be 304.1. From (4.8), we have

$$r = F^{-1}\left(1 - \frac{304.1 \cdot 0.225}{7.5 \cdot 1300}\right) = F^{-1}(0.9930) = 214.7.$$

Now, to calculate Q, we'll need to calculate $n(r)$. We can calculate $n(r)$ using $\mathscr{L}(z)$, the standard normal loss function, via (C.13), where $z = (r - \mu)/\sigma$. $\mathscr{L}(z)$, in turn, can be calculated using (C.8).

If $r = 214.7$, then $z = (r - \mu)/\sigma = 2.456$, $\mathscr{L}(z) = 0.002292$, and $n(r) = 0.002292 \cdot 43.3 = 0.0993$. Then from (4.7), we have

$$Q = \sqrt{\frac{2 \cdot 1300[8 + 7.5 \cdot 0.0993]}{0.225}} = 317.9.$$

Repeating this process:

$$r = F^{-1}\left(1 - \frac{317.9 \cdot 0.225}{7.5 \cdot 1300}\right) = F^{-1}(0.9927) = 214.0$$

$$\implies n(r) = 0.1042$$

$$Q = \sqrt{\frac{2 \cdot 1300[8 + 7.5 \cdot 0.1042]}{0.225}} = 318.6$$

$$r = F^{-1}\left(1 - \frac{318.6 \cdot 0.225}{7.5 \cdot 1300}\right) = F^{-1}(0.9927) = 214.0$$

Since r did not change since the previous iteration, the process can terminate. We have $r^* = 214.0$, $Q^* = 318.6$. The annual expected cost of this solution is

$$g(r, Q) = 0.225\left(214.0 - \frac{1300}{12} + \frac{318.6}{2}\right) + \frac{8 \cdot 1300}{318.6}$$
$$+ \frac{7.5 \cdot 1300 \cdot 0.1042}{318.6}$$
$$= 95.45.$$

☐

Table 4.1 Sample demands and stockouts.

Order Cycle	Demand	Stockouts
1	150	0
2	100	0
3	250	50

4.3.2.3 *Service Levels* The service level measures how successful an inventory policy is at satisfying the demand. There are many definitions of service level. The two most common are:

- *Type-1 service level*: the percentage of order cycles during which no stockout occurs, denoted by α

- *Type-2 service level*: the percentage of demand that is met from stock, denoted by β, sometimes called the *fill rate*

For example, suppose there are 3 order cycles with the demands and stockouts given in Table 4.1. Then the type-1 service level is 67% (because we stocked out in 1 of 3 cycles), while the type-2 service level is 90% (because we filled 450 out of 500 demands). In theory, the type-1 service level can be greater than the type-2 service level, but this rarely happens since the type-1 service level is a more rigorous measure—any cycle during which a stockout occurs is counted as a "failure," rather than just counting the individual stockouts as failures. (The type-1 service level would be greater than the type-2 service level if, for example, stockouts occur very rarely, but when they do, the number of stockouts is very large.)

One major limitation of the inventory model formulated in Section 4.3.2.1 is that p is very hard to estimate. But there is a close relationship between p and the service level: As p increases, it's more costly to stock out, so the service level should increase. In practice, many firms would rather omit the penalty cost from the objective function and add a constraint requiring the service level to be at least a certain value.

First suppose that we wish to impose a type-1 service level constraint. That is, we want to require the probability that no stockouts occur in a given cycle to be at least α. Since stockouts occur if and only if the lead-time demand is greater than r, this probability is simply $F(r)$. The expected cost function we wish to minimize is identical to (4.6) except it no longer contains a term for the stockout penalty. Therefore, we need to solve:

$$\text{minimize} \quad g(r, Q) = h \left(r - \lambda L + \frac{Q}{2} \right) + \frac{K\lambda}{Q} \tag{4.9}$$

$$\text{subject to} \quad F(r) \geq \alpha \tag{4.10}$$

At optimality, the constraint (4.10) will always hold as an equality. (Why?) Therefore, the optimal reorder point is given by $r = F^{-1}(\alpha)$, or

$$r = \mu + z_\alpha \sigma \tag{4.11}$$

since the lead-time demand is normally distributed with mean μ and standard deviation σ. As we will see in Section 4.4.2, this is exactly the form of the optimal solution to the newsvendor model. As in the newsvendor model, the first term of (4.11) represents the cycle stock (to meet the expected demand during the lead time) while the second term represents the safety stock (to meet excess demand during the lead time), since the safety stock is given by $s = r - \mu$.

What about Q? Well, once r is fixed, we can ignore the constraint, and the term $h(r - \lambda L)$ in the objective function (4.9) is a constant. What's left in (4.9) is exactly equal to the EOQ cost function (3.3). Therefore, Q^* equals the EOQ value.

This is an exact solution to the model with a type-1 service level constraint—in a sense. That is, it is an exact solution to our formulation, but our formulation is itself approximate. We'll make use of this approximation when we discuss the location model with risk pooling (LMRP) in Section 8.2. This approach can also be used when a stockout penalty (rather than a service level) is specified—we simply set $\alpha = p/(p + h)$ and calculate Q and r as described above.

Now consider a type-2 service level constraint; we want to require the fill rate to be at least β. We know that the average proportion of demands that stock out in each cycle is $n(r)/Q$, so we need to replace (4.10) with

$$\frac{n(r)}{Q} = 1 - \beta. \tag{4.12}$$

The resulting problem is significantly harder to solve: Since (4.12) contains both Q and r, we can no longer solve first for r and then solve independently for Q. Nevertheless, a reasonable approximation is simply to set $Q = $ EOQ (as in the case of type-1) and compute r using $n(r) = Q(1 - \beta)$. There is a more accurate method that involves a more complex formula for Q that is solved simultaneously with (4.8); see Nahmias (2005) for details.

□ **EXAMPLE 4.2**

Return to Example 4.1 and suppose that Joe wishes to ensure a type-1 service level of $\alpha = 0.98$. What are the optimal r and Q? What about for a type-2 service level of $\beta = 0.98$?

For the type-1 service level constraint, we have $z_\alpha = \Phi^{-1}(0.98) = 2.0538$ and

$$r = 108.3 + 2.0538 \cdot 43.3 = 197.3$$
$$Q = \text{EOQ} = 304.1$$

Using the approximate approach for the type-2 constraint, we have $Q = $ EOQ $= 304.1$. We need to solve

$$n(r) = 304.1(0.02) = 6.081.$$

You can confirm that this equation is satisfied by $r = 139.1$.   □

4.3.3 EOQB Approximation

Another well-known approximation for finding near-optimal r and Q for the exact model (i.e., without SA1 and SA2) makes use of the EOQ model with backorders discussed in Section 3.2.8. The idea is to set

$$Q = \sqrt{\frac{2K\lambda(h + p)}{hp}}$$

as in (3.27). One can show (Zheng 1992) that, for any fixed Q, the optimal r satisfies

$$g(r) = g(r + Q), \qquad (4.13)$$

where

$$g(S) = h\int_0^S (S - d)f(d)dd + p\int_S^\infty (d - S)f(d)dd. \qquad (4.14)$$

This is identical to the so-called newsvendor cost function (4.21), although in (4.21), $f(\cdot)$ is the distribution of the demand per period, while here it is the distribution of the lead-time demand. There are efficient methods to solve (4.13) for r that take advantage of the convexity of $g(S)$. (A discrete version of such a method is described in Section 4.3.4.2.)

Zheng (1992) shows that the cost of this approximate solution is no more than 12.5% worse than the optimal (r, Q) cost (again, the optimal cost of the exact model, not the approximate one formulated in Section 4.3.2). Axsäter (1996) improves this error bound, showing that the error is no more than $(\sqrt{5} - 2)/2$, or 11.8%.

☐ **EXAMPLE 4.3**

If we use the EOQB approximation to solve the problem in Example 4.1, we get

$$Q = \sqrt{\frac{2 \cdot 8 \cdot 1300(0.225 + 7.5)}{0.225 \cdot 7.5}} = 308.6.$$

Now we need to solve

$$g(r) = g(r + 308.6).$$

You can confirm that this equation is solved by $r = 128.6$. Note that this is quite different than the r we found in Example 4.1; the difference can be explained by the fact that these examples use different methods to approximate the model.   ☐

4.3.4 Exact Model with Discrete Distribution

Suppose now that the demand is discrete: Individual customers arrive randomly, each demanding one unit of the product. The number of demands in one year has a Poisson distribution with rate λ. Consequently, the lead-time demand D has a Poisson distribution with rate λL; the random variable D has pmf f and cdf F.

As in the continuous-distribution model in Section 4.3.2, as soon as the inventory position reaches r, we place an order of size Q. Q and r are both decision variables. The objective is to minimize the expected cost per year, denoted $g(r, Q)$.

Suppose we know the inventory position at time t, denoted $IP(t)$. Then the inventory level at time $t + L$, denoted $IL(t + L)$, is given by

$$IL(t + L) = IP(t) - D. \tag{4.15}$$

Why? Well, all of the items included in $IP(t)$—including items on hand and on order—will have arrived by time $t + L$. Moreover, no items ordered after time t will have arrived by time $t + L$. Therefore, all items that are on hand or on order at time t will be included in the inventory level at time $t + L$, except for the D items that have since been demanded. Equation (4.15) is a very important equation, and it applies to a wide range of other inventory models. It will be critical in the analysis below.

Note that (4.15) only holds for the lead time L; that is, if D' is a random variable representing the demand during L' years, then in general,

$$IL(t + L') \neq IP(t) - D'. \tag{4.16}$$

This is because some of the units included in $IP(t)$ may not be delivered by time $t + L'$ (if $L' < L$), or some units ordered after time t may have been delivered by time $t + L'$ (if $L' > L$).

We will first consider the special case of $Q = 1$ and then extend the results of that model to the case of general Q.

4.3.4.1 *Special Case:* $Q = 1$ Suppose Q is fixed to 1; then each time a demand occurs, we immediately place a new order for one unit. This is a continuous-review base-stock policy (see Section 4.4 for the periodic-review version), and $IP(t) = r + 1$ at all times. Therefore, (4.15) simplifies to

$$IL(t + L) = S - D,$$

where $S \equiv r + 1$. At time t, the holding and stockout costs accumulate at a rate of $h \cdot IL(t)^+ + p \cdot IL(t)^-$. Therefore (omitting some of the probability-theoretic arguments necessary to make this claim rigorously), the long-run expected holding and stockout cost per year is given by

$$
\begin{aligned}
g(S) &= hE[(S - D)^+] + pE[(S - D)^-] \\
&= h \sum_{d=0}^{S} (S - d)f(d) + p \sum_{d=S+1}^{\infty} (d - S)f(d).
\end{aligned} \tag{4.17}
$$

This is the discrete-demand analogue of the cost function given in (4.14).

Since we place an order each time a demand occurs, the expected number of orders per year is λ, and the total expected cost per year, as a function of r ($= S - 1$) and Q ($= 1$) is

$$g(S - 1, 1) = K\lambda + g(S). \tag{4.18}$$

The first term is a constant, so $g(S-1, 1)$ is optimized by optimizing $g(S)$. Analogous to Theorem 4.1 below, one can show that the minimizer of $g(S)$ is the smallest S such that

$$F(S) \geq \frac{p}{p+h}. \tag{4.19}$$

4.3.4.2 General Q   Now suppose $Q \geq 1$. Since an order is placed immediately when IP reaches r, $IP \in \{r+1, r+2, \ldots, r+Q\}$ at any time. How much time does the inventory position spend at each of these values? The answer turns out to be: *equal* time. That is, IP has a uniform distribution on the integers $r+1, \ldots, r+Q$, so $P(IP = S) = 1/Q$ for all $S = r+1, \ldots, r+Q$. (See, e.g., Zipkin (2000) for a proof of this convenient and somewhat surprising fact.) When $IP = S$, the holding and stockout costs accumulate at a rate of $g(S)$; therefore, the expected holding and stockout cost per year is given by

$$\frac{1}{Q} \sum_{S=r+1}^{r+Q} g(S),$$

and the expected total cost per year is given by

$$g(r, Q) = \frac{K\lambda + \sum_{S=r+1}^{r+Q} g(S)}{Q}, \tag{4.20}$$

since λ/Q orders are placed per year, on average. The function $g(r, Q)$ is convex in both Q and r.

Suppose we fix Q and we want to find the best r for that Q, denoted $r(Q)$. To do this, we need to choose r so that $g(r+1), \ldots, g(r+Q)$ are as small as possible. In other words, we want to find the Q best inventory positions $\{r+1, \ldots, r+Q\}$, to minimize the sum in (4.20). Since $g(S)$ is convex, these Q best inventory positions are nested, in the sense that, if $\{r+1, \ldots, r+Q\}$ is optimal for Q, then either $\{r, r+1, \ldots, r+Q\}$ or $\{r+1, \ldots, r+Q, r+Q+1\}$ is optimal for $Q+1$. If the former set yields the smaller sum in (4.20), then $r(Q+1) = r(Q) - 1$, while if the latter set is better, then $r(Q+1) = r(Q)$.

This suggests that we can find the optimal Q and r recursively, as follows. We start with $Q = 1$ and set $r = S - 1$, where S optimizes $g(S-1, 1)$ in (4.18). We then iterate through consecutive integer values of Q, determining $r(Q+1)$ using $r(Q)$ as described in the previous paragraph. Since $g(r, Q)$ is convex in Q, we can stop as soon as we find that $g(r(Q+1), Q+1) > g(r(Q), Q)$. This algorithm was introduced by Federgruen and Zheng (1992).

4.4 PERIODIC REVIEW WITH ZERO FIXED COSTS: BASE-STOCK POLICIES

We now turn our attention to periodic-review models. The time horizon consists of T time periods; T can be finite or infinite. We'll assume the lead time is zero, but most of the models in this section can be extended to handle non-zero lead times.

We'll first consider the important special case in which $K = 0$ (in this section), and then the more general case of $K \geq 0$ (in Section 4.5). We'll also assume that the costs h, p, c, and K are constant throughout the time horizon. We'll assume that $h, p > 0$, c, $K \geq 0$, and $c < p$. ·

We will model the time value of money by *discounting* future periods using a discount factor $\gamma \in (0, 1]$. That is, \$1 spent (or received) in period $t + 1$ is equivalent to \$$\gamma$ in period t. If $\gamma = 1$, then there is no discounting. For the single-period and finite-horizon problems, our objective will be to *minimize the total expected cost over the horizon*. However, the total cost over an infinite horizon will be infinite if $\gamma = 1$, and may still be infinite if $\gamma < 1$. Therefore, in the infinite-horizon case, we will minimize the *expected cost per period* if $\gamma = 1$ and the total expected cost over the horizon if $\gamma < 1$. (The solutions to the two problems turn out to be closely related.)

The sequence of events in each period t is as follows:

1. The inventory level, denoted IL_t, is observed.

2. A replenishment order of size Q_t is placed and is received instantly.

3. Demand d_t occurs; as much as possible is satisfied from inventory, and the rest is backordered.

4. Holding and stockout costs are assessed based on the ending on-hand inventory level.

The ending inventory level in period t (step 4) is equal to the starting inventory level in period $t + 1$ (step 1) and is given by $IL_{t+1} = IL_t + Q_t - d_t$.

4.4.1   Base-Stock Policies

Throughout Section 4.4, we'll assume that $K = 0$ and that the firm follows a *base-stock policy*.[2] A base-stock policy works as follows: In each time period, we observe the current inventory position and then place an order whose size is sufficient to bring the inventory position up to S. (We sometimes say we "order up to S.") S is a constant—it does not depend on the current state of the system—and is known as the *base-stock level*.

In multiple-period models, the base-stock level may be different in different periods. If the base-stock level is the same throughout the horizon, then in every period, we simply order d_{t-1} items. (Why?)

We will divide this problem into three cases—with $T = 1$, $1 \leq T < \infty$, and $T = \infty$—and find the optimal base-stock levels in each case.

4.4.2   Single Period: The Newsvendor Model

4.4.2.1   *Problem Statement*   Consider a firm selling a single product during a single time period. Single-period models are most often applied to *perishable*

---

[2]Base-stock policies are also sometimes known as *order-up-to policies*, *S-policies*, or $(S-1, S)$-*policies*.

products, which include (as you might expect) products such as eggs and flowers that may spoil, but also products that lose their value after a certain date, such as newspapers, high-tech devices, and fashion goods. The key element of the model is that the firm only has one opportunity to place an order—before the random demand is observed.

Even if the firm actually sells its products over multiple periods (as is typical), the operations in subsequent periods are not linked: Excess inventory cannot be held over until the next period, nor can excess demands (that is, unmet demands are lost, not backordered). Therefore, the firm's multi-period model can be reduced to multiple independent copies of the single-period model presented here.

This model is one of the most fundamental stochastic inventory models, and many of the models discussed subsequently in this book use it as a starting point. It is often referred to as the *newsvendor* (or *newsboy*) *model*. The story goes like this: Imagine a newsvendor who buys newspapers each day from the publisher for $0.30 each and sells them for $1.00. The daily demand for newspapers at his newsstand is normally distributed with a mean of 50 and a standard deviation of 8. If the newsvendor has unsold newspapers left at the end of the day, he cannot sell them the next day, but he can sell them back to the publisher for 12 cents (called the *salvage value*). The question is: How many newspapers should he buy from the publisher each day? If he buys exactly 50, he has an equal probability of being understocked and overstocked. But it costs more to stock out than to have excess (since stocking out costs him 70 cents in lost profit while excess newspapers cost him $30 - 12 = 18$ cents each). So he should order more than 50 newspapers each day—but how many more?

The inventory carried by the newsvendor can be decomposed into two components: cycle stock and safety stock. As noted in Section 4.1, cycle stock is the inventory that is intended to meet the expected demand—in our example, 50—whereas safety stock is extra inventory that's kept on hand to buffer against demand uncertainty—the amount over 50 ordered by the newsvendor. We will see below that the newsvendor's cycle stock depends on the mean of the demand distribution, while the safety stock depends on the standard deviation.

It is possible for the safety stock to be negative: If stocking out is less expensive than holding extra inventory, the newsvendor would want to order fewer than 50 papers. This can actually occur in practice—for example, for expensive and highly perishable products—but it is the exception rather than the rule.

4.4.2.2 *Formulation* As usual, we will use h to represent the holding cost: the cost per unit of having too much inventory on hand. In the newsvendor problem, this typically consists of the purchase cost of the unit, minus any salvage value, but may include other costs, such as processing costs. (Since inventory cannot be carried to the next period, this cost is not technically a holding cost, though we will refer to it that way anyway.) Similarly, p represents the stockout cost: the cost per unit of having too little inventory, consisting of lost profit and loss-of-goodwill costs. The holding cost is the cost per unit of positive ending inventory, while the stockout cost is the cost per unit of negative ending inventory. The costs h and p are sometimes

referred to as *overage* and *underage* costs, respectively (and some authors denote them c_o and c_u).

To keep things simple, we'll assume that $c = 0$, but we'll discuss how to modify the analysis to handle $c \neq 0$ in Section 4.4.2.6. We'll also assume the firm starts the period with $IL = 0$, but this, too, is easy to relax (see Section 4.4.2.7). Since there is only a single period, the discount factor γ won't play a role in the analysis.

Our goal is to determine the base-stock level S to minimize the *expected cost* in the single period. The strategy for solving this problem is first to develop an expression for the cost as a function of d (the observed demand) and S (call it $g(S, d)$); then to determine the expected cost $E_D[g(S, D)]$ (call it $g(S)$); and then (in Section 4.4.2.3) to determine S to minimize $g(S)$.

If the firm orders up to S and sees a demand of d units, its cost is

$$g(S, d) = h(S - d)^+ + p(d - S)^+.$$

Since the demand is stochastic, however, we must take an expectation over D:

$$
\begin{aligned}
g(S) &= E[h(S - D)^+ + p(D - S)^+] \\
&= \int_0^\infty [h(S - d)^+ + p(d - S)^+] f(d) dd \\
&= h \int_0^\infty (S - d)^+ f(d) dd + p \int_0^\infty (d - S)^+ f(d) dd \\
&= h \int_0^S (S - d) f(d) dd + p \int_S^\infty (d - S) f(d) dd
\end{aligned}
\tag{4.21}
$$

Let

$$n(x) = E[(X - x)^+] = \int_x^\infty (y - x) f(y) dy \tag{4.22}$$

$$\bar{n}(x) = E[(X - x)^-] = \int_0^x (x - y) f(y) dy \tag{4.23}$$

These functions are known as the *loss function* and the *complementary loss function*,[3] respectively. They can be defined for any probability distribution; here, we define them in terms of the demand distribution. (See Section C.2.1 for more information about these functions.) Then we can rewrite (4.21) as

$$g(S) = h\bar{n}(S) + pn(S). \tag{4.24}$$

4.4.2.3 *Optimal Solution*   The derivatives of the loss function and its complement are given by

$$n'(x) = F(x) - 1$$

---

[3] The term "complementary loss function" is our own; to the best of our knowledge, this function does not have a name in common usage.

$$\bar{n}'(x) = F(x).$$

(See Problem 4.9.) Then, using (4.24),

$$\frac{dg(S)}{dS} = hF(S) + p(F(S) - 1) = (h + p)F(S) - p. \qquad (4.25)$$

Setting this equal to 0 gives

$$(h + p)F(S) - p = 0$$

$$\implies F(S) = \frac{p}{h + p} \qquad (4.26)$$

$$\implies S^* = F^{-1}\left(\frac{p}{h + p}\right). \qquad (4.27)$$

We should also check that the function is convex:

$$\frac{d^2g(S)}{dS^2} = (h + p)f(S) \geq 0,$$

as desired.

The expression for S^* in (4.27) is an important one, so we'll state it as a theorem (which we've now proven).

Theorem 4.1 *The optimal base-stock level for a single-period model with no fixed costs (the newsvendor model) is given by*

$$S^* = F^{-1}\left(\frac{p}{h + p}\right).$$

$p/(h + p)$ is known as the *critical ratio* (or *critical fractile*). Since p and h are both positive,

$$0 < \frac{p}{h + p} < 1,$$

so $F^{-1}(p/(h + p))$ always exists. $F(S) = P(D \leq S)$, or the probability of no stockouts. This is known as the *type-1 service level* (see Section 4.4.2.5). Equation (4.27) then says that under the optimal solution, the type-1 service level should be equal to the critical ratio. It is optimal to stock out $1 - p/(h + p) = h/(h + p)$ fraction of periods. As p increases, the critical ratio increases, so S^* and the type-1 service level both increase—it is more costly to stock out, so we should do it less frequently. As h increases, the critical ratio decreases, as does S^*—it is more costly to have excess inventory, so we will order less. The type-1 service level necessarily decreases as well.

Theorem 4.1—or one very much like it—holds for a wide range of models, not just the single-period newsvendor model formulated here. Perhaps most importantly, a variant of the theorem still holds for the multi-period, infinite-horizon version of the model; see Section 4.4.4.

☐ **EXAMPLE 4.4**

In the example given at the start of this section, we have $h = 0.18$, $p = 0.70$, so

$$S^* = F^{-1}\left(\frac{0.70}{0.18 + 0.70}\right) = F^{-1}(0.795).$$

Recall that, in this example, the demand was assumed to be distributed as $N(50, 8^2)$. For this distribution, $F^{-1}(0.795) = 56.6$.

Now, this example was about newspapers, and it doesn't make sense to order a fractional number of newspapers. If the demand distribution is discrete, it is always optimal to round the solution *up*. (See Problem 4.5.) In this case, the firm should order 57 newspapers.   ☐

4.4.2.4 *Normally Distributed Demands*   In this section, we discuss results for the special case in which demands are normally distributed: $D \sim N(\mu, \sigma^2)$, with pdf f and cdf F. In what follows, we use $\phi(\cdot)$ and $\Phi(\cdot)$ to denote the pdf and cdf, respectively, of the standard normal distribution:

$$\phi(z) = \frac{1}{\sqrt{2\pi}}e^{-z^2/2} \tag{4.28}$$

$$\Phi(z) = \int_{-\infty}^{z} \phi(x)dx \tag{4.29}$$

We also use z_α to denote the αth fractile of the standard normal distribution; that is, $z_\alpha = \Phi^{-1}(\alpha)$.

As discussed in Section 4.2, we will assume that $\mu \gg \sigma$ so that the probability of negative demands is negligible.

From (4.26), we have

$$F(S^*) = \frac{p}{h + p}$$

$$\Longleftrightarrow \quad \Phi\left(\frac{S^* - \mu}{\sigma}\right) = \frac{p}{h + p}$$

$$\Longleftrightarrow \quad S^* = \mu + \sigma\Phi^{-1}\left(\frac{p}{h + p}\right).$$

If we let $\alpha = p/(h + p)$, we have

$$S^* = \mu + z_\alpha\sigma. \tag{4.30}$$

The first term of (4.30) represents the cycle stock—it depends only on μ. The second term represents the safety stock—it depends on σ. The newsvendor problem can be thought of as a problem of setting safety stock. The firm already knows that it will need μ units to satisfy the expected demand; the question is how much more to order to satisfy any demand in excess of the mean. This extra inventory is the safety stock.

Note that, as discussed in Section 4.4.2.1, the safety stock is negative if $p < h$ since, in that case, $\alpha < 0.5$ and $z_\alpha < 0$.

We next derive an expression for the expected cost under the optimal solution. If X is a normally distributed random variable, then its loss and complementary loss functions are given by

$$n(x) = \mathscr{L}(z)\sigma \qquad (4.31)$$
$$\bar{n}(x) = [z + \mathscr{L}(z)]\sigma, \qquad (4.32)$$

where $z = (x - \mu)/\sigma$ and

$$\mathscr{L}(z) = \int_z^\infty (y - z)\phi(y)dy. \qquad (4.33)$$

(See Problem 4.8.) (4.31) and (4.32) assume $F(0) = 0$; this is surely true for actual demands, but it is only approximately true for the normal distribution we use to model demand.) $\mathscr{L}(z)$ is called the *standard normal loss function*; it is equivalent to $n(x)$ in (4.22) if X has a standard normal distribution. $\mathscr{L}(z)$ is tabulated in many textbooks, or it can be computed explicitly as

$$\mathscr{L}(z) = \phi(z) - z(1 - \Phi(z)). \qquad (4.34)$$

Equation (4.34) is convenient for calculating $\mathscr{L}(z)$ in, say, Excel. Then, for our problem with normally distributed demands, the cost function (4.24) becomes

$$g(S) = h[z + \mathscr{L}(z)]\sigma + p\mathscr{L}(z)\sigma = [hz + (h + p)\mathscr{L}(z)]\sigma, \qquad (4.35)$$

where $z = (S - \mu)/\sigma$. The derivative of the loss function is given by

$$\mathscr{L}'(z) = \Phi(z) - 1, \qquad (4.36)$$

so the derivative of $g(S)$ is

$$\frac{dg(S)}{dS} = (h + p)\Phi(z) - p$$

(as in (4.25)). Setting this to zero gives us the optimal order quantity:

$$\Phi(z) = \frac{p}{h + p}$$
$$\implies z^* = \Phi^{-1}\left(\frac{p}{h + p}\right)$$
$$\implies S^* = \mu + \sigma\Phi^{-1}\left(\frac{p}{h + p}\right)$$

Now let $\alpha = p/(h + p)$; then $S^* = \mu + z_\alpha\sigma$, and $z^* = (S^* - \mu)/\sigma = z_\alpha$. As we did with the EOQ model, we will derive an expression for the optimal cost in this problem. From (4.35),

$$g(S^*) = [hz_\alpha + (h + p)\mathscr{L}(z_\alpha)]\sigma$$

$$
\begin{aligned}
&= [hz_\alpha + (h+p)\phi(z_\alpha) - (h+p)z_\alpha(1 - \Phi(z_\alpha))]\,\sigma && \text{(from (4.34))}\\
&= [hz_\alpha + (h+p)\phi(z_\alpha) - (h+p)z_\alpha(1 - \alpha)]\,\sigma\\
&= [(h+p)\phi(z_\alpha) - (h+p)z_\alpha + (h+p)z_\alpha]\,\sigma && \text{(since } (h+p)\alpha = p)\\
&= (h+p)\phi(z_\alpha)\sigma && \text{(4.37)}
\end{aligned}
$$

It seems surprising at first that (4.37) depends only on σ, not on μ. But with a little reflection, this makes sense: Since the problem comes down to setting safety stock levels, only σ should figure into the objective function. Remember that the objective function includes only holding and stockout costs—costs that result from the randomness in demand, not its magnitude.

Again, let's summarize the optimal order quantity and its cost in a theorem:

Theorem 4.2 *The optimal base-stock level for a single-period model with no fixed costs (the newsvendor model) under demands that are distributed as $N(\mu, \sigma^2)$ is given by*

$$
S^* = \mu + z_\alpha \sigma,
$$

where $z_\alpha = \Phi^{-1}(\alpha)$ and $\alpha = p/(h+p)$. The optimal cost is given by

$$
g(S^*) = (h+p)\phi(z_\alpha)\sigma.
$$

☐ **EXAMPLE 4.5**

As in Example 4.4, suppose $D \sim N(50, 8^2)$, $h = 0.18$, and $p = 0.70$. Then $z_\alpha = \Phi^{-1}(0.70/(0.18 + 0.70)) = 0.8255$. We already know that $S^* = 56.6$ for this problem. We could calculate the optimal cost by plugging S^* into (4.21), or just use (4.37):

$$
g(S^*) = (0.18 + 0.70) \cdot \phi(0.8255) \cdot 8 = 2.00.
$$

☐

4.4.2.5 Service Levels   We now return to problems with general demand distributions. We already know that, for the single-period base-stock model, the type-1 service level is given by $F(S)$, and under the optimal solution, it equals $p/(h+p)$. To calculate the type-2 service level, recall that the loss function $n(S)$ calculates the expected number of unmet demands if the firm uses a base-stock level of S. Then the type-2 service level is given by

$$
1 - \frac{E[\text{number of unmet demands}]}{E[\text{demand}]} = 1 - \frac{n(S)}{\mu},
$$

or

$$
1 - \frac{\sigma\mathscr{L}(z)}{\mu}
$$

in the case of normally distributed demands.

☐ **EXAMPLE 4.6**

What are the service levels for the solution found in Example 4.4?

$$\text{Type-1 service level} = \frac{0.7}{0.18 + 0.7} = 0.7955$$

$$\text{Type-2 service level} = 1 - \frac{8\mathscr{L}\left(\frac{56.6-50}{8}\right)}{50}$$

$$= 1 - \frac{8 \cdot 0.1150}{50} \quad \text{(using (C.8))}$$

$$= 0.9816$$

☐

4.4.2.6 Non-Zero Purchase Cost   It is easy to modify the analysis above to allow $c \neq 0$. The expected cost is simply given by

$$g(S) = cS + h \int_0^S (S-d)f(d)dd + p \int_S^\infty (d-S)f(d)dd = cS + h\bar{n}(S) + pn(S).$$
$$(4.38)$$

Then we have

$$\frac{dg(S)}{dS} = c + (h+p)F(S) - p = 0$$

$$\implies S^* = F^{-1}\left(\frac{p-c}{h+p}\right). \quad (4.39)$$

Actually, there is another way to obtain this same result, simply by adjusting h and p in our original formulation. If $c \neq 0$, then each unit on hand at the end of the period costs $h' \equiv h + c$, whereas having one additional backorder costs $p' \equiv p - c$ (we pay the stockout cost but save ourselves the purchase cost). Under these holding and stockout costs, (4.27) reduces to

$$S^* = F^{-1}\left(\frac{p'}{h'+p'}\right) = F^{-1}\left(\frac{p-c}{h+p}\right),$$

exactly the same as (4.39). In other words, the assumption $c = 0$ was made without loss of generality.

4.4.2.7 Non-Zero Starting Inventory Level   We assumed that the firm starts the period with $IL = 0$. In fact, this assumption is easy to relax (and it will be important to do so in the multi-period versions of this model). If $IL \leq S$, then the firm should order up to S, as usual. But suppose $IL > S$. The firm can't order up to S since it already has too much inventory. But should the firm order *any* units? By the convexity of $g(S)$, the answer is no: It would be better to leave the inventory level where it is. Therefore, the optimal order quantity at the start of the period is:

$$Q = \begin{cases} S - IL, & \text{if } IL \leq S \\ 0, & \text{if } IL > S. \end{cases} \quad (4.40)$$

4.4.2.8 *Forecasting and Standard Deviations*

In most real-world settings, we do not know the demand process exactly. Instead, we generate a forecast or estimate of the demand parameters required to make inventory decisions. We'll assume the demand is normally distributed. If we knew μ and σ, we would simply use them in (4.30) to determine the optimal order quantity. But suppose we don't know them; instead, suppose we have observed the demand for a long time, and let d_t be the observed demand in period t. In each period, we can generate an estimate of μ and σ from the historical data. There are many ways to do this (see Chapter 2); one of the simplest is to use a *moving average* (Section 2.2.1) to estimate μ and what we might call a *moving standard deviation* to estimate σ in period t:

$$\hat{\mu}_t = \frac{1}{N} \sum_{i=t-N}^{t-1} d_t \qquad \hat{\sigma}_t = \sqrt{\frac{1}{N-1} \sum_{i=t-N}^{t-1} (d_t - \hat{\mu}_t)^2}$$

To choose an order quantity in period t, we replace μ with $\hat{\mu}_t$ in (4.30). However, it turns out that $\hat{\sigma}_t$ is *not* the right standard deviation to use in place of σ. Instead, the correct quantity to use is the *standard deviation of the forecast error*.

Returning to our historical data, $\hat{\mu}_t$ serves as a forecast for the demand in period t. The *forecast error* (the difference between the forecast and the observed demand in a given period) is a random variable, and it has a mean, denoted μ_e, and a standard deviation, denoted σ_e. The correct quantity to replace σ with in (4.30) is σ_e. We'll omit a rigorous explanation of why this is the case (see, e.g., Nahmias (2005, Section 2.12)), but here is the intuition. The forecasting process introduces sampling error in addition to the randomness in demand, and it is this error that the firm really needs to protect itself against using safety stock. Suppose that the demand is very variable (σ is large) but we are extremely good at predicting it (μ_e and σ_e are both small). We would need very little safety stock, because we can accurately predict how much inventory we will need. Now suppose that the demand is extremely steady (σ is small) but that, for some reason, our forecast is always 100 units too large (μ_e is large, σ_e is small). Here, too, we need very little safety stock, because (knowing our forecast is always too large), we can simply revise our forecast downward. Finally, suppose that the demand is steady (σ is small) but our forecasts are all over the place—sometimes high, sometimes low (μ_e is small, σ_e is large). In this case we need a lot of safety stock to protect against the uncertainty arising from our inability to predict the demand. In all of these cases, it is the standard deviation of the forecast error that drives the inventory requirement.

Unfortunately, we don't know σ_e any more than we know σ. Instead, we can observe the forecast error in period t,

$$e_t = \hat{\mu}_t - d_t,$$

and estimate the standard deviation of the forecast error as

$$\hat{\sigma}_{e,t} = \sqrt{\frac{1}{N-1} \sum_{i=t-N}^{t-1} (e_t - \hat{\mu}_{e,t})^2},$$

where

$$\hat{\mu}_{e,t} = \frac{1}{N} \sum_{i=t-N}^{t-1} e_t$$

is the estimate of the mean of the forecast error made in period t. (If we know for sure that our forecasts are unbiased, we can replace $\hat{\mu}_{e_t}$ with 0.) We then replace σ with $\hat{\sigma}_{e,t}$ in (4.30). Of course, if the firm uses a forecasting technique other than moving average, we can simply replace the formulas above with the appropriate ones.

Now, in nearly all of the models in this book (one exception is Section 10.2.1), we assume that the demand parameters are known and stationary. In that case, the forecast $\hat{\mu}_t$ is always equal to the true demand mean μ, and the forecast error is $\mu - d_t$ with mean 0 and standard deviation

$$\hat{\sigma}_{e,t} = \sqrt{\frac{1}{N-1} \sum_{i=t-N}^{t-1} (e_t - \hat{\mu}_{e,t})^2} = \sqrt{\frac{1}{N-1} \sum_{i=t-N}^{t-1} (\mu - d_t)^2},$$

which converges to σ in the long run. Therefore, μ and σ are the appropriate parameters to use.

In general, one can show that $\sigma_e^L = c\sigma^L$ for some constant c (at least for moving average and exponential smoothing forecasts; see, e.g., Hax and Candea 1984, p. 194, or Nahmias 2005, Appendix 2-A), so in some sense the distinction between the standard deviation of the demand and that of the forecast error is academic, but it's still worth drawing.

4.4.3 Finite Horizon

Now consider a multiple-period problem consisting of a finite number of periods, T. Suppose we are at the beginning of period t. Do we need to know the history of the system (e.g., order quantities and demands through period $t - 1$) in order to make an optimal inventory decision in period t? The answer is no: All of the information we need to make the inventory decision is contained in a single quantity—the starting inventory level, IL_t. Moreover, once we decide how much to order, we can easily calculate the probability distribution of the starting inventory level in period $t + 1$ (as we'll see below). This suggests that the periods can be optimized recursively—in particular, using dynamic programming (DP). Just as in the DP algorithm we used for the Wagner-Whitin problem (Section 3.3.2), this DP will make inventory decisions for period t, assuming that optimal decisions have already been made for periods $t + 1, \ldots, T$ and using the cost of those optimal decisions to calculate the cost of the decisions in period t. However, in this DP, the optimal decisions in period t will depend on a random state variable (in particular, IL_t), whereas the decisions in the Wagner-Whitin DP depended only on the period, t.

First consider what happens at the end of the time horizon. Presumably, on-hand units and backorders must be treated differently now that the horizon has ended than they would be during the horizon. The *terminal cost function*, denoted $\theta_{T+1}(x)$, represents the additional cost incurred at the end of the horizon if we end the horizon with inventory level x. For example, we may incur a *terminal holding cost* h_{T+1} for on-hand units that must be disposed of, and a *terminal stockout cost* p_{T+1} for backorders that must be satisfied through overtime or other expensive measures. Then $\theta_{T+1}(x) = h_{T+1}x^+ + p_{T+1}x^-$. Or, maybe we can salvage excess units at the end of the horizon for a revenue of v_{T+1} per unit, in which case $\theta_{T+1}(x) = -v_{T+1}x^+ + p_{T+1}x^-$.

Let $\theta_t(x)$ be the optimal expected cost in periods $t, t+1, \ldots, T$ if we begin period t with $IL_t = x$ (and act optimally thereafter). We can define $\theta_t(x)$ recursively in terms of $\theta_s(x)$ for later periods s. In each period t, we need to decide how much to order, but we will express this optimization problem not in terms of the order quantity Q, but the *order-up-to level* y, defined as $y = x + Q$.[4] In particular:

$$\theta_t(x) = \min_{y \geq x}\{c(y - x) + g(y) + \gamma E_D[\theta_{t+1}(y - D)]\}, \tag{4.41}$$

where

$$g(y) = h \int_0^y (y - d)f(d)dd + p \int_y^\infty (d - y)f(d)dd = h\bar{n}(y) + pn(y)$$

is the single-period expected cost function (see (4.21) and (4.24)). The minimization considers all possible order-up-to levels $y \geq x$ (since Q must be non-negative) and, for each, calculates the sum of the cost to order $y - x$ units, the expected cost in period t, and the expected discounted future cost. Note that if we order up to y in period t, then the starting inventory level in period $t + 1$ will be $y - D$, where D is the (random) demand in period t; therefore, the (random) cost in periods $t+1, \ldots, T$ equals $\theta_{t+1}(y - D)$.

The DP algorithm for the finite-horizon problem can be summarized as follows:

Algorithm 4.2 (DP for Finite-Horizon Inventory Problem)

1. Compute $\theta_{T+1}(x)$ for all x and set $t \leftarrow T$.

2. Compute $\theta_t(x)$ for all x using (4.41) and set $y_t(x)$ equal to the y that minimizes the expression inside the braces.

3. Set $t \leftarrow t - 1$. If $t = 0$, STOP. Otherwise, go to 2.

The optimal expected cost for the entire horizon is given by $\theta_1(x)$, where x is the inventory level that the system starts with at time 0.

One way to think about this DP is as follows. Imagine a spreadsheet whose columns correspond to the periods $1, \ldots, T, T+1$ and whose rows correspond to the possible values of x. The value in cell (x, t) equals $\theta_t(x)$. We start by filling in the $\theta_{T+1}(x)$ values in the last column, one for each value of x. Then, we calculate the

[4]The order-up-to level y is related to, but not the same as, the base-stock level S. The order-up-to level depends on x: If $x < S$ then $y = S$ and if $x \geq S$ then $y = x$. In contrast, S is a fixed number, independent of x.

cells in column T: For each x, we calculate $\theta_T(x)$ using (4.41)—which requires us to look in column $T+1$ for the $\theta_{T+1}(x)$ values—and write the result in cell (x, T). Then we calculate the cells in column $T-1$, using the values in column T, and so on, until we solve period 1. Also imagine a second spreadsheet with identical structure but whose cells contain $y_t(x)$ rather than $\theta_t(x)$.

The completed spreadsheet tells the firm everything it needs to know about optimally managing the inventory system. If it finds itself with an inventory level of x at the start of period t, it simply looks in the second spreadsheet and orders up to the $y_t(x)$ value that is found in cell (x, t). (The corresponding cell in the first spreadsheet tells the expected current and future cost of this action.)

Two problems with this approach bear mention. First, the DP calculates $\theta_t(x)$ "for all x." But x can potentially become arbitrarily large or small, depending on the values we choose for y and on the random demands. For example, if $y_t = 100$ and $D \sim N(100, 10^2)$, it is *possible* (although extremely unlikely) that IL_{t+1} will equal $-100,000,000$, so our spreadsheet should extend at least this far. Of course, this is neither practical nor essential (since the probability is so low), so we typically *truncate* the state space to consider only "reasonable" x values. (The definition of "reasonable" depends on the specific problem at hand.)

Second, even if we consider only a reasonably narrow range of x values, if D has a continuous distribution, there are still an infinite number of possible inventory levels to consider. This problem is typically addressed by *discretizing* the demand distribution so we consider only a finite number of possible demand values. The granularity of the discretization (e.g., do we round demands to the nearest integer? to the nearest 0.001? the nearest 0.000001?) again depends on the specific problem. In general, larger ranges of x values and smaller granularity result in more accurate solutions but longer run times.

Even after we resolve these two problems, this approach is still somewhat unsatisfying, at least from a managerial point of view. The spreadsheets described above will work, but they are fairly cumbersome. It would be nice if we could boil the information contained in the spreadsheets down into a simple policy. To that end, let's look more closely at the results of the DP.

Figure 4.3 plots $y_t(x)$ for three different periods t and for a range of x values for a particular instance of the problem.[5] Essentially, each curve contains the data from a column in the second spreadsheet. Notice that all three curves are flat for a while and then climb linearly along the line $y = x$. That is, for each t, there exists some value S_t such that, for $x < S_t$, we have $y_t(x) = S_t$, and for $x \geq S_t$, we have $y_t(x) = x$. (In particular, $S_1 = 15$, $S_5 = 21$, $S_8 = 17$.) In other words, *these curves each depict a base-stock policy*! In fact, we will prove in Section 4.6.1.2 that a base-stock policy is optimal in every period of the finite-horizon model presented here—the pattern suggested by Figure 4.3 always holds.

Recognizing the optimality of a base-stock policy has simplified the results: We don't need the entire $y_t(x)$ spreadsheet to tell us how to act in each period, we just

---

[5]Actually, for a somewhat more general version of the problem in which the parameters may change (deterministically) over time. The same general results hold for both models.

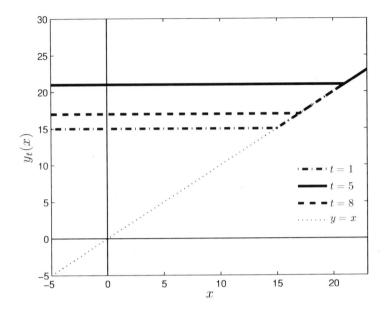

Figure 4.3   DP results, $K = 0$: $y_t(x)$.

need a list of S_t values—the optimal base-stock level for each period t. In general, these can be different for different periods, as suggested by Figure 4.3, although in some special cases, the same base-stock level is optimal in every period (see Section 4.6.1.2). However, base-stock optimality has not simplified the computation required to determine the optimal policy—we still need to solve the DP to find the optimal base-stock levels in each period. In particular, S_t is equal to $y_t(-\infty)$, or, assuming we have truncated the range of possible x values, S_t equals $y_t(x)$ for the smallest x value considered.

4.4.4   Infinite Horizon

Our third and final variety of periodic-review models with no fixed costs is the case in which $T = \infty$. This problem is sometimes known as the *infinite-horizon newsvendor model*. If the number of periods is infinite, then the total expected cost across the horizon may be infinite, too. (It certainly will be if $\gamma = 1$.) An alternate objective is to minimize the expected cost per period. The former case is known as the *discounted-cost criterion*, while the latter is known as the *average-cost criterion*. We'll consider the average-cost criterion first, then the discounted-cost criterion.

Suppose $\gamma = 1$. The expected cost in a given period if we use base-stock level S is given by

$$g(S) = h \int_0^S (S - d)f(d)dd + p \int_S^\infty (d - S)f(d)dd = h\bar{n}(S) + pn(S). \quad (4.42)$$

This is exactly the same expected cost function as in the single-period model of Section 4.4.2. Therefore, the same base-stock level—given in Theorem 4.1—is optimal, in every period!

In formulating (4.42), we glossed over two potentially problematic issues. First, why didn't we account for the purchase cost c, and second, why didn't we account for the cost in future periods? Well, in the long run, the expected number of units ordered is the same—μ—no matter what S we choose. And since $\gamma = 1$, the timing of our orders does not affect the purchase cost. Therefore, the expected cost per period is independent of c.

What about future periods? In (4.42), we didn't account for the impact of our choice of S on future periods. Is this approach sound, or do we need to account for the future cost, as in the finite-horizon DP model of Section 4.4.3? For example, if we start period t with $IL_t > S_t$, then the expected cost in period t is $g(IL_t)$ rather than $g(S_t)$. In this case, (4.42) would give an incomplete picture of the expected cost in period t since it assumes we can always order up to S. This suggests that we cannot optimize the periods independently. However, as long as $S_t \leq S_{t+1}$, we can be sure that the system starts period $t + 1$ with $IL_t \leq S_{t+1}$. (Why?) Therefore, no matter what value we choose for S_t, we know that we can always order up to S_{t+1} in period $t + 1$. And, as we will see in Section 4.6.1.3, the same base-stock level is optimal in every period. Therefore, $S_t = S_{t+1}$, so $S_t \leq S_{t+1}$ and we can optimize (4.42) to find the optimal base-stock level.

Now suppose $\gamma < 1$. Since the timing of orders now affects the cost, (4.42) is no longer valid. However, the solution turns out to be nearly as simple: The optimal base-stock level is the same in every period, and it is given by

$$S^* = F^{-1}\left(\frac{p - (1 - \gamma)c}{h + p}\right).$$

(We omit the proof.)

We summarize these conclusions in the following theorem:

Theorem 4.3 *The optimal base-stock level in every period of an infinite-horizon model with no fixed costs is given by*

$$S^* = F^{-1}\left(\frac{p - (1 - \gamma)c}{h + p}\right).$$

Note that this theorem holds for both $\gamma = 1$ and $\gamma < 1$.

If demand is normally distributed, then the results from Section 4.4.2.4 still hold, after modifying to account for γ. In particular,

$$S^* = \mu + \sigma\Phi^{-1}\left(\frac{p - (1 - \gamma)c}{h + p}\right) = \mu + z_\alpha\sigma, \tag{4.43}$$

where $\alpha = (p - (1 - \gamma)c)/(h + p)$. The comments on service levels in Section 4.4.2.5 and those on forecasting in Section 4.4.2.8 also apply here.

So far, we have assumed the lead time is zero. Suppose instead there is an L-period lead time. That is, an order placed in period t (in step 2 of the sequence of events on p. 76) is received in step 2 of period $t + L$. If we reinterpret F as the cdf of the *lead-time* demand, then Theorem 4.3 still gives the optimal base-stock level. For normally distributed demands, we have

$$S^* = L\mu + z_\alpha \sqrt{L}\sigma, \qquad (4.44)$$

where μ and σ refer to the demand per period (and so $L\mu$ is the mean and $\sqrt{L}\sigma$ is the standard deviation of lead-time demand).

In (4.44), $L\mu$ is the cycle stock and $z_\alpha \sqrt{L}\sigma$ is the safety stock. Remember that safety stock is held to protect against fluctuations in *lead time* demand, which is why the safety stock component uses the standard deviation of lead time demand. The reason the cycle stock level depends on the lead time, too, is that the base-stock level refers to the inventory position—so if the lead time is 4 weeks, we always want 4 weeks' worth of cycle stock on hand or in the pipeline.

☐ **EXAMPLE 4.7**

Return to Example 4.4. Suppose that $\gamma = 1$. If $L = 1$, we already know that $S^* = 56.6$. What if $L = 4$?

$$S^* = 4 \cdot 50 + 0.8255 \cdot \sqrt{4} \cdot 8 = 213.2.$$

Note that this is a bit less than $4S^* = 226.4$. ☐

4.5 PERIODIC REVIEW WITH NON-ZERO FIXED COSTS: (s, S) POLICIES

4.5.1 (s, S) Policies

We now consider the more general case in which the fixed cost K may be non-zero. If $K \neq 0$, it may no longer make sense to order in every period, since each order incurs a cost. Instead, the firm should order only when the inventory position becomes sufficiently low. In particular, we will assume in this section that the firm follows an (s, S)-*policy*—and in Section 4.6.2, we will prove that such policies are optimal for this system. An (s, S) policy works as follows: In each time period, we observe the current inventory position; if the inventory position is less than or equal to s, then we place an order whose size is sufficient to bring the inventory position up to S. Both s and S are constants, and $s \leq S$. The quantity s is known as the *reorder point* and S as the *order-up-to level*. The reorder point and order-up-to level may change from period to period.

In the special case in which $s = S$, we place an order in every period and the (s, S) policy is equivalent to a base-stock policy. (In the discrete-demand case, we would use $s = S - 1$; this is why base-stock policies are sometimes known as $(S - 1, S)$ policies.)

(s, S) polices and (r, Q) policies are very similar. The difference is that in an (r, Q) policy, we always order the same quantity (Q), while in an (s, S) policy, we instead order up to a fixed level (S). The two types of policies are equivalent if, in every order cycle, there exists a time at which the inventory position exactly equals the reorder point (s or r), and if we always observe the inventory at that moment. Examples include continuous-review systems with continuously distributed demand (as in Section 4.3) and periodic-review systems in which the demand in each period can only be 0 or 1.

We will discuss how to determine the optimal s and S for the single-period, finite-horizon, and infinite-horizon cases separately, just as we did in Section 4.4 for the zero-fixed-cost case. Actually, the single-period case is not nearly as useful for the $K > 0$ case as it is for the $K = 0$ case. This is because single-period models are most commonly used for perishable products that must be ordered every period; a multiple-period model thus reduces to multiple copies of a single-period one. Even if $K > 0$, we still need to order the perishable product in every period, so the fixed cost becomes a constant and can be ignored. Fixed-cost models are therefore most useful in their multiple-period incarnations. Nevertheless, we will discuss the single-period model to introduce the basic concepts.

4.5.2 Single Period

Suppose the inventory position at the start of the (single) period is x. For given s and S, the ordering rule is: If $x \leq s$, order $S - x$; otherwise, order 0. Once we order (or don't), we incur holding and stockout costs just as in the zero-fixed-cost model, except the base-stock level is replaced by S (if we order) and x (if we don't). Therefore, the total expected cost in the period—as a function of s and S—is given by

$$g(s, S) = \begin{cases} K + g(S), & \text{if } x \leq s \\ g(x), & \text{if } x > s, \end{cases}$$

where $g(S)$ is the expected cost function for the single-period problem with no fixed costs as expressed in (4.21) or (4.24). (As in the single-period model without fixed costs, we are assuming $c = 0$.)

Optimizing s and S is actually quite easy. We already know from Theorem 4.1 that $F^{-1}(p/(p+h))$ minimizes $g(S)$, so our aim should be to order up to this level unless the fixed cost makes doing so prohibitively expensive. In other words, we should set $S^* = F^{-1}(p/(p + h))$ and set s^* such that $s^* \leq S^*$ and $g(s^*) = g(S^*) + K$. (Such an s^* is guaranteed to exist for continuous demand distributions.) Because of the convexity of $g(S)$, if $x \leq s$, it is cheaper to order up to S than to leave the inventory position at x, and the reverse is true if $x > s$.

4.5.3 Finite Horizon

The finite-horizon model with non-zero fixed costs can be solved using a straightforward modification of the dynamic programming (DP) model for the zero-fixed-cost case from Section 4.4.3. Just as before, $\theta_t(x)$ represents the optimal expected cost in periods $t, \ldots, T$ if we begin period t with $IL_t = x$ (and act optimally thereafter).

Now $\theta_t(x)$ must account for the fixed cost in period t (if any), as well as the purchase cost and expected holding and stockout costs in period t, and the expected future costs, as in the $K = 0$ model. In particular:

$$\theta_t(x) = \min_{y \geq x}\{K\delta(y - x) + c(y - x) + g(y) + \gamma E_D[\theta_{t+1}(y - D)]\}, \qquad (4.45)$$

where
$$\delta(z) = \begin{cases} 1, & \text{if } z > 0 \\ 0, & \text{otherwise} \end{cases}$$

and $g(\cdot)$ is as expressed in (4.21) or (4.24).

The DP can be solved exactly as described in Section 4.4.3. Just as in that section, the results of the DP tell us exactly what to order up to in each period t for each starting inventory level x. However, just as before, we would rather have a simple policy to follow, rather than having to specify $y_t(x)$ for every t and x. And, just as before, this is always possible, because a simple policy is always optimal—in this case, an (s, S) policy.

To illustrate this, Figure 4.4 plots $y_t(x)$ for a particular instance of the problem.[6] Just as in Figure 4.3, each curve is flat for a while and then climbs along the line $y = x$. However, whereas in Figure 4.3 the two portions are continuous, here there is a discontinuity representing the point at which we stop ordering. In particular, for period t, there are values S_t and s_t such that for $x \leq s_t$, we have $y_t(x) = S_t$, and for $x > s_t$ we have $y_t(x) = x$. In other words, *these curves each depict an (s, S) policy*. We will prove in Section 4.6.2.2 that an (s, S) policy is optimal in every period of a finite-horizon model with fixed costs—the pattern suggested by Figure 4.4 always holds.

Once we solve the DP for a given instance, we still need to determine s_t and S_t from the results. This is not difficult: s_t is equal to the largest x such that $y_t(x) = S_t$, and, just as in Section 4.4.3, $S_t = y_t(-\infty)$ (or $y_t(x)$ for the smallest x value considered).

4.5.4 Infinite Horizon

Recall that the infinite-horizon model with no fixed costs (Section 4.4.4) is as simple as the single-period model (Section 4.4.2). Unfortunately, this is not the case in the fixed-cost case. The infinite-horizon model is quite a bit more difficult than its single-period or finite-horizon counterparts, and we will only sketch the approach here. We'll assume that $\gamma = 1$ and consider the average-cost criterion.

Define a cycle as the interval between two consecutive orders. For given s and S, the Renewal Reward Theorem (Ross 1995) says that the expected cost per period can be written as

$$g(s, S) = \frac{E[\text{cost per cycle}]}{E[\text{cycle length}]},$$

[6] Again, for a variant with time-varying parameters.

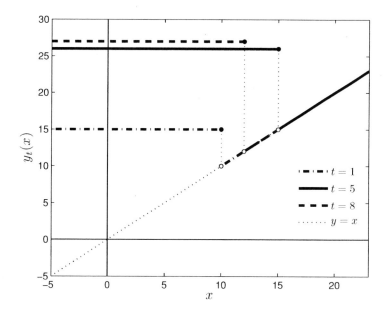

Figure 4.4   DP results, $K > 0$: $y_t(x)$.

where both the numerator and denominator of the right-hand side are functions of (s, S). Unfortunately, this still leaves us with two problems: (1) The expected cost per cycle and the expected cycle length are not trivial to calculate, and (2) the resulting expected cost function, $g(s, S)$, is not convex. However, a relatively simple, efficient algorithm, due to Zheng and Federgruen (1991), finds the exact optimal s and S. It is similar to the algorithm for (r, Q) policies discussed in Section 4.3.4.

There are several heuristics to find near-optimal s and S values. One common approach is to find the optimal r and Q for an (r, Q) policy, either exactly or heuristically—for example, using one of the methods in Section 4.3—and then to set

$$s = r$$
$$S = r + Q.$$

Another approximation involves expressing s and S as explicit functions of the parameters, as follows. Let μ and σ^2 be the mean and variance of the single-period demand, and let

$$Q = 1.30\mu^{0.494} \left(\frac{K}{h}\right)^{0.506} \left(1 + \frac{\sigma^2}{\mu^2}\right)^{0.116} \tag{4.46}$$

$$z = \sqrt{\frac{Q\,h}{\sigma\,p}}. \tag{4.47}$$

Then set

$$s = 0.973\mu + \sigma \left(\frac{0.183}{z} + 1.063 - 2.192z \right) \qquad (4.48)$$

$$S = s + Q. \qquad (4.49)$$

This approximation is known as the *power approximation* and is due to Ehrhardt and Mosier (1984). It was developed by solving a lot of (s, S) models and fitting regression models for a particular functional form to determine the coefficients. It seems complicated, but it makes some intuitive sense. First, roughly speaking, the parameter Q represents an order quantity. For a moment, suppose $\sigma = 0$ (the demand is deterministic). Then we have

$$Q = 1.30\mu^{0.494} \left(\frac{K}{h} \right)^{0.506} \approx \sqrt{2}\mu^{0.5} \left(\frac{K}{h} \right)^{0.5} = \sqrt{\frac{2K\mu}{h}},$$

in other words, the EOQ quantity! Even if $\sigma > 0$, Q is close to the EOQ quantity since the coefficient of the last term in (4.46) has a small coefficient. Note also that, since the coefficient in (4.48) is close to 1 and z does not depend on μ, s moves in roughly one-to-one correspondence with μ.

The power approximation performs quite well in practice and has the additional benefit of providing insights into the structure of the optimal solution (such as those in the previous paragraph) that are not obvious when the solution is found using an algorithm. The performance is not as good when $Q/\mu < 1.5$, but a simple modification is available for this case (Ehrhardt 1979).

☐ **EXAMPLE 4.8**

Return to Joe's corner store from Example 4.1. Suppose that Joe now operates a periodic-review system. Use the (r, Q) approximation and the power approximation to find near-optimal s and S values.

First, the (r, Q) approximation. In Example 4.1 we had $r = 214.0$ and $Q = 318.6$. Therefore

$$s = 214.0$$
$$S = 214.0 + 318.6 = 532.6.$$

Now, in Example 4.3 we used a different approximation to find $r = 128.6$ and $Q = 308.6$. This gives

$$s = 128.6$$
$$S = 128.6 + 308.6 = 437.2.$$

Finally, consider the power approximation. Recall that the lead-time demand has $\mu = 108.3$ and $\sigma = 43.3$. Then

$$Q = 1.30 \left(108.3^{0.494} \right) \left(\frac{8}{0.225} \right)^{0.506} \left(1 + \frac{43.3^2}{108.3^2} \right)^{0.116} = 81.5$$

$$z = \sqrt{\frac{81.52}{43.3} \cdot \frac{0.225}{7.5}} = 0.2377$$

$$s = 0.973 \cdot 108.3 + 43.3 \left(\frac{0.183}{0.2377} + 1.063 - 2.192 \cdot 0.2377 \right) = 162.2$$

$$S = 162.2 + 81.5 = 243.7.$$

These three methods lead to very different solutions.   □

4.6 POLICY OPTIMALITY

Now that we know how to find the optimal S for a base-stock policy (Section 4.4) and the optimal s and S for an (s, S) policy (Section 4.5), we prove that those policy types are in fact optimal for their respective problems. In a way this is a lot to ask—we are trying to show that *no* other policy, of any type, using any parameters, can outperform our chosen policy type (provided we choose the optimal parameters) in the long run. Fortunately, we do not need to prove this explicitly for every possible competing policy type. Rather, we will use the structure of the cost functions to prove that the optimal policy has the desired form.

We will first consider the zero-fixed-cost case, then the fixed-cost case, in both cases considering single-period, finite-horizon, and infinite-horizon cases separately. We will use the same assumptions and notation as in Section 4.5, as well. We continue to assume that the cost and demand parameters are stationary, but the results below still hold if these vary from period to period (deterministically).

Let's focus for a minute on finite-horizon problems with fixed costs. Recall from Section 4.5.3 that $\theta_t(x)$, the optimal cost in periods $t, \ldots, T$ if we begin period t with $IL_t = x$, can be calculated recursively as

$$\theta_t(x) = \min_{y \geq x} \{ K\delta(y - x) + c(y - x) + g(y) + \gamma E_D[\theta_{t+1}(y - D)] \}, \quad (4.50)$$

where $g(y)$ is given by (4.21) or (4.24). The zero-fixed-cost problem is a special case, obtained by setting $K = 0$, and the single-period problem is also a special case, obtained by setting $T = 1$. Note that (4.50) does not assume that any particular policy is being followed. It simply determines the optimal action (order-up-to level) for each starting inventory level x in each period t. Our goal throughout this section will be to use the structure of (4.50) to show that the optimal actions follow the policies we have conjectured are optimal.

4.6.1 Zero Fixed Costs: Base-Stock Policies

We first consider the case in which $K = 0$ and prove that—regardless of the horizon length—a base-stock policy is always optimal.

4.6.1.1 *Single Period*   In this section we'll consider the special case in which $T = 1$ and $K = 0$. We'll also assume that the terminal cost function (see Section 4.4.3) is equal to 0. This assumption is not necessary—we could instead assume only that the terminal cost function is convex—but it simplifies the analysis.

Under these assumptions, (4.50) reduces to

$$\theta(x) = \min_{y \geq x}\{c(y - x) + g(y)\}. \tag{4.51}$$

Of course, we already know how to solve this problem: Theorem 4.1 gives the optimal solution. But our goal here is not to find the optimal solution for a given set of parameters, but rather to prove that the optimal solution always has a certain structure—a base-stock policy.

It will be useful to keep the parts of (4.51) that depend on x separate from those that don't. To that end, we can rewrite $\theta(x)$ as

$$\theta(x) = \min_{y \geq x}\{H(y) - cx\}, \tag{4.52}$$

where

$$H(y) = cy + g(y). \tag{4.53}$$

Since x is a constant, from (4.52), we see that the optimal decision can be found by minimizing $H(y)$ over $y \geq x$—that is, starting at $y = x$, we want to minimize $H(y)$ looking only "to the right" of x. The question is, does this strategy give rise to a base-stock policy?

Suppose $H(y)$ has a shape like that pictured in Figure 4.5(a). In this example, $H(y)$ is minimized at $y = S$. If $x < S$, then the optimal strategy is to set $y = S$, while if $x \geq S$, the optimal strategy is to do nothing—to set $y = x$. In other words, the optimal policy is a base-stock policy. This argument works for any convex function $H(y)$—if $H(y)$ is convex, then a base-stock policy is optimal. But $H(y)$ is convex because $g(y)$ is convex, so we have now sketched the proof of the following theorem.

Theorem 4.4 *A base-stock policy is optimal for the single-period problem with no fixed costs.*

What if $H(y)$ is non-convex? (This would happen if we chose some other single-period expected cost function $g(y)$.) For example, suppose $H(y)$ has a shape like that in Figure 4.5(b). Then a base-stock policy is *not* optimal since for $x < S$, we would set $y = S$, while for $x \in (s', S']$, we would set $y = S'$. On the other hand, there are non-convex functions for which a base-stock policy is still optimal—the function in Figure 4.5(c) is an example. Even though the function has several local minima, it is still optimal to order up to S if $x < S$ and to do nothing otherwise.

4.6.1.2 *Finite Horizon*   It was simple to prove that $H(y)$ is convex, and therefore that a base-stock policy is optimal, for the single-period problem. Our main goal in this section will be to prove that the analogous functions (one per period) are also convex. This is a bit trickier than in the single-period case.

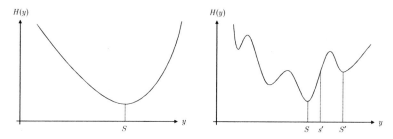

(a) $H(y)$ convex; base-stock policy is optimal. (b) $H(y)$ non-convex; base-stock policy is not
optimal.

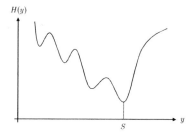

(c) $H(y)$ non-convex; base-stock policy is still
optimal.

Figure 4.5   Possible shapes of the function $H(y)$.

The finite-horizon, zero-fixed-cost version of (4.50) is:

$$\theta_t(x) = \min_{y \geq x} \{c(y - x) + g(y) + \gamma E_D[\theta_{t+1}(y - D)]\}. \qquad (4.54)$$

Here we allow the terminal cost function $\theta_{T+1}(\cdot)$ to be non-zero, and we'll add the
requirement that it is convex.

Again we re-write $\theta_t(x)$ to separate the parts that depend on x from those that
don't:

$$\theta_t(x) = \min_{y \geq x} \{H_t(y) - cx\}, \qquad (4.55)$$

where

$$H_t(y) = cy + g(y) + \gamma E_D[\theta_{t+1}(y - D)]. \qquad (4.56)$$

It is simple to argue that, if $H_t(y)$ is convex, then a base-stock policy is optimal in
period t. The tricky part is showing that $H_t(y)$ is convex for every t. We'll prove this
recursively in the next lemma, showing that if $\theta_{t+1}(x)$ is convex, then so are $H_t(y)$
and $\theta_t(x)$. Then, in Theorem 4.5, we'll get the recursion started, implying that all the
$H_t(y)$ functions are convex and that a base-stock policy is optimal in every period.

Lemma 4.1 *If $\theta_{t+1}(x)$ is convex, then:*

(a) $H_t(y)$ is convex.

(b) *A base-stock policy is optimal in period t, and any minimizer of $H_t(y)$ is an optimal base-stock level.*

(c) *$\theta_t(x)$ is convex.*

Proof.

(a) Clearly cy is convex since it is linear, and we know from Section 4.4.2.3 that $g(y)$ is convex. The third term is convex because $\theta_{t+1}(x)$ is convex (by assumption) and expectation preserves convexity.[7] Therefore $H_t(y)$ is convex, since the sum of convex functions is convex.

(b) From (a), we know that $H_t(y)$ is convex. Let S_t be a minimizer of $H_t(y)$. If $x < S_t$, then the optimal $y \geq x$ is at $y = S_t$; if $x \geq S_t$, then H_t is non-decreasing to the right of x (by convexity), so the optimal $y \geq x$ is $y = x$. This is exactly the definition of a base-stock policy.

(c) From (4.55), $\theta_t(x)$ is the minimum over y of $H_t(y)$ (minus a constant). Since minimization preserves convexity,[8] the convexity of $H_t(y)$ from (a) implies that of $\theta_t(x)$.   ∎

We have done most of the heavy lifting, but we're not done yet. All we have shown is that a base-stock policy is optimal in period t *if* $\theta_{t+1}(x)$ is convex. The next theorem establishes our main result—that a base-stock policy is optimal in every period—and the convexity of $\theta_{T+1}(\cdot)$ gets the recursion started.

Theorem 4.5 *If the terminal cost function $\theta_{T+1}(x)$ is convex, then a base-stock policy is optimal in each period of the finite-horizon problem with no fixed costs.*

Proof. By assumption, $\theta_{T+1}(x)$ is convex. Therefore, by Lemma 4.1(b), a base-stock policy is optimal in period T. Moreover, $\theta_T(x)$ is convex by Lemma 4.1(c). This implies that a base-stock policy is optimal in period $T - 1$, and that $\theta_{T-1}(x)$ is convex. Continuing this logic, a base-stock policy is optimal in every period.   ∎

Of course, this analysis says nothing about how to find the optimal base-stock levels. In general, we need to use the DP from Section 4.4.3 to find those. In most cases, the base-stock levels will change over time, and the pattern depends on what happens at the end of the horizon, i.e., the terminal value function. For example, suppose backorders that are outstanding at the end of the horizon must be cleared by, say, air-freighting inventory from overseas at a very high cost. Then the base-stock levels will increase at the end of the horizon to prevent these costly backorders. Conversely, suppose the product in question is a hazardous material that must be

---

[7]This is a well-known property of convex functions. It says that, if $f(x)$ is a convex function and Y is a random variable, then $E_Y[f(x - Y)]$ is convex.
[8]Another well-known property of convex functions: If $f(x, y)$ is convex and $g(x) = \min_y\{f(x, y)\}$, then $g(x)$ is convex (Boyd and Vandenberghe 2004, Section 3.2.3).

disposed of at a very high cost if any remains at the end of the horizon. Then the base-stock levels will decrease at the end of the horizon to ensure that the inventory is sold. But if the terminal value function is just right, the same base-stock level will be optimal in every period. Moreover, in this special case, the optimal base-stock levels can be found explicitly, without requiring an algorithm. This policy is called a *myopic policy* because it optimizes only a single period at a time, ignoring the rest of the horizon. In this special case, then, the myopic policy is optimal in every period.

The special case is defined by setting the terminal cost function to

$$\theta_{T+1}(x) = -cx.$$

This terminal cost function would be applicable if, for instance, at the end of the horizon, any excess inventory can be returned to the supplier for a full reimbursement of the order cost c and any backorders must be cleared by purchasing a new item, again at a cost of c.

First consider period T, for which it is straightforward to find the optimal base-stock level:

$$\begin{aligned} H_T(y) &= cy + g(y) + \gamma E_D[\theta_{T+1}(y - D)] \\ &= cy + g(y) + \gamma E_D[-c(y - D)] \\ &= c(1 - \gamma)y + g(y) + \gamma c\mu, \end{aligned}$$

where $\mu = E[D]$. The optimal base-stock level is a minimizer of $H_T(y)$, so we set $H_T'(y) = 0$:

$$H_T'(y) = c(1 - \gamma) + (h + p)F(y) - p = 0$$

(from (4.25)), or

$$F(y) = \frac{p - (1 - \gamma)c}{p + h}.$$

The optimal base-stock level in period T is therefore

$$S_T^* = F^{-1}\left(\frac{p - (1 - \gamma)c}{h + p}\right). \tag{4.57}$$

This is the same solution as the infinite-horizon newsvendor model in Theorem 4.3.

Now we know that (4.57) gives the optimal base-stock level in period T; it remains to show that the same base-stock level is optimal in the other periods. In period T, the solution to the minimization in (4.55) is to set $y = S_T^*$ if $x \le S_T^*$ and $y = x$ otherwise. Therefore,

$$\theta_T(x) = \begin{cases} H_T(S_T^*) - cx, & \text{if } x \le S_T^* \\ H_T(x) - cx, & \text{otherwise.} \end{cases} \tag{4.58}$$

Now let's compute $H_{T-1}(y)$ in order to derive the optimal base-stock level for period $T - 1$. From (4.56),

$$H_{T-1}(y) = cy + g(y) + \gamma E_D[\theta_T(y - D)]$$

$$= \begin{cases} cy + g(y) + \gamma E_D[H_T(S_T^*) - c(y - D)], & \text{if } y \leq S_T^* \\ [\text{something else}], & \text{if } y > S_T^*. \end{cases} \quad (4.59)$$

The first case holds because if $y \leq S_T^*$, then surely $y - D \leq S_T^*$, and therefore the first case in (4.58) holds. But the second case is harder because if $y > S_T^*$, then the first case in (4.58) will hold for some D and the second case will hold for others. Fortunately, it will turn out that we won't need to write out an expression for the second case of (4.59): If we can show that the derivative of $H_{T-1}(y)$ is 0 for some $y \leq S_T^*$, then by the convexity of $H_{T-1}(y)$ (Lemma 4.1(a)), that y minimizes $H_{T-1}(y)$ and we can ignore the case in which $y > S_T^*$. So assume that $y \leq S_T^*$. Then

$$H_{T-1}(y) = cy + g(y) + \gamma E_D[H_T(S_T^*) - c(y - D)]$$
$$= c(1 - \gamma)y + g(y) + \gamma c\mu + \gamma H_T(S_T^*),$$

which differs from $H_T(y)$ only by an additive constant. Therefore, its derivative equals 0 for the same value of y, and we have the same optimal base-stock level. Continuing this logic backwards, we get the following theorem:

Theorem 4.6 *If $\theta_{T+1}(x) = -cx$, then the myopic base-stock level, given by*

$$S^* = F^{-1}\left(\frac{p - (1 - \gamma)c}{p + h}\right),$$

is optimal in every period.

4.6.1.3 Infinite Horizon
Now suppose that $T = \infty$. The main result is the following:

Theorem 4.7 *A base-stock policy is optimal in each period of the infinite-horizon problem with no fixed costs.*

And we already know the optimal base-stock level, from Theorem 4.3. We will omit the proof of Theorem 4.7. It uses many of the ideas from the earlier proofs and is not very difficult (see, e.g., Zipkin 2000).

4.6.2 Non-Zero Fixed Costs: (s, S) Policies

We now allow $K \neq 0$ and prove that an (s, S) policy is optimal. We will present formal proofs for the single-period and finite-horizon cases but only state the result without proof for the infinite-horizon case. In the single-period case, we will argue that an (s, S) policy is optimal using the convexity of $H(y)$, just as we used the convexity of this function to prove that a base-stock policy is optimal for the zero-fixed-cost case. However, in the finite-horizon problem, $H_t(y)$ is no longer convex (except for $t = T$). Fortunately, however, it is close enough to convex (in a specific way to be made more precise later) to establish the result.

4.6.2.1 *Single Period*   Assume that $T = 1$ and (as in Section 4.6.1.1) that the terminal cost function equals 0. Then (4.50) reduces to

$$\theta(x) = \min_{y \geq x}\{K\delta(y - x) + c(y - x) + g(y)\} \tag{4.60}$$

$$= \min_{y \geq x}\{K\delta(y - x) + H(y) - cx\}, \tag{4.61}$$

where $H(y)$ is the same as before, as defined in (4.53).

Let S^* be the minimizer of $H(y)$. Since $H(y)$ is convex, we should definitely not order if $x > S^*$. What if $x \leq S^*$? We may not even wish to order in this case—it depends on how much we save by ordering versus how much it costs to order. That is, we should order up to S^* if

$$H(x) - H(S^*) \geq K \tag{4.62}$$

and do nothing otherwise. Which values of x satisfy (4.62)? By the convexity of $H(y)$, there exists an s^* such that all $x \leq s^*$ satisfy (4.62). In particular, s^* is the x such that $H(x) - H(S^*) = K$. (There may be multiple such x if $H(y)$ is not strictly convex. However, if the demand cdf $F(\cdot)$ is strictly increasing, then $g(y)$ and hence $H(y)$ are strictly convex.)

We have now proved:

Theorem 4.8 *An (s, S) policy is optimal for the single-period problem with fixed costs.*

And, as we argued in Section 4.5.2, S^* is the minimizer of $H(y)$ and $s^* \leq S^*$ satisfies $H(s^*) - H(S^*) = K$.

4.6.2.2 *Finite Horizon*   Recall the logic for proving that a base-stock policy is optimal for the finite-horizon model with no fixed costs (Lemma 4.1 and Theorem 4.5): Since $\theta_{T+1}(x)$ is convex, so is $H_T(y)$; therefore a base-stock policy is optimal in period T and $\theta_T(x)$ is convex; therefore $H_{T-1}(y)$ is convex; therefore a base-stock policy is optimal in period $T - 1$ and $\theta_{T-1}(x)$ is convex; and so on. Unfortunately, the convexity implications break down when fixed costs are present. Let's see why.

From (4.50),

$$\theta_t(x) = \min_{y \geq x}\{K\delta(y - x) + c(y - x) + g(y) + \gamma E_D[\theta_{t+1}(y - D)]\}$$

$$= \min_{y \geq x}\{H_t(y) + K\delta(y - x) - cx\},$$

where $H_t(y)$ is as defined in (4.56). Let's assume that $H_t(y)$ is convex. Is $\theta_t(x)$? Since $H_t(y)$ is convex, an (s, S) policy is optimal in period t. This implies that

$$\theta_t(x) = -cx + \begin{cases} H_t(S_t^*) + K, & \text{if } x \leq s_t^* \\ H_t(x), & \text{if } x > s_t^*. \end{cases} \tag{4.63}$$

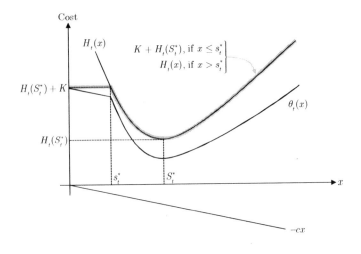

Figure 4.6   Non-convexity of $\theta_t(x)$.

Figure 4.6 sketches $\theta_t(x)$ and its constituent parts. The piecewise nature of $\theta_t(x)$ makes it non-convex, even if $H_t(y)$ is convex. Fortunately, although we used convexity to prove optimality of an (s, S) policy in the single-period case, convexity is not required—an (s, S) policy is still optimal under a weaker condition.

Let $f(x)$ be a real-valued function and let $K \geq 0$. Then f is *K-convex* if, for all x and all $a, b > 0$,

$$f(x) + a \cdot \frac{f(x) - f(x - b)}{b} \leq f(x + a) + K \qquad (4.64)$$

(Scarf 1960). This definition is identical to (one) definition of convexity, except for the $+K$ on the right-hand side. The term $[f(x) - f(x - b)]/b$ is like a derivative at x (think about b approaching 0). Then the left-hand side of (4.64) approximates $f(x+a)$ by linearizing it using the "slope" of f between $x-b$ and x. (See Figure 4.7.) So, K-convexity implies that this approximation doesn't overestimate $f(x + a)$ by more than K. (It may also underestimate it.) If f is convex, then the approximation on the left-hand side of (4.64) *always* underestimates $f(x+a)$. That is, (4.64) holds with $K = 0$. Therefore, *0-convexity is equivalent to convexity*. And K-convexity becomes weaker as K increases: If f is K_1-convex and $K_2 > K_1$, then f is also K_2-convex.

It is worth noting that, whereas some other convexity-like properties that you may be familiar with—quasiconvexity, pseudoconvexity, and so on—are used outside of inventory theory, K-convexity was developed specifically for proving the optimality of (s, S) policies and (as far as we know) is not used outside of inventory theory.

Here is another important property of K-convexity:

Lemma 4.2 *Let f be a continuous, K-convex function. Let S^* be its smallest global minimizer and let s^* be the largest $x \leq S^*$ such that $f(x) = f(S^*) + K$. Then:*

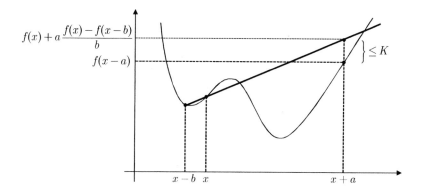

Figure 4.7 K-convexity.

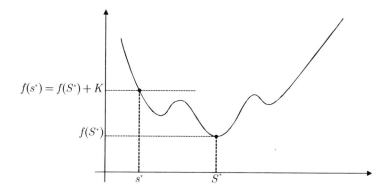

Figure 4.8   Properties of K-convex functions from Lemma 4.2.

(a) f *is non-increasing on* $(-\infty, s^*]$.

(b) *If* $s^* < x \leq S^*$, *then* $f(x) < f(s^*)$.

(c) *Suppose* $S^* < x_1 < x_2$. *Then* $f(x_1) - f(x_2) \leq K$.

Lemma 4.2 says that a K-convex function first decreases for a while, up to a point s^*; then, after a different point S^*, if it ever decreases, it never decreases by more than K. (See Figure 4.8.) This property will lead to the optimality of an (s, S) policy (as you may have suspected from our choice of notation in the lemma).

Proof.

(a) Suppose (for a contradiction) that f is *not* non-increasing on $(-\infty, s^*]$. Then there exists $x_1 < x_2 < s^*$ such that $f(x_1) < f(x_2)$. We consider two cases.

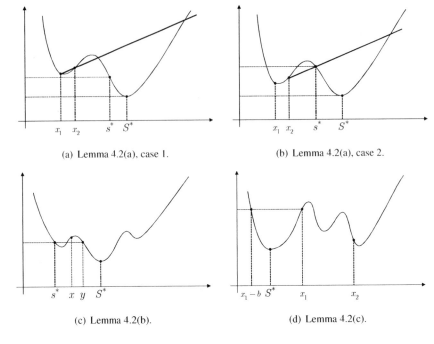

(a) Lemma 4.2(a), case 1.

(b) Lemma 4.2(a), case 2.

(c) Lemma 4.2(b).

(d) Lemma 4.2(c).

Figure 4.9   Proof of Lemma 4.2.

<u>Case 1</u>: $f(x_2) \geq f(s^*)$. (See Figure 4.9(a).)

Let $b = x_2 - x_1$ and $a = S^* - x_2$. Then

$$f(x_2) + a \cdot \frac{f(x_2) - f(x_2 - b)}{b} = f(x_2) + (S^* - x_2)\frac{f(x_2) - f(x_1)}{b}$$
$$> f(x_2) \quad (\text{since } f(x_2) - f(x_1) > 0)$$
$$\geq f(s^*) \quad (\text{by case 1 assumption})$$
$$= f(S^*) + K$$
$$= f(x_2 + a) + K.$$

This contradicts the K-convexity of f.

<u>Case 2</u>: $f(x_2) < f(s^*)$. (See Figure 4.9(b).)

Let $b = s^* - x_2$ and $a = S^* - s^*$. Then

$$f(s^*) + a \cdot \frac{f(s^*) - f(s^* - b)}{b} = f(s^*) + (S^* - s^*)\frac{f(s^*) - f(x_2)}{b}$$
$$> f(s^*) \quad (\text{since } f(s^*) - f(x_2) > 0)$$
$$= f(S^*) + K$$
$$= f(s^* + a) + K.$$

This contradicts the K-convexity of f.

Since both cases lead to a contradiction, f must be non-increasing on $(-\infty, s^*]$.

(b) Let $s^* < x \leq S^*$. Suppose (for a contradiction) that $f(x) < f(s^*)$. Then, by the continuity of $f(x)$, there is some y, $x < y < S^*$, such that $f(y) = f(s^*) = f(S^*) + K$, which violates the definition of s^* as the *largest* $x \leq S^*$ such that $f(x) = f(S^*) + K$. Therefore, $f(x) < f(s^*)$.

(c) Suppose (for a contradiction) that there exists some x_1 and x_2 such that $S^* < x_1 < x_2$ but $f(x_1) - f(x_2) > K$. (See Figure 4.9(d).)

Let b be defined such that $f(x_1 - b) = f(x_1)$. (We'll assume such a b exists. It does if $\lim_{x \to -\infty} f(x) = \infty$, which is true of the K-convex functions we'll consider below.) Let $a = x_2 - x_1$. Then

$$
\begin{aligned}
f(x_1) + a \cdot \frac{f(x_1) - f(x_1 - b)}{b} &= f(x_1) \quad (\text{since } f(x_1 - b) = f(x_1)) \\
&> f(x_2) + K \quad (\text{by assumption}) \\
&= f(x_1 + a) + K.
\end{aligned}
$$

This contradicts the K-convexity of f. ∎

The following properties of K-convex functions will be important in the results that follow. They are all generalizations of well-known results for convexity.

Lemma 4.3   (a) If $f(x)$ is K-convex, then $f(x + \epsilon)$ is K-convex for all constants ϵ.

(b) If $f_1(x)$ is K_1-convex and $f_2(x)$ is K_2-convex, then $\alpha_1 f_1(x) + \alpha_2 f_2(x)$ is $(\alpha_1 K_1 + \alpha_2 K_2)$-convex, for any $\alpha_1, \alpha_2 > 0$.

(c) If $f(x)$ is K-convex and Y is a random variable, then $E_Y[f(x - Y)]$ is K-convex.

Proof. Omitted; see Problem 4.24. ∎

Now we're finally ready to prove the optimality of (s, S) policies for the finite-horizon problem. The logic will be similar to the base-stock case: The K-convexity of $\theta_{t+1}(x)$ implies the K-convexity of $H_t(y)$, which implies the optimality of an (s, S) policy in period t and the K-convexity of $\theta_t(x)$; and so on.

Lemma 4.4 If $\theta_{t+1}(x)$ is continuous and K-convex, then:

(a) $H_t(y)$ is continuous and K-convex.

(b) An (s, S) policy is optimal in period t, with S_t^* equal to the smallest minimizer of $H_t(y)$ and s_t^* equal to the largest $x \leq S_t^*$ such that $H_t(x) - H_t(S_t^*) = K$.

(c) $\theta_t(x)$ is continuous and K-convex.

Proof.

(a) We know that

$$H_t(y) = cy + g(y) + \gamma E_D[\theta_{t+1}(y - D)].$$

The first two terms are each convex (i.e., 0-convex). Since $\theta_{t+1}(x)$ is K-convex (by assumption), so is the third term, by Lemma 4.3(c). Therefore $H_t(y)$ is $(0 + 0 + K)$-convex, or K-convex, by Lemma 4.3(b). Continuity follows from the continuity of each of the three terms.

(b) First note that Lemma 4.2 applies to $H_t(y)$ since it is K-convex, and that the definitions of S_t^* and s_t^* are identical to those of S^* and s^* in the lemma. We'll determine the optimal ordering action for each starting inventory level x. If $x < s_t^*$, then by Lemma 4.2(a), $H_t(x) \geq H_t(s_t^*) = H_t(S_t^*) + K$, so it is cheaper to order up to S_t^* than not to order (and there is no better order-up-to level since S_t^* minimizes $H_t(y)$). If $s_t^* < x \leq S_t^*$, then $H_t(x) < H_t(s_t^*)$ by Lemma 4.2(b). Therefore, $H_t(x) < H_t(S_t^*) + K$, so it is better to order nothing than to place an order. Finally, if $x > S_t^*$, then by Lemma 4.2(c), for any $y > x$, $f(x) < f(y) + K$, so it is better to order nothing than to place an order. This is exactly the definition of an (s, S) policy with parameters s_t^* and S_t^*.

(c) From (4.63), we know that

$$\theta_t(x) = -cx + \psi_t(x),$$

where

$$\psi_t(x) \equiv \begin{cases} H_t(S_t^*) + K, & \text{if } x \leq s_t^* \\ H_t(x), & \text{if } x > s_t^*. \end{cases}$$

Clearly each of the pieces of $\psi_t(x)$ is continuous, and at the breakpoint $x = s_t^*$ we have $H_t(S_t^*) + K = H_t(x)$ by definition of s_t^* from part (b). Therefore, $\psi_t(x)$ is continuous, and so is $\theta_t(x)$.

To prove K-convexity, let x be any real number and let $a, b > 0$. Since $-cx$ is convex, it suffices to prove that $\psi_t(x)$ is K-convex. (Refer to Figure 4.6.)

If $x - b > s_t^*$, then $\psi_t(x) = H_t(x)$ for $x \in [x - b, x + a]$, so the K-convexity of ψ_t follows from that of H_t.

If $x + a \leq s_t^*$, then $\psi_t(x) = H_t(S_t^*) + K$, a constant, for $x \in [x - b, x + a]$, so the K-convexity of ψ_t is trivial.

Suppose $x - b \leq s_t^* < x + a$. We consider two cases. First, if $\psi_t(x) \leq H_t(S_t^*) + K$, then

$$\psi_t(x) + a \cdot \frac{\psi_t(x) - \psi_t(x - b)}{b}$$
$$\leq \psi_t(x) \quad (\text{since } \psi_t(x) \leq H_t(S_t^*) + K = \psi_t(x - b))$$

$$\leq H_t(S_t^*) + K$$
$$\leq H_t(x + a) + K \quad \text{(since } S_t^* \text{ minimizes } H_t\text{)}$$
$$= \psi_t(x + a) + K \quad \text{(since } x + a > s_t^*\text{)}.$$

If, instead, $\psi_t(x) > H_t(S_t^*) + K$, then $x > S_t^*$ and so $\psi_t(x) = H_t(x)$. Then

$$\psi_t(x) + a \cdot \frac{\psi_t(x) - \psi_t(x - b)}{b}$$
$$= H_t(x) + a \cdot \frac{H_t(x) - (H_t(S_t^*) + K)}{b}$$
$$\leq H_t(x) + a \cdot \frac{H_t(x) - H_t(S_t^*)}{x - S_t^*} \quad \text{(since } K \geq 0 \text{ and } x - b \leq s_t^* \leq S_t^*\text{)}$$
$$\leq H_t(x + a) + K \quad \text{(by } K\text{-convexity of } H_t, \text{ letting } b' = x - S_t^*\text{)}$$
$$= \psi_t(x + a) + K \quad \text{(since } x + a > s_t^*\text{)}.$$

Therefore, $\psi_t(x)$ is K-convex, and so is $\theta_t(x)$. ∎

Theorem 4.9 *If the terminal cost function $\theta_{T+1}(x)$ is continuous and convex, then an (s, S) policy is optimal in each period of the finite-horizon problem with fixed costs.*

Proof. By assumption, $\theta_{T+1}(x)$ is continuous and convex. Therefore, by Lemma 4.4(b), an (s, S) policy is optimal in period T. Moreover, $\theta_T(x)$ is continuous and K-convex by Lemma 4.4(c). This implies that an (s, S) policy is optimal in period $T - 1$, and that $\theta_{T-1}(x)$ is continuous and K-convex. Continuing this logic, an (s, S) policy is optimal in every period. ∎

4.6.2.3   Infinite Horizon   If $T = \infty$, it is still true that an (s, S) policy is optimal in every period. And, echoing the infinite-horizon model with no fixed costs, the optimal s and S are the same in every period. However, the proof of these facts is quite a bit more difficult than the analogous proof in Section 4.6.1.3, and we omit it here. (See Zheng (1991).)

PROBLEMS

4.1   **(Three Approximate (r, Q) Policies)** Consider the model in Section 4.3. Suppose the annual demand is distributed $N(800, 40^2)$, the fixed cost is $K = 50$, and the holding and stockout costs are $h = 3.1$ and $p = 45$, respectively, per item per year. The lead time is 4 days. For each method below, report the values of r and Q you found, as well as the corresponding expected annual cost from (4.6).

   a) Solve the approximate model using the heuristic described in Section 4.3.2.2.

   b) Let $\alpha = p/(p+h)$ and solve the model with a type-1 service level constraint.

c) Solve the model using the EOQB approximation in Section 4.3.3.

4.2 **(Exact (r, Q) Model: Heuristic and Optimal)** Consider the model in Section 4.3. Suppose the demand has a Poisson distribution with a mean of $\lambda = 12$ units/month, the fixed cost is $K = 4$, and the holding and stockout costs are $h = 4$ and $p = 28$, respectively, per item per month. The lead-time is 0.5 months. For each method below, report the values of r and Q you found, as well as the corresponding expected cost per week from (4.20).

Note: If X is the lead-time demand, with mean λ, pmf $f(x)$, and cdf $F(x)$, then the cost function $g(S)$ in (4.17) can also be written as

$$g(S) = h\bar{n}(S) + pn(S), \tag{4.65}$$

where

$$n(x) = -(x - \lambda)(1 - F(x)) + \lambda f(x) \tag{4.66}$$

$$\bar{n}(x) = x - \lambda + n(x)$$

$$= (x - \lambda)F(x) + \lambda f(x). \tag{4.67}$$

($n(x)$ is the Poisson loss function.)

a) Solve the model using the EOQB approximation described in Section 4.3.3. In (4.13), $g(S)$ should be given by (4.65) rather than (4.14).

b) Solve the exact model using the algorithm described in Section 4.3.4.2.

4.3 **(Inventory of Ski Jackets)** A clothing company sells ski jackets every winter but must decide in the summer how many jackets to produce. Each jacket costs $65 to produce and ship and sells for $129 at retail stores. (For the sake of simplicity, assume the jacket is sold in a single store.) Customers who wish to buy this jacket but find it out of stock will buy a competitor's jacket; in addition to the lost revenue, the company also incurs a loss-of-goodwill cost of $15 for each lost sale. At the end of the winter, unsold jackets are sold to a discount clothing store for $22 each.

a) First suppose that the demand for the ski jackets this winter will be distributed as a normal random variable with mean 900 and standard deviation 60. What is the optimal number of jackets to produce?

b) Now suppose that the demand is distributed as a Poisson random variable with mean 900. What is the optimal number of jackets to produce?

4.4 **(Dixie's Pulled Pork)** One of the specialties at Dixie's Cafe is pulled pork, which simmers over a low flame all day. Since the cooking time is so long, Dixie must decide in the morning how many servings of pork to cook for that night's dinner service. Moreover, the pork cooked on a given day cannot be served the next day; it must be thrown away. Pulled pork is the highest-profit item on the menu at Dixie's Cafe. It earns Dixie a profit of $8 per serving, whereas all the other items earn a profit of $4. Customers who want pulled pork but find it out of stock will order one of these other items. The ingredients for pulled pork cost the Cafe $2.50.

a) First suppose that the demand for pulled pork on a given evening is normally distributed with a mean of 18 and a variance of 16. How many servings of pulled pork should Dixie prepare in the morning? (Fractional servings are OK.) What is the expected cost (ingredients and lost profit) of the optimal solution?

b) Now suppose that the demand is distributed as an exponential random variable with mean 18. How many servings should Dixie prepare?

4.5 **(The Integer Newsvendor)** Suppose that the newsvendor faces integer-valued demand and must choose an integer value of S. We make no assumptions about the demand distribution (other than that it is integer) or about the relationship between h and p. Prove that S^* is the smallest integer y such that

$$F(y) \geq \frac{p}{p+h},$$

where F is the cdf of the demand distribution. (The result implies that it is always optimal to round S^* up.)

4.6 **(Newsvendor with Forecasting)** Suppose that demands are normally distributed and that the newsvendor does not know μ and σ, but he estimates them in each period, as described in Section 4.4.2.8, using moving averages and standard deviations with $N = 5$. The observed demands in periods $t - 10, \ldots, t - 1$ are: 99, 87, 125, 106, 100, 107, 93, 114, 87, 85. The cost parameters are $h = 2$ and $p = 15$. What is the optimal order quantity for the newsvendor in period t?

4.7 **(The Cooperative Newsvendor)** Consider a newsvendor who purchases newspapers from his supplier at a cost of c per newspaper and sells them at a price of r per newspaper. If he has unsold newspapers at the end of the day, he can take them to the local recycling center, which pays him a salvage value of v per newspaper. The daily demand for newspapers has pdf $f(x)$ and cdf $F(x)$. Assume that $F(x)$ is strictly increasing.

a) Write the newsvendor's expected cost as a function of S, denoted $g_n(S)$. (Your expression may include integrals.) Show that the order quantity that minimizes $g_n(S)$ is

$$S_n^* = F^{-1}\left(\frac{r-c}{r-v}\right).$$

b) Suppose the newsvendor's supplier prints newspapers on demand; that is, she observes the newsvendor's order of S and then prints exactly S newspapers. The supplier therefore faces no uncertainty. It costs the supplier b to print one newspaper. Write the supplier's expected net cost (i.e., cost minus revenue) as a function of S, denoted $g_s(S)$. Then write the total supply chain expected cost as a function of S, denoted $g_t(S)$—that is, $g_t(S) = g_n(S) + g_s(S)$.

c) Find the order quantity S_t^* that minimizes $g_t(S)$. (If the supplier and the newsvendor were both owned by a single firm that sought to minimize its total costs, this is the order quantity it would pick.)

d) Prove that $S_n^* = S_t^*$ if and only if $c = b$—that is, if and only if the supplier earns zero profit on each newspaper she sells to the newsvendor.

e) Prove that $g_t(S_n^*) = g_t(S_t^*)$ if and only if $c = b$, and $g_t(S_n^*) > g_t(S_t^*)$ otherwise.

f) In a short paragraph, discuss the implications of the results you proved in this problem. What does it mean for two supply chain partners that are each attempting to minimize their own costs rather than minimizing the total supply chain cost?

4.8 **(Non-Standard-Normal Loss Function)** Prove equation (4.31) (also given in (C.13)).

4.9 **(Loss Function Derivatives)** Prove equations (C.6) and (C.7).

4.10 **(Worst-Case Bound for Deterministic Newsvendor Approximation)** As noted in Section 4.3.3, the papers by Zheng (1992) and Axsäter (1996) suggest bounds on the error that results from approximating a stochastic inventory model (the model of Section 4.3, for which an (r, Q) policy is optimal) by a deterministic one. Suppose we do the same thing for the newsvendor model, setting S equal to the optimal solution to the deterministic problem, i.e., $S = \mu$. Assume the demand is distributed $N(\mu, \sigma^2)$.

a) Prove that

$$\rho \equiv \frac{g(\mu)}{g(S^*)} \approx \frac{0.3989}{\phi(z_\alpha)},$$

where $g(S)$ is the expected newsvendor cost if S is the order-up-to level and $\alpha = p/(h + p)$.

b) Is it possible to identify a fixed worst-case bound $\bar{\rho}$ that holds for any values of the parameters h, p, μ, and σ? Explain your answer.

4.11 **(Working on the Chain Gang)** Lackluster Video needs to decide how may DVD copies of the new hit movie *The Supply Chain Gang* to stock in its stores. The company expects demand for DVD rentals for the movie over the next 90 days to be Poisson with a mean of λ per day. The length of time each renter keeps a DVD before returning it is exponential with a mean of $1/\mu$ days (i.e., exponential with a rate of μ).

Each copy purchased by the store costs c. Demands are backordered, in the sense that a customer wanting to rent the movie but finding that it is out of stock will return on another day to try again. Since this movie has been designated as a "guaranteed in stock" title, each backordered demand incurs a penalty cost of g, the cost of providing a free rental to the customer.

Assuming that backordered customers check back frequently to see whether the movie is in stock and rent it quickly when it is available, this system can be modeled as an $M/M/S$ queue, where S is the number of copies of the DVD owned by the store. It can be shown that the probability of a stockout in an $M/M/S$ queue is approximately

$$P[\text{stockout}] \approx 1 - \Phi \left(\frac{S - \rho - \frac{1}{2}}{\sqrt{\rho}} \right),$$

where Φ is the standard normal cdf and $\rho = \lambda/\mu$ (in queuing terminology, the "offered load").

   a) Determine the optimal number of copies to purchase (S) to minimize the purchase cost and the expected stockout cost over the next 90 days using the approximation given above. (Assume that the demand after 90 days will be negligible.) Your answer should be in closed form; that is, $S = $ [some expression].

   b) Compute the optimal S assuming that $\lambda = 22$, $\mu = \frac{1}{4}$, $c = 9$, and $g = 4.5$.

   c) Suppose the video store is worried about loss-of-goodwill costs as well as free rental costs when a demand is backordered, but it is uncomfortable estimating these costs. Instead, it would prefer to choose S so that demands are met with probability α. Prove that the smallest such S is given by

$$S \approx \rho + z_\alpha \sqrt{\rho}.$$

   d) In two or three sentences, interpret the result from part (c) in terms of cycle and safety stock.

4.12 **(A Simple Revenue Management Problem)** An airplane has n seats in coach class. Two types of travelers will purchase tickets for a certain flight on a certain date: leisure travelers, who are willing to pay only the *discounted fare* r_d, and business travelers, who are willing to pay the *full fare* r_f ($r_f > r_d$). The airline knows that the number of leisure travelers requesting tickets for this flight will be greater than n for sure, while the number of business travelers requesting tickets is a random variable X with a given cdf $F(x)$.

Assume that the leisure travelers always purchase their tickets before the business travelers do. (In practice, this is roughly true, which is why airfares increase as the flight date gets closer.) The airline wishes to sell as many seats as possible to business travelers since they are willing to pay more. However, since the number of such travelers is random and these customers arrive near the date of the flight, a sensible strategy is for the airline to allocate a certain number of seats Q for full fares and the remainder, $n - Q$, for discount fares.

The discount fares are sold first: The first $n - Q$ customers requesting tickets will be charged r_d and the remaining $\leq Q$ customers will be offered the full price r_f. Some of the customers being offered r_f will be leisure travelers; these travelers will decline to buy a ticket. Similarly, it is possible that some of the seats sold to leisure travelers for r_d could have been sold to business travelers who would have been willing to pay r_f.

   a) Show that the problem of finding the optimal number of full-fare seats, Q, is equivalent to a newsvendor problem. What should be used in place of the holding and stockout costs h and p? What is the critical ratio? What is the optimality condition (analogous to (4.26))?

b) Suppose that demand for full-fare seats is normally distributed with a mean of 40 and a standard deviation of 18. There are $n = 100$ seats on the flight and the fares are $r_d = \$189$ and $r_f = \$439$. What is the optimal number of full-fare seats? (Fractional solutions are OK.)

c) For each situation below, will the optimal Q increase, decrease, or stay the same? Will the optimal cost increase, decrease, or stay the same? Briefly explain your answers.

    i. The full-fare tickets are fully refundable, and with some probability each business traveler will cancel his or her ticket at the last minute, too late for the airline to re-sell the newly vacant seat.

    ii. A fraction of leisure travelers are willing to pay full fare if they arrive after the discount seats are sold out.

    iii. Unsold seats may be sold at the very last minute for a steeply discounted price (for example, on a discount airfare website). These tickets are made available after most (though not necessarily all) of the business travelers have requested tickets.

4.13   **(Heating Oil Replenishments)** Henry's Heating Oil company delivers oil to its customers' homes. If a customer signs up for Henry's "auto-fill" plan, the company delivers oil to the customer's home on a regular schedule based on historical oil-usage data for that customer. Suppose a given customer has an oil tank that holds C liters of oil. For each delivery to this customer, Henry's incurs a fixed cost of K, representing the cost of the truck, driver, and fuel required to make the delivery. Henry's will make a delivery to this customer every T days, where T is a decision variable, and at each delivery it will deliver enough oil to fill the tank. The number of days required for the customer to use C liters of oil is a random variable, denoted X, whose pdf and cdf are f and F, respectively. If the customer uses all C liters of oil before the next delivery, Henry's must make an emergency delivery to refill the tank. For these emergency deliveries, the normal fixed cost of K does not apply, but instead Henry's incurs a penalty cost of pT. (The penalty cost is proportional to T because, the more infrequent the deliveries, the more disruptive it is to Henry's delivery schedule to add an emergency delivery.) After the emergency delivery, the normal schedule resumes; that is, the next delivery will be T days after the last *normal* delivery. Assume the customer never needs more than one emergency shipment between two normal shipments.

    a) Write the expected cost per day as a function of T.

    b) Find the optimal delivery interval, T^*. You may assume that T is normally distributed and that $T < E[X]$.

    c) Suppose $C = 500$, $K = \$175$, $p = \$25$, and $X \sim N(22, 8^2)$. What is T^*, and what is the corresponding expected cost per day?

4.14   **(Implementing Base-Stock DP)** Consider the finite-horizon model with no fixed costs of Section 4.4.3.

a) Implement the dynamic programming model in any programming language you wish.

b) Suppose $T = 10$, $c = 1$, $h = 0.5$, $p = 10$, and $\gamma = 0.98$. Suppose the demand per period is distributed as $N(20, 5^2)$ and the terminal value function is given by

$$\theta_{T+1}(x) = h_{T+1}x^+ + p_{T+1}x^-,$$

where $h_{T+1} = h$ and $p_{T+1} = p$. Using your DP, find $y_t(x)$ and $\theta_t(x)$ for $t = 1, \ldots, 10$ and $x = -10, \ldots, 40$. Report these in two separate tables. Also report the optimal base-stock level S_t^* for periods $t = 1, \ldots, 10$.

c) Plot $y_t(x)$ for $t = 5$.

4.15   **(Implementing (s, S) DP)** Consider the finite-horizon model with fixed costs of Section 4.5.3.

a) Implement the dynamic programming model in any programming language you wish.

b) Suppose $T = 10$, $c = 1$, $K = 40$, $h = 1$, $p = 25$, and $\gamma = 0.98$. Suppose the demand per period is distributed as $N(18, 3^2)$ and the terminal value function is given by

$$\theta_{T+1}(x) = h_{T+1}x^+ + p_{T+1}x^-,$$

where $h_{T+1} = h$ and $p_{T+1} = p$. Using your DP, find $y_t(x)$ and $\theta_t(x)$ for $t = 1, \ldots, 10$ and $x = -10, \ldots, 40$. Report these in two separate tables. Also report the optimal parameters s_t^* and S_t^* for periods $t = 1, \ldots, 10$.

c) Plot $y_t(x)$ for $t = 5$.

4.16   **(Power Approximation)** Using the power approximation, determine approximate values for s and S for an infinite-horizon instance in which the demand per period is normally distributed with a mean of 190 and a standard deviation of 48, and in which the costs are given by $K = 60$, $h = 2$, and $p = 36$.

4.17   **(Ordering Capacities)** Suppose that an ordering capacity of b units is imposed in the finite-horizon model with no fixed costs of Section 4.4.3. Sketch a plot of $y_t(x)$ vs. x, analogous to Figure 4.3. (The exact numbers are not important; what is important is the shape of the curve.)

4.18   **(DP for Ordering Capacities)** Suppose that an ordering capacity of b units is imposed in the finite-horizon model with fixed costs of Section 4.5.3.

a) Explain how to modify the DP from Section 4.5.3 to account for the ordering capacity.

b) Implement your DP from part (a). Using your DP, find $y_t(x)$ and $\theta_t(x)$ for $t = 1, \ldots, 10$ and $x = -10, \ldots, 40$ for the instance described in Problem 4.15(b) using a capacity of $b = 10$. Report $y_t(x)$ and $\theta_t(x)$ in two separate tables.

4.19   **(Non-Optimality of (s, S) Policies for Ordering Capacities)** Suppose that an ordering capacity of b units is imposed in the finite-horizon model with fixed costs of Section 4.5.3. Prove, by providing a counter-example, that an (s, S) policy is *not* necessarily optimal in every period of the finite-horizon version of this problem.

4.20   (K-**Convexity Is Not a Necessary Condition**) In Section 4.6.2.2, we proved that if $H_t(y)$ is continuous and K-convex, then an (s, S) policy is optimal in period t. However, K-convexity is not a necessary condition: An (s, S) policy can still be optimal in period t even if $H_t(y)$ is not K-convex. Draw a graph of a function $H_t(y)$ that is not K-convex but for which an (s, S) policy is optimal. Explain clearly (a) why the function is not K-convex and (b) why an (s, S) policy is optimal.

4.21   (**Other Policy Forms**) Consider the single-period model with no fixed costs from Section 4.6.1.1. We know that, for a given starting inventory level x, (4.51) determines the optimal inventory position after ordering, y. In (4.51), $g(y)$ is the expected inventory-related costs (holding and stockout costs) if we order up to y. We assumed a particular form for $g(y)$ and used the convexity of this function to prove the optimality of a base-stock policy. But in principle $g(y)$ can have any form, and other policies may be optimal for other functions.

   a) Develop a function $g(y)$ such that the optimal policy has three parameters, S_1, s_2, and S_2 ($S_1 < s_2 < S_2$), and has the following form:

   - If $x \leq S_1$, then order up to S_1.

   - If $S_1 < x \leq s_2$, do nothing.

   - If $s_2 < x < S_2$, order up to S_2.

   - If $x \geq S_2$, do nothing.

      For the sake of simplicity, assume that $c = 0$. Write down the function $g(y)$ and the optimal values of the parameters S_1, s_2, and S_2, and plot $g(y)$.

   b) Now suppose that $K = 10$ so that the term $K\delta(y - x)$ is now added to the objective function, as in (4.60). Develop a function $g(y)$ such that the optimal policy has four parameters, s_1, S_1, s_2, and S_2 ($s_1 < S_1 < s_2 < S_2$), and has the following form:

      - If $x \leq s_1$, then order up to S_1.

      - If $s_1 < x \leq s_2$, do nothing.

      - If $s_2 < x < S_2$, order up to S_2.

      - If $x \geq S_2$, do nothing.

      Write down the function $g(y)$ and the optimal values of the parameters s_1, S_1, s_2, and S_2, and plot $g(y)$.

4.22   (**Single-Period Control-Band Policies**) Consider the single-period model without fixed costs of Section 4.6.1.1, and suppose we begin the period with an inventory level of $x \geq 0$. Suppose further that we can return excess inventory to the supplier in each period. That is, we can choose $Q < 0$, or equivalently, $y < x$.

For each unit we return, we earn a revenue of c', so the total revenue earned when $Q < 0$ is $-c'Q$. Normally $c' \geq 0$, but it's also possible that $c' < 0$, in which case we pay a *cost* to make the return.

Consider the following policy: There are two parameters, S and U, with $0 \leq S \leq U$. Set

$$y = \begin{cases} S, & \text{if } x < S \\ x, & \text{if } S \leq x \leq U \\ U, & \text{if } x > U. \end{cases}$$

The interval $[S, U]$ is called a *control band*, and the policy is called a *control-band policy*. The idea is to order up to S if x is below the control band, to "return down to" U if x is above the control band, and to do nothing if x is in the control band.

    a) Prove that a control-band policy is optimal for the single-period problem.

    b) Show how to calculate the optimal S^* and U^* for the single-period problem, and prove that $S^* \leq U^*$.

    c) Prove that, in the single-period problem, as $c' \to -h$ (from above), $U^* \to \infty$. In a few sentences, explain why it is logical to require $c' \geq -h$.

    d) Prove that, in the single-period problem, as $c' \to c$ (from below), $U^* - S^* \to 0$. In a few sentences, explain why it is logical to require $c' \leq c$.

    e) Suppose the demand per period is distributed as $N(60, 12^2)$. Suppose $h = 0.4$, $p = 4.8$, $c = 3$, and $c' = 1.7$. Find S^* and U^* for the single-period problem.

4.23   **(Finite-Horizon Control-Band Policies)** Return to the setup in Problem 4.22, and now consider the finite-horizon model. Prove that a control-band policy is optimal in every period of the finite-horizon model. (The parameters of the control-band policy are now indexed by time, S_t and U_t.)

4.24   **(Properties of K-Convex Functions)** Prove Lemma 4.3.

4.25   **(Alternate Terminal Value Function)** Consider the finite-horizon base-stock model described in Section 4.6.1.2. Suppose that the terminal value function is given by

$$\theta_{T+1}(x) = \begin{cases} -(h+p)x, & \text{if } x \leq 0 \\ 0, & \text{if } x > 0. \end{cases} \tag{4.68}$$

Suppose also that $h > \gamma c$.

    a) Write an expression for $H_T(y)$.

    b) Derive the optimal base-stock level in period T, in the form

$$S_T^* = F^{-1}([\text{some fraction}]).$$

    c) Write an expression for $H_{T-1}(y)$. (*Note:* Your expression may involve cases, as in (4.59).)

    d) Derive the optimal base-stock level in period $T - 1$, in the form

$$S_{T-1}^* = F^{-1}([\text{some fraction}]).$$

e) Prove that $S_{T-1}^* < S_T^*$.

CHAPTER 5

MULTI-ECHELON INVENTORY MODELS

5.1 INTRODUCTION

In this chapter, we study inventory optimization models for multi-echelon (or multi-stage) systems with shipments made among the stages. There are two common ways to interpret the stages or nodes in a multi-echelon system:

1. Stages represent locations in a supply chain network, among which physical shipments are made. Links among the stages represent physical shipments of goods. For example, the stages in Figure 5.1(a) may represent the following physical locations: a supplier in China, a factory in California, a warehouse in Chicago, and a retailer in Detroit (respectively).

2. Stages represent processes that the product must undergo during manufacturing, assembly, and/or distribution. Links among the stages represent transitions between steps in the process. For example, the stages in Figure 5.1(a) may represent the following processes: manufacturing, assembly, testing, and packaging. These four functions may take place in four different locations or all within the same building—it is largely irrelevant from the perspective of the

model. We sometimes refer to the stages as different "products," even if they really represent different phases of producing a single product.

Either interpretation is acceptable for the models that we discuss, although some models are more naturally interpreted in one way than the other. In the discussion below, we will use terms like "shipped" or "transferred" under either interpretation to mean "moved from one stage to the next."

5.1.1 Multi-Echelon Network Topologies

Multi-echelon networks can be structured in a number of ways, and the network's topology plays a large role in determining how the system is analyzed and optimized. The simplest multi-echelon topology is a *serial system* (or *series system*), in which each echelon contains exactly one stage. Put another way, every stage has exactly one predecessor and exactly one successor, except for two stages, one of which has exactly one successor and no predecessors, and the other of which has exactly one predecessor and no successors. (A *predecessor* of stage j is another stage that ships product to j, and a *successor* of j is another stage that j ships to.) See Figure 5.1(a) for an example of a serial system.

In an *assembly system*, each stage has at most one successor; see Figure 5.1(b). Interpretation (2) is most common for assembly systems: The network represents a *bill-of-materials* structure that describes how a final product is assembled from raw materials and intermediate products. In this case, the links in the network indicate "and" relationships: To make one unit of the product at stage j, we need one (or more) unit of each of j's predecessors. Assembly systems can also be viewed under interpretation (1), with links denoting the geographic flow of materials. If stage j has three predecessors, then there are three stages that make the product and ship it to stage j. Here, too, links represent "and" relationships since all three upstream stages ship product to stage j. An alternate, but less common, way to use interpretation (1) is that the links represent "or" relationships, and stage j's predecessors are multiple suppliers from which stage j can order. In a given order cycle it may order from one, more than one, or all of its predecessors, depending on their capacities, the observed demands, and so on. Under any of these interpretations, assembly systems are commonly used to model upstream portions of supply chains whose purpose is to consolidate products or locations into a few stages.

A *distribution system* (Figure 5.1(c)) is the opposite of an assembly system: Each stage has at most one predecessor. Interpretation (1) is most common for distribution systems, which are often used to model downstream portions of supply chains—the portion that moves material from a few centralized locations to a set of retailers or customers distributed throughout a large geographical region.

Tree systems (Figure 5.1(d)) are hybrids of assembly and distribution systems— each stage may have multiple predecessors and successors—but tree systems may contain no undirected cycles. (A *cycle*, in graph theory, is a portion of the graph whose links allow one to move from a starting node, through a sequence of other nodes, and back to the starting node, without repeating any other nodes links. An

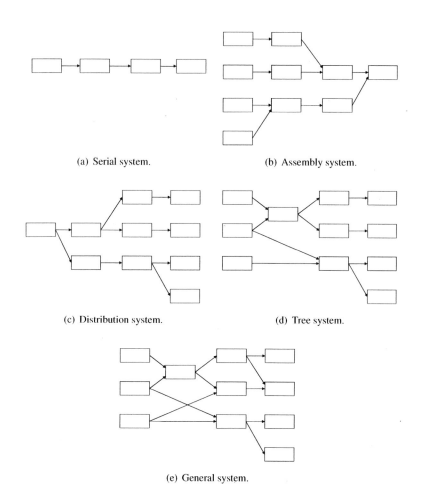

(a) Serial system.

(b) Assembly system.

(c) Distribution system.

(d) Tree system.

(e) General system.

Figure 5.1   Multi-echelon network topologies.

undirected cycle is a cycle in the graph that results from removing all of the arrows from the links so that movement can go in either direction.) Finally, *general systems* allow any number of successors and predecessors and have no restrictions on cycles. Figure 5.1(e) shows an example. General systems are the most flexible topology but are also the most difficult to analyze and optimize.

5.1.2 Stochastic vs. Guaranteed Service

The most challenging aspect of multi-echelon inventory models is that a given stage j provides stochastic lead times to its successors, even if the transportation lead time is deterministic, due to occasional stockouts at stage j. The optimal inventory parameters at stage j's successors depend on the probability distribution of these stochastic lead times, but these distributions are quite complex, even for single-stage systems (Higa et al. 1975, Sherbrooke 1975).

Two primary types of models have been developed to handle these complexities in multi-echelon base-stock systems: stochastic-service models and guaranteed-service models (Graves and Willems 2003a). In the *stochastic-service model*, each stage j sets a base-stock level S_i and meets demand from stock whenever possible using this base-stock level. The actual lead time seen by downstream stages is stochastic since some demands will not be satisfied from stock. This is the approach taken in the seminal model of Clark and Scarf (1960) and related works, discussed in Section 5.2. In the *guaranteed-service model*, stage j sets a "committed service time" (CST), denoted S_i, within which it is required to satisfy *every* demand.[1]

For example, if $S_i = 5$ periods, then every demand must be satisfied in exactly 5 periods. To make this guarantee, guaranteed-service models require the demand to be bounded above. The guaranteed-service assumption provides the strategic safety stock placement problem (SSSPP), described in Section 5.3, its tractability. There is a close relationship between the CST and the base-stock level, since a larger base-stock level allows the stage to quote a shorter CST.

Another way to view the difference between these two approaches is that guaranteed-service models allow a CST time of $S > 0$ but require a service level of $\alpha = 1$ while the stochastic-service model requires a service time of $S = 0$ but allows a less restrictive service level of $\alpha < 1$.

In Section 5.2, we first discuss stochastic-service models, describing an optimal and a heuristic approach for optimizing base-stock levels in serial systems and then briefly discussing the extent to which these methods can be extended to solve assembly and distribution systems. Then, in Section 5.3, we discuss guaranteed-service models,

---

[1] Unfortunately, the literature on stochastic-service models and that on guaranteed-service models have both laid claim to the notation S, but they use it to mean very different things. In stochastic-service models, S denotes the base-stock level, whereas in guaranteed-service models, S denotes the committed service time. We have opted to use S for both purposes to remain consistent with these two bodies of literature, at the risk of confusing the reader. It is safe to assume that S denotes a base-stock level in Section 5.2 and a committed service time in Section 5.3.

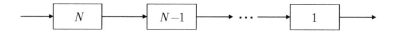

Figure 5.2 N-stage serial system in stochastic-service model.

beginning with an analysis of single-stage systems and working our way up to tree systems.

See van Houtum et al. (1996) and Graves and Willems (2003a) (among others) for further reviews of the literature on stochastic- and guaranteed-service models, respectively.

5.2 STOCHASTIC SERVICE MODELS

5.2.1 Serial Systems

Consider an N-stage serial system, with the stages labeled as in Figure 5.2. Stage 1 is farthest downstream. It faces external customer demand and places replenishment orders to stage 2, which places replenishment orders to stage 3, and so on up the line to stage N. Stage N, in turn, places replenishment orders to an external supplier that is assumed to have infinite supply.

We consider a continuous-review system, though nearly all of the results described below hold (with slight modifications) for periodic-review systems, as well. Orders placed by stage j incur a transportation lead time of L_j; that is, the order is received L_j time units later if stage $j + 1$ had sufficient stock to ship the order immediately, and more than L_j time units later otherwise. Stage j incurs a holding cost of h'_j per item per time unit, which is charged on the on-hand inventory at stage j as well as on the inventory in transit to stage $j - 1$. (One can show that the expected number of units in transit is a constant, and therefore the in-transit holding cost does not affect the optimization.) Unmet demands are backordered at all stages, but only stage 1 incurs a stockout cost, given by p per item per time unit. There are no fixed costs, and we will ignore any per-unit ordering costs.

In multi-echelon inventory theory, the *echelon* of stage j (or just "echelon j") is defined as the set of stages $\{j, j - 1, \ldots, 1\}$; that is, the set that includes j and all downstream stages. Note that this is a particular inventory-theoretic use of the term "echelon" and is different from the way we defined it in Chapter 1. Stage j's *echelon inventory* is the total inventory in echelon j, and its *local inventory* is the inventory at stage j only. Stage j's *echelon inventory level*, denoted IL_j, includes all of the on-hand inventory in echelon j, plus all of the in-transit inventory among these stages, minus the backorders at stage 1. It turns out to be more convenient to optimize stage j's echelon inventory rather than its local inventory.

The holding cost h'_j is called a *local holding cost*, and it is charged based on the number of items in stage j's local inventory. We will instead work with stage j's *echelon holding cost,* denoted h_j and defined as

$$h_j = h'_j - h'_{j+1}$$

(with $h'_{N+1} \equiv 0$). Typically, local holding costs increase as we move downstream in the supply chain since value is added to the product at each stage. Therefore, h_j represents the holding cost corresponding to the value added at stage j. It turns out that we can calculate holding costs using either echelon or local quantities:

Proposition 5.1 *If OH'_j and OH_j are the local and echelon on-hand inventory levels (respectively) at stage j, i.e., $OH_j = \sum_{i=1}^{j} OH'_i$, and h'_j and h_j are the local and echelon holding costs (respectively) at stage j, then*

$$\sum_{j=1}^{N} h_j OH_j = \sum_{j=1}^{N} h'_j OH'_j. \tag{5.1}$$

Proof. Omitted; see Problem 5.1.   ∎

The following theorem establishes the form of the optimal inventory policy for serial systems. It was proved for finite-horizon problems in the seminal paper of Clark and Scarf (1960) and for infinite-horizon problems by Federgruen and Zipkin (1984).

Theorem 5.1 *An echelon base-stock policy is optimal at each stage of a serial system with no fixed costs.*

In an *echelon base-stock policy,* each stage j has a fixed level S_j, called the *echelon base-stock level,* and it places order as needed to bring its *echelon inventory position* (defined as stage j's echelon inventory level plus any items on-order from stage $j + 1$) equal to S_j. An echelon base-stock policy is essentially the same as the base-stock policies we are already familiar with except that it is the echelon inventory, rather than the local inventory, that we compare to the base-stock level when making ordering decisions. We use **S** to denote the vector of base-stock levels, one for each stage.

We will discuss approaches for finding optimal or near-optimal echelon base-stock levels. Local base-stock levels (denoted S'_j) can be obtained from the echelon base-stock levels by setting

$$S'_j = S_j - S_{j-1}, \tag{5.2}$$

defining $S_0 \equiv 0$. This assumes that $S_j \geq S_{j-1}$. If not, we let $S_j^- = \min_{i \geq j}\{S_i\}$ and set $S'_j = S_j^- - S_{j-1}^-$, again setting $S_0^- \equiv 0$.

Let D_j be a random variable representing the lead-time demand at stage j. Since stage j's demands are ultimately generated by the external customer (via orders placed to stage 1, then to stage 2, and so on), stage j's demand per time unit has the same distribution as the customer's demand, but the distribution of stage j's lead-time demand D_j depends on L_j. Let $F_j(\cdot)$ be the cdf of D_j.

5.2.2 Exact Approach for Serial Systems

For a given base-stock vector $\mathbf{S}$, we wish to minimize the expected cost of the system,

$$C(\mathbf{S}) = E\left[\sum_{j=1}^{N} h'_j((IL'_j)^+ + IT_{j-1}) + p(IL'_1)^-\right], \qquad (5.3)$$

where IT_j is the in-transit inventory to stage j and $IT_0 \equiv 0$. One can show (see Problem 5.2) that

$$C(\mathbf{S}) = E\left[\sum_{j=1}^{N} h_j IL_j + (p + h'_1)IL_1^-\right]. \qquad (5.4)$$

$C(\mathbf{S})$ is a messy function of $\mathbf{S}$ because the inventory levels on the right-hand side depend on $\mathbf{S}$ in messy ways. In fact, since S_j affects the inventory levels at all stages downstream from j, it would seem that we need to jointly optimize all of the S_j simultaneously. Fortunately, a much simpler and more elegant procedure suffices, as demonstrated by the next theorem.

Theorem 5.2 *Let* $\underline{C}_0(x) = (p + h'_1)x^-$. *For* $j = 1, \ldots, N$, *let*

$$\hat{C}_j(x) = h_j x + \underline{C}_{j-1}(x) \qquad (5.5)$$
$$C_j(y) = E\left[\hat{C}_j(y - D_j)\right] \qquad (5.6)$$
$$S_j^* = \operatorname{argmin}\{C_j(y)\} \qquad (5.7)$$
$$\underline{C}_j(x) = C_j(\min\{s_j^*, x\}) \qquad (5.8)$$

Then $\mathbf{S}^*$ *is the optimal base-stock vector.*

Theorem 5.2 is the result of the groundwork laid by Clark and Scarf (1960) and subsequent refinements by Chen and Zheng (1994). It says that, rather than simultaneously optimizing all of the base-stock levels, we can optimize them sequentially, beginning with stage 1 and working upstream, one stage at a time. Moreover, $C_j(y)$ is known to be convex, so at each iteration we only need to minimize a single-variable, convex function. This theorem underlies much of the theory of multi-echelon stochastic-service models. (Zipkin (2000) even goes so far as to call (5.5)–(5.8) the "fundamental equation[s] of supply-chain theory.")

It is worth noting that, to evaluate the cost of a given (not necessarily optimal) base-stock vector $\mathbf{S}$, we simply skip the optimization step (5.7) and evaluate the functions using $\mathbf{S}$ instead of $\mathbf{S}^*$.

Consider the optimization problem at stage 1. We have:

$$\hat{C}_1(x) = h_1(x) + (p + h'_1)x^-$$
$$C_1(y) = E\left[\hat{C}_j(y - D_j)\right]$$

$$
\begin{aligned}
&= E\left[h_1(y - D_j) + (p + h_1')(y - D_j)^-\right] \\
&= E\left[h_1[(y - D_j)^+ - (y - D_j)^-] + (p + h_1')(y - D_j)^-\right] \\
&= E\left[h_1(y - D_j)^+ + (p + h_1' - h_1)(y - D_j)^-\right] \\
&= E\left[h_1(y - D_j)^+ + (p + h_2')(D_j - y)^+\right] \quad\quad (5.9)
\end{aligned}
$$

This function is identical in form to the newsvendor objective function (4.21), with p replaced by $p + h_2'$. Therefore, from (4.27), $C_1(y)$ it is minimized by

$$
S_1^* = F_1^{-1}\left(\frac{p + h_2'}{h_1 + p + h_2'}\right) = F_1^{-1}\left(\frac{p + \sum_{i=2}^N h_i}{p + \sum_{i=1}^N h_i}\right).
$$

At upstream stages, the functions $C_j(y)$ become more complicated and cannot be minimized in closed form. In fact, the expectation in $C_j(y)$ must be evaluated numerically for every candidate value y. Therefore, although (5.7) is a convex minimization problem, it is somewhat computationally expensive to execute, as well as cumbersome to implement.

5.2.3 Heuristic Approach for Serial Systems

Suppose we have found $S_1^*, \ldots, S_{j-1}^*$, and we now need to find S_j^*. Theorem 5.2 tells us that S_j^* does not depend on the base-stock levels at stages $j + 1, \ldots, N$, although it does indirectly depend on the echelon holding costs at those stages (because $C_j(y)$ includes h_1'). Suppose we truncate the system at stage j (i.e., remove all stages upstream from j) and replace p with $p + \sum_{i=j+1}^N h_i$. Then the S_j^* that is optimal for stage j in this truncated system is also optimal for stage j in the original system (Shang and Song 2003). In other words, the y that minimizes

$$
C_j(y) = E\left[\sum_{i=1}^j h_i'(IL')_i^+(y) + \left(p + \sum_{i=j+1}^N h_i\right) IL_1^-(y)\right] \quad\quad (5.10)
$$

also minimizes $C_j(y)$ in (5.7). (In (5.10) we have emphasized that IL is a function of y, and we have truncated the system at j; otherwise, it is identical to (5.3).) We obtained a similar result for stage 1 in (5.9).

Now, (5.10) is no easier to solve than (5.7)—except for one special case. Suppose that $h_1' = \ldots = h_j' = h'$, for some fixed h'. (Or, equivalently, $h_1 = \ldots = h_{j-1} = 0$ and $h_j = h'$.) Then it is optimal to hold all of the inventory at stage 1, because upstream inventory is not cheaper, and it requires a longer lead time to reach the customer. We can therefore replace this j-stage system with a single-stage system with a holding cost of h', a stockout cost of $p + \sum_{i=j+1}^N h_i$, and a lead time of $\sum_{i=1}^j L_i$.

This would make the problem easy to solve, but would the solution help us? It turns out that, if we choose good values for h', the resulting cost functions provide bounds on the actual cost function, and the resulting base-stock levels provide bounds on the optimal base-stock levels. Moreover, these bounds can be used to compute heuristic values for S_j^*, which turn out to be remarkably accurate. This approximation was proposed by Shang and Song (2003).

We consider two different values for h'. Let $C_j^l(y)$ be the cost function (5.10) with h_i' replaced by h_j for all i, and let $C_j^u(y)$ be the same function with h_i' replaced by $\sum_{k=1}^j h_k$ for all i. Let $\tilde{D}_j$ be the lead-time demand for a single-stage system with lead-time $\sum_{i=1}^j L_i$, i.e.,

$$\tilde{D}_j = \sum_{i=1}^j D_i,$$

and let $\tilde{F}_j(\cdot)$ be its cdf.

Then the functions $C_j^l(y)$ and $C_j^u(y)$ are minimized by

$$S_j^l = \tilde{F}_j^{-1}\left(\frac{p + \sum_{i=j+1}^N h_i}{h_j + p + \sum_{i=j+1}^N h_i}\right) = \tilde{F}_j^{-1}\left(\frac{p + \sum_{i=j+1}^N h_i}{p + \sum_{i=j}^N h_i}\right)$$

and

$$S_j^u = \tilde{F}_j^{-1}\left(\frac{p + \sum_{i=j+1}^N h_i}{\sum_{k=1}^j h_k + p + \sum_{i=j+1}^N h_i}\right) = \tilde{F}_j^{-1}\left(\frac{p + \sum_{i=j+1}^N h_i}{p + \sum_{i=1}^N h_i}\right),$$

respectively.

Theorem 5.3 (Shang and Song (2003)) *For any j and y:*

(a) $C_j^l(y) \le C_j(y) \le C_j^u(y)$

(b) $S_j^l \le S_j^* \le S_j^u$

The theorem suggests that we can approximate S_j^*, for each j, using a weighted average of S_j^l and S_j^u. In fact, Shang and Song (2003) suggest using a simple weighted average, that is,

$$\tilde{S}_j = \frac{1}{2}\left[\tilde{F}_j^{-1}\left(\frac{p + \sum_{i=j+1}^N h_i}{p + \sum_{i=j}^N h_i}\right) + \tilde{F}_j^{-1}\left(\frac{p + \sum_{i=j+1}^N h_i}{p + \sum_{i=1}^N h_i}\right)\right]. \qquad (5.11)$$

If local base-stock levels are desired, we can compute $\tilde{S}_j'$ from $\tilde{S}_j$ as described in Section 5.2.1.

This approximation performs quite well: Shang and Song (2003) report an average error of 0.24% and a maximum error of less than 1.5% on their test instances, where the errors are computed by comparing the heuristic solutions with the exact solutions from Theorem 5.2.

This heuristic can be used for periodic-review systems as well. However, in this case the lead-times must each be inflated by one unit, assuming the system uses the sequence of events on page 76. See Shang and Song (2003) for details.

5.2.4 Other Network Topologies

Assembly Systems: Assembly systems turn out to be easy to solve—or, at least, no harder than serial systems. Rosling (1989) proved that every assembly system can be transformed to an equivalent serial system. That serial system can be solved using any method available for such systems (for example, the exact method in Section 5.2.2 or the heuristic one in Section 5.2.3). The resulting solution can then be transformed back to a solution for the assembly system. The equivalence between the two systems is exact, meaning that if we solve the serial system optimally, then the transformed solution will be optimal for the assembly system.

Distribution Systems: Unfortunately, distribution systems are much more difficult. In part, the difficulty stems from the fact that, if a given stage has insufficient inventory to meet the orders placed by its successors, it must decide how to allocate the inventory that it does have among them. For example, it may assign items first-come, first-served, or randomly, or based on some priority system. Therefore, in addition to choosing a replenishment policy at each node, we must also choose an allocation policy. Under stochastic demands, even the optimal form of these policies is unknown, let alone the optimal parameters for the policies. Usually, we simply choose a plausible ordering policy (e.g., a base-stock policy) and a plausible allocation policy (e.g., a first-come, first-served policy) and then optimize the parameters under those assumptions.

The simplest type of distribution system is the *one-warehouse, multiple-retailer* (OWMR) system, a two-echelon system with one upstream stage (the "warehouse") and several downstream stages (the "retailers"). The best known exact algorithm for OWMR systems is the *projection algorithm* (Graves 1985, Axsäter 1990), which involves iterating over the possible values for S_0 (the warehouse base-stock level). For each possible value of S_0, we can find the corresponding optimal S_j for the retailers by solving a single-variable, convex optimization problem for each j. However, the total cost is not a convex function of S_0, which means that we must perform an exhaustive search to find S_0^*. Moreover, each evaluation of the objective function requires numerical convolution, a computationally costly calculation.

Several heuristics have been proposed for OWMR and more general distribution systems. Sherbrooke (1968) proposed the so-called "METRIC" model; his method approximates the stochastic lead times generated by the warehouse for the retailers by replacing them with their means. Graves (1985) proposes a two-moment approximation in which a messy distribution necessary to evaluate the cost is replaced by a simpler distribution with the same mean and variance. This approach can also be used to approximate serial systems. Gallego et al. (2007) propose the "restriction–decomposition" heuristic, which involves solving three sub-heuristics, each of which makes some simplifying assumption to render the model tractable, and then taking the best of the three resulting solutions. Özer and Xiong (2008) propose a heuristic in which the distribution system is decomposed into multiple serial systems, each of which is solved independently, and then the solutions from the serial systems

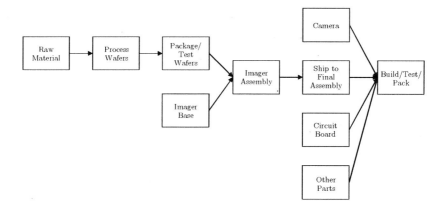

Figure 5.3   Digital camera supply chain network. Reprinted by permission, Graves and Willems, Optimizing strategic safety stock placement in supply chains, *Manufacturing and Service Operations Management*, 2(1), 2000, 68–83. ©2000, the Institute for Operations Research and the Management Sciences (INFORMS), 7240 Parkway Drive, Suite 300, Hanover, MD 21076 USA..

are summed to obtain a solution for the distribution system. A similar approach is used in the "decomposition–aggregation" heuristic by Rong et al. (2011), which uses a procedure they call "backorder matching" to convert the base-stock levels from the serial system into those for the distribution system. They also propose a more accurate, but more computationally intensive, heuristic, called the "recursive optimization" procedure, which is inspired by Theorem 5.2.

Tree and General Systems: Given the difficulty of solving distribution systems, these more general systems have received little attention in the literature.

5.3 GUARANTEED SERVICE MODELS

5.3.1 Introduction

Figure 5.3 depicts the supply chain for a digital camera made by Kodak. Each stage represents an activity (as in interpretation (2) from Section 5.1): either a processing activity like packaging or testing, or an assembly activity like combining a wafer and an "imager base" to construct an "imager assembly." These activities may occur at different locations or together at the same location. Each stage functions as an autonomous unit that can hold safety stock, place orders to upstream stages, and so on. (This network uses interpretation (2) from Section 5.1.)

The question of interest here is, which stages should hold safety stock, and how much? It may not be necessary for all stages to hold safety stock, but only a few. These stages serve as buffers to absorb all of the demand uncertainty in the supply chain. This problem is a strategic one, since the location of safety stock is a design problem that is costly to change frequently. This problem is therefore known as the *strategic safety stock placement problem* (SSSPP).

The supply chain operates in a periodic-review setting, and each stage follows a base-stock policy. Each stage quotes a lead time, or *committed service time* (CST), to its downstream stage(s) within which it promises to deliver each order. As we will see, there is a direct relationship between the CST and the safety stock required at each stage. The goal of the strategic safety stock placement model is to choose the CST (equivalently, the safety stock) at each stage in order to minimize the expected holding cost in each period.

Each stage is required to provide 100% service to its downstream stage(s). In other words, each stage is obligated to deliver every order within the CST *regardless of the size of the order*. In order to enforce this restriction, we will have to assume that the demand is bounded. We will discuss this assumption further in Section 5.3.2.

The guaranteed-service assumption was first used by Kimball in 1955 (later reprinted as Kimball 1988) and Simpson (1958). It was embedded into safety stock optimization models by Graves (1988), Inderfurth (1991), and Graves and Willems (2000), among others.

We will build gradually to tree networks like the one pictured in Figure 5.3, considering first the single-stage case, then serial systems, and finally tree networks. First we will discuss the demand process. Throughout Section 5.3, h_i will be used to represent the *local* holding cost at stage i. (In Section 5.2, it represented the echelon holding cost.)

5.3.2 Demand

We assume that the demand *in any stretch of time* is bounded. In practice, this is not a terribly realistic assumption (unless the bound is very large), but it is necessary in this model to guarantee 100% service. One way to model the demand is simply to truncate the right tail of the demand distribution. That is, if demand is normally distributed, we simply ignore any demands greater than, say, z_α standard deviations above the mean, for some constant z_α. This is the approach we will take throughout.

In particular, consider a stage that faces external demand (as opposed to serving other downstream stages). Suppose the demand per period is distributed $N(\mu, \sigma^2)$. Then we will assume that the total demand in any τ periods is bounded by

$$D(\tau) = \mu\tau + z_\alpha \sigma \sqrt{\tau} \tag{5.12}$$

for some constant z_α. In other words, we assume that the demand in τ consecutive periods is no more than z_α standard deviations above its mean, since the mean demand in τ periods is $\mu\tau$ and the standard deviation is $\sigma\sqrt{\tau}$. This implies that the demand in a single period is bounded by $\mu + z_\alpha\sigma$. The reverse implication, however, is not true: Assuming the single-period demand is bounded by $\mu + z_\alpha\sigma$ implies that the τ-period demand is bounded by $\mu\tau + z_\alpha\sigma\tau$; it does not imply the stronger result that $\mu\tau + z_\alpha\sigma\sqrt{\tau}$.

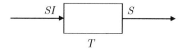

Figure 5.4 Single-stage network.

If, in actuality, the demand in a given τ-period stretch exceeds $D(\tau)$, the excess demands are assumed to be handled in some other manner—say, by outsourcing, scheduling overtime shifts, or by some other method not captured in the model.

5.3.3 Single-Stage Network

Consider a single stage that quotes a committed service time of S periods to an external customer. (Recall that S denotes a CST in this section, but a base-stock level in Section 5.2.) The stage receives raw materials from an external supplier, which promises an inbound CST of SI periods. Finally, the stage itself requires a processing time of T periods to perform its function. (See Figure 5.4.) SI and T are both constants (parameters). S is the decision variable. Our goal in this section is to determine the amount of safety stock required if the stage quotes a CST of S periods.

S is like a "demand lead time"—i.e., an advance warning of demands that must be met in the future. Conversely, SI and T both contribute to the supply lead time, since $SI + T$ periods elapse between when the stage places an order and when the products are ready to be delivered to the stage's customer. Each unit increase in demand lead time is equivalent to a unit decrease in the supply lead time. (This claim should make sense intuitively; see Hariharan and Zipkin (1995) for a rigorous proof in a somewhat different context.) Therefore, this system is equivalent to a system with no demand lead time and with $SI + T - S$ periods of supply lead time. The quantity $SI + T - S$ is called the *net lead time* (NLT).

The base-stock level required at the stage is therefore

$$\mu(SI + T - S) + z_\alpha \sigma \sqrt{SI + T - S}, \qquad (5.13)$$

using (4.44). If the base-stock level is set according to (5.13), then the stage will always be able to meet any demand within S periods. To see why, note that in time t, we place an order to bring the inventory position up to the base-stock level, call it B. By time $t + (SI + T)$, all of these units will have arrived, been processed, and been added to inventory. In other words, if no additional demands occur between period $t + 1$ and $t + (SI + T)$, the on-hand inventory at the end of period $t + (SI + T)$ will equal B. This quantity needs to be sufficient to meet all demands that are due before period $t + (SI + T)$, in other words, demands occurring between period $t + 1$ and $t + (SI + T - S)$. The demand in these $SI + T - S$ periods will be no more than $\mu(SI + T - S) + z_\alpha \sigma \sqrt{SI + T - S}$, so we should set B equal to this value, as in (5.13).

Note that this argument ignores the units that were demanded during periods $t - S + 1$ through t. These demands also must be satisfied out of the items that are on-order at time t. But these items count as backorders at time t and are subtracted from the inventory position. Therefore, the on-order items include items to meet these demands, in addition to the B items that are available in period $t + (SI + T)$.

Given the base-stock level in (5.13), the safety stock is *approximately* equal to

$$z_\alpha \sigma \sqrt{SI + T - S} \tag{5.14}$$

(since base stock = cycle stock + safety stock). The reason this expression is only approximate lies in the way we truncate the normal distribution. We have truncated the distribution z_α standard deviations above the mean, and at 0. The truncation is therefore not symmetric, and so the mean of the revised distribution no longer equals μ. Therefore, the mean demand over the net lead time is not exactly equal to $\mu(SI + T - S)$, so the safety stock is not exactly equal to the expression given in (5.14). (The true safety stock level is greater.) As z_α increases, the approximation improves. In what follows, we will treat (5.14) as though it were exact.

From (5.14), as the CST increases, the safety stock level decreases. At one extreme, the stage can quote a CST of $S = SI + T$, in which case every time the stage receives an order, it can place an order to its supplier, wait for it to arrive, process it, and deliver it in time—it has to hold 0 safety stock since $\sqrt{SI + T - (SI + T)} = 0$. At the other extreme, the stage can quote a CST of $S = 0$, in which case delivery is required immediately, so the stage must hold the maximum possible safety stock: $z_\alpha \sigma \sqrt{SI + T - S}$. Or the stage can quote some CST strictly between 0 and $SI + T$ and hold safety stock strictly between $z_\alpha \sigma \sqrt{SI + T - S}$ and 0.

If the holding cost is h per unit per time period (charged on ending inventory, as usual), then the expected holding cost per period is

$$h z_\alpha \sigma \sqrt{SI + T - S} \tag{5.15}$$

since the expected ending inventory is equal to the safety stock. From now on, we will focus on the safety stock level rather than the base-stock level since the two are essentially equivalent.

5.3.4 Serial Systems

Now consider a serial supply chain network such as the one pictured in Figure 5.5. The notation from the previous section will now include subscripts i to refer to a given stage. Note that $SI_{N-1} = S_N$ (stage $N - 1$'s inbound time is equal to stage N's outbound time), $SI_{N-2} = S_{N-1}$, and so on. And stage N's inbound time is from an external supplier rather than from another stage.

The expected holding cost per period is

$$g(\mathbf{S}) = \sum_{i=1}^{N} h_i z_\alpha \sigma \sqrt{SI_i + T_i - S_i}, \tag{5.16}$$

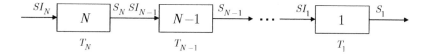

Figure 5.5 N-stage serial system in guaranteed-service model.

where $\mathbf{S} = (S_1, \ldots, S_N)$ and h_i is the local holding cost at stage i. Note that the same σ is used at all stages, since each stage places an order equal to the order that it received.

Obviously, with no constraints on the CST to the external customer (downstream from stage 1), the optimal solution would be to set $S_i = SI_i + T_i$ for all i; this solution has 0 holding cost because no safety stock is held. Therefore, we will assume that the CST to the external customer is already set to some constant s_1, and we require $S_1 \leq s_1$. But it will never be to our advantage to set $S_1 < s_1$, so in general we can assume $S_1 = s_1$. Only $S_2, \ldots, S_N$, then, are really decision variables.

For each $i = 2, \ldots, N$, g is concave in S_i since

$$\frac{\partial g}{\partial S_i} = -\frac{1}{2} h_i z_\alpha \sigma (SI_i + T_i - S_i)^{-\frac{1}{2}} + \frac{1}{2} h_{i-1} z_\alpha \sigma (S_i + T_{i-1} - S_{i-1})^{-\frac{1}{2}}$$

$$\frac{\partial^2 g}{\partial S_i^2} = -\frac{1}{4} h_i z_\alpha \sigma (SI_i + T_i - S_i)^{-\frac{3}{2}} - \frac{1}{4} h_{i-1} z_\alpha \sigma (S_i + T_{i-1} - S_{i-1})^{-\frac{3}{2}} < 0$$

Therefore, the optimal solution occurs at the extreme points—each S_i is set to its minimum or maximum feasible value. What are the minimum and maximum? Well, $S_i \leq SI_i + T_i$, otherwise the quantity under the square root for i in (5.16) is negative. Similarly, $S_i \geq S_{i-1} - T_{i-1}$, otherwise the quantity under the square root for $i - 1$ is negative. But we also know that $S_i \geq 0$. Therefore, the limits of S_i are $\max\{0, S_{i-1} - T_{i-1}\}$ and $SI_i + T_i$; the optimal solution has S_i^* taking on one of these two values. This problem can be solved as a shortest path problem or using dynamic programming (see Inderfurth 1991).

To illustrate this graphically, suppose $N = 2$. In effect, we are trying to solve the following IP:

$$
\begin{array}{lll}
\text{minimize} & h_2 z_\alpha \sigma \sqrt{SI_2 + T_2 - S_2} + h_1 z_\alpha \sigma \sqrt{S_2 + T_1 - S_1} & (5.17) \\
\text{subject to} & SI_2 + T_2 - S_2 \geq 0 & (5.18) \\
& S_2 + T_1 - S_1 \geq 0 & (5.19) \\
& S_1 \leq s_1 & (5.20) \\
& S_1, S_2 \geq 0 & (5.21)
\end{array}
$$

The feasible region for this IP is pictured in Figure 5.6, assuming that $s_1 - T_1 > 0$. (If $s_1 - T_1 < 0$, the diagonal line would not intersect the square.) If we assume that $S_1 = s_1$, then only the right-hand face of the feasible region is relevant; the extreme points on this face are $S = (s_1, SI_2 + T_2)$ and $S = (s_1, s_1 - T_1)$, as expected.

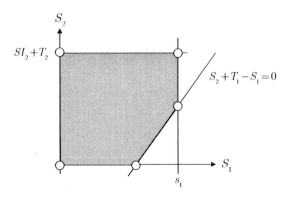

Figure 5.6   Feasible region for two-stage system.

This logic can be used to prove the following:

Theorem 5.4 *Suppose $s_1 = 0$ (immediate service is required to the customer). Then for all $i = 2, \ldots, N$, either $S_i^* = 0$ or $S_i^* = S_{i+1}^* + T_i$.*

Proof. Omitted; see Problem 5.6.   ∎

In other words, each stage follows an "all-or-nothing" inventory policy: either it holds 0 safety stock and quotes the maximum possible CST, or it holds the maximum possible safety stock and quotes 0 CST. We will see shortly that this property does not hold for the tree systems considered in Section 5.3.5.

The mathematical program (5.17)–(5.21) is not usually solved directly. Instead, we can solve this problem using dynamic programming. Let $\theta_k(SI)$ equal the optimal cost in stages $1, \ldots, k$ if stage k receives an inbound CST of SI. Then $\theta_k(SI)$ can be computed recursively as follows:

$$\theta_1(SI) = h_1 z_\alpha \sigma \sqrt{SI + T_1 - s_1} \tag{5.22}$$

$$\theta_k(SI) = \min_{0 \le S \le SI + T_k} \left\{ h_k z_\alpha \sigma \sqrt{SI + T_k - S} + \theta_{k-1}(S) \right\} \tag{5.23}$$

Equation (5.22) initializes the recursion: At stage 1, for any inbound CST SI, the net lead time is $SI + T_1 - s_1$ since the outbound CST is fixed at s_1. Then (5.23) calculates $\theta_k(SI)$ recursively: If stage k receives an inbound CST of SI and we choose an outbound CST of S, the cost at stage k is $h_k z_\alpha \sigma \sqrt{SI + T_k - S}$ and the cost at stages $1, \ldots, k-1$ is $\theta_{k-1}(S)$ since stage $k-1$ will receive an inbound CST of S. The right-hand side of (5.23) chooses the S that minimizes this cost, subject to the constraint that $0 \le S \le SI + T_k$ to ensure that S and the net lead time are both non-negative. In the next section, we will generalize this approach to solve tree systems.

5.3.5 Tree Systems

At this point we will turn our attention to tree systems. The model and algorithm described here were introduced by Graves and Willems (2000). (See also Graves and Willems (2003b) for an erratum.) General systems, which may include cycles, have not, to our knowledge, been solved. See Magnanti et al. (2006) for an alternate solution method for tree systems based on integer programming techniques.

Let A be the set of (directed) arcs in the network; then stage i is a predecessor to stage j if and only if $(i, j) \in A$.

A *demand stage* is a stage that faces external demand. We assume that a stage is a demand stage if and only if it has no successors. It is possible for a tree network to have more than one demand stage. The CST S_i for any demand stage i is set equal to $s_i \geq 0$, a constant, as in Section 5.3.4. Similarly, stages with no predecessors are called *supply stages*. If i is a supply stage, then i receives product from an external supplier with CST $SI_i \geq 0$. It is possible that a non-demand stage could have an external customer in addition to its successors, or that a non-supply stage could have an external supplier in addition to its predecessors, but we will rule out this possibility to keep things simpler.

Each demand stage i sees periodic demand distributed as $N(\mu_i, \sigma_i^2)$. Non-demand stages see demand that is derived from the stages they serve, and their safety stock levels must be set using the standard deviation of that demand. The standard deviation of demand at stage i (a non-demand stage) is

$$\sigma_i = \sqrt{\sum_{(i,j)\in A} \sigma_j^2} \tag{5.24}$$

since its variance is the sum of the variances of the downstream demands (derived or actual). The amount of safety stock required at stage i is therefore

$$z_\alpha \sigma_i \sqrt{SI_i + T_i - S_i} \tag{5.25}$$

and the expected holding cost at i is

$$h_i z_\alpha \sigma_i \sqrt{SI_i + T_i - S_i} \tag{5.26}$$

whether i is a supply stage, a demand stage, or neither. (Again, h_i is the local holding cost.)

If stage i has more than one successor, we will assume that it quotes *the same CST to all downstream neighbors*. Now, suppose stage i has more than one predecessor. Stage i cannot begin its processing until *all* of the raw materials have arrived. Therefore, if the upstream neighbors quote different CSTs, the effective inbound time at stage i is the maximum of the CSTs of the upstream neighbors. That is,

$$SI_i = \max_{(j,i)\in A} \{S_j\}. \tag{5.27}$$

All of this will be important in the algorithm we use to solve this problem.

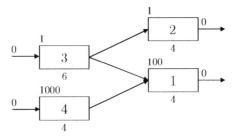

Figure 5.7   A counterexample to the "all-or-nothing" claim for tree systems.

Since the objective function is concave in every S_i, the optimal solution occurs at the extreme points, as in the serial-system case. But the "all-or-nothing" result does not hold, even if $s_i = 0$ for every demand stage. That is, it is not necessarily true that every stage either quotes 0 CST or holds 0 safety stock. An example is pictured in Figure 5.7. The processing time T_i is listed below each stage and the holding cost h_i is listed above. The inbound CST at the supply stages 3 and 4 is 0, as is the outbound CST at the demand stages 1 and 2. Stage 4 has a very large holding costs, which means it is optimal to hold no safety stock there; therefore, $S_4^* = 4$. We will show that $S_3^* = 4$ as well, even though this means stage 3 quotes a positive CST *and* holds positive safety stock. First suppose $S_3^* < 4$. Then the safety stock level at 3 increases, but there is no decrease in safety stock at stage 1 since stage 4 quotes an inbound time of 4 and $SI_1 = \max\{S_4, S_3\}$. Now suppose $S_3 > 4$. This increases the safety stock required at stage 1, which is quite expensive; the cost more than offsets any savings in holding cost at stage 3. Therefore, $S_3^* = 4$.

5.3.6   Solution Method

We will solve the SSSPP on a tree system using dynamic programming (DP). In principle, the approach is similar to the DP for the serial system in Section 5.3.4, but it is more complicated for two main reasons. First, computing the cost of a given decision is trickier than in the serial system. Second, in the serial system it is clear which stage follows a given stage, and hence how the DP recursion should be structured. In this problem, this is less clear, since each stage may have more than one upstream and/or downstream neighbor.

5.3.6.1   *Labeling the Stages*   We will address the second issue first. The DP algorithm requires us to re-label the stages so that each stage (other than stage N) *has exactly one adjacent stage with a higher index*. When we describe the algorithm, it will be clear why this is required. The re-labeling is performed using the following algorithm.

Algorithm 5.1 (Relabel Stages)

1. Start with all stages in U, the set of "unlabeled" stages.

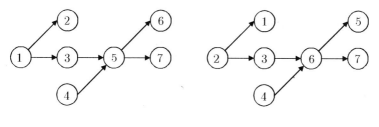

(a) Original network. (b) Relabeled network.

Figure 5.8 Relabeling the network.

2. Set $k \leftarrow 1$.

3. Choose $i \in U$ such that i is adjacent to at most one other stage in U.

4. Label i with index k. Remove stage i from U and insert it into the set L of "labeled" stages.

5. If $U = \emptyset$, STOP. Otherwise, set $k \leftarrow k + 1$ and go to 3.

☐ **EXAMPLE 5.1**

Consider the network pictured in Figure 5.8(a). Applying the procedure to this network yields the renumbered network in Figure 5.8(b). Note that in this network, every stage has exactly one neighbor (either upstream or downstream) with a higher index, other than stage 7. ☐

5.3.6.2 Functional Equations Next we describe how to evaluate the cost of a decision at a given stage. We had one recursive function, θ_k, in Section 5.3.4. In this section, we will need two. Each stage will use one function or the other based on whether the DP has already evaluated the stage's successor or its predecessor.

Let M_k be the maximum possible CST at stage k: M_k is equal to the length of the longest path through the network up to stage k, assuming each stage quotes the maximum possible CST of $SI + T$.

For a given stage k, $k = 1, \ldots, N - 1$, let $p(k)$ be the stage with the higher index in the relabeled network. Also, let N_k be the subset of $\{1, 2, \ldots, k\}$ that are connected (not necessarily adjacent) to k in the subgraph with node set $\{1, 2, \ldots, k\}$. That is,

$$N_k = \{k\} \cup \bigcup_{\substack{(i,k) \in A \\ i < k}} N_i \cup \bigcup_{\substack{(k,j) \in A \\ j < k}} N_j. \tag{5.28}$$

For example, in Figure 5.8(b),

$$N_3 = \{1, 2, 3\}$$

$$N_4 = \{4\}$$
$$N_5 = \{5\}$$

In the course of the DP, decisions made at stage k affect only those stages in N_k. The type of decision made depends on whether $p(k)$ is downstream or upstream from k:

- If $p(k)$ is *downstream* from k, then the decision to be made is the *outbound* CST S from stage k. The expected holding cost in N_k if k has an outbound CST of S is denoted $\theta_k^o(S)$. (The superscript o stands for "outbound.")

- If $p(k)$ is *upstream* from k, then the decision to be made is the *inbound* CST SI to stage k. The expected holding cost in N_k if k has an inbound CST of SI is denoted $\theta_k^i(SI)$. (The superscript i stands for "outbound.")

$\theta_k^o(S)$ and $\theta_k^i(SI)$ are the functional equations for the DP algorithm.

To compute $\theta_k^o(S)$ and $\theta_k^i(SI)$, we first compute the expected holding cost for N_k as a function of both the inbound and outbound CSTs at node k:

$$c_k(S, SI) = h_k z_\alpha \sigma_k \sqrt{SI + T_k - S}$$
$$+ \sum_{\substack{(i,k) \in A \\ i < k}} \min_{0 \leq x \leq SI} \{\theta_i^o(x)\} + \sum_{\substack{(k,j) \in A \\ j < k}} \min_{S \leq y \leq M_j - T_j} \{\theta_j^i(y)\}. \qquad (5.29)$$

The first term is simply the expected holding cost at node k. The second term is the cost at nodes in N_k that are upstream from k. For a stage i that is immediately upstream from k, if k's inbound CST is SI then i's outbound CST is *at most SI*. Why "at most" instead of "equal to"? Remember that at node k, SI is the maximum of the S's from all upstream neighbors. Forcing S to equal SI for all upstream neighbors is probably not optimal. Similarly, the third term is the cost at nodes in N_k that are downstream from k. For a stage j that is immediately downstream from k, if k's outbound CST is S then j's inbound CST is *at least S*. It's not necessarily equal to S since j might have other upstream neighbors that quote CSTs longer than S.

At stage k in the DP, we know $\theta_i^o(SI)$ for $i < k$ and $\theta_k^i(S)$ for $j < k$ because we have already visited all stages with smaller indices than k. At those stages, we have computed $\theta_i^o(S)$ for all possible values of S and $\theta_j^i(SI)$ for all possible values of SI. To compute $\theta_k^o(S)$ for a given S, we set

$$\theta_k^o(S) = \min_{SI}\{c_k(S, SI)\}. \qquad (5.30)$$

In other words, if we want to set k's outbound CST to S, we determine the cheapest possible inbound CST given that the outbound CST is S. What should the minimum be taken over (that is, what values of SI are legal)? If k is a supply node (no upstream neighbors), then there is only one possible value for SI: SI_k, a constant. But if k is not a supply node, then SI could be anywhere between $\max\{0, S - T_k\}$ (to ensure the quantity under the square root is positive) and $M_k - T_k$, where M_k is as defined above.

Similarly, to compute $\theta_k^i(SI)$ for a given SI, we set

$$\theta_k^i(SI) = \min_S \{c_k(S, SI)\}. \tag{5.31}$$

What are the limits of S? If k is a demand node (no downstream neighbors), then we have to set $S = s_k$. Otherwise, S can be anywhere between 0 and $SI + T_k$.

5.3.6.3 Dynamic Programming Algorithm   We can now state the dynamic programming algorithm.

Algorithm 5.2 (DP for Tree SSSPP)

1. For $k = 1, \ldots, N - 1$:

    (a) If $p(k)$ is downstream from k, evaluate $\theta_k^o(S)$ for $S = 0, 1, \ldots, M_k$.

    (b) If $p(k)$ is upstream from k, evaluate $\theta_k^i(SI)$ for $SI = 0, 1, \ldots, M_k - T_k$.

2. Evaluate $\theta_N^i(SI)$ for $SI = 0, 1, \ldots, M_N - T_N$.

3. Choose the SI that minimizes $\theta_N^i(SI)$, $SI = 0, 1, \ldots, M_N - T_N$.

The optimal objective value is the minimum value of $\theta_N^i(SI)$ found in step 3. The optimal solution is found by "backtracking," similar to the Wagner-Whitin algorithm.

Here's why the algorithm works. Suppose we're at stage $k < N$ in step 1. We know that k has exactly one neighbor with higher index, called $p(k)$. If $p(k)$ is downstream from k, then we compute the cost of setting k's outbound CST S to each possible value. Computing the cost for a given value, $\theta_k^o(S)$, requires knowing $c_k(S, SI)$, which in turn requires knowing $\theta_i^o(SI)$ for all stages that are immediately upstream and $\theta_j^i(S)$ for all stages that are immediately downstream from k. We know that for every upstream i, we computed $\theta_i^o(\cdot)$ in step 1(a), not $\theta_i^i(\cdot)$ in step 1(b), because i's neighbor with a higher index is k, which is downstream from it. Similarly, for every downstream j we computed $\theta_j^i(\cdot)$, not $\theta_j^o(\cdot)$, because $p(j) = k$ and k is upstream from j.

□ **EXAMPLE 5.2**

We will illustrate the algorithm on the network pictured in Figure 5.9. The numbers below the stages are the processing times T_i. The number on the inbound arrow to stage 1 indicates that $SI_1 = 1$, while the outbound numbers from stages 2 and 4 indicate the fixed CSTs s_i. The holding costs are 1 at the first echelon (stage 1), 2 at the second echelon (stage 3), and 3 at the third echelon (stages 2 and 4). Assume $z_\alpha = 1$ at all stages and $\sigma_2 = \sigma_4 = 1$; then $\sigma_1 = \sigma_3 = \sqrt{2}$. Note that the stages have already been relabeled so that each stage has exactly one neighbor with a higher index. Examining the longest path to each node, we get $M_1 = 3$, $M_2 = 5$, $M_3 = 4$, $M_4 = 5$.

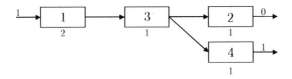

Figure 5.9 Example network for SSSPP DP algorithm.

Since $p(1) = 3$ is downstream from 1, we first compute $\theta_1^o(S)$ for $S = 0, \ldots, M_1 = 3$. Since 1 is a supply stage, the minimum over SI only considers $SI = 1$.

$$\theta_1^o(0) = \min_{SI=1}\{c_1(0, SI)\} = c_1(0, 1) = 1\sqrt{2}\sqrt{1 + 2 - 0} = 2.45$$

$$\theta_1^o(1) = \min_{SI=1}\{c_1(1, SI)\} = c_1(1, 1) = 1\sqrt{2}\sqrt{1 + 2 - 1} = 1.99$$

$$\theta_1^o(2) = \min_{SI=1}\{c_1(2, SI)\} = c_1(2, 1) = 1\sqrt{2}\sqrt{1 + 2 - 2} = 1.41$$

$$\theta_1^o(3) = \min_{SI=1}\{c_1(3, SI)\} = c_1(3, 1) = 1\sqrt{2}\sqrt{1 + 2 - 3} = 0.00$$

Next we compute $\theta_2^i(SI)$ since $p(2) = 3$ is upstream from 2; we need to consider $SI = 0, \ldots, M_2 - T_2 = 4$. Since 2 is a demand stage, the minimum over S only considers $S = 0$.

$$\theta_2^i(0) = \min_{S=0}\{c_2(S, 0)\} = c_2(0, 0) = 3\sqrt{0 + 1 - 0} = 3.00$$

$$\theta_2^i(1) = \min_{S=0}\{c_2(S, 1)\} = c_2(0, 1) = 3\sqrt{1 + 1 - 0} = 4.24$$

$$\theta_2^i(2) = \min_{S=0}\{c_2(S, 2)\} = c_2(0, 2) = 3\sqrt{2 + 1 - 0} = 5.20$$

$$\theta_2^i(3) = \min_{S=0}\{c_2(S, 3)\} = c_2(0, 3) = 3\sqrt{3 + 1 - 0} = 6.00$$

$$\theta_2^i(4) = \min_{S=0}\{c_2(S, 4)\} = c_2(0, 4) = 3\sqrt{4 + 1 - 0} = 6.71$$

Now comes the interesting case: stage 3. We need to compute $\theta_3^o(S)$ for $S = 0, \ldots, M_3 = 4$. The minimum over SI ranges from $\max\{0, S - T_3\}$ to $4 - 1 = 3$.

$$\theta_3^o(0) = \min_{0 \leq SI \leq 3}\{c_3(0, SI)\} = 8.28$$

$$c_3(0, 0) = 2\sqrt{2}\sqrt{0 + 1 - 0} + \theta_1^o(0) + \theta_2^i(0) = 2.83 + 2.45 + 3.00 = 8.28$$

$$c_3(0, 1) = 2\sqrt{2}\sqrt{1 + 1 - 0} + \theta_1^o(1) + \theta_2^i(0) = 4.00 + 1.99 + 3.00 = 8.99$$

$$c_3(0, 2) = 2\sqrt{2}\sqrt{2 + 1 - 0} + \theta_1^o(2) + \theta_2^i(0) = 4.90 + 1.41 + 3.00 = 9.31$$

$$c_3(0, 3) = 2\sqrt{2}\sqrt{3 + 1 - 0} + \theta_1^o(3) + \theta_2^i(0) = 5.66 + 0.00 + 3.00 = 8.66$$

$$\theta_3^o(1) = \min_{0 \leq SI \leq 3}\{c_3(1, SI)\} = 6.69$$

$$c_3(1, 0) = 2\sqrt{2}\sqrt{0 + 1 - 1} + \theta_1^o(0) + \theta_2^i(1) = 0.00 + 2.45 + 4.24 = 6.69$$

$$c_3(1,1) = 2\sqrt{2}\sqrt{1+1-1} + \theta_1^o(1) + \theta_2^i(1) = 2.83 + 1.99 + 4.24 = 9.05$$
$$c_3(1,2) = 2\sqrt{2}\sqrt{2+1-1} + \theta_1^o(2) + \theta_2^i(1) = 4.00 + 1.41 + 4.24 = 9.65$$
$$c_3(1,3) = 2\sqrt{2}\sqrt{3+1-1} + \theta_1^o(3) + \theta_2^i(1) = 4.90 + 0.00 + 4.24 = 9.14$$
$$\theta_3^o(2) = \min_{1 \le SI \le 3}\{c_3(2,SI)\} = 7.19$$
$$c_3(2,1) = 2\sqrt{2}\sqrt{1+1-2} + \theta_1^o(1) + \theta_2^i(2) = 0.00 + 1.99 + 5.20 = 7.19$$
$$c_3(2,2) = 2\sqrt{2}\sqrt{2+1-2} + \theta_1^o(2) + \theta_2^i(2) = 2.83 + 1.41 + 5.20 = 9.44$$
$$c_3(2,3) = 2\sqrt{2}\sqrt{3+1-2} + \theta_1^o(3) + \theta_2^i(2) = 4.00 + 0.00 + 5.20 = 9.20$$
$$\theta_3^o(3) = \min_{2 \le SI \le 3}\{c_3(3,SI)\} = 7.41$$
$$c_3(3,2) = 2\sqrt{2}\sqrt{2+1-3} + \theta_1^o(2) + \theta_2^i(3) = 0.00 + 1.41 + 6.00 = 7.41$$
$$c_3(3,3) = 2\sqrt{2}\sqrt{3+1-3} + \theta_1^o(3) + \theta_2^i(3) = 2.83 + 0.00 + 6.00 = 8.83$$
$$\theta_3^o(4) = \min_{3 \le SI \le 3}\{c_3(4,SI)\} = 6.71$$
$$c_3(4,3) = 2\sqrt{2}\sqrt{3+1-4} + \theta_1^o(3) + \theta_2^i(4) = 0.00 + 0.00 + 6.71 = 6.71$$

Finally, we compute $\theta_4^i(SI)$ for $SI = 0,\ldots,M_4 - T_4 = 4$. Again, 4 is a demand stage so the minimum ranges only over $S = 1$.

$$\theta_4^i(0) = \min_{S=1}\{c_4(S,0)\} = c_4(1,0) = 3\sqrt{0+1-1} + \theta_3^o(0) = 0.00 + 8.28 = 8.28$$
$$\theta_4^i(1) = \min_{S=1}\{c_4(S,1)\} = c_4(1,1) = 3\sqrt{1+1-1} + \theta_3^o(1) = 3.00 + 6.69 = 9.69$$
$$\theta_4^i(2) = \min_{S=1}\{c_4(S,2)\} = c_4(1,2) = 3\sqrt{2+1-1} + \theta_3^o(2) = 4.24 + 7.19 = 11.43$$
$$\theta_4^i(3) = \min_{S=1}\{c_4(S,3)\} = c_4(1,3) = 3\sqrt{3+1-1} + \theta_3^o(3) = 5.20 + 7.41 = 12.61$$
$$\theta_4^i(4) = \min_{S=1}\{c_4(S,4)\} = c_4(1,4) = 3\sqrt{4+1-1} + \theta_3^o(4) = 6.00 + 6.71 = 12.71$$

The minimum value is $\theta_4^i(0) = 8.28$, so 8.28 is the optimal cost. The optimal solution has an inbound time of 0 to stage 4, which means $S_3^* = 0$. Since $\theta_3^o(0)$ is minimized when $SI = 0$, the inbound time to stage 3 is 0, hence $S_1^* = 0$. The optimal solution is therefore $S^* = (0,0,0,1)$. The safety stock at each stage is

$$SS_1 = \sqrt{2}\sqrt{1+2-0} = 2.45$$
$$SS_2 = \sqrt{0+1-0} = 1.00$$
$$SS_3 = \sqrt{2}\sqrt{0+1-0} = 1.41$$
$$SS_4 = \sqrt{0+1-1} = 0.00$$

Note that the safety stock is pushed upstream as far as possible: Stage 2 needs to hold *some* safety stock since its processing time is 1 and its CST is 0. Since the holding cost at stages 2 and 4 is high, it is important for stage 3 to quote a CST of 0, so it, too, must hold safety stock. But the bulk of the safety stock is held at stage 1 since the holding cost is smallest there. Stage 1, then, absorbs

most of the demand uncertainty by serving as the supply chain's main buffer.
□

PROBLEMS

5.1   **(Proof of Proposition 5.1)** Prove Proposition 5.1.

5.2   **(Echelon-Based Total Cost)** Prove equation (5.4).

5.3   **(Exact Algorithm for Serial Systems)** Using the exact algorithm for serial systems with stochastic service in Section 5.2.2, find optimal base-stock levels for the following instance: $N = 2$, $p = 15$, $L_1 = L_2 = 1$, $h_1 = h_2 = 1$, and the demand per unit time is distributed $N(100, 15^2)$. Report both echelon and local base-stock levels (S_j^* and $(S')_j^*$).

5.4   **(Shang–Song Heuristic)** Using the Shang–Song heuristic discussed in Section 5.2.3, find near-optimal base-stock levels for the following instance: $N = 5$, $p = 24$, $L_1 = \ldots = L_5 = 0.5$, $h_1 = h_2 = 2$, and $h_3 = h_4 = h_5 = 1$.

    a) Assume the demand per unit time is normally distributed with a mean of 64 and a standard deviation of 8.

    b) Assume the demand per unit time has a Poisson distribution with $\lambda = 64$.

Report both echelon and local base-stock levels ($\tilde{S}_j$ and $\tilde{S}_j'$).

5.5   **(Comparison of Exact and Heuristic Approaches)** Find optimal and near-optimal base-stock levels for the following serial system using both the exact approach from Section 5.2.2 and the Shang–Song heuristic from Section 5.2.3: $N = 4$, $p = 80$, $L_1 = \ldots = L_4 = 1$, $h_j = 5 - j$ for all j, and the demand per unit time is distributed $N(20, 4^2)$. Report the echelon base-stock levels and the expected cost of each solution.

5.6   **(Proof of "All-or-Nothing" Theorem)** Prove Theorem 5.4.

    Note: You may use the fact that there exists an optimal solution in which, for all i, either $S_i = S_{i+1} + T_i$ or $S_i = \max\{0, S_{i-1} - T_{i-1}\}$.

5.7   **(Safety Stock for Ceramic Plates)** A manufacturer of ceramic plates and other tableware divides the manufacturing process into three major steps: forming, firing, and glazing. In the first step, the plates are formed out of clay; in the second, the plates are heated in a kiln, and in the third, they are painted. Forming and firing each take one day, while glazing takes two days. Clay is procured from an external vendor, which delivers orders exactly one day after they are placed. The daily demand for plates, as measured in truckloads, is distributed $N(45, 10^2)$. The company promises its customers that finished (i.e., glazed) plates will always be on-hand provided that the demand on a given day is no more than 4 standard deviations above its mean. (That is, $s_1 = 0$ and $z_\alpha = 4$.) Inventory may be held at any stage of the process. The holding cost of one truckload of plates (or its precursor products) is $2 per day for plates that have been formed but not fired, $3 for plates that have been fired but not glazed, and $4 for glazed plates. Find the optimal CST, base-stock level, and safety-stock level at each stage, as well as the optimal expected cost per day.

5.8 (Implementing Serial SSSPP DP) The file `serial10.xlsx` contains the holding costs and processing times for a 10-stage serial system. The demand per period is distributed $N(89.0, 15.8^2)$, and a service level of 98% is required. There is an inbound service time of 7 periods at stage 10, and stage 1 has a CST of 3 to the customer. Implement the dynamic programming algorithm from Section 5.3.4 and use it to find the optimal CST, base-stock level, and safety-stock level at each stage, as well as the optimal expected cost per period.

5.9 (Safety Stock for Baseball Hats) Consider the figure below, which represents the supply chain for a firm that manufactures baseball hats for college baseball fans. There are two end products. Product 1 is a Lehigh University hat, for which the firm sees a daily demand that is normally distributed with a mean of 22.0 cases and a standard deviation of 4.1 cases. Product 2 is a Lafayette College hat, whose demand is also normally distributed, with a mean of 15.3 cases and a standard deviation of 6.2 cases.

Stage 3 represents assembling the hats from two subassemblies: the cap (the part that sits on your head) and the visor (the part that sticks out in front). This generic product is then differentiated at stages 1 and 2 by dyeing the fabric and embroidering the team logos. Stage 4 represents the visor subassembly, while stage 5 represents sewing the cap subassembly out of fabric; the fabric is represented by stage 6.

The figure indicates the processing time below each stage and, above it, the value of one case's worth of the product. The firm is committed to providing a committed service time of 3 days to its customers (such as college bookstores). It has also set CSTs for the upstream stages, which are indicated on the links in the figure, but you suspect that these are not the optimal CSTs.

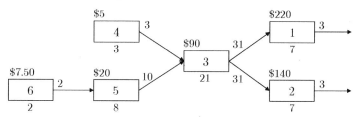

a) Calculate the base-stock level and safety-stock level required at each stage for the solution in the figure, as well as the total expected holding cost. Assume that demands are truncated 4 standard deviations above their means; i.e., $z_\alpha = 4$ in (5.12). Also assume that holding costs are calculated as 20% of the product value, per year. (Make sure to translate into days.)

b) Develop a solution to the strategic safety stock placement problem that still gives CSTs of 3 days to the end customers but is cheaper than the solution depicted above. Your solution does not need to be optimal, only better than the one above. For each stage, report the CST, base-stock level, and safety-stock level, as well as the total expected holding cost per period for the whole system.

5.10   (Implementing Tree SSSPP DP) Implement Algorithm 5.2 and use it to find the optimal solution for the instance introduced in Problem 5.9. Report the optimal CST, base-stock level, and safety-stock level at each stage, as well as the optimal expected cost per period.

5.11   (Two-Stage SSSPP) Consider a two-stage serial supply chain with guaranteed service as defined in Section 5.3.4. Assume that $0 < h_2 < h_1$. The inbound CST to stage 2, SI_2, is a constant, as is the outbound CST from stage 1, s_1. Therefore, the only decision variable is S_2. For simplicity, assume that $z_\alpha = \sigma = 1$. Then the objective function is given by

$$g(S_2) = h_2 \sqrt{SI_2 + T_2 - S_2} + h_1 \sqrt{S_2 + T_1 - s_1}.$$

a) Prove that, in the optimal solution to the strategic safety stock placement problem for the two-stage supply chain defined above:

i. Stage 1 holds safety stock if and only if $s_1 < T_1$.

ii. If stage 1 holds safety stock, then stage 2 also holds safety stock if and only if

$$h_2 \sqrt{SI_2 + T_2} + h_1 \sqrt{T_1 - s_1} < h_1 \sqrt{SI_2 + T_2 + T_1 - s_1}.$$

b) Now consider an N-stage serial supply chain, with SI_N and s_1 constants, as usual. Assume that $0 < h_N < \ldots < h_1$. Prove that if

$$\sum_{i=1}^{k} T_i < s_1,$$

then stages $1, 2, \ldots, k$ hold no safety stock.

CHAPTER 6

DEALING WITH UNCERTAINTY IN INVENTORY OPTIMIZATION

6.1 INTRODUCTION

The title of this chapter is a little misleading. After all, the inventory models in Chapter 4 deal with uncertainty in inventory optimization, too. But those models assumed a single kind of uncertainty—i.e., demand uncertainty—and assumed that inventory is the only tool for mitigating the uncertainty. In contrast, this chapter uses a broader definition of uncertainty and of the ways that we can mitigate it using inventory. The models in Sections 6.2–6.4 discuss the interactions among multiple inventory locations, and how these locations can pool together—either literally or virtually—to reduce inventory-related costs. Then, in Sections 6.5–6.8, we discuss models for mitigating a different type of uncertainty, namely, supply uncertainty.

6.2 THE RISK-POOLING EFFECT

6.2.1 Overview

Consider a network consisting of N distribution centers (DCs) or other facilities, each of which faces random demand for a single product. The DCs each hold inventory of this product. In fact, they act like N independent newsvendors, each facing $N(\mu, \sigma^2)$ demand per period. If the DCs each wish to meet a type-1 service level of α (that is, they wish to stock out in no more than $100(1 - \alpha)\%$ of the periods on average), they must each hold an amount of safety stock equal to $z_\alpha \sigma$. The total safety stock in this system is therefore $N z_\alpha \sigma$.

Now suppose that all N DCs are merged into a single DC. What are the inventory implications of this consolidation? (We're ignoring the possible increase in transportation costs and hassle the consolidation may cause.) The new DC's demand process is equal to the sum of all of the original DC's demands. This process has a mean demand of $N\mu$ and a standard deviation of $\sqrt{N}\sigma$. Therefore, to meet the same service level (α) the new DC needs to hold $\sqrt{N} z_\alpha \sigma$ of safety stock, which is less than the safety stock required when N DCs each hold inventory.

This phenomenon is known as the *risk-pooling effect* (Eppen 1979). The basic idea is that by pooling demand streams, we can reduce the amount of safety stock required to meet a given service level, and hence we can reduce the holding cost.

We next discuss the risk-pooling effect in greater generality. Our analysis is adapted from that of Eppen (1979).

6.2.2 Problem Statement

We'll assume that each DC follows a base-stock inventory policy under periodic review, with S_i the base-stock level for DC i. Excess inventory may be stored from period to period (with a holding cost of h per unit per period), and excess demand is backordered (with a penalty cost of p per unit). We assume $p > h$. Note that h and p are the same at every DC.

The demand per period seen by DC i is represented by the random variable D_i, with $D_i \sim N(\mu_i, \sigma_i^2)$. Let f_i and F_i be the pdf and cdf, respectively, of D_i. Demands may be correlated among DCs. The covariance of D_i and D_j is given by σ_{ij} and the correlation coefficient by ρ_{ij}; then $\sigma_{ij} = \sigma_i \sigma_j \rho_{ij}$.

For each DC, the sequence of events in each period is the same as in Section 4.4.

6.2.3 Decentralized System

We will refer to the system described above as the *decentralized system* since each DC operates independently of the others. S_i is the base-stock level at DC i; this is a decision variable. The expected cost per period at DC i can be expressed as a function of S_i as follows:

$$g_i(S_i) = h \int_0^{S_i} (S_i - d) f_i(d) dd + p \int_{S_i}^{\infty} (d - S_i) f_i(d) dd.$$

This formula is identical to the formula for the newsvendor cost (4.21) except for the subscripts i. Therefore, from Theorems 4.1 and 4.2, the optimal solution is

$$S_i^* = F_i^{-1}\left(\frac{p}{h + p}\right) = \mu_i + z_\alpha \sigma_i,$$

where $\alpha = p/(p+h)$ and z_α is the αth fractile of the standard normal distribution, and the optimal cost at DC i is

$$g_i(S_i^*) = (p+h)\phi(z_\alpha)\sigma_i.$$

(Recall that $\phi(\cdot)$ is the pdf of the standard normal distribution.) Defining $\eta = (p+h)\phi(z_\alpha)$ for convenience, the optimal total expected cost (at all DCs) in the decentralized system, denoted $E[C_D]$, is

$$E[C_D] = \eta \sum_{i=1}^{N} \sigma_i. \tag{6.1}$$

6.2.4   Centralized System

Now imagine that the DCs are consolidated into a single DC that serves all of the demand. We will refer to this as the *centralized system*. Let D_C be the total demand seen by this super-DC. Its mean and standard deviation are

$$\mu_C = \sum_{i=1}^{N} \mu_i$$

$$\sigma_C = \sqrt{\sum_{i=1}^{N} \sum_{j=1}^{N} \sigma_{ij}}.$$

(Note that by definition, $\sigma_{ii} = \sigma_i^2$.) Similar logic as above shows that the optimal base-stock level for the centralized system is

$$S_C^* = \mu_C + z_\alpha \sigma_C$$

with optimal expected cost

$$E[C_C] = \eta \sigma_C = \eta \sqrt{\sum_{i=1}^{N} \sum_{j=1}^{N} \sigma_{ij}}. \tag{6.2}$$

6.2.5   Comparison

Now let's compare the centralized and decentralized systems. The next theorem says that the centralized system is no more expensive than the decentralized system. This is the risk-pooling effect.

Theorem 6.1 *For the decentralized, N-DC system and the centralized, single-DC system formed by merging the DCs, $E[C_C] \leq E[C_D]$.*

Proof.

$$E[C_C] = \eta \sqrt{\sum_{i=1}^{N} \sigma_i^2 + 2 \sum_{i=1}^{N-1} \sum_{j=i+1}^{N} \sigma_i \sigma_j \rho_{ij}}$$

$$\leq \eta \sqrt{\sum_{i=1}^{N} \sigma_i^2 + 2 \sum_{i=1}^{N-1} \sum_{j=i+1}^{N} \sigma_i \sigma_j} \quad (\text{since } \rho_{ij} \leq 1)$$

$$= \eta \sqrt{\left(\sum_{i=1}^{N} \sigma_i\right)^2}$$

$$= E[C_D].$$

∎

One interpretation of the risk-pooling effect is that pooling inventory allows the firm to take advantage of random fluctuations in demand. If one DC sees unusually high demand in a given time period, it's possible that another DC sees unusually low demand. In the centralized system, the excess inventory at the low-demand DC can be used to make up the shortfall at the high-demand DC. In the decentralized system, there is no opportunity for this supply–demand matching.

A more mathematical explanation is that risk pooling occurs because the centralized system takes advantage of the concave nature of safety stock requirements. The amount of safety stock required is proportional to the standard deviation of demand. The standard deviation of demand at the centralized site is smaller than the sum of the standard deviations of the individual sites in the decentralized system since variances, not standard deviations, are additive.

Somewhat surprisingly, the *variances* of the costs of the centralized and decentralized systems are equal at optimality; that is, $\text{Var}[C_D] = \text{Var}[C_C]$, where $\text{Var}[\cdot]$ denotes variance (Schmitt et al. 2010a).

6.2.6 Magnitude of Risk-Pooling Effect

Let's try to get a handle on the magnitude of the risk-pooling effect. Let

$$v = 2 \sum_{i=1}^{N-1} \sum_{j=i+1}^{N} \sigma_i \sigma_j \rho_{ij}.$$

Note that

$$E[C_C] = \eta \sqrt{\sum_{i=1}^{N} \sigma_i^2 + v}.$$

Uncorrelated Demands: First assume that the demands are uncorrelated, i.e., $\rho_{ij} = 0$ for all i, j, so $v = 0$. Then

$$E[C_C] = \eta\sqrt{\sum_{i=1}^{N}\sigma_i^2 + v} = \eta\sqrt{\sum_{i=1}^{N}\sigma_i^2} \leq \eta\sqrt{\left(\sum_{i=1}^{N}\sigma_i\right)^2} = E[C_D].$$

The magnitude of the difference between $E[C_C]$ and $E[C_D]$ depends on the magnitude between $\sqrt{\sum \sigma_i^2}$ and $\sum \sigma_i$.

Positively Correlated Demands: Next suppose that demands are positively correlated. In fact, consider the extreme case in which $\rho_{ij} = 1$ for all i, j. Then

$$E[C_C] = \eta\sqrt{\sum_{i=1}^{N}\sigma_i^2 + v} = \eta\sqrt{\sum_{i=1}^{N}\sigma_i^2 + 2\sum_{i=1}^{N-1}\sum_{j=i+1}^{N}\sigma_i\sigma_j}$$

$$= \eta\sqrt{\left(\sum_{i=1}^{N}\sigma_i\right)^2} = \eta\sum_{i=1}^{N}\sigma_i = E[C_D],$$

so there is no risk pooling effect at all (in the extreme case of perfect correlation).

Negatively Correlated Demands: Finally, assume that demands are negatively correlated. It's difficult to identify the extreme case since ρ_{ij} can't equal -1 for all i, j. (Why?) But we can say that $v \geq -\sum_{i=1}^{N}\sigma_i^2$ since

$$\sum_{i=1}^{N}\sigma_i^2 + v = \sigma_C^2 \geq 0.$$

So let's assume as an extreme scenario that $v = -\sum_{i=1}^{N}\sigma_i^2$. Then

$$E[C_C] = \eta\sqrt{\sum_{i=1}^{N}\sigma_i^2 - \sum_{i=1}^{N}\sigma_i^2} = 0.$$

The centralized cost is 0, while the decentralized cost is not.

So the risk-pooling effect is very pronounced when demands are negatively correlated, smaller when demands are uncorrelated, and smaller still, or even non-existent, when demands are positively correlated. Why? Recall the explanation given in Section 6.2.5: The risk-pooling effect occurs because excess inventory at one DC can be used to meet excess demand at another. If demands are negatively correlated, there is a lot of opportunity to do this since demands will be very disparate at different locations. On the other hand, if demands are positively correlated, they tend to be all high or all low at the same time, so there is little opportunity for supply–demand matching.

6.2.7 Final Thoughts

The analysis above only considers holding and stockout costs; it does not consider fixed costs (to build and operate DCs) or transportation costs. Clearly, as DCs are consolidated, the fixed cost will decrease. But the transportation cost will increase, since retailers (or other downstream facilities) will be served from more distant DCs. In many cases, the magnitude of the risk pooling effect may be far outweighed by the increases or decreases in fixed and transportation cost. Any analysis of a potential consolidation of DCs must include all factors, not just risk pooling. The location model with risk pooling (LMRP), discussed in Section 8.2, attempts to incorporate all of these factors when choosing facility locations.

6.3 POSTPONEMENT

6.3.1 Introduction

Many firms have product lines containing closely related products. In many cases, multiple end products are made from a single generic product. For example, the clothing retailer Benetton sells many colors of sweater, each of which comes from the same white sweater that's dyed multiple colors (Heskett and Signorelli 1984). Hewlett-Packard sells the same printer in dozens of countries, with a different power supply module, manual, and labels in each (Lee and Billington 1993). IBM builds individualized computers by building partially finished products called "vanilla boxes" and customizing them to order (Swaminathan and Tayur 1998).

A key question in the design of the manufacturing process for each of these products is: When should the end products be differentiated? For example, consider a manufacturer of mobile phones that sells phones in many countries. The company programs each phone with a given language at the factory—the phone is "localized" when it is manufactured. The number of phones to be programmed in each language is determined based on a forecast of the demand in each country. The phones are then shipped to regional distribution centers, approximately one on each continent. The regional DCs store the phones until they are required by retailers, at which point they are shipped to individual countries. If the demand forecasts were wrong, and demand for phones in, say, Thailand was higher than expected while demand in Holland was lower than expected, the company would have to correct this discrepancy by re-programming some of the Dutch phones into Thai phones, then shipping them from the Europe DC to the Asia DC—a costly and time-consuming proposition.

Now suppose that *generic* phones are shipped to the regional DCs, and languages are programmed at the DCs once the phones are requested by retailers. Since the phones are localized on demand, there is much less risk of having too many phones of one language and too few of another. In addition, the firm holds inventory of generic phones, not localized phones, which means that fewer phones need to be held in safety stock due to the risk pooling effect, as we will see below.

This strategy is called *postponement* or *delayed differentiation*. The idea is to delay, as much as possible, the point in the manufacturing process at which end products are differentiated from one another. Of course, designing a postponement strategy may be extremely complicated, since it may require the redesign of the product and the manufacturing and distribution processes. In the mobile phone example, the regional DCs would have to be outfitted with language-programming equipment.

To take the Benetton example to an extreme, postponement might mean that sweaters are dyed in the retail stores once they are demanded by a customer. You would request, say, a red sweater, and it would be dyed for you on demand; stores would never be out of stock of the sweater you wanted. This seems silly, since the costs of implementing such a system would probably far outweigh the benefits. But some products are actually sold this way. For example, paint is mixed to order from generic white paint at your hardware store, giving you access to an enormous range of colors that would be prohibitively expensive to keep in stock. (See Lee (1996) for a discussion of the benefits and challenges of postponement, as well as for two models similar to the model presented below.)

In this section, we will present an analytical model to study the risk-pooling benefit of postponement. This model does not consider the quantitative benefits due to better matching of supply and demand, the improvements in customer satisfaction, or the costs of re-engineering the product and manufacturing process.

6.3.2 Optimization Model

Suppose there are N end products that are made from the same generic product. We will denote the demand for end product i in a given period by D_i and assume that it is normally distributed with a mean of μ_i and a standard deviation of σ_i. For simplicity, we will also assume that demands of different end products are independent of one another, though this assumption is not necessary for the analysis. The manufacturing process takes T periods from the time manufacturing begins to the time the product is sold. (It may be unreasonable to expect this time to be fixed and deterministic, especially in the case of products like Benetton sweaters that sit in inventory for a random amount of time, but we will assume this anyway.) During the first t periods of the manufacturing process, the process is the same for all products; after time t, the manufacturing process is different for each end product. In other words, the product is generic until time t, after which it becomes differentiated. (See Figure 6.1.) In the Benetton example, $t = 0$ might correspond to using dyed wool to produce sweaters (the products are differentiated before manufacturing even begins); $t = T$ corresponds to dyeing the sweaters at the time of sale; and $0 < t < T$ corresponds to an intermediate strategy—for example, dyeing the sweaters after production but before shipping to stores.

Inventory is held of both the generic product (after time t) and each finished product (after time T). Let h_0 be the holding cost per item per period for the generic product and h_i the holding cost for end product i, $i = 1, \ldots, N$. We will assume that $h_0 < h_i$ for all i since value is added as processing continues. We will assume that $t > T/2$ (mainly for mathematical convenience).

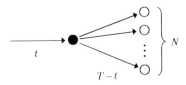

Figure 6.1   Manufacturing process with postponement.

Assuming a desired type 1 service level of α, the required amount of safety stock of the generic product is

$$z_\alpha \sqrt{t} \sqrt{\sum_{i=1}^{N} \sigma_i^2}$$

from (4.44), since the lead time for the generic product is t and the total standard deviation of demand per period is $\sqrt{\sum_i \sigma_i^2}$. The required safety stock of end product i is given by

$$z_\alpha \sqrt{T - t}\,\sigma_i.$$

Therefore, the total expected holding cost for all products is

$$C(t) = z_\alpha \left[h_0 \sqrt{t} \sqrt{\sum_{i=1}^{N} \sigma_i^2} + \sqrt{T - t} \sum_{i=1}^{N} h_i \sigma_i \right].$$

As t increases, the cost decreases since

$$\frac{dC(t)}{dt} = z_\alpha \left(\tfrac{1}{2} h_0 t^{-\frac{1}{2}} \sqrt{\sum \sigma_i^2} - \tfrac{1}{2}(T - t)^{-\frac{1}{2}} \sum h_i \sigma_i \right)$$

$$< \tfrac{1}{2} z_\alpha h_0 \left(t^{-\frac{1}{2}} \sqrt{\sum \sigma_i^2} - (T - t)^{-\frac{1}{2}} \sum \sigma_i \right)$$

$$< \tfrac{1}{2} z_\alpha h_0 \left(\left[t^{-\frac{1}{2}} - (T - t)^{-\frac{1}{2}} \right] \sum \sigma_i \right)$$

$$< 0$$

since

$$t > T/2 \implies t > T - t \implies \sqrt{t} > \sqrt{T - t} \implies t^{-\frac{1}{2}} - (T - t)^{-\frac{1}{2}} < 0.$$

Therefore, postponement results in decreased costs.

6.3.3   Relationship to Risk Pooling

The cost savings from postponement is due to the risk pooling effect: Generic products represent pooled inventory, while end products represent decentralized inventory.

This relationship can be made explicit by setting $t = 0$ and $t = T$. When $t = 0$, the total safety stock required is

$$z_\alpha \sqrt{T} \sum_{i=1}^{N} \sigma_i,$$

which is proportional to the safety stock required in the decentralized system in our discussion of risk pooling. Similarly, when $t = T$, the total safety stock required is

$$z_\alpha \sqrt{T} \sqrt{\sum_{i=1}^{N} \sigma_i^2},$$

which is proportional to the safety stock in the centralized system.

6.4 TRANSSHIPMENTS

6.4.1 Introduction

When multiple retailers stock the same product, it is sometimes advantageous for one retailer to ship items to another if the former has a surplus and the latter has a shortage. Such "lateral" transfers are called *transshipments*. Transshipments are a mechanism for improving service levels since they allow demands to be satisfied in the current period when they might otherwise be lost or backordered until the following period. In that regard, the benefit from transshipments is very similar to that from risk pooling, since transshipments use one retailer's surplus to reduce another retailer's shortfall. In this case, however, there is no physical pooling of inventory, though the strategy is sometimes referred to as "information pooling." Of course, transshipments come at a cost: Transshipments are often more expensive than replenishments from the DC because they are smaller and therefore lack the economies of scale from larger shipments.

In this section we will discuss a model for setting base-stock levels in a system with two retailers that may transship to one another. This model is adapted from Tagaras (1989). For models with more than two retailers, see Tagaras (1999) or Herer et al. (2006).

This model will assume that transshipments occur after the demand has been realized but before it must be satisfied. Therefore, these transshipments are *reactive* since they are made in reaction to realized demands. In contrast, one might consider *proactive* transshipments that are made in anticipation of demand shortages. Proactive transshipments are of interest when demands must be met instantaneously, since there is no opportunity for transshipping between demand realization and satisfaction. On the other hand, proactive transshipments are more complex to model, so we will focus only on reactive transshipments. We will develop an analytical expression for the expected cost function, but the expected cost can only be minimized using numerical methods (rather than using differentiation). We will also discuss the improvement in service levels due to transshipments.

6.4.2 Problem Statement

Consider a system with two retailers served by a single DC. The retailers receive *replenishment* shipments from the DC and are permitted to *transship* goods to each other. As stated above, transshipment occurs after the demand has been realized but before it must be satisfied. This is a periodic-review model with an infinite horizon. There is no fixed cost and no lead time, either for replenishments or transshipments. Each retailer i ($i = 1, 2$) follows a base-stock policy, with base-stock level S_i. The demand at retailer i is a random variable D_i with pdf f_i and cdf F_i. If there are excess demands at a retailer after transshipments have been made, they are backordered. The costs are as follows:

$$c_i = \text{ordering cost per unit at retailer } i, \text{ for } i = 1, 2$$
$$h_i = \text{holding cost per unit per period at retailer } i, \text{ for } i = 1, 2$$
$$p_i = \text{backorder cost per unit at retailer } i, \text{ for } i = 1, 2$$
$$c_{ij} = \text{cost per unit to transship from } i \text{ to } j, \text{ for } i = 1, 2, \ i \neq j$$

We will assume that

$$c_i - c_j + c_{ij} \geq 0. \tag{6.3}$$

In other words, it is cheaper to ship directly to c_j than to ship to i and then transship to j. This is sometimes referred to as a *triangle inequality*. We will also make the following assumptions:

(a) $h_i + p_j - c_{ij} - (c_i - c_j) \geq 0$ (i.e., if there is a shortage at j and a surplus at i, it is better to transship than not to, since the cost to transship is c_{ij}, while the cost to do nothing is $h_i + p_j + c_j - c_i$ [since we would incur the holding cost at i, the penalty cost at j, and then next period we'd order one more unit at j and one fewer at i])

(b) $c_{ij} + (c_i - c_j) - (h_i - h_j) \geq 0$ (i.e., don't transship if there is a surplus at both retailers)

(c) $c_{ij} + (c_i - c_j) + (p_i - p_j) \geq 0$ (i.e., don't transship if there is a shortage at both retailers)

These three assumptions imply that *complete pooling* is optimal: Transship if one retailer has a surplus while the other has a shortage, but if both have surpluses or both have shortages don't transship—one retailer's demand is not "more valuable" than the other's.

The sequence of events in each period is as follows:

1. Retailers observe their inventory levels.

2. Each retailer i places a replenishment order of size Q_i to the DC and receives it instantaneously.

3. Demand is observed.

4. Transshipment decisions are made. Transshipments are sent and arrive instantaneously.

5. Demand is satisfied to the extent possible, and excess demands are backordered.

6. Holding and stockout costs are assessed.

We will make use of the following random variables:

$$Q_i = \text{replenishment order quantity at retailer } i, \text{ for } i = 1, 2$$
$$Y_{ij} = \text{amount transshipped from } i \text{ to } j, \text{ for } i = 1, 2, \ i \neq j$$
$$IL_i = \text{inventory level at retailer } i \text{ after step 5, for } i = 1, 2$$
$$IL_i^+ = \text{on-hand inventory at retailer } i \text{ after step 5, for } i = 1, 2$$
$$IL_i^- = \text{backorders at retailer } i \text{ after step 5, for } i = 1, 2$$

Then

$$IL_i = IL_i^+ - IL_i^-. \tag{6.4}$$

Note that these are all random variables—they are not decision variables. The decision variables are S_i, the base stock levels for $i = 1, 2$. We will compute expectations of the random variables once the base-stock levels are set, in order to compute the expected cost.

The complete pooling policy can be stated formally as follows:

(a) If $D_i \leq S_i$ for $i = 1, 2$, then $Y_{ij} = Y_{ji} = 0$

(b) If $D_i \geq S_i$ for $i = 1, 2$, then $Y_{ij} = Y_{ji} = 0$

(c) If $D_i < S_i$ and $D_j > S_j$, then

$$Y_{ij} = \min\{S_i - D_i, D_j - S_j\}$$
$$Y_{ji} = 0.$$

This policy is represented graphically in Figure 6.2, which indicates the transshipment quantities and ending inventory levels for all possible realizations of the demand.

6.4.3 Expected Cost

The expected cost per period will be denoted $g(\mathbf{S})$, where $\mathbf{S} = (S_1, S_2)$ is the vector of base-stock levels. $g(\mathbf{S})$ is given by

$$g(\mathbf{S}) = \sum_{i=1}^{2} \left[c_i E[Q_i] + \sum_{\substack{j=1 \\ j \neq i}}^{2} c_{ij} E[Y_{ij}] + h_i E[IL_i^+] + p_i E[IL_i^-] \right]. \tag{6.5}$$

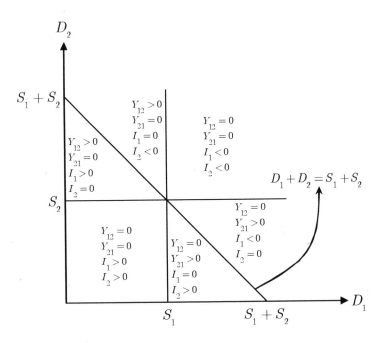

Figure 6.2   Possible realizations of transshipment and ending inventories. Adapted with permission from Tagaras, Effects of pooling on the optimization and service levels of two-location inventory systems, *IIE Transactions*, 21, 1989, 250–257. ©1989, Taylor & Francis, Ltd., http://www.informaworld.com.

In order to minimize $g(\mathbf{S})$, we need to compute $E[Q_i]$, $E[Y_{ij}]$, $E[IL_i^+]$, and $E[IL_i^-]$. First note that

$$E[Q_i] = S_i - E[IL_i] \tag{6.6}$$

$$E[IL_i] = E[IL_i^+] - E[IL_i^-]. \tag{6.7}$$

(6.6) follows from the fact that the order quantity is the difference between the target level and the ending inventory in the previous period, while (6.7) follows from (6.4).

The transshipment policy states that $Y_{ij} > 0$ if and only if $D_j > S_j$ and $D_i < S_i$. If this condition holds, the amount shipped is $\min\{S_i - D_i, D_j - S_j\}$. Therefore, we can write

$$
\begin{aligned}
E[Y_{ij}] =& E_{D_i}\left[E_{D_j}[Y_{ij}|D_i]\right] \\
=& \int_{d_i=0}^{S_i}\left[\int_{d_j=S_j}^{S_i+S_j-d_i}(d_j - S_j)f_j(d_j)dd_j\right. \\
& \left. + \int_{d_j=S_i+S_j-d_i}^{\infty}(S_i - d_i)f_j(d_j)dd_j\right]f_i(d_i)dd_i.
\end{aligned}
$$

It can be shown that

$$E[Y_{ij}] = \int_{d_i=0}^{S_i} F_i(d_i)[1 - F_j(S_i + S_j - d_i)]dd_i. \tag{6.8}$$

Figure 6.2 suggests that the ending inventory level is positive at retailer i if and only if $D_i < S_i$ and $D_j < S_j$ or $S_j < D_j \le S_i + S_j$ and $D_i < S_i + S_j - D_j$. Therefore,

$$
\begin{aligned}
E[IL_i^+] =& \int_{d_j=0}^{S_j}\int_{d_i=0}^{S_i}(S_i - d_i)f_i(d_i)f_j(d_j)dd_idd_j \\
& + \int_{d_j=S_j}^{S_i+S_j}\int_{d_i=0}^{S_i+S_j-d_j}(S_i + S_j - d_i - d_j)f_i(d_i)f_j(d_j)dd_idd_j \\
=& \int_{d_i=0}^{S_i} F_i(d_i)F_j(S_i + S_j - d_i)dd_i. \tag{6.9}
\end{aligned}
$$

Similarly, the ending inventory level is negative at retailer i if and only if $D_i > S_i$ and $D_j > S_j$ or $D_j < S_j$ and $D_i > S_i + S_j - D_j$. Therefore,

$$
\begin{aligned}
E[IL_i^-] =& \int_{d_j=S_j}^{\infty}\int_{d_i=S_i}^{\infty}(d_i - S_i)f_i(d_i)f_j(d_j)dd_idd_j \\
& + \int_{d_j=0}^{S_j}\int_{d_i=S_i+S_j-d_j}^{\infty}(d_i + d_j - S_i - S_j)f_i(d_i)f_j(d_j)dd_idd_j \\
=& E[D_i] - S_i + \int_{d_i=0}^{S_i} F_i(d_i)dd_i - \int_{d_j=0}^{S_j} F_j(d_j)dd_j
\end{aligned}
$$

$$+ \int_{d_i=S_i}^{S_i+S_j} F_i(d_i) F_j(S_i + S_j - d_i) dd_i. \tag{6.10}$$

Combining (6.7) with (6.9) and (6.10), we get

$$E[IL_i] = S_i - E[D_i] - \int_{d_i=0}^{S_i} F_i(d_i) dd_i + \int_{d_j=0}^{S_j} F_j(d_j) dd_j$$

$$+ \int_{d_i=0}^{S_i} F_i(d_i) F_j(S_i + S_j - d_i) dd_i$$

$$- \int_{d_i=S_i}^{S_i+S_j} F_i(d_i) F_j(S_i + S_j - d_i) dd_i. \tag{6.11}$$

This gives us $E[Q_i]$ using (6.6), so we now have all the components we need to compute $g(\mathbf{S})$. We won't write out $g(\mathbf{S})$ in its entirety since it's a long formula, but it's straightforward to do so using (6.5). Like several of the inventory optimization models we have seen so far, $g(\mathbf{S})$ cannot be optimized in closed form. In other words, we can't set the derivative to 0 and solve for $\mathbf{S}$ in the form $S_1^* = $ [something] and $S_2^* = $ [something]. Instead, we must use numerical methods—general-purpose nonlinear programming algorithms—to solve the problem.

6.4.4 Benefits of Transshipments

Transshipments are beneficial both by reducing costs and by improving service levels. The cost reduction is evident from assumption (a) on page 152—transshipments are less costly than holding and stockouts. Put another way, the transshipment model can be obtained from a "no-transshipment" model by relaxing a constraint—therefore, the optimal cost can only improve (or stay the same).

We will next examine the effect of transshipments on both type-1 and type-2 service levels. (See Section 4.3.2.3 for definitions.) Let

$\alpha_i^0(\mathbf{S})$ =type-1 service level at retailer i if transshipments are not allowed
   and base-stock levels are set to $\mathbf{S}$

$\alpha_i(\mathbf{S})$ =type-1 service level at retailer i if transshipments are allowed
   and base-stock levels are set to $\mathbf{S}$

$\beta_i^0(\mathbf{S})$ =type-2 service level at retailer i if transshipments are not allowed
   and base-stock levels are set to $\mathbf{S}$

$\beta_i(\mathbf{S})$ =type-2 service level at retailer i if transshipments are allowed
   and base-stock levels are set to $\mathbf{S}$

We will show that transshipments improve both types of service levels. In fact, we will quantify the improvement. We will prove that transshipments improve the service levels for a *given* base-stock level, but this, in turn, implies that the *optimal* solution with transshipments has a higher service level than the optimal solution without transshipments. (Why?)

Theorem 6.2 *Transshipments increase the type-1 service level by the marginal decrease in the expected transshipment quantity for a unit increase in the base-stock level; that is,*

$$\alpha_i(\mathbf{S}) = \alpha_i^0(\mathbf{S}) + \left| \frac{\partial E[Y_{ji}]}{\partial S_i} \right|$$

for i = 1, 2.

Proof. Since $\alpha_i^0(\mathbf{S})$ is the probability that no stockout occurs in a given period with no transshipments,

$$\alpha_i^0(\mathbf{S}) = F_i(S_i). \tag{6.12}$$

Now, no stockouts occur at retailer i in the system with transshipments if either $D_i \leq S_i$ or $D_i > S_i$ and retailer j has sufficient excess inventory to meet i's excess demand. Therefore,

$$
\begin{aligned}
\alpha_i(\mathbf{S}) &= P(D_i \leq S_i) + P(D_j < S_j \text{ and } S_i < D_i < S_i + S_j - D_j) \\
&= F_i(S_i) + \int_{d_j=0}^{S_j} \left[\int_{d_i=S_i}^{S_i+S_j-d_j} f_i(d_i)dd_i \right] f_j(d_j)dd_j \\
&= F_i(S_i) + \int_{d_j=0}^{S_j} [F_i(S_i + S_j - d_j) - F_i(S_i)]f_j(d_j)dd_j \\
&= F_i(S_i) + \int_{d_j=0}^{S_j} F_i(S_i + S_j - d_j)f_j(d_j)dd_j - F_i(S_i)F_j(S_j) \tag{6.13}
\end{aligned}
$$

Now, differentiating (6.8) with respect to S_i using Leibniz's rule (C.19) gives

$$\frac{\partial E[Y_{ji}]}{\partial S_i} = F_i(S_i)F_j(S_j) - \int_{d_j=0}^{S_j} F_i(S_i + S_j - d_j)f_j(d_j)dd_j. \tag{6.14}$$

Therefore,

$$\alpha_i = \alpha_i^0 - \frac{\partial E[Y_{ji}]}{\partial S_i}, \tag{6.15}$$

but since

$$\frac{\partial E[Y_{ji}]}{\partial S_i} = -\int_{d_j=0}^{S_j} \left[\int_{d_i=S_i}^{S_i+S_j-d_j} f_i(d_i)dd_i \right] f_j(d_j)dd_j < 0,$$

(from (6.13) and (6.14)), we can write (6.15) as

$$\alpha_i = \alpha_i^0 + \left| \frac{\partial E[Y_{ji}]}{\partial S_i} \right|, \tag{6.16}$$

as desired. ∎

Theorem 6.3 *Transshipments increase the type-2 service level at retailer i by the ratio of the expected transshipment quantity from j to i to the expected demand at i; that is,*

$$\beta_i(\mathbf{S}) = \beta_i^0(\mathbf{S}) + \frac{E[Y_{ji}]}{E[D_i]}$$

for $i = 1, 2$.

Proof. Omitted; see Problem 6.7.   ∎

As you might expect, the larger the base-stock levels are, the better the post-transshipment service levels are:

Theorem 6.4 *The type-1 and type-2 service levels (with transshipments) at both i and j are non-decreasing with S_i.*

Proof. Omitted.   ∎

With more than two retailers, transshipment problems become much harder to analyze. It is often true that a base-stock *replenishment* policy is still optimal in this case (Robinson 1990). In general it is difficult to determine the optimal *transshipment* policy, so some authors use heuristic policies such as "grouping" policies in which retailers are divided into groups using some logical rules, and then transshipments are allowed only within groups. Models with a small number of retailers, say 3, usually assume complete pooling, even though this policy may not be strictly optimal. Other transshipment policies are possible, of course—for example, Tagaras (1999) compares complete pooling to a random transshipment policy (in which, for example, we choose randomly between two retailers with positive inventory to ship to a retailer with negative inventory) and a risk-balancing policy (which tries to account for the risk of stockout in at least the next period). Fortunately, it is usually true that a base-stock replenishment policy is optimal even if a non-optimal transshipment policy is used.

Often these models are so complex that even the expected cost cannot be calculated using formulas, and instead must be estimated using simulation. In this case an optimization-by-simulation procedure, such as infinitesimal perturbation analysis (IPA), is used to find the optimal base-stock levels (Herer et al. 2006). One insight to come from these papers is that a small increase in the flexibility with which transshipments are allowed can lead to large decreases in cost. Therefore, more flexible transshipment policies are preferable, even if they are more difficult to analyze and implement.

6.5 INTRODUCTION TO SUPPLY UNCERTAINTY

Supply chains are subject to many types of uncertainty, and many approaches have been proposed for modeling uncertainty in the supply chain. So far, we have primarily considered uncertainty in demand. In this section (and again in Section 8.4), we study models that consider uncertainty in supply; in other words, what happens when a firm's suppliers, or the firm's own facilities, are unreliable.

Supply uncertainty may take a number of forms. These include:

- *Disruptions.* A disruption interrupts the supply of goods at some stage in the supply chain. Disruptions tend to be binary events—either there's a disruption or there isn't. During a disruption, there's generally no supply available. Disruptions may be due to bad weather, natural disasters, strikes, suppliers going out of business, etc.

- *Yield Uncertainty.* Sometimes the quantity that a supplier can provide falls short of the amount ordered; the amount actually supplied is random. This is called yield uncertainty. It can be the result of product defects, or of batch processes in which only a certain percentage of a given batch (the yield) is usable.

- *Lead Time Uncertainty.* Uncertainty in the supply lead time can result from stockouts at the supplier, manufacturing or transit delays, and so on. In this case, the lead time L that figures into many of the models in this book must be treated as a random variable rather than a constant.

In this section we will discuss the first two types of supply uncertainty. We will discuss models for setting inventory levels in the presence of disruptions in Section 6.6 and in the presence of yield uncertainty in Section 6.7. In both sections, we will cover models that are analogous to the classical EOQ and infinite-horizon newsvendor models (the models from Sections 3.2 and 4.4.4). Next we discuss the risk-diversification effect, a supply-uncertainty version of the risk-pooling effect.

In most of the models in this section, we will assume that demand is deterministic. We do this for tractability, but also, more importantly, to highlight the effect of supply uncertainty, in the absence of demand uncertainty.

In some ways, there is no conceptual difference between supply uncertainty and demand uncertainty. After all, having too little supply is the same as having too much demand. A firm might use similar strategies for dealing with the two types of uncertainty, as well—for example, holding safety stock, utilizing multiple suppliers, or improving its forecasts of the uncertain events. But, as we will see, the ways in which we model these two types of uncertainty, and the insights we get from these models, can be quite different. (For more on this issue, see Snyder and Shen (2006).)

For reviews of the literature on disruptions, see Snyder et al. (2010) and Vakharia and Yenipazarli (2008), and for yield uncertainty, see Yano and Lee (1995) and Grosfeld Nir and Gerchak (2004). For an overview of models with lead-time uncertainty, see Zipkin (2000).

6.6 INVENTORY MODELS WITH DISRUPTIONS

Disruptions are usually modeled using a two-state Markov process in which one state represents the supplier operating normally and the other represents a disruption.

These states may be known as up/down, wet/dry, on/off, normal/disrupted, and so on. (We'll use the terms up/down.) Not surprisingly, continuous-review models (such as the one in Section 6.6.1) use continuous-time Markov chains (CTMCs) while periodic-review models (Section 6.6.2) use discrete-time Markov chains (DTMCs). The time between disruptions, and the length of disruptions, are therefore exponentially or geometrically distributed (in the case of CTMCs and DTMCs, respectively). The models presented here assume the inventory manager knows the state of the supplier at all times.

Some papers also consider more general disruption processes than the ones we consider here—for example, non-stationary disruption probabilities (Snyder and Tomlin 2006) or partial disruptions (Güllü et al. 1999). These disruption processes can also usually be modeled using Markov processes.

6.6.1   The EOQ Model with Disruptions

6.6.1.1   Problem Statement   Consider the classical EOQ model with fixed order cost K and holding cost h per unit per year. The demand rate is d units per year (a change from our notation in Section 3.2). Suppose that the supplier is not perfectly reliable—that it functions normally for a certain amount of time (an up interval) and then shuts down for a certain amount of time (a down interval). The transitions between these intervals are governed by a continuous-time Markov chain (CTMC). During down intervals, no orders can be placed, and if the retailer runs out of inventory during a down interval, all demands observed until the beginning of the next up interval are lost, with a stockout cost of p per lost sale. Both types of intervals last for a random amount of time. Every order placed by the retailer is for the same fixed quantity Q. Our goal is to *choose Q to minimize the expected annual cost.*

This problem, which is known as the *EOQ with disruptions* (EOQD), was first introduced by Parlar and Berkin (1991), but their analysis contained two errors that rendered their model incorrect. A correct model was presented by Berk and Arreola-Risa (1994), whose treatment we follow here.

Let X and Y be the duration of a given up and down interval, respectively. X and Y are exponentially distributed random variables, X with rate λ and Y with rate μ. (Recall that if $X \sim \exp(\lambda)$, then $f(x) = \lambda e^{-\lambda x}$, $F(x) = 1 - e^{-\lambda x}$, and $E[X] = 1/\lambda$.) The parameters λ and μ are called the *disruption rate* and *recovery rate*, respectively. These are the transition rates for the CTMC.

The EOQ inventory curve now looks something like Figure 6.3. Note that the inventory position never becomes negative because excess demands are lost, not backordered. The time between successful orders is called a *cycle*. The length of a cycle, T, is a random variable. If the supplier is in an up interval when the inventory level reaches 0, then $T = Q/d$, otherwise, $T > Q/d$.

Note: In the EOQ, we ignored the per-unit ordering cost c because the annual per-unit cost is independent of Q (since d units are ordered every year, regardless of Q). It is not strictly correct to ignore c in the EOQD because, in the face of lost sales, the number of units ordered each year may not equal d, and in fact it depends on Q. Nevertheless, we will ignore c for tractability reasons.

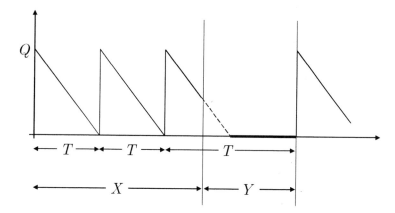

Figure 6.3   EOQ inventory curve with disruptions.

6.6.1.2   *Expected Cost*   Let ψ be the probability that the supplier is in a down interval when the inventory level hits 0. One can show that

$$\psi = \frac{\lambda}{\lambda + \mu}\left(1 - e^{-\frac{(\lambda+\mu)Q}{d}}\right). \tag{6.17}$$

Let $f(t)$ be the pdf of T, the time between successful orders. Then

$$f(t) = \begin{cases} 0, & \text{if } t < Q/d \\ 1 - \psi, & \text{if } t = Q/d \\ \psi\mu e^{-\mu(t-Q/d)}, & \text{if } t > Q/d. \end{cases}$$

Note that $f(t)$ has an atom at Q/d and is continuous afterwards.

Each cycle lasts at least Q/d years. After that, with probability $1 - \psi$, it lasts an additional 0 years, and with probability ψ, it lasts, on average, an additional $1/\mu$ years (because of the memoryless property of the exponential distribution). Therefore, the expected length of a cycle is given by

$$E[T] = \frac{Q}{d} + \frac{\psi}{\mu}. \tag{6.18}$$

We're interested in finding an expression for the expected cost per year. It's difficult to write an expression for this cost directly. On the other hand, we can calculate the expected cost of one cycle, as well as the expected length of a cycle. Moreover, the system state is always the same at the beginning of each cycle—we have Q units on hand, and the supplier is in an up interval. In situations like these, the well-known *Renewal Reward Theorem* is helpful. (See, e.g., Ross (1995).) In particular, the Renewal Reward Theorem tells us that the expected cost per year, $g(Q)$, is given by

$$g(Q) = \frac{E[\text{cost per cycle}]}{E[\text{cycle length}]}. \tag{6.19}$$

The denominator is given by (6.18); it remains to find an expression for the numerator.

In each cycle we place exactly one order, incurring a fixed cost of K. The inventory in a given cycle is positive for exactly Q/d years (regardless of whether there's a disruption), so the holding cost is based on the area of one triangle in Figure 6.3, namely $Q^2/2d$. Finally, we incur a penalty cost if the supplier is in a down interval when the inventory level hits 0. This happens with probability ψ, and if it does happen, the expected remaining duration of the down interval is $1/\mu$. Therefore, the expected stockout cost per cycle is $pd\psi/\mu$. Then the total expected cost per cycle is

$$K + \frac{hQ^2}{2d} + \frac{pd\psi}{\mu}. \tag{6.20}$$

We can use (6.18)–(6.20) to derive the expected cost per year; the result is stated in the next proposition.

Proposition 6.1 *In the EOQD, the expected cost per year is given by*

$$g(Q) = \frac{K + hQ^2/2d + pd\psi/\mu}{Q/d + \psi/\mu}. \tag{6.21}$$

6.6.1.3   *Solution Method*   Remember that ψ is a function of Q, and in fact it's a pretty messy function of Q. Therefore, (6.21) can't be solved in closed form—that is, we can't take a derivative, set it equal to 0, and solve for Q. Instead, it must be solved numerically using line search techniques such as bisection search. These techniques rely on $g(Q)$ having certain nice properties like convexity. Unfortunately, it is not known whether $g(Q)$ is convex with respect to Q, but it is known that $g(Q)$ is *quasiconvex* in Q. A quasiconvex function has only one local minimum, which is a sufficient condition for most line search techniques to work.

There's nothing wrong with solving the EOQD numerically, insofar as the algorithm for doing so is quite efficient. On the other hand, it's desirable to have a closed-form solution for it for two main reasons. One is that we may want to embed the EOQD into some larger model rather than implementing it as-is. (See, e.g., Qi et al. (2010).) Doing so may require a closed-form expression for the optimal solution or the optimal cost. The other reason is that we can often get insights from closed-form solutions that we can't get from solutions we have to obtain numerically.

Although we can't get an exact solution for the EOQD in closed form, we can get an approximate one. In particular, Snyder (2009) approximates ψ by ignoring the exponential term:

$$\hat{\psi} = \frac{\lambda}{\lambda + \mu}. \tag{6.22}$$

$\hat{\psi}$ is the probability that the supplier is in a down interval at an arbitrary point in time. But ψ refers to a specific point in time, i.e., the point when the inventory level hits 0, and the term $(1 - e^{-(\lambda+\mu)Q/d})$ in the definition of ψ accounts for the knowledge that, when this happens, we were in an up interval as recently as Q/d years ago.

By replacing ψ with $\hat{\psi}$, then, we are essentially assuming that the system approaches steady state quickly enough that when the inventory level hits 0, we can ignore this bit of knowledge, i.e., ignore the transient nature of the system at this moment. The approximation is most effective, then, when cycles tend to be long; e.g., when Q/d is large. If Q/d is large, then $(\lambda + \mu)Q/d$ is large, $e^{-(\lambda+\mu)Q/d}$ is small, and $\hat{\psi} \approx \psi$. The approximation tends to be quite tight for reasonable values of the parameters.

The advantage of using $\hat{\psi}$ in place of ψ is that the resulting expected cost function no longer has any exponential terms, and we can set its derivative to 0 and solve for Q in closed form. This allows us to perform some of the same analysis on the EOQD that we do on the EOQ—for example, we can perform sensitivity analysis, develop worst-case bounds for power-of-two policies, and so on. It also allows an examination of the cost of using the classical EOQ solution when disruptions are possible; as it happens, the cost of this error can be quite large.

6.6.2   The Newsvendor Problem with Disruptions

In this section we consider the infinite-horizon newsvendor problem of Section 4.4.4, except that in place of demand uncertainty we have supply uncertainty, in the form of disruptions. We know from Section 4.4.4 that in the case of demand uncertainty, a base-stock policy is optimal, with the optimal base-stock level given by

$$S^* = \mu + \sigma\Phi^{-1}\left(\frac{p}{p+h}\right) \qquad (6.23)$$

(if demand is normally distributed and $\gamma = 1$). We will see that the optimal solution for the problem with supply uncertainty has a remarkably similar form.

The model we discuss below can be viewed as a special case of models introduced by Güllü et al. (1997) and by Tomlin (2006). Elements of our analysis are adapted from Tomlin (2006) and from the unabridged version of that paper (Tomlin 2005). Some of the analysis can also be found in Schmitt et al. (2010b).

6.6.2.1   Problem Statement   As in Section 6.6.1 on the EOQD, we assume that demand is deterministic; it's equal to d units per period. (d need not be an integer.) On-hand inventory and backorders incur costs of h and p per unit per period, respectively. There is no lead time. The sequence of events is identical to that described in Section 4.4, except that in step 2, no order is placed if the supplier is disrupted.

The probability that the supplier is disrupted in the next period depends on its state in the current period. In other words, the disruption process follows a two-state discrete-time Markov chain (DTMC). Let

$$\alpha = P(\text{down next period}|\text{up this period})$$
$$1 - \beta = P(\text{down next period}|\text{down this period}).$$

We refer to α as the *disruption probability* and β as the *recovery probability*. These are the transition probabilities for the DTMC. The up and down periods both constitute geometric processes, and these processes are the discrete-time analogues to the continuous-time up/down processes in Section 6.6.1.

Given the transition probabilities α and β, we can solve the Chapman-Kolmogorov equations to derive the steady-state probabilities of being in an up or down state as:

$$\pi_u = \frac{\beta}{\alpha + \beta} \tag{6.24}$$

$$\pi_d = \frac{\alpha}{\alpha + \beta} \tag{6.25}$$

It turns out to be convenient to work with a more granular Markov chain that indicates not only whether the supplier is in an up or down period, but also how long the current down interval has lasted. In particular, state n in this Markov chain represents being in a down interval that has lasted for n consecutive periods. If $n = 0$, we are in an up period.

Let π_n be the steady-state probability that the supplier is in a disruption that has lasted n periods. Furthermore, define

$$F(n) = \sum_{i=0}^{n} \pi_n. \tag{6.26}$$

$F(n)$ is the cdf of this process and represents the steady-state probability that the supplier is in a disruption that has lasted n periods or fewer (including the probability that it is not disrupted at all). These probabilities are given explicitly in the following lemma, but often, we will ignore the explicit form of the probabilities and just use π_n and $F(n)$ directly.

Lemma 6.1 *If the disruption probability is α and the recovery probability is β, then*

$$\pi_0 = \frac{\beta}{\alpha + \beta}$$

$$\pi_n = \frac{\alpha\beta}{\alpha + \beta}(1 - \beta)^{n-1}, \quad n \geq 1$$

$$F(n) = 1 - \frac{\alpha}{\alpha + \beta}(1 - \beta)^n, \quad n \geq 0.$$

Proof. Omitted; see Problem 6.14. ∎

6.6.2.2 Form of the Optimal Policy

Our objective is to make inventory decisions to minimize the expected holding and stockout cost per period. What type of inventory policy should we use? It turns out that a base-stock policy is optimal for this problem:

Theorem 6.5 *A base-stock policy is optimal in each period of the infinite-horizon newsvendor problem with deterministic demand and stochastic supply disruptions.*

We omit the proof of Theorem 6.5; it follows from a much more general theorem proved by Song and Zipkin (1996). Note that a base-stock policy works somewhat differently in this problem than in previous problems, since we might not be able to order up to the base-stock level in every period—in particular, we can't order *anything* during down periods. So a base-stock policy means that we order up to the base-stock level during up periods and order nothing during down periods. The extra inventory during up periods is meant to protect us against down periods.

6.6.2.3 Expected Cost   Suppose the supplier is in state $n = 0$; that is, an up period. If we order up to a base-stock level of S at the beginning of the period, we incur a cost at the end of the period of

$$h(S - d)^+ + p(d - S)^+. \tag{6.27}$$

In state $n = 1$, we incur a cost of

$$h(S - 2d)^+ + p(2d - S)^+, \tag{6.28}$$

and in general, we incur a cost of

$$h\left[S - (n + 1)d\right]^+ + p\left[(n + 1)d - S\right]^+ \tag{6.29}$$

in state n, for $n = 0, 1, \ldots$,

Therefore, the expected holding and stockout costs per period can be expressed as a function of S as follows:

$$g(S) = \sum_{n=0}^{\infty} \pi_n \left[h\left[S - (n + 1)d\right]^+ + p\left[(n + 1)d - S\right]^+\right]. \tag{6.30}$$

In addition, we can say the following:

Lemma 6.2 *The optimal base-stock level S^* is an integer multiple of d.*

Proof (sketch). The proof follows from the fact that g is a piecewise-linear function of S, with breakpoints at multiples of d.   ∎

Normally, we would find the optimal S by taking a derivative of $g(S)$, but since S is discrete (by Lemma 6.2), we need to use a *finite difference* instead. A finite difference is very similar to a derivative except that, instead of measuring the change in the function as the variable changes infinitesimally, it measures the change as the variable changes by one unit. In particular, S^* is the smallest S such that $\Delta g(S) \geq 0$, where

$$\Delta g(S) = g(S + d) - g(S). \tag{6.31}$$

(Normally, we would define $\Delta g(S)$ as $g(S + 1) - g(S)$, but since S can only take on values that are multiples of d, it's sufficient to define $\Delta g(S)$ as in (6.31).)

$$\Delta g(S) = g(S + d) - g(S)$$

$$= \sum_{n=0}^{\infty} \pi_n \left[h\,[S - nd]^+ + p\,[nd - S]^+ \right.$$
$$\left. - h\,[S - (n+1)d]^+ - p\,[(n+1)d - S]^+ \right]$$

Now,

$$[S - nd]^+ - [S - (n+1)d]^+ = \begin{cases} d, & \text{if } n < \frac{S}{d} \\ 0, & \text{otherwise} \end{cases}$$

and

$$[nd - S]^+ - [(n+1)d - S]^+ = \begin{cases} -d, & \text{if } n \geq \frac{S}{d} \\ 0, & \text{otherwise.} \end{cases}$$

Therefore,

$$\Delta g(S) = d \left[h \sum_{n=0}^{\frac{S}{d}-1} \pi_n - p \sum_{n=\frac{S}{d}}^{\infty} \pi_n \right]$$
$$= d \left[hF\left(\frac{S}{d} - 1\right) - p\left(1 - F\left(\frac{S}{d} - 1\right)\right) \right]$$
$$= d \left[(h + p)F\left(\frac{S}{d} - 1\right) - p \right],$$

where F is as defined in (6.26). Then S^* is the smallest multiple of d such that

$$(h + p)F\left(\frac{S}{d} - 1\right) - p \geq 0 \qquad (6.32)$$

$$\Longleftrightarrow S \geq d + dF^{-1}\left(\frac{p}{p + h}\right). \qquad (6.33)$$

The notation in (6.33) is a little sloppy since $F^{-1}(\gamma)$ only exists if γ happens to be one of the discrete values that $F(n)$ can take. If $p/(p + h)$ is not one of these values, then (6.32) implies it is always optimal to "round up." Interpreted this way, $F^{-1}(\gamma)$ is an integer for all γ, the right-hand side of (6.33) is automatically a multiple of d, and we can drop the "smallest multiple of d" language and replace the inequality in (6.33) with an equality.

We have now proved the following:

Theorem 6.6 *In the infinite-horizon newsvendor problem with deterministic demand and stochastic supply disruptions, the optimal base-stock level is given by*

$$S^* = d + dF^{-1}\left(\frac{p}{p + h}\right), \qquad (6.34)$$

where F is as defined in (6.26).

Notice that the optimal base-stock level under supply uncertainty has a very similar structure to that under demand uncertainty, as given in (6.23). First, it uses the familiar newsvendor critical fractile $p/(p + h)$, but here the inverse cdf F refers not to the demand distribution but to the supply distribution.

Second, the right-hand side of (6.34) has a natural cycle stock–safety stock interpretation, just like in the demand uncertainty case. Here, d is the cycle stock—the inventory to meet this period's demand—and $dF^{-1}(\gamma)$, where $\gamma = p/(p + h)$, is the safety stock—the inventory to protect against uncertainty (in this case, supply uncertainty).[1]

Just like in the demand-uncertainty case, the optimal solution specifies what fractile of the distribution we should protect against. Here, we should have enough inventory to protect against any disruption whose length is no more than $F^{-1}(\gamma)$ periods. The probability of a given period being in a disruption that has lasted longer than this is $1 - \gamma$, so, as in the demand-uncertainty case, the type-1 service level is given by γ. As usual, the base-stock level increases with p and decreases with h.

6.7 INVENTORY MODELS WITH YIELD UNCERTAINTY

In some cases, the number of items received from the supplier may not equal the number ordered. This may happen because of stockouts or machine failures at the supplier, or because the production process is subject to defects. The quantity actually received is called the *yield*. If the yield is deterministic—e.g., we always receive 80% of our order size—then the problem is easy: we just multiply our order size by $1/0.8 = 1.25$. More commonly, however, there is a significant amount of uncertainty in the yield. The optimal solution under *yield uncertainty* generally involves increasing the order quantity, as under imperfect but deterministic yield, but it should account for the variability in yield, not just the mean—just as in the case of demand uncertainty.

In the sources of yield uncertainty mentioned above, we'd expect that the actual yield should always be less than or equal to the order quantity—we shouldn't receive more than we order. But yield uncertainty can also occur in batch production processes—e.g., for chemicals or pharmaceuticals. In this case, it's not a matter of items being "defective," but rather of not knowing in advance precisely how much usable product will result from the process. In this case, the amount received may be more than the amount expected, and we can't necessarily place an upper bound on the yield.

In this section, we consider how to set inventory levels under yield uncertainty. As in Section 6.6, we consider both a continuous-review setting, based on the EOQ model, and a periodic-review setting, based on the newsvendor problem. As before, we will assume that demand is deterministic.

There are many ways to model yield uncertainty. We will consider two that are intuitive and tractable.

The first is an *additive yield* model in which we assume that if an order of size Q is placed, then the yield (the amount received) equals $Q + Y$. Y is a continuous

---

[1] In earlier chapters we used $\alpha = p/(p + h)$; here we use γ since α has a new meaning in this section.

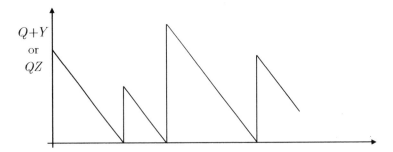

Figure 6.4   EOQ inventory curve with yield uncertainty.

random variable with pdf f_Y and cdf F_Y. Y need not be normal, or even symmetric. Y might be bounded from above by 0 if the yield can never exceed the order quantity; in this case, it might have an "atom" at 0 (otherwise the yield would equal 100% with 0 probability). Typically the yield distribution is truncated at $-Q$ (since we can't receive a negative amount), but we'll use $-\infty$ as its lower bound, primarily because it's inconvenient to have the yield distribution depend on the order size.

The second approach is a *multiplicative yield* approach in which the yield is given as QZ, where Z is a continuous, non-negative random variable with pdf f_Z and cdf F_Z. Again, Z need not be symmetric. If the yield cannot exceed Q, then $Z \leq 1$.

In both cases, we assume that the yield distribution (f_Y or f_Z) does not depend on Q. This assumption may or may not be realistic; it is made primarily for mathematical convenience.

6.7.1   The EOQ Model with Yield Uncertainty

6.7.1.1   Problem Statement   The setup for this problem is just like the EOQ model, except that if an order is placed for Q units, the actual number of units received may differ from Q. Unlike the EOQD in Section 6.6.1, the supplier never experiences down intervals, so it's always possible to place an order, even if the quantity delivered falls short of the quantity ordered. That means that, unlike the EOQD, we never have stockouts in the EOQ with yield uncertainty. (See Figure 6.4.)

As in the EOQD, we'll derive the expected cost per year as a function of Q using the Renewal Reward Theorem. Here, we can define a renewal cycle simply as the time between orders. We need to derive expressions for the expected cost per cycle and the expected cycle length.

6.7.1.2   Additive Yield   Let's first consider the additive yield approach, in which the yield is given by $Q + Y$. In each cycle, we place exactly one order, so the fixed order cost is given by K. The expected holding cost is given by h times the area of one triangle in Figure 6.4, but these triangles have varying heights and widths. In particular, if the yield is $Q + Y$, then the holding cost is $h(Q + Y)^2/2d$. Therefore, the expected cost per cycle is given by

$$
\begin{aligned}
K + \int_{-\infty}^{\infty} \frac{h}{2d}(Q+y)^2 f_Y(y)dy &= K + \frac{h}{2d}\left[Q^2 \int_{-\infty}^{\infty} f_Y(y)dy \right.\\
&\qquad\left. + 2Q \int_{-\infty}^{\infty} y f_Y(y)dy + \int_{-\infty}^{\infty} y^2 f_Y(y)dy \right]\\
&= K + \frac{h}{2d}\left[Q^2 + 2QE[Y] + E[Y^2] \right]\\
&= K + \frac{h}{2d}\left[Q^2 + 2QE[Y] + \mathrm{Var}[Y] + E[Y]^2 \right]\\
&= K + \frac{h}{2d}\left[(Q + E[Y])^2 + \mathrm{Var}[Y] \right]. \qquad (6.35)
\end{aligned}
$$

The expected cycle length is given by

$$
\frac{Q + E[Y]}{d}. \qquad (6.36)
$$

Using the Renewal Reward Theorem, the total expected cost per year is then

$$
g(Q) = \frac{2Kd + h\left[(Q+E[Y])^2 + \mathrm{Var}[Y]\right]}{2(Q+E[Y])} = \frac{2Kd + h\mathrm{Var}[Y]}{2(Q+E[Y])} + \frac{h(Q+E[Y])}{2}. \qquad (6.37)
$$

$g(Q)$ is clearly convex with respect to Q, so we can find a minimum by setting its derivative to 0:

$$
\begin{aligned}
\frac{dg}{dQ} &= -\frac{2Kd + h\mathrm{Var}[Y]}{2(Q+E[Y])^2} + \frac{h}{2} = 0\\
&\implies h(Q+E[Y])^2 = 2Kd + h\mathrm{Var}[Y]\\
&\implies Q + E[Y] = \sqrt{\frac{2Kd + h\mathrm{Var}[Y]}{h}}\\
&\implies Q^* = \sqrt{\frac{2Kd}{h} + \mathrm{Var}[Y]} - E[Y]
\end{aligned}
$$

Note that if $\mathrm{Var}[Y] = 0$ (i.e., the yield differs from the order quantity but is no longer uncertain), then the solution is equivalent to the classical EOQ solution shifted by $E[Y]$—i.e., order $\sqrt{2Kd/h}$, but if we will always receive 20 units fewer than we order ($E[Y] = -20$), then add 20 units to our order. If, in addition $E[Y] = 0$, then we have the EOQ solution precisely.

Notice also that the optimal solution does not depend on the *distribution* of Y, only its first two moments. The optimal order quantity increases with $\mathrm{Var}[Y]$ but decreases with $E[Y]$, since we need to over-order less if the additive term is greater.

6.7.1.3 Multiplicative Yield Now consider the multiplicative yield approach, in which the yield is given by QZ. In analogy to (6.35), the expected cost per cycle is

$$
K + \frac{hQ^2}{2d} \int_0^{\infty} z^2 f_Z(z)dz. \qquad (6.38)
$$

Similarly, the expected cycle length is $QE[Z]/d$, so the expected cost per year is

$$g(Q) = \frac{2Kd + hQ^2 \int_0^\infty z^2 f_Z(z)dz}{2QE[Z]}$$

$$= \frac{Kd}{QE[Z]} + \frac{hQ(\text{Var}[Z] + E[Z]^2)}{2E[Z]}. \tag{6.39}$$

Again, we take a derivative with respect to Q:

$$\frac{dg}{dQ} = -\frac{Kd}{Q^2 E[Z]} + \frac{h(\text{Var}[Z] + E[Z]^2)}{2E[Z]} = 0$$

$$\Longrightarrow Q^* = \sqrt{\frac{2Kd}{h(\text{Var}[Z] + E[Z]^2)}}$$

As in the additive yield case, the optimal solution reduces to the EOQ solution, scaled by $E[Z]$, if $\text{Var}[Z] = 0$. If, in addition, $E[Z] = 1$, then we have the EOQ solution exactly.

Here, too, the optimal solution depends only on the first two moments of Z, not its distribution. As before, Q^* decreases with $E[Z]$, but here it also decreases with $\text{Var}[Y]$. This is somewhat strange behavior. The explanation lies in what Yano and Lee (1995) call the "portfolio effect," which basically means that if the yield is very variable, it's preferable to use smaller batches to increase our chances of getting a "good" batch the next time.

6.7.2 The Newsvendor Problem with Yield Uncertainty

6.7.2.1 *Problem Statement*   Next we consider the same newsvendor-type problem as in Section 6.6.2, except that the supplier suffers from yield uncertainty rather than disruptions. As before, we assume that the demand is deterministic and equal to d per period.

We consider only the additive yield model. (The multiplicative yield model is significantly more complex.)

6.7.2.2 *Additive Yield*   If we choose a base-stock level of S, then we have $S+Y$ on hand after the shipment arrives but before demand is realized, and the inventory level at the end of the period is $(S + Y - d)$. This inventory level is positive if $Y > d - S$ and negative otherwise. Therefore, the expected cost per period is given by

$$g(S) = h \int_{d-S}^\infty ((S+y) - d) f_Y(y)dy + p \int_{-\infty}^{d-S} (d - (S+y)) f_Y(y)dy. \tag{6.40}$$

We can convert this to a newsvendor function by letting $R \equiv d - S$. ($-R$ represents the safety stock: the amount ordered in excess of the demand to protect against yield uncertainty.) Equation (6.40) can then be written as

$$g(R) = p \int_{-\infty}^R (R - y) f_Y(y)dy + h \int_R^\infty (y - R) f_Y(y)dy. \tag{6.41}$$

This equation is identical in form to (4.21) (but note the reversal of the cost coefficients). Therefore, using (4.27) we know that

$$R^* = F^{-1}\left(\frac{h}{h+p}\right),$$

so

$$S^* = d - F^{-1}\left(\frac{h}{h+p}\right).$$
(6.42)

Note that the critical ratio has h in the numerator, not p.

If Y is normally distributed, then

$$S^* = d - \left[E[Y] + \Phi^{-1}\left(\frac{h}{h+p}\right)\sqrt{\mathrm{Var}[Y]}\right].$$

Again, S^* decreases with $E[Y]$. Since $h < p$ (typically), $\Phi^{-1}(h/(h+p)) < 0$, so, like the EOQ model with additive yield in Section 6.7.1.2, S^* increases with $\mathrm{Var}[Y]$.

6.8 THE RISK-DIVERSIFICATION EFFECT

6.8.1 Problem Statement

Consider the N-DC system described in Section 6.2, except that now the demand is deterministic and equal to d per period ($\mu_i = d$, $\sigma_i^2 = 0$ for all i) but the supply may be disrupted. All DCs follow a periodic-review base-stock policy, as in Section 6.6.2. Disruptions follow the same two-state Markov process described in Section 6.6.2, with disruption probability α and recovery probability β. As before, π_n is the pmf of the disruption process and $F(n)$ is the cdf.

The central question is, would it be preferable to consolidate the N DCs into a single DC? That is, is a centralized system preferable to a decentralized one? It turns out that the decentralized system is preferable in this case, but not because it has a lower expected cost. In fact, the two systems have the *same* expected cost, but the decentralized system has a lower variance. Therefore, risk-averse decision makers would prefer the decentralized system.

This phenomenon—whereby the cost variance (but not the mean cost) is smaller when inventory is held at a decentralized set of locations—is called the *risk-diversification effect*. Intuitively, it occurs because a given DC (or its portion of the central DC) is disrupted the same number of times, on average, in both systems, but disruptions are more severe in the centralized system. The supply chain benefits by not having all its eggs in one basket. The risk-diversification effect was first described by Snyder and Shen (2006), who demonstrated it using simulation; the theoretical analysis in this section is based on Schmitt et al. (2010a).

Note the parallels to the risk-pooling effect: Whereas the risk-pooling effect says that the mean cost (but not the variance (Schmitt et al. 2010a)) is lower in a centralized system under demand uncertainty, the risk-diversification effect says that the cost variance is lower (and the mean cost is equal) in a decentralized system under supply uncertainty.

In fact, Snyder and Shen (2006) comment that supply uncertainty often has a mirror-image effect in relation to demand uncertainty, and that the optimal strategy under one type of uncertainty is often the exact opposite of that under the other type of uncertainty. The risk-diversification effect is an example of this mirror-image phenomenon, in the sense that supply chains under supply uncertainty behave in the opposite way to the ways we've observed them behaving previously, under demand uncertainty.

6.8.2   Notation

For a given base-stock level S, let $E[C]$ and $\mathrm{Var}[C]$ be the mean and variance of the optimal cost. ($E[C]$ has the same meaning as $g(S)$ in Section 6.6.2.) We'll use subscripts D and C to refer to the costs in the decentralized and centralized systems, respectively, and no subscript when we're discussing a single-stage system. Asterisks denote optimal solutions.

6.8.3   Optimal Solution

The optimal base-stock level for a single-stage newsvendor system with disruptions is given by Theorem 6.6:

$$S^* = d + dF^{-1}\left(\frac{p}{p+h}\right). \tag{6.43}$$

(Remember that most of the time, $F^{-1}(p/(p+h))$ does not exist since F is a discrete distribution; in these cases, we "round up.")

Now, in the decentralized system, each DC acts like a single-stage system, so the optimal base-stock level at each DC is $S_D^* = S^*$, where S^* is given by (6.43). In the centralized system, the warehouse acts as a single stage facing a demand of Nd. Therefore, its optimal base-stock level is

$$S_C^* = Nd + NdF^{-1}\left(\frac{p}{p+h}\right) = NS_D^* = NS^*.$$

Thus, the total inventory is the same in both the centralized and decentralized systems. (In contrast, the total inventory is smaller in the centralized system under the risk-pooling effect, assuming $h < p$.)

6.8.4   Mean and Variance of Optimal Cost

Next we examine the mean and variance of the cost when we use the optimal base-stock levels in each system. In the decentralized system, since each DC acts like a single-stage system, the total expected cost is just N times the total expected cost in a single-stage system: $E[C_D] = NE[C]$. In the centralized system, the optimal cost at the warehouse is obtained by substituting NS^* in place of S and Nd in place of d in (6.30):

$$E[C_C] = \sum_{n=0}^{\infty} \pi_n \left[h(NS^* - (n+1)Nd)^+ + p((n+1)Nd - NS^*)^+ \right]$$

$$= N \sum_{n=0}^{\infty} \pi_n \left[h(S^* - (n+1)d)^+ + p((n+1)d - S^*)^+ \right]$$

$$= NE[C] = E[C_D] \tag{6.44}$$

Therefore, the expected cost is the same in the centralized and decentralized systems when we set the base-stock levels optimally in each. In both systems, each DC experiences disruption-related stockouts in the same percentage of periods. Moreover, during non-disrupted periods, the two systems have the same amount of inventory. Therefore, the optimal expected cost is the same in both systems.

Rather than improving the mean cost, decentralization improves the cost variance. Intuitively, this is because disruptions in the centralized system are less frequent but more severe, and therefore they cause greater variability. To prove this mathematically, first note that

$$\text{Var}[C_D] = N\text{Var}[C] \tag{6.45}$$

because the decentralized system consists of N individual single-stage systems. Recall that $\text{Var}[X] = E[X^2] - E[X]^2$ and note that, for a single-stage system,

$$E[C^2] = \sum_{n=0}^{\infty} \pi_n \left[h^2 \left((S^* - (n+1)d)^+ \right)^2 + p^2 \left(((n+1)d - S^*)^+ \right)^2 \right]. \tag{6.46}$$

Similarly, in the centralized system,

$$E[(C_C)^2] = \sum_{n=0}^{\infty} \pi_n \left[h^2 \left(NS^* - (n+1)Nd)^+ \right)^2 + p^2 \left((n+1)Nd - NS^*)^+ \right)^2 \right]$$

$$= N^2 \sum_{n=0}^{\infty} \pi_n \left[h^2 \left(S^* - (n+1)d)^+ \right)^2 + p^2 \left((n+1)d - S^*)^+ \right)^2 \right]$$

$$= N^2 E[(C)^2] \tag{6.47}$$

Then the variance in the centralized system is given by

$$\begin{aligned}
\text{Var}[C_C] &= E[(C_C)^2] - E[C_C]^2 \\
&= N^2 E[(C)^2] - (NE[C])^2 \text{ (by (6.47) and (6.44))} \\
&= N^2 (E[(C)^2] - E[C]^2) \\
&= N^2 \text{Var}[C] \\
&> N\text{Var}[C] = \text{Var}[C_D]
\end{aligned}$$

Therefore, the variance is smaller in the decentralized system—this is the risk-diversification effect. We summarize the preceding results in the following theorem:

Theorem 6.7 *For the decentralized N-DC system with supply disruptions and deterministic demand, and the centralized, single-DC system formed by merging the DCs:*

1. $S_C^* = NS_D^* = NS_C^*$

2. $E[C_C] = E[C_D] = NE[C]$

3. $\text{Var}[C_C] = N\text{Var}[C_D] = N^2\text{Var}[C]$

6.8.5 Supply Disruptions and Stochastic Demand

Suppose now that demand is uncertain, as in Section 6.2. Disruptions are also still present, as in the preceding analysis.

Under demand uncertainty, the risk-pooling effect says that centralization is preferable, while under supply uncertainty, the risk-diversification effect says that decentralization is preferable. So, if both types of uncertainty are present, which strategy is better? We cannot answer this question analytically since the expected cost function cannot be optimized in closed form for either system. Instead, we evaluate the question numerically.

Most decision makers are risk averse—they are willing to sacrifice a certain amount of expected cost in order to reduce the variance of the cost. One way of modeling risk aversion is using a *mean–variance objective*, popularized by Markowitz in the 1950s:

$$(1 - \kappa)E[C] + \kappa\text{Var}[C], \tag{6.48}$$

where $\kappa \in [0, 1]$ is a constant. If κ is small, then the decision maker is fairly risk neutral; the larger κ is, the more risk-averse the decision maker is. Typically κ is less than, say, 0.05.

One can write out $E[C]$ and $\text{Var}[C]$ for the systems with disruptions and demand uncertainty, but we omit the formulas here. Schmitt et al. (2010a) perform a computational study to determine which system is preferable to the risk-averse decision maker. They numerically optimize (6.48) for both the centralized and decentralized systems and determine which system gives the smaller optimal objective value.

They find that the decentralized system is almost always optimal, i.e., that the risk-diversification effect almost always trumps the risk-pooling effect. For example, under a given set of problem parameters, the decentralized system is optimal whenever $\kappa \geq 0.0008$ and $p/(p + h) \geq 0.5$—in other words, whenever the decision maker is even slightly risk averse and the required service level is at least 50%.

PROBLEMS

6.1 **(Risk-Pooling Example)** Three distribution centers (DCs) each face normally distributed demands, with $D_1 \sim N(22, 8^2)$, $D_2 \sim N(19, 4^2)$, and $D_3 \sim N(17, 3^2)$. All three DCs have a holding cost of $h = 1$ and $p = 15$, and all three follow a periodic-review base-stock policy using their optimal base-stock levels.

a) Calculate the expected cost of the decentralized system.

b) Suppose demands are uncorrelated among the three DCs: $\rho_{12} = \rho_{13} = \rho_{23} = 0$. Calculate the expected cost of the centralized system.

c) Suppose $\rho_{12} = \rho_{13} = \rho_{23} = 0.75$. Calculate the expected cost of the centralized system.

d) Suppose $\rho_{12} = 0.75$, $\rho_{13} = \rho_{23} = -0.75$. Calculate the expected cost of the centralized system.

6.2   (**No Soup for You**) A certain New York City soup vendor sells 15 varieties of soup. The number of customers who come to the soup store on a given day has a Poisson distribution with a mean of 250. A given customer has an equal probability of choosing each of the 15 varieties of soup, and if his or her chosen variety of soup is out of stock (no pun intended), he or she will leave without buying any soup.

You may assume (although it is not necessarily a good assumption) that the demands for different varieties of soup are independent; that is, if the demand for variety i is high on one day, that doesn't indicate anything about the demand for variety j.

Every type of soup sells for $5 per bowl, and the ingredients for each bowl of soup cost the soup vendor $1. Any soups (or ingredients) that are unsold at the end of the day must be thrown away.

a) How many ingredients of each variety of soup should the soup vendor buy? What is the restaurant's total expected underage and overage cost for the day?

b) What is the probability that the vendor stocks out of a given variety of soup?

c) Now suppose that the soup vendor wishes to streamline his offerings by reducing the selection to 8 varieties of soup. Assume that the total demand distribution does not change, but now the total demand is divided among 8 soup varieties instead of 15. As before, assume that a customer finding his or her choice of soup unavailable will leave without purchasing anything. Now how many ingredients of each variety of soup should the vendor buy? What is the restaurant's total expected underage and overage cost for the day?

d) In a short paragraph, explain how this problem relates to risk pooling.

Note: You may use the normal approximation to the Poisson distribution, but make sure to specify the parameters you are using.

6.3   (**Mile-High Trash**) On a certain airline, the flight attendants collect trash during flights and deposit it all into a single receptacle. Airline management is thinking about instituting an on-board recycling program in which waste would be divided by the flight attendants and placed into three separate receptacles: one for paper, one for cans and bottles, and one for other trash.

The volume of each of the three types of waste on a given flight is normally distributed. The airline would maintain a sufficient amount of trash-receptacle space on each flight so that the probability that a given receptacle becomes full under the new system is the same as the probability that the single receptacle becomes full under the old system.

Would the new policy require the same amount of space, more space, or less space for trash storage on each flight? Explain your answer in a short paragraph.

6.4 **(Days-of-Supply Policies)** Rather than setting safety stock levels using base-stock or (r, Q) policies, some companies set their safety stock by requiring a certain number of "days of supply" to be on hand at any given time. For example, if the daily demand has a mean of 100 units, the company might aim to keep an extra 7 days of supply, or 700 units, in inventory. This policy uses μ instead of σ to set safety stock levels.

Consider the N-DC system described in Section 6.2.1, with independent demands across DCs ($\rho_{ij} = 0$ for $i \neq j$). You may assume that all DCs are identical: $\mu_i = \mu$ and $\sigma_i = \sigma$ for all i. Assume that μ and σ refer to *weekly* demands, and that orders are placed by the DCs once per week. Finally, assume that each DC follows a days-of-supply policy with k days of supply required to be on hand as safety stock; each DC's order-up-to level is then

$$S = \mu + \frac{k}{7}\mu.$$

a) Prove that the centralized and decentralized systems have the *same amount* of total inventory.

b) Derive expressions for $E[C_D]$ and $E[C_C]$, the total expected costs of the decentralized and centralized systems. Your expressions may *not* involve integrals; they *may* involve the standard normal loss function, $\mathcal{L}(\cdot)$.

  Hint: Since the DCs are not following the optimal stocking policy, the cost is analogous to (4.35), not to (4.37).

c) Prove that $E[C_C] < E[C_D]$.

d) Explain in words how to reconcile parts (a) and (c)—how can the centralized cost be smaller even though the two systems have the same amount of inventory?

6.5 **(Negative Safety Stock)** Consider the N-DC system described in Section 6.2.1, with independent demands across DCs ($\rho_{ij} = 0$). Suppose that the holding cost is greater than the penalty cost: $h > p$.

a) Prove that *negative* safety stock is required at DC i—that the base-stock level is less than the mean demand.

b) Prove that the total inventory (cycle stock and safety stock) required in the decentralized system (each DC operating independently) is *less* than the total inventory required in the centralized system (all DCs pooled into one). (This is the opposite of the result in Section 6.2.)

c) Prove that, despite the result from part (b), the total expected cost of the centralized system is less than that of the decentralized system ($E[C_C] < E[C_D]$).

d) Explain in words how to reconcile parts (b) and (c)—how can it be less expensive to hold more inventory?

6.6   (Rationalizing DVR Models) A certain brand of digital video recorder (DVR) is available in three models, one that holds 40 hours of TV programming, one that holds 80 hours, and one that holds 120 hours. The lifecycle for a given DVR model is short, roughly 1 year. Because of long manufacturing lead times, the company must manufacture all of the units it intends to sell before the DVRs go on the market, and it will not have another opportunity to manufacture more before the end of the products' 1-year life cycles.

Demand for DVRs is highly volatile, and customers are very picky. A customer who wants a given model but finds that it's out of stock will almost never change to a different model—instead, he or she will buy a competitor's product. In this case, the firm incurs both the lost profit and a loss-of-goodwill cost. Moreover, any DVRs that are unsold at the end of the year are taken off the market and destroyed, with no salvage value (or cost).

The three models have the following parameters:

Storage Space	Manufacturing Cost (c_i)	Selling Price (r_i)	Goodwill Cost (g_i)	Mean Annual Demand (μ_i)	SD of Annual Demand (σ_i)
40	80	120	150	40,000	12,000
80	90	150	150	55,000	15,000
120	100	250	150	25,000	8,000

Demands are normally distributed with the parameters specified in the table. Moreover, demands for the 80- and 120-hour models are negatively correlated, with a correlation coefficient of $\rho_{80,120} = -0.4$. (Demands for the 40-hour model are independent of those for the other two models.)

The company is currently designing its three models for next year, and a very smart supply chain manager noticed that although the models sell for different prices, they cost nearly the same amount to manufacture. The manager thus proposed that the firm manufacture only a *single* model, containing 120 hours of storage space. When customers purchase a DVR, they specify how much storage space they'd like it to have (either 40, 80, or 120 hours) and pay the corresponding price, and the unit is activated with that much space. If the customer asks for 40 or 80 hours, the remaining storage space simply goes unused. This change can be made with software rather than hardware and therefore costs very little to make.

a) Let Q_i be the quantity of model i manufactured, $i = 1, \ldots, 3$, if the supply chain manager's proposal is *not* followed. Write the firm's expected profit for model i as a function of Q_i.

b) Find the optimal order quantities Q_i^* and the corresponding total optimal expected profit (for all three models).

c) Let Q be the quantity of the single model manufactured if the manager's proposal *is* followed. Write the firm's total expected profit as a function of Q. Although it is not entirely accurate to do so, you may assume that the expected selling price for the single model is given by a weighted average of the r_i, with weights given by the μ_i.

d) Find the optimal order quantity Q and the corresponding optimal expected profit. Based on this analysis, should the firm follow the manager's suggestion?

e) What other factors should the firm consider before deciding whether to implement the manager's proposal?

6.7   **(Proof of Theorem 6.3)** Prove Theorem 6.3.

6.8   **(Transhipment Simulation)** Build a spreadsheet simulation model for the two-retailer transshipment problem from Section 6.4. Your spreadsheet should include columns for the demand at each location; the inventory at each location at the start of the period, before transshipments, and after transshipments; the amount transshipped; and the costs for the period. Assume that demands are Poisson with mean λ_i per period and that

$$\begin{array}{ll} \lambda_1 = 30 & \lambda_2 = 20 \\ c_1 = 1.2 & c_2 = 1.7 \\ h_1 = 0.6 & h_2 = 0.8 \\ p_1 = 8.0 & p_2 = 8.0 \\ c_{12} = 3.0 & c_{21} = 3.0. \end{array}$$

Use $S_1 = 33$ and $S_2 = 22$ as the base-stock levels, and assume that both retailers begin the simulation with $S_i - \lambda_i$ units on-hand (that is, at the start of period 1, retailer i needs to order λ_i units to bring its inventory position to S_i).

a) Simulate the system for 500 periods and include the first 10 rows of your spreadsheet in your report.

b) Compute the average ordering, transshipment, holding, and penalty costs per period from your simulation.

c) Compute the expected transshipment quantity from retailer 1 to retailer 2 $(E[Y_{12}])$ and the expected ending inventory at retailer 1 $(E[IL_1^+])$ using (6.8) and (6.9). To compute these quantities, you will need to evaluate some integrals numerically.

d) Compare the results from parts (a) and (c). How closely do the simulated and actual quantities match?

e) By trial and error, try to find the values of S_1 and S_2 that minimize the simulated cost. What are the optimal values, and what is the optimal expected cost?

6.9   **(Binary Transshipments)** Consider the transshipment model from Section 6.4, except now suppose the demands are binary. That is, the demands can only equal 0 or 1, and they are governed by a Bernoulli distribution: $D_i = 1$ with probability q_i and $D_i = 0$ with probability $1 - q_i$, for $i = 1, 2$. All of the remaining assumptions from Section 6.4.2 hold.

Your goal in this problem will be to formulate the expected cost and evaluate several feasible values for the base-stock levels (S_1, S_2). Assume that S_i must be an integer.

a) Explain why $S_1^* + S_2^* \leq 2$.

b) For each possible solution (S_1, S_2) below, write the expected values of the state variables Q_i, Y_{ij}, IL_i^+, and IL_i^-, and then write the expected cost $g(S_1, S_2)$.

1. $(S_1, S_2) = (0, 0)$

2. $(S_1, S_2) = (1, 1)$

3. $(S_1, S_2) = (1, 0)$

4. $(S_1, S_2) = (2, 0)$

(The cases in which $(S_1, S_2) = (0, 1)$ or $(0, 2)$ are similar to the cases above, so we'll skip them.)

Hint 1: If $S_i = 0$, that does *not* mean that stage i never orders!

Hint 2: To check your cost functions, we'll tell you the following: If $c_i = h_i = p_i = 1$, $c_{ij} = 3$, and $q_i = 0.5$ for all $i = 1, 2$, then $g(0, 0) = 4$, $g(1, 1) = 2$, $g(1, 0) = 2.25$, and $g(2, 0) = 3$. Note, however, that these parameters do not satisfy the assumptions on page 152.

c) Prove that, if $h_i \leq p_i$ and $q_i \geq 0.5$ for $i = 1, 2$, and if the assumptions on page 152 are satisfied, then $g(0, 0) \geq g(1, 1)$.

d) Find an instance for which $(S_1^*, S_2^*) = (1, 1)$. Your instance must satisfy the assumptions on page 152.

e) Find a *symmetric* instance for which $(S_1^*, S_2^*) = (1, 0)$. Your instance must satisfy the assumptions on page 152. A symmetric instance is one for which the parameters for the two retailers are identical ($c_1 = c_2$, $h_1 = h_2$, etc.). (It's a little surprising that a symmetric instance can produce a non-symmetric solution, but it can.)

f) Prove or disprove the following claim: $g(2, 0) \geq g(1, 1)$ for all instances that satisfy the assumptions on page 152.

6.10 (**EOQD Approximation**) Suppose that, in the EOQD model of Section 6.6.1, we replace ψ (a function of Q) with

$$\hat{\psi} = \frac{\lambda}{\lambda + \mu}$$

(which is independent of Q). Let $\hat{g}$ be the cost function that results from replacing ψ with $\hat{\psi}$ in (6.21). It is known that $\hat{g}$ is convex (you do not need to prove this).

a) Prove that the derivative of $\hat{g}(Q)$ is

$$\hat{g}'(Q) = \frac{\frac{h\mu^2}{2}Q^2 + \hat{\psi}dh\mu Q - (Kd\mu + d^2 p\hat{\psi})\mu}{(Q\mu + \hat{\psi}d)^2}.$$

b) Prove that $\hat{Q}^*$, the Q that minimizes $\hat{g}$, is given by

$$\hat{Q}^* = \frac{-\hat{\psi}dh + \sqrt{(\hat{\psi}dh)^2 + 2hd\mu(K\mu + dp\hat{\psi})}}{h\mu}. \qquad (6.49)$$

6.11   **(Implementing EOQD Approximation)** Consider an instance of the EOQD with $K = 35$, $h = 4$, $p = 22$, $d = 30$, $\lambda = 1$, and $\mu = 12$.

   a) Find Q^* for this instance using optimization software of your choice. Report the expected cost, $g(Q^*)$.

   b) Consider the following heuristic for the EOQD:

   1. Set Q equal to the EOQ.

   2. Calculate ψ using the current value of Q.

   3. Find Q using (6.49) from Problem 6.10, setting $\hat{\psi}$ equal to the current ψ from step 2.

   4. If Q has changed more than ϵ since the previous iteration (for fixed $\epsilon > 0$), then go to 2; otherwise, stop.

   Using this heuristic and any software package you like, find a near-optimal Q using $\epsilon = 10^{-3}$. Report the Q you found, its cost $g(Q)$, and the percentage difference between $g(Q)$ and $g(Q^*)$ from part (a).

6.12   **(Disruption-Prone Bicycle Parts)** A bicycle manufacturer buys a particular cable used in its bicycles from a single supplier located in South America. The manufacturer follows a periodic-review base-stock policy, placing an order with the supplier every week. The supplier occasionally experiences disruptions due to hurricanes, labor actions, and other events. These disruptions follow a Markov process with disruption probability $\alpha = 0.1$ and recovery probability $\beta = 0.4$. When not disrupted, the supplier's lead time is negligible. Cables are used by the manufacturer at a constant rate of 6000 per week. Inventory incurs a holding cost of \$0.002 per cable per week. If the manufacturer runs out of cables, it must delay production, resulting in a cost that amounts to \$0.05 per cable per week.

   a) On average, how many weeks per year is the supplier disrupted? On average, how long does each disruption last?

   b) What is the optimal base-stock level for cables?

6.13   **(Optimal Cost for Base-Stock Policy with Disruptions)** Prove that, in the base-stock problem with disruptions discussed in Section 6.6.2, the optimal cost is given by

$$g(S^*) = d \left[p \sum_{n=R+1}^{\infty} \pi_n n - h \sum_{n=0}^{R} \pi_n n \right],$$

where $R = F^{-1}(p/(p+h))$ and $F(x)$ is as defined in (6.26). You may assume that h and p are set so that $p/(p+h)$ exactly equals one of the possible values of $F(x)$.

6.14   **(Proof of Lemma 6.1)** Prove Lemma 6.1.

6.15   **(Disruptions = Stochastic Demand?)**

   a) Develop a *stochastic demand process* that is equivalent to the *stochastic supply process* in the base-stock model with disruptions from Section 6.6.2.

In particular, formulate a demand distribution such that, if the demand is iid stochastic following your distribution but the supply is deterministic, the expected cost is equal to the expected cost given by (6.30), assuming we order up to the same S in every period. Prove that the two expected costs are equal. Make sure you specify both the possible values of the demand and the probability of each value, i.e., the pmf.

b) In part (a) you proved that, under the optimal solution, the expected cost is the same in both models. Is the entire distribution of the random variable representing the cost also the same in both models?

6.16 **(Random Yield for Steel)** Return to Problem 3.1. Suppose that the amount of steel delivered by the supplier differs randomly from the order quantity, and the auto manufacturer must accept whatever quantity the supplier delivers. Let Q be the order quantity.

a) Suppose the delivery quantity is given by $Q + Y$, where $-Y \sim \exp(0.02)$. What is Q^*?

b) Suppose the delivery quantity is given by QZ, where $Z \sim U[0.8, 1.0]$. What is Q^*?

6.17 **(Staffing Truck Drivers)** The U.S. trucking industry suffers from notoriously high employee turnover, with turnover rates often well in excess of 100% (Paz-Frankel 2006). This makes advance planning difficult since it is difficult to predict how many drivers will be available when needed. Suppose a trucking company needs 25 drivers every day. If the company asks S drivers to report to work on a given day, the number of drivers who actually show up is given by $S + Y$, where $Y \sim U[-5, 0]$. Drivers who report to work but are not needed must still be paid their daily wage of $150. For each driver fewer than 25 that show up, the company will be unable to deliver a load, incurring a cost of $1200. Find S^*, the optimal number of drivers to ask to report to work.

CHAPTER 7

FACILITY LOCATION MODELS

7.1 INTRODUCTION

One of the major strategic decisions faced by firms is the number and locations of factories, warehouses, retailers, or other physical facilities. This is the purview of a large class of models known as *facility location problems*. The key tradeoff in most facility location problems is between the facility cost and customer service. If we open a lot of facilities (Figure 7.1(a)), we incur high facility costs (to build and maintain them) but we can provide good service, since most customers are close to a facility. On the other hand, if we open few facilities (Figure 7.1(b)), we reduce our facility costs but must travel farther to reach our customers (or they to reach us).

Most (but not all) location problems make two related sets of decisions: (1) where to locate, and (2) which customers are assigned or allocated to which facilities. Therefore, facility location problems are also sometimes known as *location–allocation problems*.

A huge range of approaches has been considered for modeling facility location decisions. These differ in terms of how they model facility costs (for example, some include the costs explicitly while others impose a constraint on the number of facilities to be opened) and how they model customer service (for example, some include a

Fundamentals of Supply Chain Theory, First Edition. Lawrence V. Snyder, Zuo-Jun Max Shen.
© 2011 John Wiley & Sons, Inc. Published 2011 by John Wiley & Sons, Inc.

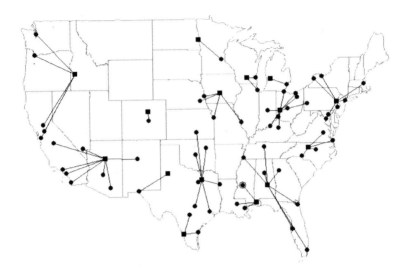

(a) Many facilities open.

(b) Few facilities open.

Figure 7.1   Facility location configurations. Squares represent facilities; circles represent customers.

transportation cost while others require all or most facilities to be *covered*—that is, served by a facility that is within some specified distance). Facility location problems come in a great variety of flavors based on what types of facilities are to be located, whether the facilities are capacitated, which (if any) elements of the problem are stochastic, what topology the facilities may be located on (e.g., on the plane, in a network, or at discrete points), how distances or transportation costs are measured, and so on. Our treatment of facility location will only scratch the surface of this large body of literature. Several excellent textbooks provide additional material for the interested reader; for example, see Mirchandani and Francis (1990), Daskin (1995), Drezner (1995), or Drezner and Hamacher (2002).

In addition to supply chain facilities like plants and warehouses, location models have been applied to public-sector facilities like bus depots and fire stations, as well as to telecommunications hubs, satellite orbits, bank accounts, and other items that are not really "facilities" at all. In addition, many operations research problems can be formulated as facility location problems or have subproblems that resemble them. Facility location problems are often easy to state and formulate but are difficult to solve; this makes them a popular testing ground for new optimization tools. For all of these reasons, facility location problems are an important topic in operations research, and in supply chain management in particular, in both theoretical and applied work.

In this chapter, we will discuss a classical facility location model, the uncapacitated fixed-charge location problem (UFLP). The UFLP and its descendants have been deployed more widely in supply chain management than perhaps any other location model. One reason for this is that the UFLP is very flexible and, although it is NP-hard, lends itself to a variety of effective solution methods. Another reason is that the UFLP includes explicit costs for both key elements of the problem—facilities and customer service—and is therefore well suited to supply chain applications.

In Section 7.2, we discuss the UFLP (including its capacitated cousin in Section 7.2.5). We then discuss a multi-echelon, multi-product extension of the UFLP in Section 7.3.

7.2   THE UNCAPACITATED FIXED-CHARGE LOCATION PROBLEM

7.2.1   Problem Statement

The *uncapacitated fixed-charge location problem* (UFLP) chooses facility locations in order to minimize the total cost of building the facilities and transporting goods from facilities to customers. The UFLP makes location decisions for a single echelon, and the facilities in that echelon are assumed to serve facilities in a downstream echelon, all of whose locations are fixed. We will tend to refer to the facilities in the upstream echelon as *distribution centers* (DCs) or *warehouses* and to those in the downstream echelons as *customers*. However, the model is generic, and the two echelons may instead contain other types of facilities—for example, factories and warehouses, or regional and local DCs, or even fire stations and homes. Sometimes it's also useful to think of an upstream echelon, again with fixed location(s), that serves the DCs.

Each potential DC location has a *fixed cost* that represents building (or leasing) the facility; the fixed cost is independent of the volume that passes through the DC. There is a *transportation cost* per unit of product shipped from a DC to each customer. There is a single product. The DCs have no capacity restrictions—any amount of product can be handled by any DC. (We'll relax this assumption in Section 7.2.5.) The problem is to choose facility locations to minimize the fixed cost of building facilities plus the transportation cost to transport product from DCs to customers, subject to constraints requiring every customer to be served by some open DC.

As noted above, the key tradeoff in the UFLP is between fixed and transportation costs. If too few facilities are open, the fixed cost is small but the transportation cost is large because many customers will be far from their assigned facility. On the other hand, if too many facilities are open, the fixed cost is large but the transportation cost is small. The UFLP tries to find the right balance, and to optimize not only the number of facilities, but also their locations.

7.2.2 Formulation

Define the following notation:

Sets

I = set of customers

J = set of potential facility locations

Parameters

h_i = annual demand of customer $i \in I$

c_{ij} = cost to transport one unit of demand from facility $j \in J$ to customer $i \in I$

f_j = fixed (annual) cost to open a facility at site $j \in J$

Decision Variables

x_j = 1 if facility j is opened, 0 otherwise

y_{ij} = the fraction of customer i's demand that is served by facility j

The transportation costs c_{ij} might be of the form $k \times$ distance for some constant k (if the shipping company charges \$$k$ per mile per unit) or may be more arbitrary (for example, based on airline ticket prices, which are not linearly related to distance). In the former case, distances may be computed in a number of ways:

- *Euclidean Distance*: The distance between (a_1, b_1) and (a_2, b_2) is given by

$$\sqrt{(a_1 - a_2)^2 + (b_1 - b_2)^2}.$$

  This is an intuitive measure of distance but is not usually applicable in supply chain contexts because Cartesian coordinates are not useful for describing real-world locations.

- *Manhattan or Rectilinear Metric*: The distance is given by

$$|a_1 - a_2| + |a_1 - a_2|.$$

This metric assumes that travel is only possible parallel to the x- or y-axis, e.g., travel along city streets.

- *Great Circle*: This method for calculating distances takes into account the curvature of the earth and, more importantly, takes latitudes and longitudes as inputs and returns distances in miles or kilometers. Great circle distances assume that travel occurs over a great circle, the shortest route over the surface of a sphere. Let (α_1, β_1) and (α_2, β_2) be the latitude and longitude of two points, and let $\Delta\alpha \equiv \alpha_1 - \alpha_2$ and $\Delta\beta \equiv \beta_1 - \beta_2$ be the differences in the latitude and longitude (respectively). Then the great-circle distance between the two points is given by

$$2r \arcsin \left(\sqrt{\sin^2 \left(\frac{\Delta\alpha}{2} \right) + \cos\alpha_1 \cos\alpha_2 \sin^2 \left(\frac{\Delta\beta}{2} \right)} \right),$$

where r is the radius of the Earth, approximately 3958.76 miles or 6371.01 km (on average).

- *Highway/Network*: The distance is computed as the shortest path within a network, for example, the U.S. highway network. This is usually the most accurate method for calculating distances in a supply chain context. However, since they require data on the entire road network, they must be obtained from geographic information systems (GIS) or from on-line services such as Mapquest or Google Maps. (In contrast, the distance measures above can be calculated from simple formulas using only the coordinates of the facilities and customers.)

- *Matrix*: Sometimes a matrix containing the distance between every pair of points is given explicitly. This is the most general measure, since all others can be considered a special case. It is also the only possible measure when the distances follow no particular pattern.

In general, we won't be concerned with how transportation costs are computed—we'll assume they are given to us already as the parameters c_{ij}.

The UFLP is formulated as follows:

$$\text{(UFLP)} \quad \text{minimize} \quad \sum_{j \in J} f_j x_j + \sum_{i \in I} \sum_{j \in J} h_i c_{ij} y_{ij} \tag{7.1}$$

$$\text{subject to} \quad \sum_{j \in J} y_{ij} = 1 \qquad \forall i \in I \tag{7.2}$$

$$y_{ij} \le x_j \qquad \forall i \in I, \forall j \in J \tag{7.3}$$

$$x_j \in \{0, 1\} \qquad \forall j \in J \tag{7.4}$$

$$y_{ij} \ge 0 \qquad \forall i \in I, \forall j \in J \tag{7.5}$$

The objective function (7.1) computes the total (fixed plus transportation) cost. In the discussion that follows, we'll use z^* to denote the optimal objective value of (UFLP).

Constraints (7.2) require the full amount of every customer's demand to be assigned, to one or more facilities. These are often called *assignment constraints*. Constraints (7.3) prohibit a customer from being assigned to a facility that has not been opened. These are often called *linking constraints*. Constraints (7.4) require the location (x) variables to be binary, and constraints (7.5) require the assignment (y) variables to be non-negative.

Constraints (7.2) and (7.5) together ensure that $0 \leq y_{ij} \leq 1$. In fact, it is always optimal to assign each customer solely to its nearest open facility. (Why?) Therefore, there always exists an optimal solution in which $y_{ij} \in \{0, 1\}$ for all $i \in I$, $j \in J$. It is therefore appropriate to think of the y_{ij} as binary variables and to talk about "the facility to which customer i is assigned."

Another way to write constraints (7.3) is

$$\sum_{i \in I} y_{ij} \leq |I| x_j \qquad \forall j \in J. \tag{7.6}$$

If $x_j = 1$, then y_{ij} can be 1 for any or all $i \in I$, while if $x_j = 0$, then y_{ij} must be 0 for all i. These constraints are equivalent to (7.3) for the IP. But the LP relaxation is weaker (i.e., it provides a weaker bound) if constraints (7.6) are used instead of (7.3). This is because there are solutions that are feasible for the LP relaxation with (7.6) that are not feasible for the LP relaxation with (7.3). To take a trivial example, suppose there are 2 facilities and 10 customers with equal demand, and suppose each facility serves 5 customers in a given solution. Then it is feasible to set $x_1 = x_2 = \frac{1}{2}$ for the problem with (7.6) but not with (7.3). Since the feasible region for the problem with (7.6) is larger than that for the problem with (7.3), its objective value is no greater. It is important to understand that the IPs have the *same* optimal objective value, but the LPs have different values—one provides a weaker LP bound than the other.

7.2.3   Solution Methods

The UFLP is NP-hard. A number of solution methods have been proposed in the literature over the past several decades, both exact algorithms and heuristics.

Some of the earliest exact algorithms involve simply solving the IP using branch and bound. Today, this would mean solving (UFLP) as-is using CPLEX or another off-the-shelf IP solver, although such general-purpose solvers did not exist when the UFLP was first formulated. This approach works quite well using modern solvers, in part because the LP relaxation of (UFLP) is usually extremely tight, and in fact it often results in all-integer solutions "for free." (ReVelle and Swain (1970) discuss this property in the context of a related problem, the P-median problem.) Current versions of CPLEX can solve instances of the UFLP with thousands of potential facility sites in a matter of minutes. However, when it was first proposed that branch-and-bound be used to solve the UFLP (by Efroymson and Ray (1966)), IP technology was much less advanced, and this approach could only be used to solve problems of modest size. Therefore, a number of other optimal approaches were developed. These include a "dual-ascent" algorithm called DUALOC (Erlenkotter

1978), decomposition methods like Dantzig-Wolfe or Benders decomposition, and Lagrangian relaxation (to be discussed further in Section 7.2.4).

Heuristics for combinatorial problems such as the UFLP fall into two categories: *construction heuristics* and *improvement heuristics*. Construction heuristics build a feasible solution from scratch, whereas improvement heuristics start with a feasible solution and attempt to improve it.

The most basic construction heuristics for the UFLP are *greedy* heuristics such as the "greedy-add" procedure (Kuehn and Hamburger 1963): Start with all facilities closed and open the single facility that can serve all customers with the smallest objective function value; then at each iteration open the facility that gives the largest decrease in the objective, stopping when no facility can be opened that will decrease the objective. A reverse approach is called the "greedy-drop" heuristic, which starts with all facilities open and sequentially closes the facility that decreases the objective the most.

One important improvement heuristic is the *swap* or *exchange* algorithm (Teitz and Bart 1968), which attempts to find a pair j, k of facilities with j open and k closed such that if j were closed and k opened (and the customers re-assigned as needed), the objective value would decrease. If such a pair can be found, the swap is made and the procedure continues. Other procedures attempt to find closed facilities that can be opened to reduce the objective function, or open facilities that can be closed. A somewhat more sophisticated heuristic is the *neighborhood search* heuristic (Maranzana 1964), which considers the neighborhood of a given open facility (defined as the set of customers assigned to it) and attempts to find a different facility that could serve the neighborhood less expensively. If such a facility can be found, the two facilities are swapped, the neighborhoods are re-defined, and the procedure repeats.

The heuristics mentioned here have proven to perform well in practice, which means they return good solutions *and* execute quickly. Metaheuristics, such as tabu search, genetic algorithms, and simulated annealing, have also been widely applied to the UFLP and other facility location problems (Mladenovic et al. 2007).

7.2.4 Lagrangian Relaxation

7.2.4.1 Introduction   One of the methods that has proven to be most effective for the UFLP and other location problems is Lagrangian relaxation, a standard technique for integer programming (as well as other types of optimization problems). The basic idea behind Lagrangian relaxation is to remove a set of constraints to create a problem that's easier to solve than the original. But instead of just removing the constraints, we include them in the objective function by adding a term that penalizes solutions for violating the constraints. This process gives a *lower bound* on the optimal objective value of the UFLP, but it does not necessarily give a feasible solution. Feasible solutions must be found using some other method (to be described below); each feasible solution provides an *upper bound* on the optimal objective value. When the upper and lower bounds are close (say, within 1%), we know that the feasible solution we have found is close to optimal.

For more details on Lagrangian relaxation, see Appendix D. See also Fisher (1981, 1985) for excellent overviews. Lagrangian relaxation was proposed as a method for solving a UFLP-like problem by Cornuejols et al. (1977).

We want to use Lagrangian relaxation on the UFLP formulation given in Section 7.2.2. The question is, which constraints should we relax? There are only two options: (7.2) and (7.3). (Constraints (7.4) and (7.5) can't be relaxed using Lagrangian relaxation.) Relaxing either (7.2) or (7.3) results in a problem that is quite easy to solve, and both relaxations produce the same bound (for reasons discussed below). But relaxing (7.2) involves relaxing fewer constraints, which is generally preferable (also for reasons that will be discussed below). Therefore, we will relax constraints (7.2), although in Section 7.2.4.7 we will briefly discuss what happens when constraints (7.3) are relaxed.

7.2.4.2 *Relaxation*   We relax constraints (7.2), removing them from the problem and adding a penalty term to the objective function:

$$\sum_{i\in I}\lambda_i\left(1-\sum_{j\in J}y_{ij}\right)$$

The λ_i are called *Lagrange multipliers*. There is one for each relaxed constraint. Their purpose is to ensure that violations in the constraints are penalized by just the right amount—more on this later. We'll use λ to represent the vector of λ_i's.

For now, assume the λ are fixed. Relaxing constraints (7.2) gives us the following problem, known as the *Lagrangian subproblem*:

$$\begin{aligned}
\text{(UFLP-LR}_\lambda) \quad \text{minimize} \quad & \sum_{j\in J}f_jx_j + \sum_{i\in I}\sum_{j\in J}h_ic_{ij}y_{ij} + \sum_{i\in I}\lambda_i\left(1-\sum_{j\in J}y_{ij}\right) \\
= & \sum_{j\in J}f_jx_j + \sum_{i\in I}\sum_{j\in J}(h_ic_{ij}-\lambda_i)y_{ij} + \sum_{i\in I}\lambda_i \quad (7.7)
\end{aligned}$$

$$\begin{aligned}
\text{subject to} \quad & y_{ij}\le x_j && \forall i\in I, \forall j\in J && (7.8)\\
& x_j\in\{0,1\} && \forall j\in J && (7.9)\\
& y_{ij}\ge 0 && \forall i\in I, \forall j\in J && (7.10)
\end{aligned}$$

(The subscript λ on the problem name reminds us that this problem depends on λ as a parameter.) Since the λ_i are all constants, the last term of (7.7) can be ignored during the optimization.

How can we solve this problem? It turns out that the problem is quite easy to solve by inspection—we don't need to use an IP solver or any sort of complicated algorithm. Suppose that we set $x_j=1$ for a given facility j. By constraints (7.8), setting $x_j=1$ allows y_{ij} to be set to 1 for any $i\in I$. For which i would y_{ij} be set to 1 in an optimal solution to the problem? Since this is a minimization problem, y_{ij}

would be set to 1 for all i such that $h_i c_{ij} - \lambda_i < 0$. So if x_j were set to 1, the *benefit* (or contribution to the objective function) would be

$$\beta_j = \sum_{i \in I} \min\{0, h_i c_{ij} - \lambda_i\}. \tag{7.11}$$

Now the question is, which x_j should be set to 1? It's optimal to set $x_j = 1$ if and only if $\beta_j + f_j < 0$; that is, if the benefit of opening the facility outweighs its fixed cost. So an optimal solution to (UFLP-LR_λ) can be found by setting

$$x_j = \begin{cases} 1, & \text{if } \beta_j + f_j < 0 \\ 0, & \text{otherwise} \end{cases} \tag{7.12}$$

$$y_{ij} = \begin{cases} 1, & \text{if } x_j = 1 \text{ and } h_i c_{ij} - \lambda_i < 0 \\ 0, & \text{otherwise} \end{cases} \tag{7.13}$$

We'll use $z_{\text{LR}}(\lambda)$ to denote the optimal objective value of (UFLP-LR_λ). Then

$$z_{\text{LR}}(\lambda) = \sum_{j \in J} \min\{0, \beta_j + f_j\} + \sum_{i \in I} \lambda_i.$$

Notice that in solutions to (UFLP-LR_λ), customers may be assigned to 0 or more than 1 facility since the constraints requiring exactly one facility per customer have been relaxed.

Why is this problem so much easier to solve than the original problem? The answer is that (UFLP-LR_λ) decomposes by j, in the sense that we can focus on each $j \in J$ individually since there are no constraints tying them together. In the original problem, constraints (7.2) tied the j's together—we could not make a decision about y_{ij} without also making a decision about y_{ik} since i had to be assigned to exactly 1 facility.

7.2.4.3   *Lower Bound*   We've now solved (UFLP-LR_λ) for given λ_i. How does this help us? Well, from Theorem D.1, we know that, for any λ, the optimal objective value of (UFLP-LR_λ) is a lower bound on the optimal objective value for the original problem:

$$z_{\text{LR}}(\lambda) \leq z^*. \tag{7.14}$$

The point of Lagrangian relaxation is not to generate feasible solutions, since the solutions to (UFLP-LR_λ) will generally be infeasible for (UFLP). Instead, the point is to generate good (i.e., high) lower bounds in order to prove that a feasible solution we've found some other way is good. For example, if we've found a feasible solution for the UFLP (using any method at all) whose objective value is 1005 and we've also found a λ so that $z_{\text{LR}}(\lambda) = 1000$, then we know our solution is no more than $(1005 - 1000)/1000 = 0.5\%$ away from optimal. (It may in fact be *exactly* optimal, but given these two bounds we can only say it's within 0.5%.)

Now, if we pick λ at random, we're not likely to get a particularly good bound— that is, $z_{\text{LR}}(\lambda)$ won't be close to z^*. We have to choose λ cleverly so that we get the best possible bound—so that $z_{LR}(\lambda)$ is as large as possible. That is, we want to solve problem (LR) given in (D.8), which, for the UFLP, can be written as follows:

$$(LR) \quad \max_\lambda \quad \begin{cases} \min_{x,y} & \sum_{j\in J} f_j x_j + \sum_{i\in I}(h_i c_{ij} - \lambda_i)y_{ij} + \sum_{i\in I}\lambda_i \\ \text{s.t.} & y_{ij} \leq x_j \quad \forall i \in I, \forall j \in J \\ & x_j \in \{0,1\} \quad \forall j \in J \\ & y_{ij} \geq 0 \quad \forall i \in I, \forall j \in J \end{cases}$$

(7.15)

We'll talk more later about how to solve this problem. For now, let's assume we know the optimal λ^* and that the optimal objective value is $z_{LR} \equiv z_{LR}(\lambda^*)$. How large can z_{LR} be? Theorem D.1 tells us it cannot be larger than z^*, but how close can it get? The answer turns out to be related to the LP relaxation of the problem. From Theorem D.2, we have

$$z_{LP} \leq z_{LR}, \quad (7.16)$$

where z_{LP} is the optimal objective value of the LP relaxation of (UFLP) and z_{LR} is the optimal objective value of (LR).

Combining (7.14) and (7.16), we now know that

$$z_{LP} \leq z_{LR} \leq z^*. \quad (7.17)$$

For most problems, $z_{LP} \lneq z^*$, so where in the gap does z_{LR} fall? Recall from Appendix D that an IP is said to have the *integrality property* if its LP relaxation naturally has an all-integer optimal solution. You should be able to convince yourself that (UFLP-LR$_\lambda$) has the integrality property for all λ since it is never better to set x and y to fractional values. Therefore, the following is a corollary to Lemma D.1:

Corollary 7.1 *For the UFLP,* $z_{LP} = z_{LR}$.

Combining (7.17) and Corollary 7.1, we have

$$z_{LR} = z_{LP} \leq z^*.$$

This means that if the LP relaxation bound from the UFLP is not very tight, the Lagrangian relaxation bound won't be very tight either. Fortunately, as noted in Section 7.2.3, the UFLP tends to have very tight LP relaxation bounds. This raises the question of why we'd want to use Lagrangian relaxation at all since the LP bound is just as tight.

There are several possible answers to this question. The first is that when Lagrangian relaxation was first applied to the UFLP, computer implementations of the simplex method were quite inefficient, and even the LP relaxation of the UFLP could take a long time to solve, whereas the Lagrangian subproblem could be solved quite quickly. Recent implementations of the simplex method, however (for example, recent versions of CPLEX), are much more efficient and are able to solve reasonably large instances of the UFLP—LP or IP—pretty quickly. Nevertheless, Lagrangian relaxation is still an important tool for solving the UFLP. One advantage of this method is that it can often be modified to solve extensions of the UFLP that IP solvers can't solve—for example, nonlinear problems like the location model with risk-pooling (LMRP), which we discuss in Section 8.2.

It is important to distinguish between z_{LR} (the best possible lower bound achievable by Lagrangian relaxation) and $z_{LR}(\lambda)$ (the lower bound achieved at a given iteration of the procedure). At any given iteration, we have

$$z_{LR}(\lambda) \leq z_{LR} = z_{LP} \leq z^* \leq z(x, y), \qquad (7.18)$$

where $z_{LR}(\lambda)$ is the objective value of the Lagrangian subproblem for the particular λ at the current iteration, and $z(x, y)$ is the objective value of the particular feasible solution found at the current iteration.

7.2.4.4 *Upper Bound*
Now that we've obtained a lower bound on the optimal objective of (UFLP) using (UFLP-LR$_\lambda$), we need to find an upper bound. Upper bounds come from feasible solutions to (UFLP). How can we build good feasible solutions? One way would be using construction and/or improvement heuristics like those described in Section 7.2.3. But we'd like to take advantage of the information contained in the solutions to (UFLP-LR$_\lambda$); that is, we'd like to convert a solution to (UFLP-LR$_\lambda$) into one for (UFLP). Remember that solutions to (UFLP-LR$_\lambda$) consist of a set of facility locations (identified by the x variables) and a set of assignments (identified by the y variables). It is the y variables that make the solution infeasible for (UFLP), since customers might be assigned to 0 or more than 1 facility. (If every customer happens to be assigned to exactly 1 facility, the solution is also feasible for (UFLP). In fact, it is *optimal* for (UFLP) since it has the same objective value for both (UFLP-LR$_\lambda$), which provides a lower bound, and (UFLP), which provides an upper bound. But we can't expect this to happen in general.)

Generating a feasible solution for (UFLP) is easy: We just open the facilities that are open in the solution to (UFLP-LR$_\lambda$) and then assign each customer to its nearest open facility. The resulting solution is feasible and provides an upper bound on the optimal objective value of (UFLP). Sometimes an improvement heuristic (like the swap or neighborhood search algorithms) is applied to each feasible solution found, but this is optional.

7.2.4.5 *Updating the Multipliers*
Each λ gives a single lower bound and (using the method in Section 7.2.4.4) a single upper bound. The Lagrangian relaxation process involves many iterations, each using a different value of λ, in the hopes of tightening the bounds. It would be impractical to try every possible value of λ; we want to choose λ cleverly.

Using the logic of Section D.3, if λ_i is too small, there's no real incentive to set the y_{ij}'s to 1 since the penalty will be small. On the other hand, if λ_i is too large, there will be an incentive to set *lots* of y_{ij}'s to 1, making the term inside the parentheses negative and the overall penalty large and negative. (Remember that (UFLP-LR$_\lambda$) is a minimization problem.) By changing λ_i, we'll encourage fewer or more y_{ij} variables to be 1.

So:

- If $\sum_{j \in J} y_{ij} = 0$, then λ_i is too small; it should be increased.

- If $\sum_{j \in J} y_{ij} > 1$, then λ_i is too large; it should be decreased.

- If $\sum_{j \in J} y_{ij} = 1$, then λ_i is just right; it should not be changed.

Here's another way to see the effect of changing λ_i. Remember that if $x_j = 1$ in the solution to (UFLP-LR$_\lambda$), y_{ij} will be set to 1 if

$$h_i c_{ij} - \lambda_i < 0.$$

Increasing λ_i makes this hold for more facilities j, while decreasing it makes it hold for fewer.

There are several ways to make these adjustments to λ. Perhaps the most common is *subgradient optimization*, discussed in Section D.3. For the UFLP, the step size at iteration t (denoted Δ^t) is given by

$$\Delta^t = \frac{\alpha^t (\text{UB} - \mathcal{L}^t)}{\sum_{i \in I} \left(1 - \sum_{j \in J} y_{ij}\right)^2}, \tag{7.19}$$

where $\mathcal{L}^t$ is the lower bound found at iteration t (i.e., the value of $z_{\text{LR}}(\lambda)$ for the current value of λ), UB is the best upper bound found (i.e., the objective value of the best feasible solution found so far), and α^t is a constant that is generally set to 2 at iteration 1 and divided by 2 after a given number (say 20) of consecutive iterations have passed during which the best known lower bound has not improved. The step direction for iteration i is simply given by

$$1 - \sum_{j \in J} y_{ij}$$

(the violation in the constraint).

To obtain the new multipliers (call them λ^{n+1}) from the old ones (λ^n), we set

$$\lambda_i^{t+1} = \lambda_i^t + \Delta^t \left(1 - \sum_{j \in J} y_{ij}\right). \tag{7.20}$$

Note that since $\Delta^t > 0$, this follows the rules given above: If $\sum_{j \in J} y_{ij} = 0$, then λ_i increases; if $\sum_{j \in J} y_{ij} > 1$, then λ_i decreases; and if $\sum_{j \in J} y_{ij} = 1$, then λ_i stays the same.

The process of solving (UFLP-LR$_\lambda$), finding a feasible solution, and updating λ is continued until some stopping criteria are met. (See Section D.4.)

At the first iteration, λ can be initialized using a variety of ways: For example, set $\lambda_i = 0$ for all i, set it to some random number, or set it according to some other ad-hoc rule.

If the Lagrangian procedure stops before the upper and lower bounds are sufficiently close to each other, we can use branch-and-bound to close the optimality gap; see Section D.6. The Lagrangian procedure is summarized in Section D.7.

7.2.4.6 Variable Fixing   Sometimes the Lagrangian relaxation procedure terminates with the lower and upper bounds farther apart than we'd like. Before executing
branch-and-bound to close the gap, we may be able to fix some of the x_j variables
to 0 or 1 based on the facility benefits and the current bounds. The variables can be
fixed permanently, throughout the entire branch-and-bound tree. The more variables
we can fix, the faster the branch-and-bound procedure is likely to run. Essentially,
the method works by "peeking" down a branch of the tree and running a quick check
to determine whether the next node down the branch would be fathomed.

Theorem 7.1 *Let UB be the best upper bound found during the Lagrangian procedure, let λ be a given set of Lagrange multipliers that were used during the procedure,
let β_j be the facility benefits (7.11) under λ, and let $z_{LR}(\lambda)$ be the lower bound (the
optimal objective value of (UFLP-LR$_\lambda$)) under λ. If $x_j = 0$ in the solution to
(UFLP-LR$_\lambda$) and*

$$z_{LR}(\lambda) + \beta_j + f_j > UB, \tag{7.21}$$

*then $x_j = 0$ in every optimal solution to (UFLP). If $x_j = 1$ in the solution to
(UFLP-LR$_\lambda$) and*

$$z_{LR}(\lambda) - (\beta_j + f_j) > UB, \tag{7.22}$$

then $x_j = 1$ in every optimal solution to (UFLP).

Proof. Suppose we were to branch on x_j, setting $x_j = 0$ for one child node and
$x_j = 1$ for the other, and suppose we use λ as the initial multipliers for the Lagrangian
procedure at each child node.

At the "$x_j = 1$" node, the same facilities would be open as in the root-node
solution, except that now facility j is also open. The cost of this solution for
(UFLP-LR$_\lambda$) is the cost of the original solution, $z_{LR}(\lambda)$, plus $\beta_j + f_j$. Therefore
we would obtain $z_{LR}(\lambda) + \beta_j + f_j$ as a lower bound at this node. Since this lower
bound is greater than the best-known upper bound, we would fathom the tree at this
node, and the optimal solution would be contained in the other half of the tree—the
"$x_j = 0$" half.

A similar argument applies to the second case. At the "$x_j = 0$" node, we obtain
a lower bound of $z_{LR}(\lambda) - (\beta_j + f_j)$, and if this is greater than UB, we fathom the
tree at this node. ∎

Note that, in the second part of the theorem, if $x_j = 1$ then, by (7.12), $\beta_j + f_j < 0$,
which is why the left-hand side of (7.22) might be greater than UB.

This trick has been applied successfully to a variety of facility location problems;
see, e.g., Daskin et al. (2002), Snyder and Daskin (2005). Typically the conditions
in Theorem 7.1 are checked twice after processing has terminated at the root node,
once using the most recent multipliers λ and once using the multipliers that produced
the best-known lower bound. The time required to check these conditions for every
j is negligible.

7.2.4.7 *Alternate Relaxation*   As stated above, we could have chosen instead to relax constraints (7.3). In this case, the Lagrangian subproblem becomes

$$(\text{UFLP-LR}_\lambda) \quad \text{minimize} \quad \sum_{j \in J} f_j x_j + \sum_{i \in I} \sum_{j \in J} h_i c_{ij} y_{ij} + \sum_{i \in I} \sum_{j \in J} \lambda_{ij} (x_j - y_{ij})$$

$$= \sum_{j \in J} \left(\sum_{i \in I} \lambda_{ij} + f_j \right) x_j + \sum_{i \in I} \sum_{j \in J} (h_i c_{ij} - \lambda_{ij}) y_{ij} \tag{7.23}$$

$$\text{subject to} \quad \sum_{j \in J} y_{ij} = 1 \qquad \forall i \in I \tag{7.24}$$

$$x_j \in \{0, 1\} \qquad \forall j \in J \tag{7.25}$$

$$y_{ij} \geq 0 \qquad \forall i \in I, \forall j \in J \tag{7.26}$$

Now every customer must be assigned to a single facility, but that facility need not be open. There are no constraints linking the x and y variables, so the problem can be written as two separate problems:

$$(x\text{-problem}) \quad \text{minimize} \quad \sum_{j \in J} \left(\sum_{i \in I} \lambda_{ij} + f_j \right) x_j \tag{7.27}$$

$$\text{subject to} \quad x_j \in \{0, 1\} \qquad \forall j \in J \tag{7.28}$$

$$(y\text{-problem}) \quad \text{minimize} \quad \sum_{i \in I} \sum_{j \in J} (h_i c_{ij} - \lambda_{ij}) y_{ij} \tag{7.29}$$

$$\text{subject to} \quad \sum_{j \in J} y_{ij} = 1 \quad \cdot \quad \forall i \in I \tag{7.30}$$

$$y_{ij} \geq 0 \qquad \forall i \in I, \forall j \in J \tag{7.31}$$

To solve the x-problem, we simply set $x_j = 1$ for all j such that $\sum_{i \in I} \lambda_{ij} + f_j < 0$. (Note that since the constraints relaxed are $\leq$ constraints, $\lambda \leq 0$; see Section D.5.1.) To solve the y-problem, for each i we set $y_{ij} = 1$ for the j that minimizes $h_i c_{ij} - \lambda_{ij}$. The rest of the procedure is similar, except that the step-size calculation becomes

$$\Delta^t = \frac{\alpha^t (\text{UB} - \mathcal{L}^t)}{\sum_{i \in I} \sum_{j \in J} (x_j - y_{ij})^2} \tag{7.32}$$

and the multiplier-updating formula becomes

$$\lambda_{ij}^{t+1} = \lambda_{ij}^t + \Delta^t (x_j - y_{ij}). \tag{7.33}$$

In practice, relaxing the assignment constraints (7.2) tends to work better than relaxing the linking constraints (7.3). One reason for this is that the former relaxation involves relaxing fewer constraints, which generally makes it easier to find good multipliers using subgradient optimization. Another reason is that since y_{ij} will be 0 for many j that are open, there will be many constraints such that $y_{ij} < x_j$. It is often difficult to get good results when relaxing inequality constraints if many of them are slack.

7.2.5 Capacitated Version

In the UFLP, we assumed that there are no capacity restrictions on the facilities. Obviously, this is an unrealistic assumption in many practical settings. The UFLP can be easily modified to account for capacity restrictions; the resulting problem (not surprisingly) is called the *capacitated fixed-charge location problem*, or CFLP. Suppose v_j is the maximum demand that can be served by facility j per year. The CFLP can be formulated as follows:

$$\text{(CFLP)} \quad \text{minimize} \quad \sum_{j \in J} f_j x_j + \sum_{i \in I} \sum_{j \in J} h_i c_{ij} y_{ij} \tag{7.34}$$

$$\text{subject to} \quad \sum_{j \in J} y_{ij} = 1 \qquad \forall i \in I \tag{7.35}$$

$$y_{ij} \leq x_j \qquad \forall i \in I, \forall j \in J \tag{7.36}$$

$$\sum_{i \in I} h_i y_{ij} \leq v_j \qquad \forall j \in J \tag{7.37}$$

$$x_j \in \{0,1\} \qquad \forall j \in J \tag{7.38}$$

$$y_{ij} \geq 0 \qquad \forall i \in I, \forall j \in J \tag{7.39}$$

This IP is identical to (UFLP) except for the new capacity constraints (7.37).

Many approaches have been proposed to solve this problem. We briefly outline a method very similar to the method discussed for the UFLP. We relax the assignment constraints (7.35) to obtain the following Lagrangian subproblem:

$$\text{(CFLP-LR}_\lambda) \quad \text{minimize} \quad \sum_{j \in J} f_j x_j + \sum_{i \in I} \sum_{j \in J} h_i c_{ij} y_{ij} + \sum_{i \in I} \lambda_i \left(1 - \sum_{j \in J} y_{ij} \right)$$

$$= \sum_{j \in J} f_j x_j + \sum_{i \in I} \sum_{j \in J} (h_i c_{ij} - \lambda_i) y_{ij} + \sum_{i \in I} \lambda_i \tag{7.40}$$

$$\text{subject to} \quad y_{ij} \leq x_j \qquad \forall i \in I, \forall j \in J \tag{7.41}$$

$$\sum_{i \in I} h_i y_{ij} \leq v_j \qquad \forall j \in J \tag{7.42}$$

$$x_j \in \{0,1\} \qquad \forall j \in J \tag{7.43}$$

$$y_{ij} \geq 0 \qquad \forall i \in I, \forall j \in J \tag{7.44}$$

As in the UFLP, this problem separates by j, but now computing the benefit β_j is a little more complicated because of the capacity constraint. In particular, for each $j \in J$ we need to solve a problem of the form

$$(\text{P}_j) \quad \text{minimize} \quad \beta_j = \sum_{i \in I} a_i z_i \tag{7.45}$$

$$\text{subject to} \quad \sum_{i \in I} h_i z_i \leq v \tag{7.46}$$

$$0 \leq z_i \leq 1 \qquad \forall i \in I, \tag{7.47}$$

where $a_i = h_i c_{ij} - \lambda_i$, $z_i = y_{ij}$, and $v = v_j$. This is a continuous knapsack problem, which can be solved efficiently by sorting the i's so that

$$a_1 h_1 \leq a_2 h_2 \leq \ldots \leq a_{|I|} h_{|I|}.$$

We then set $z_i = 1$ for $i = 1, \ldots, r$, where r is the largest number so that

$$\sum_{i=1}^{r} h_i \leq v_j$$

and set $z_{r+1} = v_j - \sum_{i=1}^{r} h_i$. Other aspects of the Lagrangian procedure (finding upper bounds, subgradient optimization, branch and bound) are similar to those discussed in Section 7.2.4, although the upper-bounding procedure must take into account the capacity constraints.

Generally, the optimal solution to (CFLP) will not have $y_{ij} \in \{0, 1\}$ as in (UFLP). (Why?) This means that some customers will receive product from more than one DC. Sometimes it is important to prohibit this from happening by requiring $y_{ij} \in \{0, 1\}$; this is called a *single-sourcing constraint*. The CFLP with single-sourcing constraints is harder to solve because (P_j) becomes an integer knapsack problem, which is NP-hard. On the other hand, good algorithms exist for the knapsack problem, and since the knapsack problem does not have the integrality property, the Lagrangian bound will be tighter than the LP bound. This highlights the important tradeoff between the quality of the Lagrangian bound and the ease with which the subproblem can be solved.

7.3   A MULTI-ECHELON, MULTI-COMMODITY MODEL

7.3.1   Introduction

The UFLP and CFLP make decisions about which facilities to open in only a single echelon (the DCs). In this section, we present a model that makes location decisions about two echelons and can be extended to consider a general number of echelons. In addition, this model considers multiple products and joint capacity constraints that reflect the limited capacity in each facility that the several products "compete" for.

The seminal paper on multi-echelon facility location problems is by Geoffrion and Graves (1974), which presents a three-echelon (plant–DC–customer) model. This paper considers location decisions only at the DC echelon, but it optimizes product flows among all three echelons. The model we will present in this section also considers location decisions at the plant echelon. It is adapted from Pirkul and Jayaraman (1996).

7.3.2 Problem Statement

This problem is concerned with a three-echelon system consisting of plants, DCs, and customers. The customer locations are fixed but the plant and DC locations are to be optimized. In addition, the model considers multiple products and limited capacity at the plants and DCs. As in the UFLP and CFLP, the objective is to minimize the total fixed and transportation cost.

We will use the following notation:

Sets

I	= set of customers
J	= set of potential DC locations
K	= set of potential plant locations
L	= set of products

Demands and Capacities

h_{il}	= annual demand of customer $i \in I$ for product $l \in L$
v_j	= capacity of DC $j \in J$
b_k	= capacity of plant $k \in K$
s_l	= units of capacity consumed by one unit of product $l \in L$

Costs

f_j	= fixed (annual) cost to open a DC at site $j \in J$
g_k	= fixed (annual) cost to open a plant at site $k \in K$
c_{ijl}	= cost to transport one unit of product $l \in L$ from DC $j \in J$ to customer $i \in I$
d_{jkl}	= cost to transport one unit of product $l \in L$ from plant $k \in K$ to DC $j \in J$

Decision Variables

x_j	= 1 if DC j is opened, 0 otherwise
z_k	= 1 if plant k is opened, 0 otherwise
y_{ijl}	= number of units of product l shipped from DC j to customer i
w_{jkl}	= number of units of product l shipped from plant k to DC j

The space parameter s_l must be expressed in the same units used to express the capacities v_j and c_k. That is, if capacities are expressed in square feet, then s_l is the number of square feet taken up by one unit of product l. If capacities are expressed in person-hours of work available per year, then s_l is the number of person-hours of work required to process one unit of product l. And so on.

The transportation variables y and w indicate the amount of product l shipped along each link, from plants to DCs (w) and from DCs to customers (y). There is an alternate way to formulate a model like this in which we define a single set of transportation variables, call it y_{ijkl}, that specifies the amount of product l shipped from plant k to customer i via DC j. (Geoffrion and Graves (1974) use this approach.) This type of formulation is more compact and has certain attractive structural properties. However, this strategy requires $|I||J||K||L|$ transportation variables, which is generally larger than the $|I||J||L| + |J||K||L|$ variables required by the formulation below.

Moreover, the strategy of defining a new set of transportation variables for each pair of consecutive echelons allows us to extend this model to more than three echelons. The number of such variables in the alternate approach grows multiplicatively with the number of echelons, while the approach taken here grows only additively.

Note that while in the UFLP, the y_{ij} variables indicated the *fraction* of i's demand served by j, here y_{ijl} is a *quantity*.

7.3.3 Formulation

The multi-echelon location problem can be formulated as an integer programming problem as follows:

$$\text{minimize} \quad \sum_{j \in J} f_j x_j + \sum_{k \in K} g_k z_k + \sum_{l \in L} \left[\sum_{j \in J} \sum_{i \in I} c_{ijl} y_{ijl} + \sum_{k \in K} \sum_{j \in J} d_{jkl} w_{jkl} \right] \tag{7.48}$$

$$\text{subject to} \quad \sum_{j \in J} y_{ijl} = h_{il} \qquad \forall i \in I, \forall l \in L \tag{7.49}$$

$$\sum_{i \in I} \sum_{l \in L} s_l y_{ijl} \leq v_j x_j \qquad \forall j \in J \tag{7.50}$$

$$\sum_{k \in K} w_{jkl} = \sum_{i \in I} y_{ijl} \qquad \forall j \in J, \forall l \in L \tag{7.51}$$

$$\sum_{j \in J} \sum_{l \in L} s_l w_{jkl} \leq b_k z_k \qquad \forall k \in K \tag{7.52}$$

$$x_j, z_k \in \{0, 1\} \qquad \forall j \in J, \forall k \in K \tag{7.53}$$

$$y_{ijl}, w_{jkl} \geq 0 \qquad \forall i \in I, \forall j \in J, \forall k \in K, \forall l \in L \tag{7.54}$$

The objective function (7.48) computes the total fixed and transportation cost. Constraints (7.49) require the total amount of product l shipped to customer i to equal i's demand for l. These constraints are analogous to constraints (7.2) in the UFLP. Constraints (7.50) ensure that the total amount shipped out of DC j is no more than the DC's capacity, and that nothing is shipped out if DC j is not opened. Constraints (7.51) require the total amount of product l shipped into DC j to equal the total amount shipped out. Constraints (7.52) are capacity constraints at the plants and prevent product from being shipped from plant k if k has not been opened. Finally, constraints (7.53) and (7.54) are integrality and non-negativity constraints.

The UFLP and CFLP are special cases of this problem, and hence it is NP-hard. We will discuss a Lagrangian relaxation algorithm for solving it.

7.3.4 Lagrangian Relaxation

We will solve the multi-echelon location problem using Lagrangian relaxation. Before we do, though, we'll add a new set of constraints to the model:

$$y_{ijl} \leq h_{il} \qquad \forall i \in I, \forall j \in J, \forall l \in L \qquad (7.55)$$

These constraints simply say that the amount of product l shipped to customer i cannot exceed i's demand for l. They are redundant in the original model in the sense that they are satisfied by every feasible solution. However, they will not be redundant after we relax some of the original constraints. Adding constraints (7.55) tightens the relaxation, as we will see below.

We relax the assignment constraints (7.49) (as in the UFLP) as well as the "balance" constraints (7.51). We use Lagrange multipliers λ_{il} for the first set of constraints and μ_{jl} for the second. The resulting subproblem is as follows:

$$
\text{minimize} \quad \sum_{j \in J} f_j x_j + \sum_{k \in K} g_k z_k + \sum_{l \in L} \left[\sum_{j \in J} \sum_{i \in I} c_{ijl} y_{ijl} + \sum_{k \in K} \sum_{j \in J} d_{jkl} w_{jkl} \right]
$$

$$
+ \sum_{i \in I} \sum_{l \in L} \lambda_{il} \left(h_{il} - \sum_{j \in J} y_{ijl} \right) + \sum_{j \in J} \sum_{l \in L} \mu_{jl} \left(\sum_{i \in I} y_{ijl} - \sum_{k \in K} w_{jkl} \right) \quad (7.56)
$$

subject to

$$y_{ijl} \leq h_{il} \qquad \forall i \in I, \forall j \in J, \forall l \in L \qquad (7.57)$$

$$\sum_{i \in I} \sum_{l \in L} s_l y_{ijl} \leq v_j x_j \qquad \forall j \in J \qquad (7.58)$$

$$\sum_{j \in J} \sum_{l \in L} s_l w_{jkl} \leq b_k z_k \qquad \forall k \in K \qquad (7.59)$$

$$x_j, z_k \in \{0, 1\} \qquad \forall j \in J, \forall k \in K \qquad (7.60)$$

$$y_{ijl}, w_{jkl} \geq 0 \qquad \forall i \in I, \forall j \in J, \forall k \in K, \forall l \in L \qquad (7.61)$$

The first two sets of constraints involve only the x and y variables while the third set involves only the z and w variables. This allows us to decompose the subproblem into two separate subproblems:

$$(xy\text{-problem}) \quad \text{minimize} \quad \sum_{j \in J} f_j x_j + \sum_{i \in I} \sum_{j \in J} \sum_{l \in L} (c_{ijl} - \lambda_{il} + \mu_{jl}) y_{ijl} \quad (7.62)$$

subject to $\qquad y_{ijl} \leq h_{il} \qquad \forall i \in I, \forall j \in J, \forall l \in L \qquad (7.63)$

$$\sum_{i \in I} \sum_{l \in L} s_l y_{ijl} \le v_j x_j \quad \forall j \in J \tag{7.64}$$

$$x_j \in \{0, 1\} \quad \forall j \in J \tag{7.65}$$

$$y_{ijl} \ge 0 \qquad \forall i \in I, \forall j \in J, \forall l \in L \tag{7.66}$$

(zw-problem)   minimize $$\sum_{k \in K} g_k z_k + \sum_{k \in K} \sum_{j \in J} \sum_{l \in L} (d_{jkl} - \mu_{jl}) w_{jkl} \tag{7.67}$$

subject to $$\sum_{j \in J} \sum_{l \in L} s_l w_{jkl} \le b_k z_k \quad \forall k \in K \tag{7.68}$$

$$z_k \in \{0, 1\} \quad \forall k \in K \tag{7.69}$$

$$w_{jkl} \ge 0 \qquad \forall j \in J, \forall k \in K, \forall l \in L \tag{7.70}$$

Both problems are quite easy to solve. First consider the xy-problem. If we set $x_j = 1$ for a given j, then we are allowed to set some of the y_{ijl}'s to something greater than 0. The problem of determining values for the y_{ijl}'s (assuming $x_j = 1$) is a continuous knapsack problem. Here's where constraints (7.55) come into play. If we didn't have these constraints in the formulation, we would set $y_{ijl} = v_j / s_l$ for only a single i and l. By imposing bounds on the y_{ijl} variables, we obtain a solution that is much closer to the true optimal solution and hence provides a tighter lower bound. For each j, we solve the continuous knapsack problem, and if the optimal objective value is less than $-f_j$, we set $x_j = 1$; otherwise, we set $x_j = 0$. Solving the zw-problem is very similar, except that there are no explicit upper bounds on the w_{jkl} variables.

As in the UFLP, upper bounds are found using a greedy-type heuristic, and the Lagrange multipliers are updated using subgradient optimization. In computational tests reported by Pirkul and Jayaraman (1996), this algorithm could solve small-to-medium-sized problems in roughly 1 minute.

PROBLEMS

7.1   (Locating DCs for Toy Stores) A toy store chain operates 100 retail stores throughout the United States. The company currently ships all products from a central distribution center (DC) to the stores, but it is considering closing the central DC and instead operating multiple regional DCs that serve the retail stores. It will use the UFLP to determine where to locate DCs. Planners at the company have identified 24 potential cities in which regional DCs may be located. The file `toy-stores.xlsx` lists the longitude and latitude for all of the locations (stores and DCs), as well as the annual demand (measured in pallets) at each store and the fixed annual location cost at each potential DC location. Using optimization software of your choice, implement the UFLP model from Section 7.2.2 and solve it using the data provided. Assume that transportation from DCs to stores costs $1 per mile, as measured by the great-circle distance between the two locations. Report the optimal cities to locate DCs in and the optimal total annual cost.

7.2   (Easy or Hard Modifications?) Which of the following costs can be implemented in the UFLP by modifying the parameters only, without requiring structural changes to the model; that is, without requiring modifications to the variables, objective function, or constraints?

a) A per-unit cost to ship items from a supplier to facility j. (The cost may be different for each j.)

b) A per-unit processing cost at facility j. (The cost may be different for each j.)

c) A fixed cost to ship items from facility j to customer i. (The cost is independent of the quantity shipped but may be different for each i and j.)

d) A transportation cost from facility j to customer i that is a non-linear function of the quantity shipped (for example, one of the quantity discount structures discussed in Section 3.2.7).

e) A fixed capacity-expansion cost that is incurred if the demand served by facility j exceeds a certain threshold.

7.3   (LP Relaxation of UFLP) Develop a simple instance of the UFLP for which the optimal solution to the LP relaxation has fractional values of the x_j variables. This solution must be strictly optimal—that is, you can't submit an instance for which the LP relaxation has an optimal solution with all integer values, even if there's another optimal solution, that ties the integer one, with fractional values. Your instance must have $I = J$, that is, all customer nodes are also potential facility sites. Your instance must have at most 4 nodes.

Include the following in your report:

1. A diagram of the nodes and arcs.

2. The values of h_i, f_j, and c_{ij} for all i, j.

3. The optimal solution (x_{LP} and y_{LP}) and optimal objective value (z_{LP}) for the LP relaxation.

4. The optimal solution (x^* and y^*) and optimal objective value (z^*) for the IP.

7.4   (Ignoring Some Customers in the UFLP) The UFLP includes a constraint that requires every customer to be assigned to some facility. It is often the case that a small handful of customers in remote regions of the geographical area are difficult to serve and can influence the solution disproportionately. In this problem, you will formulate a version of the UFLP in which a certain percentage of the demands may be ignored when calculating the objective function.

Let α be the minimum fraction of demands to be assigned; that is, a set of customers whose cumulative demand is no more than $100(1 - \alpha)\%$ of the total demand may be ignored. The parameter α is fixed, but the model decides endogenously which customers to ignore. Customers must be either assigned or not—they cannot be assigned fractionally.

a) Using the notation introduced in Section 7.2.2, formulate this problem— we'll call it the "partial assignment UFLP" (PAUFLP)—as a linear integer programming problem. Explain each of your constraints in words.

b) Now consider adding a dummy facility, call it u, to the original UFLP. Facility u has a fixed capacity, so we are really dealing with the capacitated fixed-charge location problem (CFLP), not the UFLP. (See Section 7.2.5 for more on the CFLP.) Assigning customers to this dummy facility in the CFLP represents choosing not to assign them in the PAUFLP. Explain how to set the dummy facility's parameters—its fixed cost, capacity, and transportation cost to each customer—so that solving the CFLP with the dummy facility is equivalent to solving the PAUFLP. Formulate the resulting integer programming problem.

c) Using Lagrangian relaxation, relax the assignment constraints in your model from part (b). Formulate the Lagrangian subproblem, using λ_i as the Lagrange multiplier for the assignment constraint for customer i.

d) Explain how to solve the Lagrangian subproblem you wrote in part (c) for fixed values of λ.

e) Once you have a solution to the Lagrangian subproblem for fixed values of λ, how can you convert it to a feasible solution to the CFLP?

7.5   (Warehouses for Quikflix) Quikflix is a mail-order DVD-rental company. You choose which DVDs to rent on Quikflix's web site, and the company mails the DVDs to you. When you've finished watching the movies, you mail them back to Quikflix. Quikflix's business plan depends on fast shipping times (otherwise customers will get impatient). But overnight delivery services like FedEx are prohibitively expensive. Instead, Quikflix has decided to open enough DCs so that roughly 90% of their customers enjoy 1-day delivery times.

In this problem, you will formulate and solve a model to determine where Quikflix should locate DCs to ensure that a desired percentage of the U.S. population is within a 1-day mailing range while minimizing the fixed cost to open the DCs. (You may assume that the per-unit cost of processing and shipping DVDs is the same at every DC.)

a) Formulate the following problem as an integer programming problem: We are given a set of cities, as well as the population of each city and the fixed cost to open a DC in that city. The objective is to decide in which cities to locate DCs in order to minimize the total fixed cost while also ensuring that at least α fraction of the population is within a 1-day mailing range.

Define your notation clearly, and indicate which items are parameters (inputs) and which are decision variables. Explain each of your constraints in words.

b) Implement your model using a modeling language of your choice. Solve the problem using the data set provided in `quikflix.xlsx`, which gives the locations and populations of the 150 largest cities in the U.S. (according to the 2000 U.S. Census), as well as the average annual fixed cost to open a DC in the city (which are fictitious). The file also contains the distance between each pair of cities in the data set, in miles. Assume that two cities are within a 1-day mailing radius if they are no more than 150 miles apart.

Using these data and a coverage percentage of $\alpha = 0.9$, find the optimal solution to the Quikflix DC location problem. Include a printout of your model file (data not necessary) in your report. Report the total cost of your solution and the total number of DCs open.

7.6   (Solving the Quikflix Problem) In Problem 7.5, you formulated an IP model to solve Quikflix's problem of locating DCs to ensure that a given fraction (α) of the population is within a 1-day mailing range of its nearest DC. In this problem you will develop a method for solving this IP using Lagrangian relaxation.

The IP formulation for Problem 7.5 contains two decision variables. We'll assume that the x variables represent location decisions, while the y variables indicate whether or a city is covered (i.e., is within a 1-day mailing radius of an open facility). If you defined y as a continuous variable, make sure you have added a constraint requiring it to be less than or equal to 1. (This constraint is not strictly necessary since it is implied by other constraints, but it strengthens the Lagrangian relaxation formulation.)

The IP formulation also has a set of constraints that allow city i to be covered only if there is an open facility that is less than 150 miles away. If necessary, rewrite your model so that those constraints are written as $\leq$ constraints. Then relax those constraints, and let λ_i be the Lagrange multiplier for the constraint corresponding to node $i \in J$, where J is the set of cities.

a) Write out the Lagrangian subproblem that results from this relaxation.

b) The subproblem should decompose into two separate problems, one containing only the x variables and one containing only the y variables. Write out these two separate problems.

c) Explain how to solve each of the two subproblems, the x-subproblem and the y-subproblem. Your solution method may *not* rely on using the simplex method or any other general-purpose LP or IP algorithm.

d) Suppose that the problem parameters and Lagrange multipliers are given by the following values:

i	f_i	h_i	λ_i
1	100	80	-50
2	100	120	-50
3	100	40	-40
4	100	90	-200

Suppose also that $\alpha = 0.7$ and that node 1 covers nodes 1, 2, 3; node 2 covers nodes 1, 2, and 4; node 3 covers nodes 1 and 3; and node 4 covers nodes 2 and 4.

Determine the optimal values of x and y, as well as the optimal objective value, for this iteration of the Lagrangian subproblem.

7.7   **(LR Iteration for UFLP)** The file LR-UFLP.xlsx contains data for a 50-node instance of the UFLP, as well as the Lagrange multipliers for a single iteration of the Lagrangian relaxation algorithm described in Section 7.2.4. For each facility $j \in J$, column B lists the fixed cost f_j. For each customer $i \in I$, row 2 lists the demand h_i and row 3 lists the Lagrange multiplier λ_i. Finally, the cells in the range C6:AZ55 contain the matrix of transportation costs c_{ij}.

    a) For each $j \in J$, calculate the benefit β_j, the optimal value of x_j, and the optimal objective value of (UFLP-LR_λ). The worksheet labeled "solution" contains spaces to list β_j (column B), x_j (column C), and the objective value (cell C5).

        Hint 1: You should not have to do *anything* 50 times manually in your spreadsheet. Instead, use the spreadsheet software's copy and paste feature and built-in functions, making clever use of absolute and relative references. If you are using Microsoft Excel, the functions SUMIF, SUMPRODUCT, and OFFSET may help you to automate your calculations. If you prefer, you may instead solve this problem using VBA, C++, or another programming language.

        Hint 2: To double-check your calculations, we'll tell you that if $i = 6$ and $j = 3$, then $h_i c_{ij} - \lambda_i = 12422.34$.

    b) Using the method described in Section 7.2.4.4, generate a feasible solution to the UFLP. In row 2 of the "solution" worksheet, list the index of the facility that each customer is assigned to in your solution. In cell C6, list the objective value of your solution.

7.8   **(Maxisum Location Problem)** Consider the following problem: We must locate exactly p facilities, for fixed p. The objective is to *maximize* the sum of the demand-weighted distances between each customer and its nearest facility. (Such problems are called *maxisum location problems* since the objective is to maximize the sum of the distances, in contrast to *minisum location problems* like the UFLP. Maxisum problems are useful in locating "obnoxious" facilities such as nuclear waste sites.) Formulate this problem as an IP. Define any new notation clearly. Explain the objective function and each of the constraints in words.

7.9   **(Error Bias)** Suppose the transportation costs are estimated badly in the UFLP. It is natural to expect that the true cost of the solution found under the erroneous data has an equal probability of being larger or smaller than the cost calculated when solving the problem. Test this hypothesis by solving the instance given in random-errors.xlsx 100 times, each time perturbing the transportation costs by multiplying them by $U[0.75, 1.25]$ random variates. For each instance generated this way, record the objective function value, as well as the objective function of the same solution when the correct costs are used. If the hypothesis is correct, the objective function should be less than the true cost for roughly half of the instances and greater for the other half. Do your results confirm the hypothesis? In a few sentences, explain your results, and why they occurred. Also comment on the implications your results have for the importance of having accurate data when choosing facility locations.

7.10 **(1-Center on a Tree)** The *p-center problem* addresses the problem of minimizing the maximum distance that a customer must travel to reach its closest facility, subject to a constraint that we may locate at most p facilities. There are two categories of center problems: absolute and vertex. In an *absolute center problem*, facilities can be located anywhere on the network (i.e., on the vertices or on the links), whereas in a *vertex center problem*, facilities can only be located on the vertices of the network.

Consider the 1-center problem on a tree network in which all of the demands are 1. Prove that the following algorithm finds the optimal solution to both the absolute and the vertex 1-center problem.

Algorithm 7.1 (1-CENTER)

1. Choose any point on the tree and find the vertex that is farthest away from the point that was chosen. Call this vertex v_1.

2. Find the vertex that is farthest from v_1 and call this vertex v_2.

3. The absolute 1-center of the tree is at the midpoint of the (unique) path from v_1 to v_2. The vertex 1-center of the tree is on the vertex of the tree that is closest to the absolute 1-center.

7.11 **(2-Center on a Tree)** Prove that the following algorithm finds the optimal solution to the absolute 2-center problem. (See Problem 7.10 for a description of the p-center problem.)

Algorithm 7.2 (2-CENTER)

1. Using Algorithm 7.1, find the absolute 1-center of the tree.

2. Delete from the tree the link containing the absolute 1-center. (If the absolute 1-center is on a vertex, delete one of the links incident to the center on the path from v_1 to v_2.) This divides the tree into two disconnected subtrees.

3. Use the 1-center algorithm to find the absolute 1-center of each of the subtrees. These constitute a solution to the absolute 2-center problem.

7.12 **(N-Echelon Location Problem)** By extending the approach used in Section 7.3, formulate a facility location model with N echelons, for general $N \geq 3$. Echelon N ships products to echelon $N - 1$, which ships products to echelon $N - 2$, and so on; echelon 1 serves the end customer. Define any new notation clearly. Explain the objective function and each of the constraints in words. *Note*: No decision variables should have more than 3 indices.

CHAPTER 8

DEALING WITH UNCERTAINTY IN FACILITY LOCATION

8.1 INTRODUCTION

The facility location models in Chapter 7 are deterministic—they assume that all of the parameters in the model are known with certainty, and that facilities always operate as expected. However, the life span of a typical factory, warehouse, or other facility is measured in years or decades, and over this long time horizon, many aspects of the environment in which the facility operates may change. It is a good idea to anticipate these eventualities when designing the facility network so that the facilities perform well even in the face of uncertainty.

In this chapter, we discuss three types of models that incorporate stochastic elements into facility location models. All three models are based on the UFLP discussed in Section 7.2. The first model, the location model with risk pooling (LMRP; Section 8.2), assumes that the facilities hold inventory in order to protect against uncertain demand and incorporates the costs of this inventory in the objective function. In Section 8.3, we discuss scenario-based approaches for coping with uncertainty in facility location models. Like the LMRP, these models consider stochastic demand, but they assume that changes in demand occur gradually over time (for example, as populations shift, or as demand for the firm's products increases). Inventory is not an appropriate tool for coping with this type of uncertainty. Rather, the uncertainty is modeled using *scenarios*, and the model chooses facility locations that perform well under all of these scenarios. Finally, in Section 8.4, we turn our attention to supply uncertainty. We discuss the reliable fixed-charge location model (RFLP), which assumes that facilities may be disrupted and that demand must be re-routed through the network when this happens.

8.2   THE LOCATION MODEL WITH RISK POOLING

8.2.1   Introduction

In an inventory system, both the cycle stock and the safety stock tend to be concave functions of the demand served. To take a simple example, suppose the demand is distributed as $N(\xi\mu, \xi\sigma^2)$ for $\xi \geq 0$. As we increase ξ, we scale both the mean and variance. If the cycle stock is set using the EOQ formula (we will see below why this is a reasonable assumption), then

$$\text{cycle stock} = \sqrt{2K\xi\mu/h}. \tag{8.1}$$

And, again for reasons to be discussed below, the safety stock is given by

$$\text{safety stock} = z_\alpha \sigma \sqrt{\xi}, \tag{8.2}$$

where α is the desired service level. The right-hand sides of both (8.1) and (8.2) are concave functions of ξ.

The upshot of this analysis is that, given the choice between many small facilities or few large facilities to serve a geographically dispersed demand, inventory costs would always favor the latter—both because of the economies of scale present in cycle stock costs and because of the risk-pooling effect with regard to safety stock costs (see Section 6.2). Of course, this doesn't mean we should always locate only a single DC. Rather, we must consider the fixed costs of the DCs and their locations (and hence transportation costs) before deciding how many DCs to open, and where. The *location model with risk pooling* (LMRP),[1] introduced by Daskin et al. (2002) and Shen et al. (2003), simultaneously optimizes all of these factors.

As we will see below, the LMRP is structured much like the UFLP, with two extra nonlinear terms in the objective function that represent the cycle- and safety-stock costs. Importantly, these costs are calculated *without including any decision variables to represent inventory decisions*. Despite its nonlinear (in fact, concave) objective function, the LMRP can be solved quite efficiently using extensions of algorithms for the UFLP.

---

[1]The name "location model with risk pooling" is actually a bit misleading, since it suggests that risk pooling of safety stock is the only inventory aspect considered in the location model. On the contrary, the LMRP considers economies of scale in both cycle and safety stocks. In fact, the cycle stock costs tend to drive the results of the LMRP much more than the safety stock costs. This model is also commonly known as the "location–inventory model," although that term is also sometimes used to describe a more general class of models.

Imagine a set of retailers, each with random demand. Some of these retailers will be converted to DCs, which will then serve the non-DC retailers (as well as their own demand). The discussion of the UFLP in Section 7.2 referred to "customers" instead of "retailers," but the terms are interchangeable—both refer to some source of demand. Also, by stating that some retailers will be "converted" into DCs, we are assuming that $I = J$ (using the notation of Section 7.2.2). We can make this assumption without loss of generality since if there is a retailer that is not a potential facility site, we can set its fixed cost to ∞, while if there is a potential facility site that is not a retailer, we can set its demand to 0.

The original motivation for the LMRP was a study of a Chicago-area blood bank system, in which inventories of blood platelets (an expensive and perishable component of donated blood) were being stored at individual hospitals, which ordered them from the blood bank's main headquarters. The hospitals were doing a poor job of managing these inventories: Some hospitals were routinely throwing away expired platelets because they had ordered too much, while others were chronically under-stocked and were requesting expensive emergency shipments from the blood bank. The hope was that certain hospitals could be established as distribution centers that would serve their own demand as well as those of nearby hospitals. This would allow the total amount of inventory to remain low while meeting the same service level requirements, due to the risk pooling effect. Moreover, the cost of shipments (both regular and emergency) would decrease since hospitals would now be located closer to their suppliers (Daskin et al. 2002).

8.2.2 Problem Statement

Let I be the set of retailers, each of which faces normally distributed daily demands. Demands are assumed to be independent both among retailers and from day to day. The objective of the LMRP is to determine how many DCs to locate, where to locate them, and which retailers to assign to each DC to minimize the total expected location, transportation, and inventory costs, while ensuring a specified level of service. Each DC receives product from a single supplier. Each DC is assumed to follow an (r, Q) policy to maintain its inventory, with a type-1 service level requirement. The cost of such a policy is approximated in the LMRP using the heuristic method described in Section 4.3.2.3: Q is set using by the deterministic EOQ formula, and r is set using a formula akin to (4.11).

8.2.3 Notation

Define the following notation:

Set
$\quad I \quad$ = set of retailers/potential facility sites
Parameters
$\quad$ *Demand*
$\quad\quad \mu_i \quad$ = mean daily demand of retailer i

σ_i^2 = variance of daily demand at retailer i

Costs

f_j = fixed (daily) cost to open a DC at site j

K_j = fixed cost for DC j to place an order from the supplier, including fixed components of both ordering and transportation costs

c_j = per-unit cost for each item ordered by DC j from the supplier, including per-unit inbound transportation costs

d_{ij} = per-unit outbound transportation cost from DC j to retailer i

h_j = holding cost per unit per day at DC j

Other

L_j = lead time (in days) for orders placed by DC j to the supplier

α = desired fraction of DC order cycles during which no stockout occurs

Decision Variables

x_j = 1 if retailer j is selected as a DC, 0 otherwise

y_{ij} = 1 if retailer i is served by DC j, 0 otherwise

8.2.4   Objective Function

The objective function will be of the form

minimize   [location cost] + [per-unit costs] + [cycle stock cost] + [safety stock cost].

Location Cost: The fixed location cost is given by

$$\sum_{j\in I} f_j x_j. \tag{8.3}$$

Per-Unit Costs: The per-unit costs have two parts: the inbound cost (which includes both purchase and transportation costs from the supplier), given by

$$\sum_{j\in J}\sum_{i\in I} \mu_i c_j y_{ij}, \tag{8.4}$$

and the outbound cost, given by

$$\sum_{j\in I}\sum_{i\in I} \mu_i d_{ij} y_{ij}. \tag{8.5}$$

Combining (8.7)–(8.5), we get the following objective function:

$$\sum_{j\in I}\left[f_j x_j + \sum_{i\in I}\mu_i(c_j + d_{ij})y_{ij} + \sqrt{2K_j h_j \sum_{i\in I}\mu_i y_{ij}} + h_j z_\alpha \sqrt{\sum_{i\in I} L_j \sigma_i^2 y_{ij}} \right]. \tag{8.6}$$

Cycle Stock Cost: First suppose that DC j is open and that it serves a total (expected) annual demand of D. The fixed cost per order is K_j, the per-unit cost is c_j, and the holding cost is h_j. From (3.5), we know that if the DC follows the optimal EOQ policy, its annual cost will be

$$\sqrt{2K_j D h_j}.$$

Now, using the notation introduced in Section 8.2.3, we know that $D = \sum_{i \in I} \mu_i y_{ij}$. Therefore, the cycle stock cost at DC j is given by

$$\sqrt{2K_j h_j \sum_{i \in I} \mu_i y_{ij}}. \qquad (8.7)$$

Note that this concise formulation for the cycle stock cost would not be possible if we didn't have a closed-form expression for the optimal EOQ cost, as in (3.5). If, to calculate the optimal EOQ cost, it was necessary to run an algorithm to find Q^* and then to plug Q^* into the cost function, then we'd need to include a variable for Q_j and somehow optimize these when we optimize all the other decision variables. This would complicate the model and algorithm considerably.

Safety Stock Cost: From (4.11) we know that the amount of safety stock required is $z_\alpha \sigma$, where σ is the standard deviation of *lead-time* demand seen by the DC. (Remember that the safety stock level for an (r, Q) policy is given by $r - \mu$.) The variance of *daily* demand seen by DC j is $\sum_{i \in I} \sigma_i^2 y_{ij}$, so

$$\sigma = \sqrt{\sum_{i \in I} L_j \sigma_i^2 y_{ij}}. \qquad (8.8)$$

Therefore, the total safety stock cost at DC j is given by

$$h_j z_\alpha \sqrt{L_j \sum_{i \in I} \sigma_i^2 y_{ij}}. \qquad (8.9)$$

The risk-pooling effect can be seen directly in this expression: As more demand is added to DC j, the amount of safety stock increases as the square root of the demand served. Adding a new retailer's demand to DC j moves the cost along the flat part of the square-root curve, while establishing the retailer as its own DC starts it all over again at the steep part.

8.2.5 NLIP Formulation

The LMRP can now be formulated as a nonlinear integer program (NLIP):

$$(\text{LMRP}) \quad \text{minimize} \quad \sum_{j \in I} \left[f_j x_j + \sum_{i \in I} \mu_i (c_j + d_{ij}) y_{ij} + \sqrt{2K_j h_j \sum_{i \in I} \mu_i y_{ij}} \right.$$

$$\left. + h_j z_\alpha \sqrt{\sum_{i \in I} L_j \sigma_i^2 y_{ij}} \right] \qquad (8.10)$$

$$\text{subject to} \qquad \sum_{j \in J} y_{ij} = 1 \qquad \forall i \in I \tag{8.11}$$

$$y_{ij} \leq x_j \qquad \forall i \in I, \forall j \in I \tag{8.12}$$

$$x_j \in \{0,1\} \qquad \forall j \in I \tag{8.13}$$

$$y_{ij} \in \{0,1\} \qquad \forall i \in I, \forall j \in I \tag{8.14}$$

Constraints (8.11) require each retailer to be assigned to some DC, and constraints (8.12) require that DC to be open. Constraints (8.13) and (8.14) are integrality constraints. Notice that the LMRP has the exact same constraints as the UFLP—only the objective function is different. (Actually, in the UFLP, constraints (7.5) are non-negativity constraints, not integrality constraints. But as we said in Section 7.2.2, the non-negativity constraints in the UFLP can be replaced with integrality constraints without changing the problem.) This suggests that the Lagrangian relaxation method described in Section 7.2.4 might be adapted to solve the LMRP. That is exactly the approach that Daskin et al. (2002) take, and the approach we discuss in Section 8.2.6. In addition, in Section 8.2.7, we discuss a column generation algorithm, introduced by Shen et al. (2003).

8.2.6   Lagrangian Relaxation

As in the UFLP, we will solve the LMRP by relaxing the assignment constraints (8.11) to obtain the following Lagrangian subproblem:

(LMRP-LR_λ)

$$\begin{aligned}
\text{minimize} \quad & \sum_{j \in I} \left[f_j x_j + \sum_{i \in I} \mu_i(c_j + d_{ij}) y_{ij} + \sqrt{2 K_j h_j \sum_{i \in I} \mu_i y_{ij}} \right.\\
& \left. + h_j z_\alpha \sqrt{\sum_{i \in I} L_j \sigma_i^2 y_{ij}} \right] + \sum_{i \in I} \lambda_i \left(1 - \sum_{j \in I} y_{ij} \right) \\
= & \sum_{j \in I} \left[f_j x_j + \sum_{i \in I} (\mu_i(c_j + d_{ij}) - \lambda_i) y_{ij} + \sqrt{2 K_j h_j \sum_{i \in I} \mu_i y_{ij}} \right.\\
& \left. + h_j z_\alpha \sqrt{\sum_{i \in I} L_j \sigma_i^2 y_{ij}} \right] + \sum_{i \in I} \lambda_i
\end{aligned} \tag{8.15}$$

$$\text{subject to} \quad y_{ij} \leq x_j \qquad \forall i \in I, \forall j \in I \tag{8.16}$$

$$x_j \in \{0,1\} \qquad \forall j \in I \tag{8.17}$$

$$y_{ij} \in \{0,1\} \qquad \forall i \in I, \forall j \in I \tag{8.18}$$

8.2.6.1 *Solving the Subproblem*
Just like the subproblem for the UFLP, (LMRP-LR$_\lambda$) decomposes by j. Unfortunately, computing the benefit β_j is not as straightforward as it was for the UFLP because of the square-root terms. Instead, for each j, we need to solve the following problem:

$$(\text{P}_j) \quad \beta_j = \text{minimize} \quad \sum_{i \in I}(\mu_i(c_j + d_{ij}) - \lambda_i)y_{ij} + \sqrt{2K_j h_j \sum_{i \in I} \mu_i y_{ij}}$$

$$+ h_j z_\alpha \sqrt{\sum_{i \in I} L_j \sigma_i^2 y_{ij}} \tag{8.19}$$

$$\text{subject to} \quad y_{ij} \in \{0, 1\} \quad \forall i \in I \tag{8.20}$$

Although (P_j) is a concave integer minimization problem, it can be solved relatively efficiently—in order $O(|I|^2 \log |I|)$ time, using an algorithm developed by Shu et al. (2005). We won't discuss this algorithm. Instead, we'll discuss an even more efficient algorithm that relies on the following assumption:

Assumption 8.1 *The ratio of the demand variance to the demand mean is identical for all retailers. That is, for all $i \in I$, $\sigma_i^2 / \mu_i = \gamma$ for some constant $\gamma \geq 0$.*

At first glance, this seems like an unreasonable assumption to make. However, if the demands come from a Poisson process (as is commonly assumed), Assumption 8.1 holds exactly, since the variance of a Poisson process equals its mean (hence $\sigma_i^2 / \mu_i = 1$ for all i). Now (8.19) can be rewritten as follows:

$$\sum_{i \in I}(\mu_i(c_j + d_{ij}) - \lambda_i)y_{ij} + \sqrt{2K_j h_j \sum_{i \in I} \mu_i y_{ij}} + h_j z_\alpha \sqrt{\sum_{i \in I} L_j \sigma_i^2 y_{ij}}$$

$$= \sum_{i \in I}(\mu_i(c_j + d_{ij}) - \lambda_i)y_{ij} + \sqrt{2K_j h_j \sum_{i \in I} \mu_i y_{ij}} + h_j z_\alpha \sqrt{\sum_{i \in I} L_j \gamma \mu_i y_{ij}}$$

$$= \sum_{i \in I}(\mu_i(c_j + d_{ij}) - \lambda_i)y_{ij} + \left(\sqrt{2K_j h_j} + h_j z_\alpha \sqrt{L_j \gamma}\right)\sqrt{\sum_{i \in I} \mu_i y_{ij}}$$

We have gotten rid of one of the square-root terms. Now (P_j) can be written as follows:

$$(\text{P}_j') \quad \beta_j = \text{minimize} \quad \sum_{i \in I} a_i y_i + \sqrt{\sum_{i \in I} b_i y_i} \tag{8.21}$$

$$\text{subject to} \quad y_i \in \{0, 1\} \quad \forall i \in I \tag{8.22}$$

where

$$a_i = \mu_i(c_j + d_{ij}) - \lambda_i$$

$$b_i = \mu_i \left(\sqrt{2K_j h_j} + h_j z_\alpha \sqrt{L_j \gamma}\right)^2$$

$$y_i = y_{ij}.$$

It turns out that (P'_j) can be solved even more efficiently than (P_j), in $O(|I| \log |I|)$ time. We will describe the algorithm shortly. First, let $I^- = \{i \in I | a_i < 0\}$; that is, I^- is the set of retailers that have negative a_i. Let $I_1^- = \{i \in I^- | b_i > 0\}$ and $I_2^- = \{i \in I^- | b_i = 0\}$. Note that $I_1^- \cup I_2^- = I^-$ since $b_i \geq 0$ for all i. We will further assume that the elements of I_1^- are indexed and sorted such that

$$\frac{a_1}{b_1} \leq \frac{a_2}{b_2} \leq \cdots \leq \frac{a_m}{b_m},$$

where $m = |I_1^-|$. The algorithm for solving (P'_j) relies on the following theorem:

Theorem 8.1 *There exists an optimal solution y^* to (P'_j) such that the following property holds:*

(1) $y_i^* = 0$ for all $i \in I \setminus I^-$

Moreover, for every optimal solution y^* to (P'_j), the following two properties hold:

(2) $y_i^* = 1$ for all $i \in I_2^-$

(3) If $y_k^* = 1$ for some $k \in I_1^-$, then $y_l^* = 1$ for all $l \in \{1, \ldots, k-1\}$

Proof. (1) follows from the fact that for all i, $b_i \geq 0$; if $a_i \geq 0$ as well, then the objective function does not increase when $y_i = 1$ as opposed to $y_i = 0$. (2) follows from the fact that if $b_i = 0$ and $a_i < 0$, then setting $y_i = 1$ decreases the objective function.

To prove (3), suppose, for a contradiction, that y^* is an optimal solution such that $y_k^* = 1$ for some $k \in I_1^-$ but $y_l^* = 0$ for some $l \in \{1, \ldots, k-1\}$. Define two new solutions y' and y'' as follows:

$$y_i' = \begin{cases} 1, & \text{if } i = l \\ y_i^*, & \text{otherwise} \end{cases}$$

$$y_i'' = \begin{cases} 0, & \text{if } i = k \\ y_i^*, & \text{otherwise} \end{cases}$$

In other words, $y' = y^*$ except that y_l^* is changed to 1, and $y'' = y^*$ except that y_k^* is changed to 0. (See Figure 8.1.) Let z^*, z', and z'' be the objective values of y^*, y', and y'', respectively.
   Let $R = \{i \in I_1^- | y_i^* = 1\}$ and

$$B = \sum_{i \in R} b_i.$$

Then

$$z' - z^* = a_l + \sqrt{B + b_l} - \sqrt{B}$$

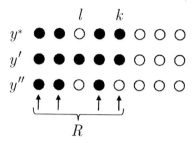

$l \quad k$

$y^* \quad \bullet \bullet \circ \bullet \bullet \circ \circ \circ$

$y' \quad \bullet \bullet \bullet \bullet \bullet \circ \circ \circ$

$y'' \quad \bullet \bullet \circ \bullet \circ \circ \circ \circ$

R

Figure 8.1 Proof of Theorem 8.1(c). Filled circles represent $y_i = 1$; open circles represent $y_i = 0$.

and

$$z^* - z'' = a_k + \sqrt{B} - \sqrt{B - b_k}.$$

Next, note that

$$\frac{a_l}{b_l} \leq \frac{a_k}{b_k} \tag{8.23}$$

by assumption and that

$$\frac{\sqrt{B + b_l} - \sqrt{B}}{b_l} < \frac{\sqrt{B} - \sqrt{B - b_k}}{b_k} \tag{8.24}$$

by the strict concavity of the square-root function. Therefore,

$$
\begin{aligned}
\frac{z' - z^*}{b_l} &= \frac{a_l}{b_l} + \frac{\sqrt{B + b_l} - \sqrt{B}}{b_l} \\
&\leq \frac{a_k}{b_k} + \frac{\sqrt{B + b_l} - \sqrt{B}}{b_l} \quad \text{(by (8.23))} \\
&< \frac{a_k}{b_k} + \frac{\sqrt{B} - \sqrt{B - b_k}}{b_k} \quad \text{(by (8.24))} \\
&= \frac{z^* - z''}{b_k} \\
&\leq 0 \quad \text{(since } y^* \text{ is optimal and } b_k > 0).
\end{aligned}
$$

Since $b_l > 0$, we have that $z' - z^* < 0$. In other words, y' is a strictly better solution than y^*, violating the assumption that y^* is optimal. Therefore, y^* satisfies (3). ∎

The upshot of Theorem 8.1 is that an optimal solution to (P_j) exists that has the form shown in Figure 8.2. (P_j) can therefore be solved using the following algorithm.

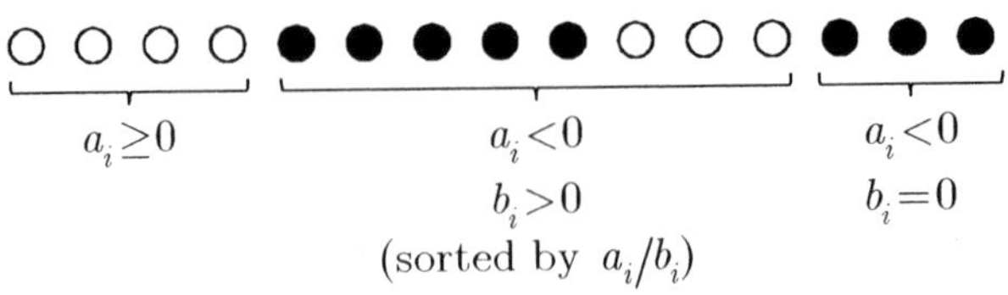

Figure 8.2   Solution to problem (P_j). Filled circles represent $y_i = 1$; open circles represent $y_i = 0$.

Algorithm 8.1 (Solution for (P'_j))

1. Set $y_i = 0$ for all $i \in I \setminus I^-$.

2. Set $y_i = 1$ for all $i \in I^-$ such that $b_i = 0$.

3. Sort the elements in I_1^- in increasing order of a_i/b_i.

4. For each $r \in \{0\} \cup I_1^-$, compute

$$S_r = \sum_{i=1}^{r} a_i + \sqrt{\sum_{i=1}^{r} b_i}. \tag{8.25}$$

   (If $r = 0$, then $S_r = 0$.)

5. Choose the r that minimizes S_r and set $y_i = 1$ for $i = 1, \ldots, r$.

The step with the most iterations is step 3, the sorting step, which can be done in $O(|I| \log |I|)$ time. The algorithm, therefore, can be performed in $O(|I| \log |I|)$ time for each j. At each iteration of the Lagrangian procedure, we must solve (P_j) for each j, so the total effort required at each iteration is $O(|I|^2 \log |I|)$. To solve (LMRP-LR$_\lambda$), we set $x_j = 1$ if $\beta_j + f_j < 0$ and set $y_{ij} = 1$ if $x_j = 1$ and if $y_i = 1$ in the optimal solution to (P'_j).

The proof of Theorem 8.1 did not use any special properties of the square-root function except its concavity. Therefore, Theorem 8.1 still holds if we replace the square-root term in (8.21) with *any* concave function of the total mean demand served by DC j. (Note that this square-root term is a concave function not only of $\sum_i b_i y_i$, but also of $\sum_i \mu_i y_i$, the total mean demand served by DC j, since b_i equals μ_i times a constant that is independent of i.) This means that the Lagrangian relaxation algorithm discussed here can be used to solve (LMRP) if the sum of the square-root terms in the objective function is replaced by any concave function of the total mean demand served by DC j. This property has allowed the LMRP to be extended in a number of ways; see, e.g., Qi et al. (2010).

8.2.6.2 Finding Upper Bounds As in the Lagrangian relaxation algorithm for the UFLP, at each iteration we want to convert a solution to the Lagrangian subproblem into a feasible solution for the original problem. As before, we start by opening the facilities that are open in the optimal solution to (LMRP-LR$_\lambda$). Unlike in the UFLP, however, retailers are not always assigned to their nearest open facilities in the LMRP since assignment costs are based on inventory as well as transportation. In other words, the savings from the risk-pooling effect may outweigh the increased transportation cost if a retailer is assigned to a more distant facility. (See Problem 8.3.) In fact, it is possible for the following strange thing to happen in an optimal solution to the LMRP: A DC is opened in, say, Chicago, but the retailer in Chicago is served by a DC in Minneapolis instead of the DC in Chicago. This would probably never happen in practice, though, so it's a little inconvenient that our model would allow this to be optimal. Fortunately, if Assumption 8.1 holds, it can be shown that this situation is never optimal.

Once we choose which DCs to open, we assign retailers to DCs as follows. First, we loop through all retailers with $\sum_j y_{ij} \geq 1$ in the optimal solution to (LMRP-LR$_\lambda$) (retailers that are assigned to at least one facility) and assign each retailer to the facility j with $y_{ij} = 1$ that minimizes the increase in cost based on the assignments already made. Next, we loop through all retailers with $\sum_j y_{ij} = 0$ and assign these retailers to the open facility that minimizes the increase in cost based on the assignments already made. Note that we only allow retailers with $\sum_j y_{ij} \geq 1$ to be assigned to DCs for which $y_{ij} = 1$, while we allow retailers with $\sum_j y_{ij} = 0$ to be assigned to any open DC.

After assigning retailers to DCs in this manner, we may want to apply two *improvement heuristics*:

- *Retailer reassignment*: For each retailer i, determine whether there is a DC that i can be assigned to instead of its current DC that would decrease the objective value. If so, reassign the retailer. If the reassignment means that the old DC no longer has any retailers assigned to it, it can be closed, saving the fixed cost, as well.

- *DC exchange*: Loop through the DCs, looking for an open DC j and a closed DC k such that if j were closed and k were opened (and retailers reassigned as needed), the objective value would decrease. If such a pair can be found, the DCs are exchanged and the heuristic continues.

8.2.6.3 Other Aspects of the Algorithm The remaining aspects of the Lagrangian relaxation algorithm (subgradient optimization, branch and bound) are identical to the algorithm described for the UFLP in Section 7.2.4.

8.2.6.4 Computational Results Most papers that introduce Lagrangian relaxation algorithms test the algorithm on one or more data sets. These data sets may come from real-life problems, but more commonly, they are randomly generated since real-life data are hard to come by. There are several performance measures of interest when evaluating a Lagrangian relaxation algorithm. For example:

- How quickly does the algorithm solve the test problems? CPU times of under a minute are generally considered to be quite fast; but times of an hour or longer can be acceptable as well, depending on the context. Some people argue that for strategic problems like facility location, which might be solved only once every few years, it's acceptable for the algorithm to take several hours. Others argue that these models are typically run many times during the process of fine-tuning the data and running what-if scenarios, in which case long run times may be unacceptable.

- How large are the test problems? CPU times will be dependent on the size of the test data sets, so they should be evaluated with this in mind. Ideally, the data sets tested should include a range of sizes (in this case, number of retailers) so that the reader gets a sense of how fast the CPU time grows with the problem size and how large a problem the algorithm can handle before it gets too slow.

- How tight are the bounds achieved by the Lagrangian process, before branch-and-bound begins (i.e., at the root node of the branch-and-bound tree)? Just like in the standard LP-based branch-and-bound algorithm, it is important to have tight bounds at the root node, otherwise too much branching may be required before the optimality gap is closed.

- How many branch-and-bound nodes are required before the optimal solution is found (and proven optimal)? This goes hand-in-hand with the previous question, since large root-node gaps will probably mean that many branch-and-bound nodes are required. Note that the optimal solution may be found quite early, but many branch-and-bound nodes may be required to *prove* optimality. That is, if the root-node gap is large, it's possible that we've already found the optimal solution but that branch-and-bound will be required to prove that it is optimal.

The algorithm discussed in this section turns out to be quite efficient by these measures. Daskin et al. (2002) report that they solved problems with up to 150 nodes in under 20 seconds on a desktop computer, with no more than 3 branch-and-bound nodes required for each problem. Root-node gaps are generally less than 1%.

The authors report the following managerial insights. First, the optimal number of DCs increases as the transportation cost increases and decreases as the holding cost increases. (This result is not surprising, but it is important for validating the model.) Second, although the optimal solution may involve a few retailers that are assigned to facilities other than the closest (see p. 219), forcing retailers to be assigned to their closest facilities (for reasons of convenience) does not generally increase the cost by too much. Finally, fewer DCs are located when inventory is taken into account. That is, a firm that solves the UFLP instead of the LMRP, ignoring inventory, will build too many DCs, because it ignores the tendency toward consolidation brought about by the economies of scale in inventory costs.

8.2.7   Column Generation

Shen et al. (2003) present a different algorithm for solving the LMRP. Their method
involves formulating the problem as a *set covering problem* and solving it using
column generation. Here's a brief overview of how it works.

First suppose that we could write down every possible subset $R \subseteq I$. (There are
$2^{|I|}$ such subsets.) Let $\mathcal{R}$ be the collection of all of these subsets. For each subset
$R \in \mathcal{R}$ and for each facility $j \in R$, let $c_{R,j}$ be the cost of serving all of the retailers
in R from a DC located at j:

$$c_{R,j} = f_j + \sum_{i \in R} \mu_i(c_j + d_{ij}) + \sqrt{2K_j h_j \sum_{i \in R} \mu_i} + h_j z_\alpha \sqrt{\sum_{i \in R} L_j \sigma_i^2}.$$

Then choose the cheapest facility in R and call its cost c_R:

$$c_R = \min_{j \in R}\{c_{R,j}\}.$$

The idea behind modeling this problem as a set covering problem is to choose several
sets from $\mathcal{R}$ so that every retailer is contained in exactly one set. Each set corresponds
to a group of retailers that will be served by a single facility; c_R represents the cost
of this group.

The set covering model has a single decision variable for each $R \in \mathcal{R}$:

$Z_R = 1$ if set R is in the solution, 0 otherwise

The model is formulated as follows:

(LMRP-SC)   minimize $\quad \sum_{R \in \mathcal{R}} c_R z_R \quad$ (8.26)

subject to $\quad \sum_{R \in \mathcal{R}: i \in R} z_R \geq 1 \qquad \forall i \in I \quad$ (8.27)

$z_R \in \{0, 1\} \qquad \forall R \in \mathcal{R} \quad$ (8.28)

The objective function (8.26) computes the cost of all of the sets chosen. Constraints
(8.27) say that every retailer must be included in at least one chosen set—that is,
every retailer must be assigned to some open facility. Although (8.27) is written
with a $\geq$, any optimal solution will have each retailer assigned to *exactly* one facility
(why?), so the constraints could be written with an $=$. This is called a "set covering"
model because the idea is to choose a number of sets to "cover" every element in I.

It seems like we've lost two aspects of the original problem in formulating it as a
set covering problem. First, (LMRP-SC) is linear while (LMRP) is nonlinear. What
happened to the nonlinearity? Computing each cost c_R requires solving a nonlinear
problem, so the nonlinearity in (LMRP) is present in the setup to (LMRP-SC), not
in (LMRP-SC) itself. Second, nothing in the formulation of (LMRP-SC) indicates
which j are chosen—only which sets are chosen. That is, if $R = \{2, 4, 7, 11\}$ and
$z_R = 1$, we know that retailers 2, 4, 7, and 11 are served by the same DC, and that

that DC is either 2, 4, 7, or 11, but which one is it? The answer to this question, too, is hidden in the computation of c_R. To compute c_R, we had to compute $c_{R,j}$ for $j = 2, 4, 7, 11$; whichever was smallest became c_R. Somewhere we would have recorded which j gave the best cost, and we'd use that to convert a solution to (LMRP-SC) into a solution to the original problem.

In principle, we could solve the **LMRP** by enumerating all the sets in $\mathcal{R}$ and then solving (LMRP-SC). Unfortunately, there are two problems with this approach. First, there are $2^{|I|}$ elements in $\mathcal{R}$—far too many to enumerate. Second, even if we could enumerate $\mathcal{R}$, it's not clear how we would solve (LMRP-SC). The solution to the first problem is to enumerate a small handful of elements of $\mathcal{R}$ first, then identify new elements as needed as the algorithm proceeds. (How do we do this? We'll find out below.) The solution to the second problem is to solve the LP relaxation of (LMRP-SC), then use branch-and-bound if the resulting solution is not integer. It turns out that the set covering problem usually has a very tight LP bound. Sometimes the solution to the LP relaxation is naturally all-integer; if not, it doesn't usually take much branching to find an optimal integer solution. So in what follows, we'll focus on solving the LP relaxation of (LMRP-SC), not (LMRP-SC) itself.

Suppose we have enumerated a subset of $\mathcal{R}$—call it $\mathcal{R}'$. We might do this by generating random sets, or using some heuristic. We need to solve the LP relaxation of (LMRP-SC) including only the sets in $\mathcal{R}'$, not all of $\mathcal{R}$. This problem is called the *restricted master problem*; we will denote it by $(\overline{\text{LMRP-SC}})$:

$$(\overline{\text{LMRP-SC}}) \quad \text{minimize} \quad \sum_{R \in \mathcal{R}'} c_R z_R \tag{8.29}$$

$$\text{subject to} \quad \sum_{R \in \mathcal{R}': i \in R} z_R \geq 1 \qquad \forall i \in I \tag{8.30}$$

$$0 \leq z_R \leq 1 \qquad \forall R \in \mathcal{R}' \tag{8.31}$$

Suppose we solve $(\overline{\text{LMRP-SC}})$. Let $\bar{z}_R$ $(R \in \mathcal{R}')$ be an optimal solution. Recall from basic LP theory that any optimal solution to an LP has a corresponding optimal *dual solution*. Let $\bar{\pi}_i$ $(i \in I)$ be the optimal dual solution corresponding to $\bar{z}$. Recall also that a solution to a minimization LP is optimal if every variable has non-negative reduced cost with respect to the dual variables. Therefore, if we were to solve $(\overline{\text{LMRP-SC}})$ with all of $\mathcal{R}$ instead of just $\mathcal{R}'$, $\bar{z}$ would still be optimal provided that

$$c_R - \sum_{i \in R} \bar{\pi}_i \geq 0 \tag{8.32}$$

for each $R \in \mathcal{R}$. So even if we didn't solve $(\overline{\text{LMRP-SC}})$ over all of $\mathcal{R}$, we can check whether a given solution is optimal by checking (8.32) for all $R \in \mathcal{R}$. Of course, we don't want to check (8.32) for all $R \in \mathcal{R}$ since we can't enumerate $\mathcal{R}$. Instead, we search for an $R \in \mathcal{R}$ that *violates* (8.32). But how?

Suppose R_j^* is the set in $\mathcal{R}$ that uses j as its designated DC and has the minimum reduced cost. If R_j^* has non-negative reduced cost for all $j \in I$, then every $R \in \mathcal{R}$ has non-negative reduced cost. For each j, we can find R_j^* by solving the following problem:

$$\text{minimize} \quad f_j + \sum_{i \in I} \mu_i (c_j + d_{ij}) y_{ij} + \sqrt{2K_j h_j \sum_{i \in I} \mu_i y_{ij}}$$

$$+ h_j z_\alpha \sqrt{\sum_{i \in I} L_j \sigma_i^2 y_{ij}} - \sum_{i \in I} \bar{\pi}_i y_{ij}$$

$$= f_j + \sum_{i \in I} (\mu_i (c_j + d_{ij}) - \bar{\pi}_i) y_{ij} + \sqrt{2K_j h_j \sum_{i \in I} \mu_i y_{ij}}$$

$$+ h_j z_\alpha \sqrt{\sum_{i \in I} L_j \sigma_i^2 y_{ij}} \qquad (8.33)$$

$$\text{subject to} \quad y_{ij} \in \{0, 1\} \quad \forall i \in I \qquad (8.34)$$

A solution to this problem can be converted to a set R_j^* by setting

$$R_j^* = \{ j \in I | y_{ij} = 1 \}.$$

Does this problem look familiar? Of course it does—this is the same problem as (P_j) (see p. 215), plus a constant (f_j) and with λ_i replaced by $\bar{\pi}_i$. We already know how to solve this problem.

So, at each iteration of the algorithm, we solve $(\overline{\text{LMRP-SC}})$, then solve the problem above for each j. If the objective function is nonnegative for every j, we have found the optimal solution to $(\overline{\text{LMRP-SC}})$. If it is negative for some j, then we add the corresponding set R_j^* to $\mathcal{R}'$ and solve $(\overline{\text{LMRP-SC}})$ again. This method is called *column generation* since it consists of generating good variables (columns) on the fly.

The computational results reported by Shen et al. (2003) suggest that this algorithm executes quickly, but not quite as quickly as the Lagrangian relaxation algorithm.

8.3 STOCHASTIC AND ROBUST LOCATION MODELS

8.3.1 Introduction

In this section, we discuss approaches for optimizing facility location decisions when the model parameters are stochastic. The stochastic parameters are modeled using *scenarios*, each of which specifies all of the parameters in one possible future state. We must choose facility locations now, before we know which scenario will occur, but we may re-assign customers to facilities after we know the scenario. That is, facility locations are *first-stage decisions*, while customer assignments are *second-stage decisions*.

In some models, we know the probability distribution of the scenarios (i.e., the probability that each scenario occurs), while in others we do not. Models in which the probability distribution is known fall under the domain of *stochastic programming*, while those in which it is not are part of *robust optimization*. In stochastic programming models, the objective is usually to minimize the expected cost over the scenarios. Several objectives are used for robust facility location models, the most common of which is to minimize the worst-case cost over the scenarios. We will discuss both stochastic and robust approaches for facility location in this section.

Suppose a given set of facilities is meant to operate for 20 years. There are several ways to interpret the way scenarios occur over this time. One way is to assume that we build the facilities today, and then a single scenario occurs tomorrow and lasts for all 20 years. Another is to assume that a new scenario occurs, say, every year or every month, drawn in an iid manner from the scenario distribution. Either interpretation is acceptable for the models we consider in this section.

Choosing the scenarios to include in the model is a difficult task, as much art as science. Expert judgment plays an important role in this process, as can the demand modeling techniques described in Chapter 2. The number of scenarios chosen plays a role in the computational performance of these models: They generally take longer to solve as the number of scenarios increases.

A wide range of approaches for modeling and solving stochastic location problems has been proposed. We discuss only a small subset of them. For a more thorough review, see Snyder (2006).

We introduce the following new notation, which we will use throughout this section:

Set

S = set of scenarios

Parameters

h_{is} = annual demand of customer $i \in I$ in scenario $s \in S$

c_{ijs} = cost to transport one unit of demand from facility $j \in J$ to customer $i \in I$ in scenario $s \in S$

q_s = probability that scenario q occurs

Decision Variables

y_{ijs} = the fraction of customer i's demand that is served by facility j in scenario s

Otherwise, the notation is identical to the notation for the UFLP introduced in Section 7.2.2.

8.3.2 The Stochastic Fixed-Charge Location Problem

Suppose we know the scenario probabilities q_s. Our objective is to minimize the total expected cost of locating facilities and then serving customers. We will refer to this problem as the *stochastic fixed-charge location problem* (SFLP). It was formulated by Mirchandani (1980) and Weaver and Church (1983). The SFLP is an example of *stochastic programming*, a field of optimization that considers optimization under uncertainty. (In particular, this formulation is an example of a *deterministic equivalent* problem.) Usually, the objective is to optimize the expected value of the objective function under all scenarios, and that is the approach we will take here.

The SFLP is formulated as follows:

$$\text{(SFLP)} \quad \text{minimize} \quad \sum_{s \in S} q_s \left[\sum_{j \in J} f_j x_j + \sum_{i \in I} \sum_{j \in J} h_{is} c_{ijs} y_{ijs} \right] \tag{8.35}$$

$$\text{subject to} \quad \sum_{j \in J} y_{ijs} = 1 \qquad \forall i \in I, \forall s \in S \tag{8.36}$$

$$y_{ijs} \le x_j \qquad \forall i \in I, \forall j \in J, \forall s \in .S \tag{8.37}$$

$$x_j \in \{0,1\} \qquad \forall j \in J \tag{8.38}$$

$$y_{ijs} \ge 0 \qquad \forall i \in I, \forall j \in J, \forall s \in S \tag{8.39}$$

The objective function (8.35) computes the total expected (fixed plus transportation) cost. Note that, since the fixed costs and location decisions are scenario independent, and since the q_s sum to 1, the objective can be rewritten as:

$$\text{minimize} \quad \sum_{j \in J} f_j x_j + \sum_{s \in S} \sum_{i \in I} \sum_{j \in J} q_s h_{is} c_{ijs} y_{ijs} \tag{8.40}$$

Constraints (8.36) and (8.37) are multi-scenario versions of the assignment and linking constraints, respectively. Constraints (8.38) require the location (x) variables to be binary, and constraints (8.39) require the assignment (y) variables to be non-negative. Note that, if $|S| = 1$, this problem is identical to the classical UFLP. (Therefore, the SFLP is NP-hard.)

The SFLP can be solved using a straightforward modification of the Lagrangian relaxation algorithm for the UFLP (Section 7.2.4). We relax constraints (8.36) to obtain the following Lagrangian subproblem:

(SFLP-LR$_\lambda$)

$$\text{minimize} \quad \sum_{j \in J} f_j x_j + \sum_{i \in I} \sum_{j \in J} \sum_{s \in S} h_{is} c_{ijs} y_{ijs} + \sum_{i \in I} \sum_{s \in S} \lambda_{is} \left(1 - \sum_{j \in J} y_{ijs} \right)$$

$$= \sum_{j \in J} f_j x_j + \sum_{i \in I} \sum_{j \in J} \sum_{s \in S} (h_{is} c_{ijs} - \lambda_{is}) y_{ijs} + \sum_{i \in I} \sum_{s \in S} \lambda_{is} \tag{8.41}$$

$$\text{subject to} \quad y_{ijs} \le x_j \qquad \forall i \in I, \forall j \in J, \forall s \in S \tag{8.42}$$

$$x_j \in \{0,1\} \qquad \forall j \in J \tag{8.43}$$

$$y_{ijs} \ge 0 \qquad \forall i \in I, \forall j \in J, \forall s \in S \tag{8.44}$$

Just as for the UFLP, this problem can be solved easily by inspection. The benefit of opening facility j is

$$\beta_j = \sum_{i \in I} \sum_{s \in S} \min\{0, h_{is} c_{ijs} - \lambda_{is}\}.$$

An optimal solution to (SFLP-LR_λ) can be found by setting

$$x_j = \begin{cases} 1, & \text{if } \beta_j + f_j < 0 \\ 0, & \text{otherwise} \end{cases}$$

$$y_{ijs} = \begin{cases} 1, & \text{if } x_j = 1 \text{ and } h_{is}c_{ijs} - \lambda_{is} < 0 \\ 0, & \text{otherwise.} \end{cases}$$

The objective value of this solution is given by

$$\sum_{j \in J} \min\{0, \beta_j + f_j\} + \sum_{i \in I} \sum_{s \in S} \lambda_{is}.$$

Upper bounds can be obtained from feasible solutions that are constructed by opening the facilities for which $x_j = 1$ in the Lagrangian subproblem and then assigning each customer to its nearest open facility in each scenario. (Since the transportation cost may vary by scenario, so may the optimal assignments.) The remainder of the Lagrangian relaxation algorithm is similar to that for the UFLP.

The SFLP can actually be interpreted as a special case of the deterministic UFLP obtained by replacing the customer set I with $I \times S$. That is, think of creating multiple instances of each customer, one per scenario, and using this as the customer set. Viewed in that light, the formulation and algorithm for SFLP are identical to those for UFLP. This means that an instance of the SFLP with 100 nodes and 10 scenarios is equivalent to an instance of the UFLP with 1000 nodes and can be solved equally quickly.

In fact, the SFLP can also be interpreted another way. Imagine a deterministic problem with multiple products, each of which has its own set of demands and transportation costs. The formulation for SFLP models this situation exactly, so long as we interpret S as the set of products rather than scenarios.

8.3.3 The Minimax Fixed-Charge Location Problem

In this section, we discuss the *minimax fixed-charge location problem* (MFLP), which minimizes the maximum (i.e., worst-case) cost over all scenarios. Minimax problems are an example of *robust optimization*. Robust optimization takes many forms, but the general objective of all of them is to find a solution that performs well no matter how the random variables are realized. Most robust models (including the MFLP) assume that no probabilistic information is known about the random parameters. This is one of the main advantages of robust optimization, since scenario probabilities can be very difficult to estimate. On the other hand, robust optimization problems are generally more difficult to solve than stochastic programming problems. Moreover, minimax models are often criticized for being overly conservative their solutions are driven by a single scenario, which may be unlikely to occur. Nevertheless, they are an important class of problems, both within facility location and in robust optimization in general.

Conceptually, the MFLP can be formulated as follows:

$$\text{minimize} \quad \max_{s \in S} \left\{ \sum_{j \in J} f_j x_j + \sum_{i \in I} \sum_{j \in J} h_{is} c_{ijs} y_{ijs} \right\} \qquad (8.45)$$

subject to the same constraints as in (SFLP). However, this is not a valid objective function for a linear integer program (because of the "max"), so instead we introduce a new variable, w, that represents the maximum cost over all the scenarios. The MFLP can then be formulated as follows:

$$\text{(MFLP)} \quad \text{minimize} \quad w \qquad (8.46)$$

$$\text{subject to} \quad \sum_{j \in J} y_{ijs} = 1 \qquad \forall i \in I, \forall s \in S \qquad (8.47)$$

$$y_{ijs} \leq x_j \qquad \forall i \in I, \forall j \in J, \forall s \in S \qquad (8.48)$$

$$\sum_{j \in J} f_j x_j + \sum_{i \in I} \sum_{j \in J} h_{is} c_{ijs} y_{ijs} \leq w \qquad \forall s \in S \qquad (8.49)$$

$$x_j \in \{0, 1\} \qquad \forall j \in J \qquad (8.50)$$

$$y_{ijs} \geq 0 \qquad \forall i \in I, \forall j \in J, \forall s \in S \qquad (8.51)$$

Constraints (8.49) ensure that w is at least as large as the cost in each scenario. Since the objective function (8.46) minimizes w, we are guaranteed that w will *equal* the maximum cost over all scenarios. The remaining constraints are identical to those in (SFLP).

Unfortunately, facility location problems that minimize the worst-case cost, such as the MFLP, are generally much more difficult to solve than their stochastic counterparts. The Lagrangian relaxation algorithm from Section 8.3.2, and most other algorithms for stochastic location problems, cannot be readily adapted for robust problems. Therefore, these problems are generally solved heuristically (e.g., Serra et al. 1996, Serra and Marianov 1998), or solved exactly for special cases such as locating single facilities or locating facilities on specialized networks such as trees (e.g., Vairaktarakis and Kouvelis 1999). Additional results are sometimes possible if the uncertain parameters are modeled using intervals in which the parameters are guaranteed to lie rather than scenarios (e.g., Chen and Lin 1998, Averbakh and Berman 2000a,b).

Another common approach for robust optimization is to minimize the worst-case regret (rather than cost). The *regret* of a given solution in a given scenario is defined as the difference between the cost of that solution in that scenario and the cost of the optimal solution for that scenario. In other words, it's the difference between how well your solution performs in a given scenario and how well you *could have* done if you had known that that scenario would be the one to occur. The *absolute regret* calculates the absolute difference in cost, whereas the *relative regret* reports this difference as a fraction of the optimal cost. If (x, y) is the solution to a facility location problem and $z_s(x,y)$ is the cost of that solution in scenario s, then the absolute regret of (x,y) in scenario s is given by

$$z_s(x,y) - z_s(x_s^*, y_s^*)$$

and the relative regret is given by

$$\frac{z_s(x,y) - z_s(x_s^*, y_s^*)}{z_s(x_s^*, y_s^*)},$$

where (x_s^*, y_s^*) is the optimal solution for scenario s.

Minimax-regret models are closely related to minimax-cost models. In fact, the MFLP can be modified easily to minimize the worst-case regret rather than the worst-case cost simply by subtracting $z_s(x_s^*, y_s^*)$ from the left-hand side of (8.49) (to minimize absolute regret) and by also dividing the left-hand side of (8.49) by $z_s(x_s^*, y_s^*)$ (to minimize relative regret). The constants $z_s(x_s^*, y_s^*)$ must be calculated ahead of time by solving $|S|$ single-scenario problems. Since we are modifying constraints by adding and multiplying constants, the structure of the problem does not change (though the optimal solutions might). Therefore, solutions methods for minimax-cost problems are often applicable for minimax-regret problems, and vice-versa.

8.4   A FACILITY LOCATION MODEL WITH DISRUPTIONS

8.4.1   Introduction

The uncapacitated fixed-charge location problem (UFLP) introduced in Section 7.2 chooses facility locations and customer assignments to minimize fixed and transportation costs. The model assumes that facilities always operate as planned. However, facilities are occasionally disrupted by weather conditions, labor actions, or natural disasters. These disruptions may result in increased costs as customers previously served by these facilities must now be served by more distant ones. The model presented in this section chooses facility locations to minimize the expected cost after accounting for disruptions. We call the ability of a system to perform well even when parts of the system are disrupted the *reliability* of the system. Our goal is to choose facility locations that are both inexpensive and reliable.

Figure 8.3 shows the optimal UFLP solution for a data set consisting of the capitals of the lower 48 United States plus Washington, DC (Daskin 1995). In this solution, the fixed cost is $348,000 and the transportation cost is $509,000. Now suppose that the facility in Sacramento, CA is disrupted. During the disruption, Sacramento's customers are re-routed to their nearest open facilities, in Springfield, IL and Austin, TX (Figure 8.4). This new solution has a transportation cost of $1,081,000, an increase of 112%.

Table 8.1 lists the *disruption costs* (the transportation cost when a site is disrupted) of the five optimal DCs, as well as their assigned demands. From the table, it is evident

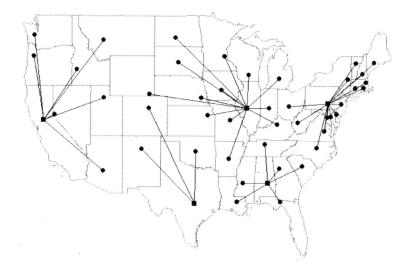

Figure 8.3   UFLP solution for 49-node data set. Reprinted by permission, Snyder and Daskin, Reliability models for facility location: The expected failure cost case, *Transportation Science*, 39(3), 2005, 400–416. ©2005, the Institute for Operations Research and the Management Sciences, 7240 Parkway Drive, Suite 300, Hanover, MD 21076 USA.

Figure 8.4   UFLP solution for 49-node data set, after disruption of facility in Sacramento. Reprinted by permission, Snyder and Daskin, Reliability models for facility location: The expected failure cost case, *Transportation Science*, 39(3), 2005, 400–416. ©2005, the Institute for Operations Research and the Management Sciences, 7240 Parkway Drive, Suite 300, Hanover, MD 21076 USA.

Table 8.1   Disruption costs for optimal DCs. Reprinted by permission, Snyder and Daskin, Reliability models for facility location: The expected failure cost case, *Transportation Science*, 39(3), 2005, 400–416. ©2005, the Institute for Operations Research and the Management Sciences, 7240 Parkway Drive, Suite 300, Hanover, MD 21076 USA.

Location	% Demand Served	Disruption Cost	% Increase
Sacramento, CA	19%	1,081,229	112%
Harrisburg, PA	33%	917,332	80%
Springfield, IL	22%	696,947	37%
Montgomery, AL	16%	639,631	26%
Austin, TX	10%	636,858	25%
Transportation cost w/no disruptions		508,858	0%

that the reliability of a facility can depend either on its distance from other facilities or on the demand it serves, or both. For example, Sacramento, CA serves a relatively small portion of the total demand, but it has a large disruption cost because its nearest "backup" facilities are far away. Harrisburg, PA also has a high disruption cost, even though it is relatively close to two good backup facilities; the high disruption cost occurs because Harrisburg serves one-third of the total demand. Springfield, IL is the second-largest facility in terms of demand served, but its disruption cost is much smaller because it is centrally located, close to good backup facilities.

It is possible to choose facility locations that are more resilient to disruptions— that is, that have lower disruption costs. For example, suppose we locate facilities in the capitals of CA, NY, TX, PA, OH, AL, OR, and IA. (See Figure 8.5.) In this solution, every disruption cost is less than or equal to than $640,000. On the other hand, three additional facilities are used in this solution. Is the improvement in reliability worth the increased facility cost? One of the goals of the model in this section is to demonstrate that the answer is often "yes." In other words, substantial improvements in reliability can often be obtained without large increases in the UFLP cost. This means that by taking reliability into account at design time, one can find a near-optimal UFLP solution that has much better reliability.

We will present an extension of the UFLP that minimizes the expected post-disruption cost, given a certain probability that each facility is disrupted. Multiple facilities may be disrupted simultaneously. We refer to this model as the *reliable fixed-charge location problem* (RFLP). The model we present is a simplified version of the model introduced by Snyder and Daskin (2005). A similar model was studied by Berman et al. (2007). For reviews on facility location models with disruptions, see Snyder et al. (2006) or Snyder and Daskin (2007).

8.4.2   Notation

As in the UFLP, let I be the set of customers and J the set of potential facility sites. Let h_i be the demand at customer i, c_{ij} the transportation cost from facility j to customer i, and f_j the fixed cost to open facility j.

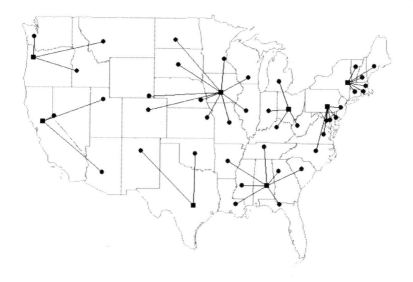

Figure 8.5 Reliable solution for 49-node data set.

Each facility in J has the same probability q of being disrupted, which is interpreted as the long-run fraction of time the facility is non-operational. In some cases, q may be estimated based on historical data (e.g., for weather-related disruptions), while in others q must be estimated subjectively (e.g., for disruptions due to labor strikes). We can assume that facility disruptions follow a two-state Markov process, as in Section 6.6, but the exact disruption process is not important. It is important, however, that disruptions are statistically independent from facility to facility.

The assumption that every facility has the same disruption probability q is generally unrealistic, but it makes the model considerably easier to solve. Several approaches have been proposed for relaxing this assumption; see, e.g., Berman et al. (2007), Shen et al. (2010), Li and Ouyang (2010), Cui et al. (2010), and also Problem 8.9.

Associated with each customer i is a cost θ_i that represents the cost of not serving the customer—for example, if all open facilities are disrupted—per unit of demand. θ_i may be a lost-sales cost, or the cost of serving i by purchasing product from a competitor on an emergency basis. Instead of modeling this eventuality explicitly, we perform a modeling trick: We add an "emergency" facility u that cannot be disrupted and we force $x_u = 1$. This facility has fixed cost $f_j = 0$ and transportation cost $c_{iu} = \theta_i$ for every customer $i \in I$. From this point forward, the set J is assumed to contain u, as well.

The strategy behind the formulation of the RFLP is to assign each customer to a primary facility that will serve it under normal circumstances, as well as to a set of backup facilities that serve it when the primary facility is disrupted. Since multiple disruptions may occur simultaneously, each customer needs a first backup facility in case its primary facility is disrupted, a second backup facility in case its first backup is disrupted, and so on.

There are two sets of decision variables in this model:

$$x_j = \begin{cases} 1, & \text{if facility } j \in J \text{ is selected} \\ 0, & \text{otherwise} \end{cases}$$

$$y_{ijr} = \begin{cases} 1, & \text{if customer } i \text{ is assigned to facility } j \text{ as a level-}r \text{ assignment} \\ 0, & \text{otherwise} \end{cases}$$

A "level-r" assignment is one for which there are r closer facilities that are open. If $r = 0$, this is a primary assignment; otherwise, it is a backup assignment. Each customer i has a level-r assignment for each $r = 0, \ldots, |J| - 1$, unless i is assigned to the emergency facility u at level s, where $s < r$. In other words, customer i is assigned to one facility at level 0, another facility at level 1, and so on until i has been assigned to facility u at some level. If a customer is assigned to facility u at a level r, with $r < |J| - 1$, then it is preferable to lose that customer's demand than to serve it from the remaining facilities if the first r facilities have failed.

8.4.3 Formulation

The objective function of the RFLP is given by

$$\sum_{j \in J} f_j x_j + \sum_{i \in I} \sum_{\substack{j \in J \\ j \neq u}} \sum_{r=0}^{|J|-1} h_i c_{ij} q^r (1 - q) y_{ijr} + \sum_{i \in I} \sum_{r=0}^{|J|-1} h_i c_{iu} q^r y_{iur}.$$

This expression calculates the fixed cost plus the expected transportation cost. Each customer i is served by its level-r facility (call it j) if the r closer facilities are disrupted (this occurs with probability q^r) and if j itself is not disrupted (this occurs with probability $1 - q$, unless $j = u$, in which case it occurs with probability 1). For notational convenience, we define

$$\psi_{ijr} = \begin{cases} h_i c_{ij} q^r, & \text{if } j = u \\ h_i c_{ij} q^r (1 - q), & \text{if } j \neq u. \end{cases}$$

Then the RFLP can be formulated as an IP as follows:

(RFLP)

$$\text{minimize} \quad \sum_{j \in J} f_j x_j + \sum_{i \in I} \sum_{j \in J} \sum_{r=0}^{|J|-1} \psi_{ijr} y_{ijr} \tag{8.52}$$

$$\text{subject to} \quad \sum_{j \in J} y_{ijr} + \sum_{s=0}^{r-1} y_{ius} = 1 \qquad \forall i \in I, r = 0, \ldots, |J| - 1 \tag{8.53}$$

$$y_{ijr} \le x_j \qquad \forall i \in I, j \in J, r = 0, \ldots, |J| - 1 \tag{8.54}$$

$$\sum_{r=0}^{|J|-1} y_{ijr} \le 1 \qquad \forall i \in I, j \in J \tag{8.55}$$

$$x_u = 1 \tag{8.56}$$

$$x_j \in \{0, 1\} \qquad \forall j \in J \tag{8.57}$$

$$y_{ijr} \in \{0, 1\} \qquad \forall i \in I, j \in J, r = 0, \ldots, |J| - 1 \tag{8.58}$$

Constraints (8.53) require that for each customer i and each level r, either i is assigned to a level-r facility or it is assigned to facility u at a level $s < r$. (By convention we take $\sum_{s=0}^{r-1} y_{ijs} = 0$ if $r = 0$.) Constraints (8.54) prohibit an assignment to a facility that has not been opened. Constraints (8.55) prohibit a customer from being assigned to a given facility at more than one level. Constraint (8.56) requires the emergency facility u to be opened. Constraints (8.57) and (8.58) are integrality constraints.

You may be wondering why there are no constraints requiring the assignments to occur in order of distance—that is, for a customer's level-r facility to be closer than its level-$(r + 1)$ facility. It turns out that this assignment strategy is always optimal, so it does not need to be enforced by constraints.

Theorem 8.2 *In any optimal solution to (RFLP), if* $y_{ijr} = y_{i,k,r+1} = 1$ *for* $i \in I$, $j, k \in J$, $0 \le r < |J| - 2$, *then* $c_{ij} \le c_{ik}$.

Proof. Omitted; see Problem 8.8. ∎

8.4.4 Lagrangian Relaxation

We solve (RFLP) by relaxing constraints (8.53) using Lagrangian relaxation. For given Lagrange multipliers λ, the subproblem is as follows:

(RFLP-LR$_\lambda$)

minimize $\displaystyle \sum_{j \in J} f_j x_j + \sum_{i \in I} \sum_{j \in J} \sum_{r=0}^{|J|-1} \psi_{ijr} y_{ijr} +$

$$\sum_{i \in I} \sum_{r=0}^{|J|-1} \lambda_{ir} \left(1 - \sum_{j \in J} y_{ijr} - \sum_{s=0}^{r-1} y_{ius} \right) \tag{8.59}$$

subject to $\quad y_{ijr} \le x_j \qquad \forall i \in I, j \in J, r = 0, \ldots, |J| - 1 \tag{8.60}$

$$\sum_{r=0}^{|J|-1} y_{ijr} \le 1 \qquad \forall i \in I, j \in J \tag{8.61}$$

$$x_u = 1 \tag{8.62}$$

$$x_j \in \{0,1\} \quad \forall j \in J \tag{8.63}$$

$$y_{ijr} \in \{0,1\} \quad \forall i \in I, j \in J, r = 0, \ldots, |J| - 1 \tag{8.64}$$

The non-fixed-cost portion of the objective function (8.59) can be re-written as follows:

$$\sum_{i \in I} \sum_{j \in J} \sum_{r=0}^{|J|-1} (\psi_{ijr} - \lambda_{ir}) y_{ijr} + \sum_{i \in I} \sum_{r=0}^{|J|-1} \lambda_{ir} - \sum_{i \in I} \sum_{r=0}^{|J|-1} \sum_{s=0}^{r-1} \lambda_{ir} y_{ius}$$

$$= \sum_{i \in I} \sum_{j \in J} \sum_{r=0}^{|J|-1} (\psi_{ijr} - \lambda_{ir}) y_{ijr} + \sum_{i \in I} \sum_{r=0}^{|J|-1} \lambda_{ir} - \sum_{i \in I} \sum_{s=0}^{|J|-1} \sum_{r=0}^{s-1} \lambda_{is} y_{iur}$$

(by swapping the indices r and s in the last term)

$$= \sum_{i \in I} \sum_{j \in J} \sum_{r=0}^{|J|-1} (\psi_{ijr} - \lambda_{ir}) y_{ijr} + \sum_{i \in I} \sum_{r=0}^{|J|-1} \lambda_{ir} - \sum_{i \in I} \sum_{\substack{r=0,\ldots,|J|-1 \\ s=0,\ldots,|J|-1 \\ r<s}} \lambda_{is} y_{iur}$$

$$= \sum_{i \in I} \sum_{j \in J} \sum_{r=0}^{|J|-1} (\psi_{ijr} - \lambda_{ir}) y_{ijr} + \sum_{i \in I} \sum_{r=0}^{|J|-1} \lambda_{ir} - \sum_{i \in I} \sum_{r=0}^{|J|-1} \left(\sum_{s=r+1}^{|J|-1} \lambda_{is} \right) y_{iur}$$

Therefore, the objective function can be written as

$$\sum_{j \in J} f_j x_j + \sum_{i \in I} \sum_{j \in J} \sum_{r=0}^{|J|-1} \tilde{\psi}_{ijr} y_{ijr} + \sum_{i \in I} \sum_{r=0}^{|J|-1} \lambda_{ir}, \tag{8.65}$$

where

$$\tilde{\psi}_{ijr} = \begin{cases} \psi_{ijr} - \lambda_{ir}, & \text{if } j \neq u \\ \psi_{ijr} - \lambda_{ir} - \sum_{s=r+1}^{|J|-1} \lambda_{is} = \psi_{ijr} - \sum_{s=r}^{|J|-1} \lambda_{is}, & \text{if } j = u \end{cases} \tag{8.66}$$

For given λ, problem (RFLP-LR$_\lambda$) can be solved easily. Since the assignment constraints (8.53) have been relaxed, customer i may be assigned to zero, one, or more than one open facility at each level, but it may be assigned to a given facility at at most one level r. Suppose that facility j is opened. Customer i will be assigned to facility j at level r if $\tilde{\psi}_{ijr} < 0$ and $\tilde{\psi}_{ijr} \leq \tilde{\psi}_{ijs}$ for all $s = 0, \ldots, |J| - 1$. Therefore, the benefit of opening facility j is given by

$$\beta_j = \sum_{i \in I} \min \left\{ 0, \min_{r=0,\ldots,|J|-1} \{\tilde{\psi}_{ijr}\} \right\}. \tag{8.67}$$

Once the benefits β_j have been computed for all j, we set $x_j = 1$ for the emergency facility u and for any j for which $\beta_j + f_j < 0$; we set $y_{ijr} = 1$ if (1) facility j is open, (2) $\tilde{\psi}_{ijr} < 0$, and (3) r minimizes $\tilde{\psi}_{ijs}$ for $s = 0, \ldots, |J| - 1$. The optimal objective value for (RFLP-LR$_\lambda$) is

$$\sum_{j \in J} (\beta_j + f_j) x_j + \sum_{i \in I} \sum_{r=0}^{|J|-1} \lambda_{ir},$$

and this provides a lower bound on the optimal objective value of (RFLP).

One can obtain upper bounds by first opening the facilities that are open in the solution to (RFLP-LR$_\lambda$), then assigning customers to level-r facilities in increasing order of distance. As in the UFLP, improvement heuristics (e.g., exchange heuristics) can be applied to improve the solution found.

The Lagrange multipliers are updated using subgradient optimization in a manner very similar to that described in Section 7.2.4.5. If the procedure terminates without a provably optimal solution, branch-and-bound can be used to close the gap, as described in Section D.6 in Appendix D.

8.4.5 Tradeoff Curves

The RFLP can alternately be modeled as a multi-objective optimization problem in which one objective represents the normal UFLP cost (ignoring disruptions) and the other objective represents the expected transportation cost (accounting for disruptions). Multi-objective optimization allows the decision maker to express her preference between the two objectives. For example, a firm that is used to thinking only about the classical UFLP objective may weight the problem toward this objective, while a firm that is very concerned about disruptions may favor the other objective.

The two objectives can be formulated as follows:

$$w_1 = \sum_{j \in J} f_j x_j + \sum_{i \in I} \sum_{j \in J} h_i c_{ij} y_{ij0}$$

$$w_2 = \sum_{i \in I} \sum_{j \in J} \sum_{r=0}^{|J|-1} \psi_{ijr} y_{ijr}.$$

Objective w_1 calculates the "operating" cost—the classical UFLP cost of opening facilities and serving customers from their primary facilities. Objective w_2 computes the expected transportation cost, accounting for both normal and disrupted modes. We can then replace the RFLP objective function (8.52) with

$$\text{minimize} \quad \alpha w_1 + (1 - \alpha) w_2, \tag{8.68}$$

where α is a parameter specified by the user, $0 \le \alpha \le 1$. Large values of α place more emphasis on objective 1, small values on objective 2. (Setting $\alpha = 1$ is equivalent to solving the UFLP.) The decision maker might select a single value of α, but more commonly, the goal is to generate the *tradeoff curve* that depicts the

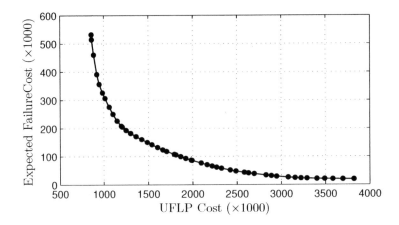

Figure 8.6   Sample RFLP tradeoff curve. Reprinted by permission, Snyder and Daskin, Reliability models for facility location: The expected failure cost case, *Transportation Science*, 39(3), 2005, 400–416. ©2005, the Institute for Operations Research and the Management Sciences, 7240 Parkway Drive, Suite 300, Hanover, MD 21076 USA.

relationship between the two objectives. In essence, the tradeoff curve (also known as the *Pareto curve* or *efficient frontier*) tells us how much of one objective we must sacrifice in order to improve the other objective.

How can we generate such a tradeoff curve? The brute-force approach would be to simply solve the RFLP (with objective (8.68)) for every value of α between 0 and 1 in increments of, say, 0.001. But it is preferable to use a much more elegant and efficient approach called the *weighting method*. We won't describe the details of this approach; see instead Cohon (1978). The tradeoff curve for the 49-node problem discussed in Section 8.4.1 is pictured in Figure 8.6. Each point represents a different solution to the RFLP, and the axes represent the two objectives. The left-most point is the UFLP solution ($\alpha = 1$). The left portion of the tradeoff curve is "steep," indicating that large improvements in reliability can be attained with only small increases in the classical UFLP cost. For example, the third point on the tradeoff curve has a 3.1% increase in UFLP cost from the original UFLP solution but a 13.4% decrease in expected disruption cost, and the fourth point has a 7.3% increase in cost but a 26.5% decrease in expected disruption cost.

PROBLEMS

8.1   (LR Iteration for LMRP) The file LR-LMRP.xlsx contains a_i and b_i values for a 50-node instance of problem (P'_j) ((8.21)–(8.22)) for a single iteration of the Lagrangian relaxation algorithm described in Section 8.2.6 and for a single value of j. Using the algorithm described in Section 8.2.6.1, solve this instance of problem (P'_j). List the optimal values of y^* in column D and the optimal objective value (β_j) in cell H2. (Hint 1 for Problem 7.7 applies here, too.)

8.2 **(Non-Convexity of S_r in LMRP Algorithm)** Theorem 8.1 allows us to solve problem (P'_j) by first sorting a subset of the i's and then computing the partial sums given by (8.25), choosing the r that minimizes S_r and setting $y_i = 1$ for $i = 1, \ldots, r$. It is tempting to think that S_r is convex with respect to r, since then we could consider each r in turn as long as S_r is decreasing, and then stop as soon as S_r increases (or use an even more efficient method like binary search). Unfortunately, this claim is *not* true. Provide a counterexample with 4 variables such that $a_i < 0$ and $b_i > 0$ for all i, and such that

$$S_1 > S_2 < S_3 > S_4 \quad \text{and} \quad S_2 > S_4.$$

8.3 **(Non-Closest Assignments in LMRP)** Consider the 3-node instance of the LMRP pictured below. Each circle represents a retailer, and each retailer is eligible to be converted to a DC. The numbers on the links indicate the transportation cost (c_{ij}) between retailers; the transportation cost between a retailer and itself is 0. Construct an example, using this instance, for which there is a retailer in the optimal solution that is assigned to a DC that is not its closest. That is, this problem is asking you to choose values for the parameters $(f_j, \mu_i, \sigma_i, K_j,$ etc., but not including d_{ij} since those are given in the diagram) and demonstrate that in the optimal solution, there is a retailer assigned to a DC other than its closest. You do not need to enumerate the objective value of every possible solution, but you should argue rigorously that your candidate solution is optimal.

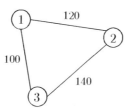

8.4 **(Retailer Assignment is NP-Hard)** Suppose the facility locations in the LMRP are already fixed. Prove that the problem of optimally assigning retailers to facilities is NP-hard.

8.5 **(Location of Power Generators)** Consider the problem of locating generators within an electricity network.

a) First consider a single generator. Suppose the generator's load (i.e., the total demand for electricity from the generator) is given by $D \sim N(\mu, \sigma^2)$, where D is measured in kilowatt-hours (kWh). The cost to generate enough electricity to meet a load of d kWh is given by $\frac{1}{2}\gamma d^2$, where $\gamma > 0$ is a constant. Prove that the expected generation cost is given by $\frac{1}{2}\gamma(\mu^2 + \sigma^2)$.

b) Now consider an electricity network consisting of multiple generators, whose locations we need to choose. Let I be the set of loads (demand nodes), with load i having a daily demand distributed $N(\mu_i, \sigma_i^2)$. Let J be the set of potential generators. The daily fixed cost if generator j is open is f_j, and the generation cost coefficient for j is γ_j. Formulate the problem of choosing generator locations and assigning loads to generators in order to minimize the expected daily cost of the system. Assume that, once location and assignment decisions are made, the power network for a given generator and its loads is disconnected from the remaining generators and loads (so that the physics of power flows can be ignored). Also assume that the cost to transmit power is negligible.

8.6   **(Stochastic Location for Toy Stores)** Return to Problem 7.1, and suppose now that the demands are stochastic. The file `toy-stores-stochastic.xlsx` gives the demands for five scenarios, as well as the probability that each scenario occurs.

   a) Implement the stochastic fixed-charge location problem in a modeling language of your choice. Find the optimal solution for the instance given in `toy-stores-stochastic.xlsx`. Report the optimal set of facilities and the corresponding cost.

   b) Now implement and solve the minimax fixed-charge location problem. Report the optimal set of facilities and the corresponding cost.

8.7   **(Pre-positioning for Disaster Relief)** A humanitarian relief agency wishes to pre-position stockpiles of emergency supplies (food, water, blankets, medicine, etc.) for use in the aftermath of disasters. Its objective is to locate the smallest possible number of stockpiles while ensuring a low probability that, for each population center, a disaster strikes and the population center cannot be served by any stockpile. Whether a given stockpile can serve a given population center depends on their physical distance as well as on the disaster that strikes.

Disasters are represented by scenarios. A scenario can be thought of as a disaster type, magnitude, and location (e.g., magnitude 7.5 earthquake in city A, influenza pandemic in city B, etc.). However, mathematically each scenario simply specifies whether a given population center can be served by a given stockpile during a given disaster.

Let I be the set of population centers, and let J be the set of potential stockpile locations. Let S be the set of scenarios (including the scenario in which no disaster occurs), and let q_s be the probability that scenario s occurs. Stockpile j is said to "cover" population center i in scenario s if *either* stockpile j can serve population center i in scenario s *or* population center i does not need disaster relief in scenario s. Let $a_{ijs} = 1$ if stockpile j covers population center i in scenario s. Assume each stockpile is sufficiently large to serve the needs of the entire population it covers.

Formulate a linear integer programming problem that chooses where to locate stockpiles in order to minimize the total number of stockpiles located while ensuring that, for each $i \in I$, the probability that i is not covered by any open stockpile is less than or equal to α, for given $0 \leq \alpha \leq 1$. Clearly define any new notation you introduce. Explain the objective function and all constraints in words.

8.8   **(Proof of Theorem 8.2)** Prove Theorem 8.2.

8.9   **(Facility-Dependent Disruption Probabilities)** Suppose we want each facility to have a different disruption probability q_j in the RFLP model from Section 8.4. If we were to use similar logic as the RFLP, the objective function would become very messy since the q^r terms would be replaced by a product of y_{ijr} variables. Develop an alternate formulation for this problem in which the q_j may be different for each j.

a) Write out your formulation. Your formulation must be linear. Define any new notation that you introduce, and explain the objective function and each of the constraints in words.

b) In a short paragraph, discuss the advantages and disadvantages of your formulation versus the original model.

CHAPTER 9

PROCESS FLEXIBILITY

9.1 INTRODUCTION

Manufacturers in most industries today face increasingly demanding customers and increasingly fierce competition. These factors have led to a huge proliferation in product varieties offered by manufacturers of everything from breakfast cereals to automobiles. For example, the number of car and light truck models for sale in the United States rose from 195 in 1984 to 282 in 2004 (Van Biesebroeck 2007). This so-called *product proliferation* leads to increased diversity and unpredictability of demand. At the same time, firms are under increasing financial pressure to keep capacity as tight as possible, which makes it crucial for manufacturing facilities to have the flexibility to produce a range of products.

The importance of flexibility can be demonstrated by some examples from the automotive industry:

- BMW designs its factory to build cars with the specific colors, features, and options requested by customers. (In contrast, many other auto manufacturers offer a more limited range of combinations, which are ordered by dealers, not

Fundamentals of Supply Chain Theory, First Edition. Lawrence V. Snyder, Zuo-Jun Max Shen. **241**
© 2011 John Wiley & Sons, Inc. Published 2011 by John Wiley & Sons, Inc.

by individual customers.) A customer can even change the specifications of his or her car as late as five days before the car is built (Henry 2009).

- In 2000–2001, Chrysler saw an unexpectedly large demand for its new PT Cruiser model, while the demand for another car, the Neon, was lower than forecast. As a result, there was a shortage of the PT Cruiser while a manufacturing plant in Belvidere, IL that built only Neons—which have many similar parts as the PT Cruiser—had excess capacity. Chrysler's lack of flexibility to reassign PT Cruiser production to the Belvidere plant cost the company nearly $500 million in lost profit (Biller et al. 2006).

- Learning from this mistake, Chrysler invested heavily in the mid-2000s to ensure that its factories are more flexible and can each make more than one type of vehicle. The Belvidere plant began to make three additional models, and it produced roughly twice as many vehicles in 2006 as it did in 2005. Chrysler Group's CEO, Thomas LaSorda, said that the extra flexibility "gives us a wider margin of error" (Boudette 2006).

- Ford Motor Company invested $485 million to retool two Canadian engine plants with flexible systems. The redesigned plants can produce multiple types of engines and, just as importantly, can switch production from one to another in a matter of hours or days, rather than months. Chris Bolen, the manager of one of the plants, said that "the initial investment is slightly higher, but long-term costs are lower in multiples." The company also had a plan to convert the systems at most of its other engine and transmission plants all over the world to flexible ones (Phelan 2002).

- In the late 1990s, Honda invested $400 million to make its three plants in Ohio flexible. The increased flexibility allowed the company to keep its production closely in line with demand patterns that changed rapidly during the 2000s due to wide fluctuations in gasoline prices and to the global recession. Because most Honda vehicles are designed to be assembled using a similar process, plants can be flexible and can change production from one product to another in as little as five minutes (Linebaugh 2008).

Flexibility can provide a firm with a competitive advantage by allowing it to react quickly to changing demand patterns and supply conditions. It is becoming an increasingly prevalent practice in a wide range of industries, including apparel (DesMarteau 1999) and semiconductors and electronics (McCutcheon 2004). Greater flexibility entails a greater up-front investment, however, and this tradeoff must be carefully considered.

In this chapter, we discuss models for evaluating the effectiveness of, and optimizing, *process flexibility*, by which we mean the ability to manufacture a variety of products at the same facility, the ability to manufacture a given product at multiple facilities, or both.

9.2 FLEXIBILITY DESIGN GUIDELINES

One of the most important questions in designing a flexible supply chain is, "How much flexibility is enough?" If there is no flexibility, then each plant is assigned to a unique product. If the demand for one product is unexpectedly high while that for another product is low, the firm will stock out of the high-demand product and have excess capacity at the plant that makes the low-demand one. At the other extreme, every plant can produce every product, leaving the firm much better able to reconfigure production in response to demands. Jordan and Graves (1995) describe a simple simulation model that shows that, for a particular set of assumptions, the full-flexibility structure resulted in approximately a 12% increase in sales and capacity utilization. On the other hand, this additional flexibility requires additional capital investments. Is full flexibility really required, or would some in-between strategy be sufficient? As we will see below, it is often possible to choose a partial-flexibility strategy that achieves most of the benefit of the full-flexibility structure with a much smaller resource requirement.

It is common to model process flexibility problems using bipartite graphs (i.e., graphs whose nodes are partitioned into two sets such that no edge has both endpoints in the same set). One set of nodes represents the plants while the other represents the products. If a plant node and a product node are connected by an edge in the network, then the plant is capable of manufacturing the product. Greater flexibility therefore means more edges in the graph. For example, if there are n plants and n products, then in the dedicated (i.e., no-flexibility) system, there are n edges in the graph, whereas in the full-flexibility system, there are n^2. (See Figures 9.1(a) and 9.1(b).)

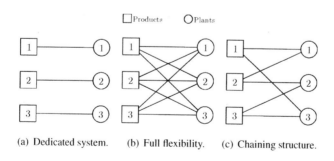

(a) Dedicated system.   (b) Full flexibility.   (c) Chaining structure.

Figure 9.1 Examples of flexibility configurations.

We would like to evaluate the effectiveness of a given flexibility structure (i.e., a given set of edges connecting plants and products). There are many possible ways to define and measure this effectiveness. Typically, we assume that, once the demands for each product in a given period are known, the firm assigns production to the various plants, following the plant–product capabilities implied by the edges and satisfying a fixed capacity constraint at each. One of the most popular ways to measure the effectiveness of a flexibility structure is to evaluate the total *shortfall* (i.e., stockouts) that occurs after the production is optimized and demands are satisfied.

The problem of optimizing production to minimize the shortfall (or, equivalently, maximizing the sales) when the demands are known can be formulated as follows (Jordan and Graves 1995). Let $G = (V_1, V_2, E)$ be a bipartite graph consisting of a set V_1 of products, a set V_2 of plants, and an edge set E. Every edge in E has one endpoint in V_1 and one in V_2, indicating a plant–product capability. For example, the full-flexibility structure has edge set $E = \{(i,j)|i \in V_1, j \in V_2\}$. Let d_i be the observed demand realization for product $i \in V_1$ and let C_j be the capacity of plant $j \in V_2$. Let s_i be the shortfall, i.e., the unsatisfied demand, for product i, and let y_{ij} be the number of units of product i produced at plant j, for all $(i,j) \in E$. (s and y are decision variables.) Then, given an observed realization of demand, the production allocation decisions can be optimized, and the minimum total shortfall of a flexibility structure E can be determined by solving the following optimization problem.

$$\text{minimize} \quad \sum_{i \in V_1} s_i \qquad (9.1)$$

$$\text{subject to} \quad \sum_{i \in V_1 : (i,j) \in E} y_{ij} \leq C_j \qquad \forall j \in V_2 \qquad (9.2)$$

$$\sum_{j \in V_2 : (i,j) \in E} y_{ij} + s_i = d_i \qquad \forall i \in V_1 \qquad (9.3)$$

$$y_{ij} \geq 0 \qquad \forall (i,j) \in E \qquad (9.4)$$

$$s_i \geq 0 \qquad \forall i \in V_1 \qquad (9.5)$$

The objective function (9.1) calculates the total shortfall over all products. (Alternately, we could weight the shortfalls differently, if some products are more important than others.) Constraints (9.2) enforce the capacity restriction at each plant, and constraints (9.3) require the shortfall variable s_i to equal the difference between the demand for product i and the total amount of it produced. Constraints (9.4) and (9.5) are non-negativity constraints. This problem can be generalized to handle multi-echelon supply chains; see Graves and Tomlin (2003), Chou et al. (2008b).

This problem is equivalent to a maximum-flow problem and can therefore be solved efficiently. However, we are interested in evaluating the performance of a given flexibility guideline under *random* demands D_i rather than deterministic demands d_i. (After all, if we knew the demands, we would not need flexibility.) Therefore, we need to solve a stochastic version of the problem, in which we minimize the expected total shortfall over all possible demand realizations. Unfortunately, this problem has a complicated combinatorial and stochastic structure, and finding an optimal solution is challenging. Therefore, researchers have developed intuitive flexibility guidelines that can yield shortfalls that are nearly as low as the shortfall generated by the full-flexibility structure. Moreover, they use far fewer edges and are therefore much less costly to implement. We discuss two of these gs next.

We next discuss two flexibility guidelines that provide some insight into how supply chains can be configured to achieve a high level of flexibility with a small number of edges in the flexibility graph.

Chaining Guideline: Perhaps the best-known flexibility guideline is the *chaining guideline* proposed by Jordan and Graves (1995). (See Figure 9.1(c).) Assume first that $|V_1| = |V_2| = n$. Then the chaining guideline is defined as follows:

- Plant 1 makes products 1 and 2

- Plant 2 makes products 2 and 3

- ...

- Plant j makes products j and $j + 1$

- ...

- Plant n makes products n and 1.

This structure uses $2n$ edges. Jordan and Graves (1995) report that chaining can achieve well above 90% of the benefits of the full-flexibility configuration, while using only a fraction of that configuration's n^2 edges. This intuitive result is believed to be true in a wide variety of settings, both analytically and in practice, and has been applied successfully in many industries.

The number of edges is not the only consideration when determining the effectiveness of a chaining guideline. Consider the two flexibility structures in Figure 9.2. Both are chaining structures, both have 12 edges, and in both, every plant makes two products and every product is made at two plants. The structure in Figure 9.2(a) uses a single chain for all products and plants, while that in Figure 9.2(b) partitions the system into three separate chains. The single-chain structure is much more effective, though, achieving nearly twice the benefits (in terms of expected sales) as the three-chain structure in a simulation discussed by Jordan and Graves (1995). The reason is that the single-chain structure allows a greater degree of flexibility in reassigning products to plants than the three-chain structure. For example, if the demand for product 1 is very high and plant 5 has excess capacity, the single-chain structure can take advantage of the discrepancy while the three-chain structure cannot.

Lim et al. (2009) examine the chaining guideline for systems with random supply disruptions that can affect either nodes (representing a disruption of an entire plant) or edges (representing disruptions for particular plant–product pair). For node disruptions, they confirm Jordan and Graves's intuition that longer chains are better, but they find that short chains are preferable when edge failures are the issue.

The discussion so far assumes that the number of products and plants is the same, that the products are identical, as are the plants, and that any plant could be configured to make any product. Real-life situations do not follow this idealized model. Jordan and Graves (1995) outline three guidelines for adding flexibility to chains in more realistic situations:

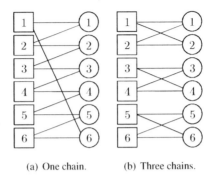

(a) One chain.   (b) Three chains.

Figure 9.2   Two chaining structures.

1. All products should be made by roughly the same number of plants; more precisely, the total capacity of the plants making each product should be roughly the same.

2. All plants should make roughly the same number of products; more precisely, the total expected demand of the products made at each plant should be roughly the same.

3. Longer chains are better than shorter ones.

Node-Expansion Guideline: A more connected guideline is inherently more flexible. With this in mind, Chou et al. (2007) propose the *node-expansion guideline*. The guideline is used to augment a given flexibility structure by adding links iteratively to improve the *node-expansion ratio*. The node-expansion ratio of product $i \in V_1$ is the total capacity of the plants capable of making product i divided by the expected demand for i:

$$\delta_i = \frac{\sum_{j \in V_2 : (i,j) \in E} C_j}{E[D_i]}$$

Similarly, the node-expansion ratio of plant $j \in V_2$ is the total expected demand of the products that can be made at plant j divided by the capacity of plant j:

$$\delta_j = \frac{\sum_{i \in V_1 : (i,j) \in E} E[D_j]}{C_j}$$

Smaller node-expansion ratios suggest products or plants that do not have enough flexibility. The node-expansion guideline says that, at each iteration, we add an edge that is not yet in E in order to increase all node-expansion ratios as much as possible; that is, to increase

$$\delta = \min \left\{ \min_{i \in V_1} \delta_i, \min_{j \in V_2} \delta_j \right\}$$

as much as possible. One heuristic for doing this is to add, at each iteration, an edge connecting the product and the plant with the lowest node-expansion ratios, skipping any edges that have already been added. This procedure repeats until the number of edges reaches a predetermined limit.

9.3 A PROCESS FLEXIBILITY OPTIMIZATION MODEL

So far we have discussed flexibility guidelines for symmetric networks, in which all plants have the same capacity and all products have independent, identical demand distributions. However, real systems are much more complex. Jordan and Graves's (1995) three rules of thumb listed on p. 245 provide some guidance, but it would be helpful to have a more rigorous, optimization-based approach to design flexibility structures. In addition, the models we have discussed so far ignore the possibility that the investment and operating costs of different flexible resources can be different. For example, it is generally cheaper for a plant to produce two similar products than two very different products.

In addition, some flexible plants are designed for one primary product (or product family), and when it is called upon to produce a different product, production costs may increase—for example, due to additional costs for training workers to produce the new product, or to the change-over time required to switch products on an assembly line. These "recourse" costs are ignored in many process flexibility models. One exception is Chou et al. (2008a), who assume that it costs more for a plant to manufacture products other than those it is primarily designed for. Their results show that chaining can be less beneficial relative to full flexibility when recourse costs are taken into consideration, but that chaining still yields significant benefits over the no-flexibility structure.

Another paper that accounts for recourse costs, as well as nonhomogeneous products and plants, is that of Mak and Shen (2009), which *optimizes* the flexibility structure to maximize the firm's expected profit, accounting for the costs to invest in process flexibility. We discuss their model in this section.

9.3.1 Formulation

As in earlier parts of this chapter, we consider set V_1 of products, indexed by i, and a set V_2 of plants, indexed by j, each with n elements.[1] Demands for the products are random.

This is a two-stage stochastic programming model, like the stochastic facility location model in Section 8.3.2. In the first stage, we decide which edges $(i, j) \in E$ to construct, i.e., which plants should be made capable of producing which products. There is a fixed investment cost of a_{ij} to add edge (i, j), representing the cost of retooling the manufacturing process or purchasing a flexible technology. At the beginning of the second stage, we observe the random demands and then choose production levels for each product at each plant, subject to the flexibility structure

---

[1]To be consistent with the literature we assume that $|V_1| = |V_2| = n$. However, it is trivial to allow these numbers to be different; see Mak and Shen (2009).

chosen in the first stage. There is a production cost of c_{ij} for each unit of plant j's capacity that is used to produce product i and a selling price of p_i for each unit of product i sold. The objective is to maximize the profit, which equals the sales revenue minus the costs of production and flexibility investments.

We model the random product demands using scenarios: The demand for product i in scenario s is given by d_{is}, and the probability that scenario s occurs is q_s.[2]

We summarize the notation as follows:

Sets

V_1 = set of products
V_2 = set of plants
S = set of scenarios

Parameters

a_{ij} cost to invest in technology that allows plant j to produce product i
c_{ij} cost to produce one unit of product i at plant j
p_i revenue from selling one unit of product i
C_j capacity of plant j
d_{is} demand for product i in scenario s
q_s probability that scenario s occurs

Decision Variables

$x_{ij} = 1$ if plant j is configured to produce product i, 0 otherwise
$y_{ijs}=$ the number of units of product i produced at plant j in scenario s

We formulate the model for optimizing process flexibility as follows:

$$\text{maximize} \quad \sum_{i \in V_1} \sum_{j \in V_2} \left[-a_{ij}x_{ij} + \sum_{s \in S} q_s(p_i - c_{ij})y_{ijs} \right] \quad (9.6)$$

$$\text{subject to} \quad \sum_{i \in V_1} y_{ijs} \leq C_j \qquad \forall j \in V_2, \forall s \in S \quad (9.7)$$

$$\sum_{j \in V_2} y_{ijs} \leq d_{is} \qquad \forall i \in V_1, \forall s \in S \quad (9.8)$$

$$y_{ijs} \leq d_{is}x_{ij} \qquad \forall i \in V_1, \forall j \in V_2, \forall s \in S \quad (9.9)$$

$$x_{ij} \in \{0,1\} \qquad \forall i \in V_1, \forall j \in V_2 \quad (9.10)$$

$$y_{ijs} \geq 0 \qquad \forall i \in V_1, \forall j \in V_2, \forall s \in S \quad (9.11)$$

The objective function (9.6) calculates the expected profit—the expected sales revenue minus investment costs and expected production costs. Constraints (9.7) enforce the capacity limit at each plant in each scenario. Constraints (9.8) require the amount of product i produced in scenario s to be less than or equal to the demand. Without these constraints, the model might choose to produce more than the demand in order to increase the profit. Note, however, that the formulation does not require the

[2]Mak and Shen (2009) consider a much more general multivariate demand model. We consider the scenario-based approach here for the sake of simplicity.

demand to be met in full. A product's demand may not be met in full, or at all, if there is insufficient capacity or if it is not profitable to meet the demand. Constraints (9.9) allow production of product i at plant j in scenario s only if that capability was established in the first stage. Constraints (9.10) and (9.11) require the x variables to be binary and the y variables to be non-negative.

The second stage of this problem (i.e., the problem in the y variables) is similar to the deterministic model (9.1)–(9.5) except that (1) the goal is to maximize profit rather than minimize shortfall, and (2) the plant–product capabilities are first-stage decisions rather than exogenous factors.

9.3.2 Lagrangian Relaxation

We now describe a Lagrangian relaxation algorithm to solve the process flexibility design model. We relax constraints (9.8) and (9.9) with Lagrange multipliers τ and η respectively. Since we are relaxing $\leq$ constraints in a maximization problem, τ and η are both restricted to be non-negative (see Section D.5 in Appendix D). The Lagrangian subproblem becomes:

$$
\begin{aligned}
\text{maximize} \quad & \sum_{i \in V_1} \sum_{j \in V_2} \left[-a_{ij}x_{ij} + \sum_{s \in S} q_s(p_i - c_{ij})y_{ijs} \right] \\
& + \sum_{i \in V_1} \sum_{s \in S} \left[\tau_{is}\left(d_{is} - \sum_{j \in V_2} y_{ijs}\right) + \sum_{j \in V_2} \eta_{ijs}(d_{is}x_{ij} - y_{ijs}) \right] \\
= & \sum_{i \in V_1} \sum_{j \in V_2} \left(-a_{ij} + \sum_{s \in S} \eta_{ijs}d_{is} \right) x_{ij} \\
& + \sum_{i \in V_1} \sum_{j \in V_2} \sum_{s \in S} [q_s(p_i - c_{ij}) - \tau_{is} - \eta_{ijs}]y_{ijs} + \sum_{i \in V_1} \sum_{s \in S} \tau_{is}d_{is}
\end{aligned}
$$

(9.12)

$$
\begin{aligned}
\text{subject to} \quad & \sum_{i \in V_1} y_{ijs} \leq C_j && \forall j \in V_2, \forall s \in S && (9.13) \\
& x_{ij} \in \{0,1\} && \forall i \in V_1, \forall j \in V_2 && (9.14) \\
& y_{ijs} \geq 0 && \forall i \in V_1, \forall j \in V_2, \forall s \in S && (9.15)
\end{aligned}
$$

This problem decouples into two subproblems, one involving only x and one involving only y. The x-problem is trivial to solve: We simply set $x_{ij} = 1$ if

$$ -a_{ij} + \sum_{s \in S} \eta_{ijs}d_{is} > 0 $$

and set $x_{ij} = 0$ otherwise. Solving the y-problem amounts to solving the following problem for each j and s:

$$ (\mathrm{P}_{js}) \quad \text{maximize} \quad \sum_{i \in V_1} a_i y_i \tag{9.16} $$

$$\text{subject to} \quad \sum_{i \in V_1} y_i \leq C_j \quad\quad (9.17)$$

$$y_i \geq 0 \quad\quad \forall i \in V_1 \quad\quad (9.18)$$

where

$$a_i = q_s(p_i - c_{ij}) - \tau_{is} - \eta_{ijs}$$
$$y_i = y_{ijs}.$$

This problem, too, is easy: We simply set $y_i = C_j$ for the i that has the largest a_i and $y_i = 0$ for all other i. (If $a_i \leq 0$ for all i, then we set $y_i = 0$ for all i.) The problem could be strengthened somewhat by adding a constraint

$$y_{ijs} \leq d_{is} \quad \forall i \in V_1, \forall j \in V_2, \forall s \in S$$

to the original problem. This constraint is redundant in the original problem but strengthens the y-problem by reducing its optimal objective value (or leaving it the same), thereby tightening the Lagrangian upper bound. If we do this, the y-problem becomes a continuous knapsack problem, which is still easy to solve.

In Mak and Shen's (2009) formulation of this problem, the demands are modeled using a continuous, multivariate distribution, rather than the discrete scenarios used here. In effect, this means that there are an infinite number of demand scenarios, and hence we must relax an infinite number of constraints of type (9.8) and (9.9). To handle this issue, Mak and Shen propose the use of scenario-independent Lagrange multipliers; that is, to omit the subscript s from τ and η and to use the same multipliers for all scenarios. This results in a weaker upper bound from the Lagrangian subproblem than if the multipliers depend on the scenario, but it also leads to a more tractable Lagrangian dual problem. In general, the quality of the bound is better if the demand variability is relatively small. (See, for example, Kunnumkal and Topaloglu (2008) for a discussion.) This approach has been used successfully in stochastic network flow and stochastic dynamic programming problems (Cheung and Powell 1996, Topaloglu 2009).

Feasible solutions to the original problem can be obtained from solutions to the Lagrangian subproblem in order to obtain lower bounds. To do this, we set the first-stage (x) variables to their values from the subproblem. Once these variables are fixed, the y variables can be determined by solving a network flow problem for each scenario s. (For the continuous-demand case in Mak and Shen (2009), the y variables must be determined by solving a stochastic linear program.)

Mak and Shen (2009) compare the solutions obtained from this flexibility optimization model with the simple chaining structure. When the products are identical in terms of demand distribution and production cost, the two approaches produce solutions with similar expected profit. For non-homogenous products, the performance of the chaining strategy can be sensitive to the sequences of the products and plants. For example, if there are two high-demand products and two low-demand products, then the solutions will be different if we number the high-demand products as $i = 1, 2$ than if we number them as $i = 1, 3$. (See Figure 9.3.) Therefore, the

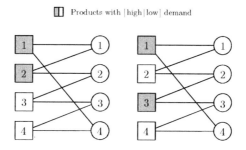

Products with [high][low] demand

Figure 9.3   Examples of different chaining structures for non-homogeneous demand case.

performance of the straightforward chaining structure, in which plant j produces products $i = j$ and $j + 1$, may depend on how the products happen to be indexed. On the other hand, the process flexibility design model discussed in this section accounts with these non-homogeneities explicitly. As a result, this approach outperforms the simple chaining approach considerably for some problem instances.

PROBLEMS

9.1   (Three-Stage Flexibility) Consider the three-stage supply chain flexibility design problem pictured below.

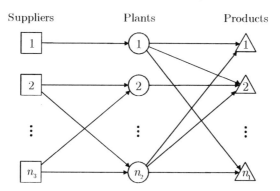

There are n_1 products, n_2 plants, and n_3 suppliers. In the full-flexibility structure, each product can be produced at any plant using raw materials sourced from any supplier. We assume that each unit of product consumes one unit of material from each supplier and uses one unit of capacity at each plant. We assume further that the production capacities at the plants are C_j, $j = 1, \ldots, n_2$, and that the suppliers have a limited amount B_k of raw materials, $k = 1, \ldots, n_3$. The demand for each product is random and is denoted by the random variable D_i, $i = 1, \ldots, n_1$.

a) Derive an expression for the expected sales in the full-flexibility structure.

b) Let y_{ijk} be a decision variable representing the amount of raw materials from supplier k used to produce product i at plant j. Formulate the flexibility design problem for this three-stage supply chain.

9.2 (Capacity Investment) Recall the formulation of the flexibility design problem (9.6)–(9.11). Suppose now that the capacity is also a decision, to be made jointly with the network design problem. In particular, the capacities C_j are first-stage decision variables, together with the flexibility investment variables x_{ij}. We assume a linear investment cost function for the capacity, with constant marginal investment cost v_j per unit.

a) Write down the new objective function after adding the capacity-investment cost term.

b) Discuss a method for solving this new problem.

9.3 (Auto Repair) A small car repair shop has four certified technicians, Irene, Larry, Max, and Suzanne. The shop specializes in four types of vehicles, labeled A, B, C, and D. Each technician has been trained to repair one type of vehicle. On average, the repair of each type of vehicle takes 4 hours. It is estimated that the number of customers who want a type-A vehicle fixed during a given week is equally likely to be 8, 10 or 12. That is, the probability is $\frac{1}{3}$ for each of the possible outcomes, 8, 10 or 12 customers. Each of the other three vehicle types has the same demand distribution for repairs. Furthermore, the demands are iid across time and type. Each technician has a nominal work week of 40 hours at $55 per hour and will be paid for 40 hours even if he or she works fewer than 40 hours in the week. But if a technician works more than 40 hours, then the overtime rate is 150% of the normal pay. The overtime rate applies only to the hours in excess of 40.

a) Find the probability distribution for the total demand, as well as the overtime required for each possible value of the total demand.

b) Calculate the expected yearly cost of the dedicated system, in which Irene, Larry, Max, and Suzanne can only repair vehicles of type A, B, C, and D, respectively.

c) After reading this chapter, the repair shop's manager decides to try a flexible system that follows a chaining structure in which Irene will be trained to repair type-B vehicles, Larry to repair type-C vehicles, Max to repair type-D vehicles, and Suzanne to repair type-A vehicles. Suppose the cost of training one technician to repair a new vehicle type is $10,000. Calculate the expected number of years until the shop recoups the investment cost to convert the dedicated system to the partial flexible system with the chaining structure.

d) Calculate the expected number of years to recoup the investment cost if the shop instead chooses the full-flexibility system in which every technician is trained to repair all four vehicle models. Compare this to the result from part (c).

9.4   (**Max-Flow Formulation**) The production-allocation problem (9.1)–(9.5) can also be formulated using a max-flow formulation.

   a) Formulate the problem as a max-flow problem, using the notation already defined in the chapter.

   b) Research has shown that when demands are independent, chaining can achieve most (roughly 97%) of the benefits of full flexibility as the number of nodes n approaches ∞. Show that if the demands are correlated, the situation can be very different.

CHAPTER 10

THE BULLWHIP EFFECT

10.1 INTRODUCTION

In the early 1990s, executives at Procter and Gamble (P&G) noticed a peculiar trend in the orders for Pampers, a brand of baby diapers. As you might expect, demand for diapers at the consumer level is pretty steady since babies use them at a fairly constant rate. But P&G noticed that the orders placed by retailers (e.g., CVS, Target) to distributors were quite variable over time—high one week, low the next. The distributors' orders to P&G were even more variable, and P&G's orders to its own suppliers (e.g., 3M) were still more variable. (See Figure 10.1.)

This phenomenon is known as the *bullwhip effect* (BWE), a phrase coined by P&G executives that refers to the way a wave's amplitude increases as it travels the length of a whip. Sometimes it's also known as the "whiplash" or "whipsaw" effect. The bullwhip effect has been observed in many industries other than diapers. For example, Hewlett-Packard (HP) noticed large variability in the orders retailers placed to HP for printers, even though demand for printers is fairly steady. Similarly, the demand for DRAM (a component of computers) is more volatile than the demand for computers themselves. Wide swings in order sizes can cause big increases in inventory costs (for both raw materials and finished goods), overtime and idling

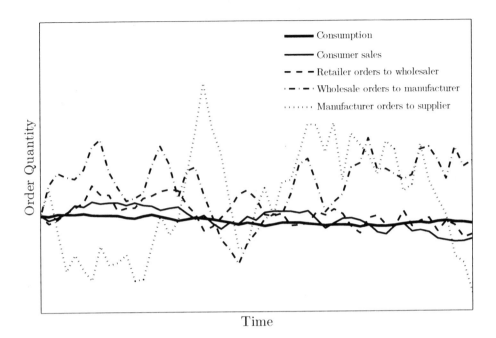

Figure 10.1   Increase in order variability in upstream supply chain stages.

expenses, and emergency shipment costs. These factors are estimated to increase costs by as much as 12.5% to 25% (Lee et al. 1997a).

The BWE was described in the literature as early as the 1950s (Forrester 1958). Sterman (1989) described how the BWE could be caused by *irrational* behavior by supply chain managers: for example, overreacting to a small shortage one week by ordering far too much the next week. His paper uses the now-famous "beer game" to demonstrate this relationship empirically. Then, two papers by Lee et al. (1997a,b) demonstrated that the BWE can occur even if all players act *rationally*—following the logical, optimized policies of the type we discuss in this book. They identified four primary causes for the BWE:

1. **Demand signal processing.** Many firms use forecasting techniques to estimate the mean and standard deviation of current or future demands. Each time a new demand is observed, the estimates are updated. If the previous period's demand was high, the new estimate will be higher than the previous one, thus raising the target inventory level. The orders will be more exaggerated than the demands. This phenomenon is amplified by the lead time if the base-stock level is set using (4.44), that is,

$$\mu L + z_\alpha \sigma \sqrt{L},$$

where μ and σ are the mean and standard deviation of the demand per period and L is the lead time. In practice, the firm doesn't know μ and σ, so it estimates them based on historical data. These estimates change periodically, and any change in the estimates are magnified by the lead time when setting base-stock levels, so long lead times produce large shifts in order sizes.

2. **Rationing game.** When distributors don't have enough inventory to meet retailers' orders, they often allocate product according to order size: If retailer 1 orders 100 units and retailer 2 orders 150 units but there are only 200 units available, then the distributor will give $200 \times (100/250) = 80$ units to retailer 1 and $200 \times (150/250) = 120$ units to retailer 2. If the retailers anticipate the shortage, they may artificially inflate their orders to try to get a larger allocation of the inventory. Once the shortage is over, the retailers' orders will return to their normal levels, or even lower. Thus, the variance in retailer orders is larger than the variance in actual demands.

3. **Order batching.** It is common for all players in a supply chain to place orders in bulk: Parents buy diapers in packages of 50, retailers buy them by the case, distributors buy them by the truckload. The theoretical explanation for the optimality of bulk ordering is that there is a fixed cost to place each order, so it's better to place fewer orders if possible. (For parents, the fixed cost is in the form of inconvenience and time: They don't want to go to the drug store every time their baby uses another diaper.) Moreover, bulk buying is encouraged by sellers by offering quantity discounts, another common practice. But order batching means that orders may be high one week, then low for the next few weeks as retailers use up the stock they've accumulated. Another reason for order batching is that many firms use materials requirements planning (MRP) software that evaluates the firm's requirements for every part it uses and automatically places orders with suppliers once per month. That means the supplier sees large demand during a few days of the month as its customers' MRP systems place orders and small demand for the rest of the month; this is sometimes known as the "hockey stick" phenomenon.

4. **Price speculation.** Prices change all the time, and firms tend to stock up while prices are low and order less when prices are high. This is most pronounced at upstream stages in the supply chain whose raw materials are commodities like plastic, steel, fuel, and so on—prices for these commodities change constantly, and speculation is common among buyers. It's also obvious at the other end of the supply chain, as customers buy more when retailers offer sales and promotions. In the middle of the supply chain, sales and promotions are common, too, causing retailers and other players to stock up when prices drop. All of this leads to large variability in buying patterns.

In Section 10.2, we'll discuss mathematical models explaining these causes and demonstrating that they occur even when each player in the supply chain is a rational "optimizer." Then, in Section 10.3, we'll discuss strategies for reducing the BWE. Finally, in Section 10.4, we'll examine the extent to which sharing demand information with upstream supply chain members can reduce or eliminate the BWE.

Figure 10.2   Serial supply chain network.

Most of the analysis in this section is adapted from Lee et al. (1997a) and Chen et al. (2000). For reviews of recent literature on the BWE, see McCullen and Towill (2002), Lee et al. (2004), or Geary et al. (2006).

10.2 PROVING THE EXISTENCE OF THE BULLWHIP EFFECT

Consider a serial supply chain like the one pictured in Figure 10.2. We will examine this system in the context of an infinite horizon under periodic review. Each stage places orders from its upstream stage and supplies product to its downstream stage. Stage N serves the end customer.

Our strategy will be to focus on one stage and to show that the variance of orders it places to its supplier is larger than the variance of orders it receives from its customer. That, in turn, implies the BWE as a whole: Stage N's orders are more variable than its demands, so stage $N - 1$'s orders are even more variable, so stage $N - 2$'s orders are even more variable, and so on.

Suppose the following conditions hold at each stage:

1. Demands are independent over time, and the parameters of the demand distribution are known

2. The stage's supplier always has sufficient inventory and satisfies orders with a fixed lead time that is independent of the order size

3. There is no fixed ordering cost

4. The purchase cost is constant over time

If all four of these conditions hold, it is optimal for the stage to follow a stationary base-stock policy. As we know from Section 4.4, that means that in each period, the order placed by the stage is exactly equal to the demand seen by the stage in the previous time period, so the orders placed by the stage and the demand seen by it have the same variance—*the bullwhip effect does not occur.*

However, relaxing each of the conditions given above (one at a time) gives us the four causes of the BWE: demand signal processing (when the demand parameters are unknown and hence forecasting techniques must be used to estimate them), rationing game (when supply is limited), order batching (when there is a fixed cost for ordering), and price speculation (when the purchase price can change over time).

We discuss models for each of these causes next. In each of the four sections that follow, we will consider only a single stage in the supply chain and show that the orders placed by the stage to its supplier have larger variance than the demands received by the stage. Without loss of generality we will refer to this stage as the "retailer."

10.2.1 Demand Signal Processing

In this section we relax both parts of assumption #1 on page 258: We assume that the demands are *serially correlated*—that is, demands in one time period are statistically dependent on demands in the previous time period—and that the parameters of the demand process are unknown and must be estimated. Each stage in the supply chain makes its own estimate of the demand parameters based on the orders it receives. We will show that this processing of the demand signal can lead to the BWE.

We assume that the demands seen by the retailer follow a first-order autoregressive $AR(1)$ process; that is, the demand follows a model of the form

$$D_t = d + \rho D_{t-1} + \epsilon_t, \tag{10.1}$$

where D_t is the demand in period t (a random variable), $d \geq 0$ is a constant, ρ is a correlation constant with $-1 < \rho < 1$, and ϵ_t is an error term that is distributed $N(0, \sigma^2)$. If ρ is close to 1, then a large demand tends to be followed by another large demand, while if ρ is close to -1, then a large demand tends to be followed by a small one.

It's tempting to think of d as the mean of this process, but it is not, unless $\rho = 0$. In fact, it can be shown that

$$E[D_t] = \frac{d}{1 - \rho} \tag{10.2}$$

$$\text{Var}[D_t] = \frac{\sigma^2}{1 - \rho^2} \tag{10.3}$$

$$\text{Cov}[D_t, D_{t-k}] = \frac{\rho^k \sigma^2}{1 - \rho^2} = \rho^k \text{Var}[D_t] \tag{10.4}$$

Note that the mean, variance, and covariance are the same in every period. If $\rho = 0$, the demands are iid with mean d and variance σ^2.

The retailer follows a base-stock policy. Let D_t^L be the lead-time demand for an order placed in period t; that is,

$$D_t^L = \sum_{k=0}^{L-1} D_{t+k}. \tag{10.5}$$

If the retailer knew the mean $\mu_t^L = E[D_t^L]$ and standard deviation $\sigma_t^L = \sqrt{\text{Var}[D_t^L]}$ of the lead-time demand (which it could calculate if it knew d, σ, and ρ—see Problem 10.3), then, analogous to (4.44), the optimal base-stock level would be given by

$$S_t = \mu_t^L + z_\alpha \sigma_t^L. \tag{10.6}$$

However, the retailer does not know μ_t^L and σ_t^L but instead must forecast them based on observed demands using, for example, one of the methods in Chapter 2. One of the most common forecasting techniques, and the one we'll use here, is a *moving average* (Section 2.2.1), which simply consists of the average of the demands from the previous m time periods. The estimate for μ_t^L, computed at time t and denoted $\hat{\mu}_t^L$, is

$$\hat{\mu}_t^L = L\left(\frac{\sum_{i=1}^m D_{t-i}}{m}\right). \tag{10.7}$$

As for the standard deviation, it turns out that instead of estimating the standard deviation of lead-time demand (σ_t^L), we want to estimate the standard deviation of the *forecast error* of the lead-time demand, σ_{et}^L. (See Section 4.4.2.8.) The estimate of σ_{et}^L at time t is given by

$$\hat{\sigma}_{et}^L = C_{L\rho}\sqrt{\frac{\sum_{i=1}^m (e_{t-i})^2}{m}} \tag{10.8}$$

where

$$e_t = D_t - \hat{\mu}_t^1$$

is the one-period forecast error and $C_{L\rho}$ is a constant depending on L, ρ, and m; we omit the derivation of this equation and the exact form of $C_{L\rho}$. The base-stock level is then set using

$$S_t = \hat{\mu}_t^L + z_\alpha \hat{\sigma}_{et}^L. \tag{10.9}$$

This policy is optimal for iid normal demands (i.e., if $\rho = 0$) and is approximately optimal otherwise. (It is only approximately optimal because these estimates of μ_t^L and σ_{et}^L do not take into account the autocorrelation of the demand; that is, they assume that the demand will have the same distribution in each period of the lead time. It would be more accurate to account for the correlation, i.e., using (10.1), when estimating the lead-time demand parameters. This is relatively straightforward to do if d, ρ, and σ are known—see Problem 10.3—but is quite a bit harder when the parameters are unknown and are estimated as described above.)

In period t, the retailer computes $\hat{\mu}_t^L$ and $\hat{\sigma}_{et}^L$ using the previous m periods' demands, then sets the base-stock level S_t using (10.9) and places an order of size $Q_t = S_t - S_{t-1} + D_{t-1}$ (why?). (It is possible that $Q_t < 0$. In this case, we assume that the firm *returns* $-Q_t$ units to the supplier and receives a full refund for the returned units.) We can write Q_t as

$$
\begin{aligned}
Q_t &= S_t - S_{t-1} + D_{t-1} \\
&= \hat{\mu}_t^L + z_\alpha \hat{\sigma}_{et}^L - (\hat{\mu}_{t-1}^L + z_\alpha \hat{\sigma}_{e,t-1}^L) + D_{t-1} \\
&= \hat{\mu}_t^L - \hat{\mu}_{t-1}^L + z_\alpha(\hat{\sigma}_{et}^L - \hat{\sigma}_{e,t-1}^L) + D_{t-1} \\
&= L\left(\frac{\sum_{i=1}^m D_{t-i} - \sum_{i=1}^m D_{t-1-i}}{m}\right) + D_{t-1} + z_\alpha(\hat{\sigma}_{et}^L - \hat{\sigma}_{e,t-1}^L) \\
&= L\left(\frac{D_{t-1} - D_{t-m-1}}{m}\right) + D_{t-1} + z_\alpha(\hat{\sigma}_{et}^L - \hat{\sigma}_{e,t-1}^L)
\end{aligned}
$$

$$= \left(1 + \frac{L}{m}\right) D_{t-1} - \frac{L}{m} D_{t-m-1} + z_\alpha(\hat{\sigma}_{et}^L - \hat{\sigma}_{e,t-1}^L)$$

We want to compute $\text{Var}[Q_t]$ so that we can compare it to $\text{Var}[D_t]$ to demonstrate the BWE. Using the fact that

$$\text{Var}[aX + bY] = a^2\text{Var}[X] + b^2\text{Var}[Y] + 2ab\text{Cov}[X, Y], \qquad (10.10)$$

we have

$$
\begin{aligned}
\text{Var}[Q_t] =& \text{Var}\left[\left(1 + \frac{L}{m}\right) D_{t-1} - \frac{L}{m} D_{t-m-1}\right] + \text{Var}\left[z_\alpha(\hat{\sigma}_{et}^L - \hat{\sigma}_{e,t-1}^L)\right] \\
&+ 2\text{Cov}\left[\left(1 + \frac{L}{m}\right) D_{t-1} - \frac{L}{m} D_{t-m-1}, z_\alpha(\hat{\sigma}_{et}^L - \hat{\sigma}_{e,t-1}^L)\right] \quad (10.11)
\end{aligned}
$$

Let's examine the $\text{Cov}[\cdot]$ term. Recall that

$$\text{Cov}\left[\sum_{i=1}^{m} a_i X_i, \sum_{j=1}^{n} b_j Y_j\right] = \sum_{i=1}^{m}\sum_{j=1}^{n} a_i b_j \text{Cov}[X_i, Y_j].$$

Then

$$
\begin{aligned}
\text{Cov}[\cdot] =& \left(1 + \frac{L}{m}\right) z_\alpha \text{Cov}[D_{t-1}, \hat{\sigma}_{et}^L] - \left(1 + \frac{L}{m}\right) z_\alpha \text{Cov}[D_{t-1}, \hat{\sigma}_{e,t-1}^L] \\
&- \frac{L}{m} z_\alpha \text{Cov}[D_{t-m-1}, \hat{\sigma}_{et}^L] + \frac{L}{m} z_\alpha \text{Cov}[D_{t-m-1}, \hat{\sigma}_{e,t-1}^L]. \quad (10.12)
\end{aligned}
$$

To evaluate this further, we'll need the following lemma:

Lemma 10.1 $\text{Cov}[D_{t-i}, \hat{\sigma}_{et}^L] = 0$ *for all* $i = 1, \dots, m$.

Proof. Omitted; see Ryan (1997). ∎

Therefore the first and last terms of (10.12) are equal to 0. As for the middle terms,

$$
\begin{aligned}
&- \left(1 + \frac{L}{m}\right) z_\alpha \text{Cov}[D_{t-1}, \hat{\sigma}_{e,t-1}^L] \\
=& - \left(1 + \frac{L}{m}\right) z_\alpha \text{Cov}[d + \rho D_{t-2} + \epsilon_{t-1}, \hat{\sigma}_{e,t-1}^L] \quad \text{(by (10.1))} \\
=& - \left(1 + \frac{L}{m}\right) z_\alpha \rho \text{Cov}[D_{t-2}, \hat{\sigma}_{e,t-1}^L] \quad \text{(since } D, \epsilon \text{ are independent)} \\
=& \, 0 \quad \text{(by Lemma 10.1)}
\end{aligned}
$$

and

$$- \frac{L}{m} z_\alpha \text{Cov}[D_{t-m-1}, \hat{\sigma}_{et}^L]$$

$$= -\frac{L}{m} z_\alpha \text{Cov} \left[\frac{1}{\rho} (D_{t-m} - d - \epsilon_{t-m}), \hat{\sigma}_{et}^L \right] \qquad \text{(by (10.1))}$$

$$= -\frac{L}{m} z_\alpha \frac{1}{\rho} \text{Cov}[D_{t-m}, \hat{\sigma}_{et}^L] \qquad \text{(since } D, \epsilon \text{ are independent)}$$

$$= 0. \qquad \text{(by Lemma 10.1)}$$

Therefore we can ignore the $\text{Cov}[\cdot]$ term in (10.11). Then using (10.10) again, we have

$$\text{Var}[Q_t] = \left[\left(1 + \frac{L}{m} \right)^2 \text{Var}[D_{t-1}] + \left(\frac{L}{m} \right)^2 \text{Var}[D_{t-m-1}] \right.$$
$$\left. -2 \left(1 + \frac{L}{m} \right) \left(\frac{L}{m} \right) \text{Cov}[D_{t-1}, D_{t-m-1}] \right]$$
$$+ z_\alpha^2 \text{Var}[\hat{\sigma}_{et}^L - \hat{\sigma}_{e,t-1}^L]$$
$$= \left(1 + \frac{2L}{m} + \frac{2L^2}{m^2} \right) \text{Var}[D] - \left(\frac{2L}{m} + \frac{2L^2}{m^2} \right) \rho^m \text{Var}[D]$$
$$+ z_\alpha^2 \text{Var}[\hat{\sigma}_{et}^L - \hat{\sigma}_{e,t-1}^L] \qquad \text{(by (10.4))}$$
$$= \left[1 + \left(\frac{2L}{m} + \frac{2L^2}{m^2} \right) (1 - \rho^m) \right] \text{Var}[D] + z_\alpha^2 \text{Var}[\hat{\sigma}_{et}^L - \hat{\sigma}_{e,t-1}^L].$$

This gives us the following theorem:

Theorem 10.1

$$\frac{\text{Var}[Q]}{\text{Var}[D]} \geq 1 + \left(\frac{2L}{m} + \frac{2L^2}{m^2} \right) (1 - \rho^m) \qquad (10.13)$$

The bound is tight when $z_\alpha = 0$.

Theorem 10.1 demonstrates that demand forecasting in the presence of positive lead times is sufficient to create the BWE at a single stage. Moreover, it provides a lower bound on the percentage increase in variability. For shorthand, let B equal the lower bound on $\text{Var}[Q]/\text{Var}[D]$, i.e., the right-hand side of (10.13). Theorem 10.1 demonstrates that:

- As m increases, B decreases. This is intuitive since larger m means smoother forecasts, so less variability in the order sizes.

- As L increases, B increases. This is also reasonable since longer lead times make it harder to forecast demand, so the forecasts themselves, and hence the order sizes, will be more variable.

- If $\rho \geq 0$ (positively correlated demand), then as ρ increases, B decreases. The intuitive explanation is that stronger positive correlation means there is more information available to make forecasts since each demand observation also provides information about past and future demands.

- If $\rho < 0$ (negatively correlated demand), then as $|\rho|$ increases, B decreases if m is even and increases if m is odd. At first it seems surprising that the directional change in B should depend on whether m happens to be odd or even, but here is an explanation. Suppose $\rho \approx -1$, so that the demand alternates between large and small values. If m is even, then the moving average always includes the same number of large and small values, so the forecast does not change much from period to period. On the other hand, if m is odd, then the moving average itself will alternate between large and small values. Therefore, B will be smaller if m is even than if it is odd, and the difference between these two cases will be more exaggerated as $\rho \to -1$.

- If $z_\alpha = 0$, then the bound given in Theorem 10.1 is tight. In this case, no safety stock is held and stockouts occur in 50% of the periods. Simulation results given by Chen et al. (2000) suggest that even when $z_\alpha \neq 0$, the bound given by the theorem is reasonably tight.

Theorem 10.1 establishes that the BWE occurs when the demand is autocorrelated *and* the parameters are unknown. In fact, either of these conditions, by itself, is sufficient to cause the BWE. If demands are independent over time (i.e., $\rho = 0$ and the retailer knows this) but d and σ are still unknown, then Theorem 10.1 still applies and $B > 1$, so the BWE occurs. If, on the other hand, demands are still serially correlated but d, ρ, and σ are known, then the BWE occurs as well; see Problem 10.4 or Zhang (2004).

10.2.2 Rationing Game

Suppose the supply for a given product may be insufficient to meet the demand from multiple retailers and that the supplier will ration the available supply according to the fraction of demand accounted for by each retailer: If a retailer accounted for 8% of the total demand, it will receive 8% of the available supply. The BWE occurs when retailers anticipate the shortage since they have an incentive to inflate their orders to try to gain a larger share of the available supply. This behavior is called the *rationing game* because retailers play a "game" (in the game-theory sense) to try to obtain a larger allocation in the face of the supplier's rationing.

We will consider the following simple model. There are two identical retailers, each facing demand with pdf $f(\cdot)$ and cdf $F(\cdot)$ (the same distribution for both retailers). There is no inventory carryover between periods and unmet demands at the retailers are lost; therefore, we can model a single period and treat the multi-period problem as multiple copies of the single-period one. The cost of each unit on hand at the end of a period incurs a cost of h, and each lost sale incurs a stockout penalty of p. The lead time is $L = 1$: An order placed at the end of one period is received at the start of the next.

Let Q^* be the optimal order quantity if the supply were infinite; that is,

$$Q^* = F^{-1}\left(\frac{p}{h+p}\right)$$

(from (4.27)). We assume that the available supply A can take on two quantities: It will equal A_1 with probability r and ∞ with probability $1 - r$, with $A_1 < 2Q^*$. That is, with probability r there will be a supply shortage and with probability $1 - r$ there will be adequate supply. (Lee et al. (1997a) consider a model with N retailers and a more general supply process, but the simpler model presented here conveys most of the same insights.)

If a retailer expects a supply shortage, it has an incentive to order more than Q^*. We will evaluate the *Nash equilibrium* solution—the order quantities chosen by the two retailers such that neither retailer, knowing the other's order quantity, would want to change its own. Put another way, a retailer's Nash equilibrium solution is the order quantity it chooses assuming it knows the other retailer's order quantity already.

Let Q_i be the order size for retailer i, $i = 1, 2$. If $A = A_1$, then retailer i will receive $A_1 Q_i / (Q_1 + Q_2)$ units. For convenience, define retailer 1's allocation as

$$a(Q) = \frac{A_1 Q}{Q + Q_2}.$$

If Q_2 is fixed, retailer 1's expected cost is given by

$$
g_1(Q_1) = (1 - r) \left[h \int_0^{Q_1} (Q_1 - d) f(d) dd + p \int_{Q_1}^{\infty} (d - Q_1) f(d) dd \right]
$$
$$
+ \quad r \left[h \int_0^{a(Q_1)} (a(Q_1) - d) f(d) dd + p \int_{a(Q_1)}^{\infty} (d - a(Q_1)) f(d) dd \right].
$$

$$(10.14)$$

The first term of (10.14) represents the expected cost given $A = \infty$ while the second term assumes $A = A_1$. An analogous expression describes retailer 2's expected cost.

Theorem 10.2 *Both retailers choose an order quantity Q that is larger than the optimal newsvendor order quantity, Q^*.*

Proof. Retailer 1 minimizes (10.14) by setting its first derivative to 0:

$$
\frac{dg_1}{dQ_1} = r \left[h \int_0^{a(Q_1)} \frac{A_1 Q_2}{(Q_1 + Q_2)^2} f(d) dd + p \int_{a(Q_1)}^{\infty} - \frac{A_1 Q_2}{(Q_1 + Q_2)^2} f(d) dd \right]
$$
$$
+ (1 - r) \left[h \int_0^{Q_1} f(d) dd + p \int_{Q_1}^{\infty} - f(d) dd \right] \quad \text{(using Leibniz's rule (C.19))}
$$
$$
= r \left[(h + p) \frac{A_1 Q_2}{(Q_1 + Q_2)^2} F(a(Q_1)) - p \frac{A_1 Q_2}{(Q_1 + Q_2)^2} \right]
$$
$$
+ (1 - r) \left[(h + p) F(Q_1) - p \right]
$$

Since retailers 1 and 2 are identical, they will make exactly the same decisions: $Q_1 = Q_2 = Q$. Then $a(Q_1) = A_1/2$. Each retailer will set

$$
r \frac{A_1}{4Q} \left[(h + p) F \left(\frac{A_1}{2} \right) - p \right] + (1 - r)[(h + p) F(Q) - p] = 0.
$$

Now,

$$F\left(\frac{A_1}{2}\right) < F\left(\frac{2Q^*}{2}\right) = F(Q^*) = \frac{p}{h+p}$$

since $A_1 < 2Q^*$ and $F(\cdot)$ is strictly increasing. Therefore

$$(h+p)F\left(\frac{A_1}{2}\right) - p < (h+p)\frac{p}{h+p} - p = 0.$$

So the optimal Q satisfies

$$(h+p)F(Q) - p = [\text{something positive}] \qquad (10.15)$$

while the optimal Q from the newsvendor problem satisfies

$$(h+p)F(Q) - p = 0. \qquad (10.16)$$

Since $F(\cdot)$ is strictly increasing, it takes a *larger* value of Q to satisfy (10.15) than to satisfy (10.16). ∎

Therefore, in the presence of supply shortages, order quantities will be inflated. However, this, by itself, does not prove that the BWE occurs in the rationing game, since inflated order quantities do not necessarily imply inflated variances. However, Lee et al. (1997a) argue that the theorem

> ...implies the bullwhip effect when the mean demand changes over time. Re-tailers' equilibrium order quantity may be identical or close to the newsvendor solution for low-demand periods, while it will be larger than the newsvendor solution for high-demand periods. Hence, the variance is amplified at the retailer.

It takes some additional work to prove this claim rigorously. In fact, it can be shown that, if the mean demand changes over time as described in the quote above, then there is *no* finite Nash equilibrium in the rationing game defined by Lee et al. (1997a). That is, the retailers will keep inflating their order quantities in response to one another *ad infinitum*. However, under some minor modifications, a Nash equilibrium does exist, and its variance is greater than that of the demand, as suggested in the quote. (See Rong et al. (2010) for these results.)

10.2.3 Order Batching

We will model the batching of orders by assuming that a given retailer will not place an order in every time period. Instead, each retailer uses a periodic-review base-stock policy with a *review period* of R periods—that is, every Rth period, the retailer places an order whose size is equal to the demand seen by the retailer in the previous R periods. If the supplier serves several retailers, we will show that the variance of the orders seen by the supplier is larger than the variance of the orders seen by the retailers.

Suppose that there are N retailers; retailer i sees a demand of D_{it} in period t, with $D_{it} \sim N(\mu, \sigma^2)$. Demands are independent among retailers and across time periods. We consider three cases corresponding to how the retailers' orders line up with one another: random ordering, positively correlated ordering, and balanced ordering.

10.2.3.1 Random Ordering Suppose each retailer's ordering day is chosen randomly from $1, \ldots, R$ with equal probability. Let X be a random variable indicating the number of orders seen by the supplier in a given time period. Since each retailer orders with probability $1/R$ in a given time period, X is a binomial random variable with parameters N and $1/R$, and

$$E[X] = \frac{N}{R}$$

$$\text{Var}[X] = \frac{N}{R} \left(1 - \frac{1}{R} \right).$$

Let Q_t^r be the total size of the orders received by the supplier in period t. Without loss of generality, assume that retailers $1, \ldots, X$ are the retailers that order in period t and retailers $X + 1, \ldots, N$ are the retailers that do not. Then

$$Q_t^r = \sum_{i=1}^{X} \sum_{k=t-R}^{t-1} D_{ik}.$$

(The superscript r stands for "random.") Then

$$E[Q_t^r] = E[E[Q_t^r | X]] = E[XR\mu] = N\mu,$$

where the notation $E[E[Q_t^r | X]]$ means we take the expectation of Q_t^r for fixed X, then take the expectation over X. Similarly,

$$\begin{aligned}
\text{Var}[Q_t^r] &= E[\text{Var}[Q_t^r | X]] + \text{Var}[E[Q_t^r | X]] \\
&= E[XR\sigma^2] + \text{Var}[XR\mu] \\
&= N\sigma^2 + R^2\mu^2 \frac{N}{R} \left(1 - \frac{1}{R} \right) \\
&= N\sigma^2 + \mu^2 N(R - 1) \\
&\geq N\sigma^2.
\end{aligned}$$

(The first equality is a well known identity for variance.) Therefore, the variance of orders seen by the supplier is greater than or equal to that of the demands seen by the retailers. Note that if $R = 1$ (no order batching: every retailer orders every time period), the variances are equal, as expected.

10.2.3.2 Positively Correlated Ordering We'll consider the extreme case in which all retailers order in the same period. For example, if R is one week, then all retailers order on Monday (say) and not on other days of the week. This is the MRP "hockey stick" taken to its extreme. The distribution function of X (the number of retailers ordering on a given day) is then

$$P(X = i) = \begin{cases} 1 - 1/R, & \text{if } i = 0 \\ 1/R, & \text{if } i = N \\ 0, & \text{otherwise,} \end{cases}$$

with

$$E[X] = \frac{N}{R}$$

$$\text{Var}[X] = \frac{N^2}{R}\left(1 - \frac{1}{R}\right).$$

Let Q_t^c be the total size of the orders received by the supplier in period t. Then

$$E[Q_t^c] = E[E[Q_t^c|X]] = E[XR\mu] = N\mu$$

and

$$\text{Var}[Q_t^c] = E[XR\sigma^2] + \text{Var}[XR\mu]$$
$$= N\sigma^2 + R^2\mu^2 \frac{N^2}{R}\left(1 - \frac{1}{R}\right)$$
$$= N\sigma^2 + \mu^2 N^2(R - 1)$$
$$\geq N\sigma^2.$$

Again, the variance of orders is greater than the variance of demands, unless $R = 1$.

10.2.3.3 Balanced Ordering
Finally, suppose that the retailers' orders are evenly spread throughout the R-period review period. We'll write the number of retailers N as $N = MR + k$ for integers M and k. M is like N div R and k is like N mod R. For example, if $R = 7$ (one-week review period) and $N = 38$, then $M = 5$ and $k = 3$. Three days a week, 6 retailers order, and four days a week, 5 retailers order. More generally, the retailers are divided into R groups, each ordering on a different day. k of the groups have size $M + 1$ and $R - k$ of them have size M.

We get:

$$P(X = i) = \begin{cases} 1 - k/R, & \text{if } i = M \\ k/R, & \text{if } i = M + 1 \\ 0, & \text{otherwise} \end{cases}$$

Then

$$E[X] = M\left(1 - \frac{k}{R}\right) + \frac{(M + 1)k}{R} = \frac{N}{R}$$

$$\text{Var}[X] = \left(1 - \frac{k}{R}\right)M^2 + \frac{(M + 1)^2 k}{R} - \left(\frac{N}{R}\right)^2$$
$$= \frac{k}{R}\left(1 - \frac{k}{R}\right).$$

Let Q_t^b be the total size of the orders received by the supplier in period t. Then

$$E[Q_t^b] = E[E[Q_t^b|X]] = E[XR\mu] = N\mu$$

and

$$\text{Var}[Q_t^b] = E[XR\sigma^2] + \text{Var}[XR\mu]$$
$$= N\sigma^2 + R^2\mu^2\frac{k}{R}\left(1 - \frac{k}{R}\right)$$
$$= N\sigma^2 + \mu^2 k(R - k)$$
$$\geq N\sigma^2.$$

Once again, the variance of orders is greater than or equal to that of demands. If $k = 0$ or $k = R$, then exactly the same number of retailers place orders on each day, and the variances are equal.

We now have the following theorem.

Theorem 10.3 *Let Q_t^r, Q_t^c, and Q_t^b be random variables representing the orders received by the supplier in period t in the cases of random ordering, correlated ordering, and balanced ordering, respectively. Then:*

(a) $E[Q_t^c] = E[Q_t^r] = E[Q_t^b] = N\mu$

(b) $\text{Var}[Q_t^c] \geq \text{Var}[Q_t^r] \geq \text{Var}[Q_t^b] \geq N\sigma^2$

Proof. The analysis above proves (a) and the last inequality in (b). It remains to show $\text{Var}[Q_t^c] \geq \text{Var}[Q_t^r] \geq \text{Var}[Q_t^b]$:

$$\text{Var}[Q_t^c] = N\sigma^2 + \mu^2 N^2(R - 1)$$
$$\geq N\sigma^2 + \mu^2 N(R - 1)$$
$$= \text{Var}[Q_t^r]$$

since $N \geq 1$, and

$$\text{Var}[Q_t^r] = N\sigma^2 + \mu^2 N(R - 1)$$
$$\geq N\sigma^2 + \mu^2 k(R - k)$$
$$= \text{Var}[Q_t^b]$$

since $k(R - k) \leq N(R - 1)$ for all $k = 1, \ldots, R$. ∎

Therefore, the orders placed to the supplier have the same mean as those placed to the retailers, but larger variance. Moreover, correlated demand produces the largest bullwhip effect, then random, then balanced.

10.2.4   Price Speculation

We will consider a single retailer whose supplier alternates between two prices, c^L and c^H, with $c^L < c^H$. With probability r, the price will be c^L and with probability

Time Period	Starting Inventory	Demand	Price (L/H)	Order Size
1	100	77	L	77
2	100	67	H	17
3	50	82	L	132
4	100	93	L	93
etc.				

Figure 10.3   Bullwhip effect simulation.

$1 - r$, the price will be c^H. The optimal inventory policy in this case can be shown to be a modified base-stock policy: When the price is c^L, order enough to bring the inventory position to S^L, and when the price is c^H, order enough to bring the inventory position to S^H. If the inventory level is greater than the applicable base-stock level in a given period, returns are not allowed; instead, the retailer orders 0. It is clear that $S^H \leq S^L$, but finding the optimal S^H and S^L can be difficult. We omit the details here. The net result is the following theorem:

Theorem 10.4 $\mathrm{Var}[Q] > \mathrm{Var}[D]$

Therefore, price fluctuations produce the BWE.

You can get a feel for how this works by building a spreadsheet simulation model. For example, Figure 10.3 shows the first few rows of a spreadsheet that has columns for starting inventory, demand (we used $N(80, 100)$ to generate demand), price (low or high; we used $r = 0.7$), and order size (we used $S^L = 100$, $S^H = 50$ to compute these, but these are not the optimal base-stock levels). The results of the simulation are displayed graphically in Figure 10.4. The orders clearly display a larger variance than the demands.

10.3   REDUCING THE BULLWHIP EFFECT

A number of strategies have been proposed for addressing the four causes of the bullwhip effect. We discuss some of these next.

10.3.1   Demand Signal Processing

The analysis given above suggests that the BWE is amplified as we move upstream in the supply chain since stage i uses stage $(i+1)$'s orders as though they were demands, when in fact they are more variable than demands. This can be mitigated by sharing *point-of-sale* (POS) demand information with upstream members of the supply chain. That is, when the retailer places an order with the wholesaler, it relays not only the order size but also the size of the most recent demands. The proliferation of bar code scanners at checkout lines makes this technologically easy, but retailers are often reluctant to give demand data, which they treat as proprietary, to their suppliers. In addition, even if upstream stages see this "sell-through" data, they may each use

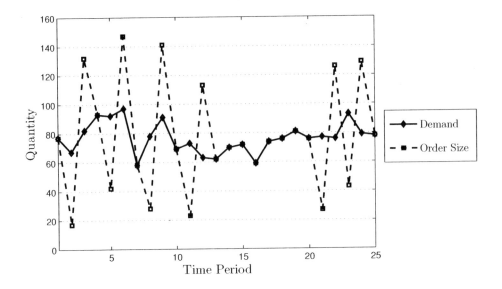

Figure 10.4 Bullwhip effect caused by price fluctuations.

different forecasting techniques or inventory policies, and this will exacerbate the BWE as well. We will analyze the effect of sell-through data on the BWE in Section 10.4.

Vendor-managed inventory (VMI) is a distribution strategy whereby the vendor (say, Coca-Cola) manages the inventory at the retailer (say, Walmart). The Coca-Cola company sets up the Coke displays at Walmart and, more importantly, monitors the inventory level and replenishes as necessary. In many cases, Coke actually owns the merchandise until it is sold—Walmart only takes ownership of the product for a split second as it's being scanned at the checkout line. Walmart benefits because Coke pays some of the costs of holding and managing the inventory. Coke benefits because it can keep tighter control over the displays of its products at stores, and also because its distribution is more efficient when it, not its customers, decides when to replenish the stock at each store. Moreover, since Coke gets to see actual sales data, the BWE is reduced.

As we saw earlier, longer lead times make the BWE worse. Therefore, one strategy for reducing the BWE is to shorten lead times. There are various ways to accomplish this, though it is often easier said than done.

10.3.2 Rationing Game

Rather than rationing according to order sizes in the current period, the supplier could allocate the available supply based on each retailer's orders in the *previous* period, or based on market share or some other mechanism that's independent of this period's orders. That eliminates the incentive to over-order during shortages.

Alternatively, the supplier could restrict each retailer's orders to be no more than a certain percentage (say 10%) larger than its order in the previous period, or charge a small "reservation payment" for each item ordered, whether or not it is received. Finally, the supplier can avoid the rationing game to a certain extent by sharing supply information with downstream members (note the symmetry with the demand signal processing case), allowing the retailers to use actual data instead of conjecture when making ordering decisions.

10.3.3   Order Batching

Recall from the EOQ model (Section 3.2) that as the fixed order cost increases, so does the order size. The batching of orders, then, can be reduced by reducing the fixed order cost. Nowadays, most communication uses a technique known as *electronic data interchange* (EDI), in which communication is performed electronically instead of on paper. This reduces the cost in both time and money of placing each order. Another innovation that reduces the setup cost of each order is *third-party logistics* (3PL) providers. 3PLs allow smaller companies to attain large economies of scale by taking advantage of the 3PL's size. For example, if a firm wants to ship a single package to a customer, it doesn't have to contract for a full truck—it can just use UPS, one of the world's largest 3PLs. Since UPS has lots of packages going all over the world, it attains huge economies of scale and passes some of these savings to its customers.

Suppliers can also encourage less batching by offering retailers volume discounts based on their total order, not based on orders for individual products. For example, P&G used to give bulk discounts if retailers ordered an entire truckload of one product (say, Pampers); now they give the same discounts even if the truck carries a variety of P&G products. This allows retailers to order Pampers more frequently (possibly with every order) as opposed to only ordering Pampers when they need a full truckload.

If batching is unavoidable, suppliers can force the orders to be balanced over time by assigning each retailer a specific period during which it may place orders. For example, one retailer might have to place orders only on Tuesdays while another may place orders on Thursdays. This strategy will reduce, but not avoid, the BWE, as we saw in Theorem 10.3.

10.3.4   Price Speculation

One way to avoid the variability introduced by price fluctuations is simply to keep prices fixed. Although this seems obvious, it has introduced a shift in the pricing schemes of many major manufacturers like P&G, Kraft, and Pillsbury. The strategy is called *everyday low pricing* (EDLP), and the basic idea is that prices stay at a constant low rate: there are no sales or promotions. EDLP is widely used upstream in the supply chain, but it is also increasingly used for retail sales. You may have seen stores that advertise "everyday low prices" and assumed it is merely a marketing ploy, without realizing the substantial benefit the retailer may be gaining by reducing the BWE.

In some cases, price fluctuations are unavoidable or desirable, and a natural consequence is that retailers will buy more when the price is low. The supplier can still reduce the BWE, however, by proposing contracts in which the retailer agrees to buy a large quantity of goods at a discount but to spread the receipt of the goods over time. The manufacturer can plan production more efficiently, but the retailer can continue to buy when prices are low.

10.4   CENTRALIZING DEMAND INFORMATION

In Section 10.3 we suggested that sharing POS demand information with upstream supply chain members reduces the BWE: Instead of seeing the retailer's orders, which are already more variable than the demands, the supplier sees the actual demands and uses these to make its own ordering decisions. But can this strategy eliminate the BWE entirely? If not, how much can it reduce the BWE?

In this section, we will analyze the impact of demand sharing on the BWE using the model introduced in Section 10.2.1, extending the analysis now to multiple stages as pictured in Figure 10.2. We will consider a *centralized* system in which each stage sees the actual customer demands; we will then compare this system to a *decentralized* system in which demand information is not shared and each stage sees only the orders placed by its immediate downstream neighbor.

The lead time for goods being transported from stage i to stage $i + 1$ is given by L_{i+1}. Each stage uses a moving average forecast with m observations. The moving average is used to compute estimates of the lead time demand mean, μ_t^L, and the standard deviation of the forecast error of lead-time demand, σ_{et}^L, which are in turn used to compute the base-stock levels.

10.4.1   Centralized System

In the centralized system, demand information is available to all stages of the supply chain. There is no "information lead time"—all stages see customer demands at exactly the same moment, when the demands arrive. Stage i can build its moving average forecast using actual customer demands. Its estimates of μ_t^L and σ_{et}^L will be as given in (10.7) and (10.8), and it will use these to compute base-stock levels as in (10.9).

Conceptually, there is no difference between (a) goods being shipped from i to $i + 1$ to ... to N to the customer, with a total lead time of $L_{i+1} + L_{i+2} + \ldots + L_N$, and (b) goods being shipped directly from i to the customer with the same lead time. Therefore, we can think of stage i as serving the end customer demand directly with a transportation lead time of $L_{i+1} + L_{i+2} + \ldots + L_N$. Using the same logic as in Section 10.2, we get the following theorem, which quantifies the increase in variability between the customer demands and the orders placed by a given stage:

Theorem 10.5 *In a centralized serial supply chain, the variance of the orders placed by stage* i, *denoted* Q_i, *satisfies*

$$\frac{\text{Var}[Q_i]}{\text{Var}[D]} \geq 1 + \left(\frac{2\sum_{j=i+1}^{N} L_j}{m} + \frac{2\left(\sum_{j=i+1}^{N} L_j\right)^2}{m^2} \right)(1 - \rho^m)$$

for all $i = 1, \ldots, N$.

Thus, even if (1) demand information is visible to all supply chain members, (2) all supply chain members use the same forecasting technique, and (3) all supply chain members use the same inventory policy, *the bullwhip effect still exists*. Sharing demand information does not eliminate the bullwhip effect. But does it reduce it? We will answer this question in the next section by comparing this system to one in which demand information is not shared.

10.4.2   Decentralized System

Consider the same system as in the previous section except that demand information is not shared: Each stage only sees the orders placed by its downstream stage. For simplicity, we will assume that $\rho = 0$ (demands are uncorrelated across time). We will also assume that $z_\alpha = 0$ (a 50% service level is acceptable), which means no safety stock is held. (Firms sometimes use inventory policies of this form, inflating L_i artificially to provide a buffer against uncertainty. For example, the firm might increase L_i by 7 days, requiring 7 extra *days of supply* of inventory to be on hand at any given time. Firms generally refer to this inflated lead time as *safety lead time*, but we can think of safety lead time as essentially an alternate method of setting safety stock.)

The "demands" seen by stage i are really the orders placed by stage $i + 1$. The variance of these orders is at least $1 + 2L_{i+1}/m + 2L_{i+1}^2/m^2$ times the variance of the orders received by stage $i + 1$, by Theorem 10.1. By following this logic through to stage N, we get the following theorem:

Theorem 10.6 *In a decentralized serial supply chain with* $\rho = 0$ *and* $z_\alpha = 0$, *the variance of the orders placed by stage* i, *denoted* Q_i, *satisfies*

$$\frac{\text{Var}[Q_i]}{\text{Var}[D]} \geq \prod_{j=i+1}^{N} \left(1 + \frac{2L_j}{m} + \frac{2L_j^2}{m^2} \right)$$

for all $i = 1, \ldots, N$.

Therefore, the increase in variability is additive in the centralized system but multiplicative in the decentralized system. Sharing demand information can significantly reduce the BWE. Although our analysis of the decentralized system assumed $\rho = z_\alpha = 0$, the qualitative result (additive vs. multiplicative variance increase) still holds in the more general case, though the math is uglier.

Table 10.1   Bounds on variability increase: Decentralized vs. centralized.

i	Decentralized	Centralized
1	12.7	7.2
2	6.7	5.0
3	3.6	3.2
4	1.9	1.9

To get a sense of the difference in magnitude between the bounds provided by Theorems 10.5 and 10.6, consider the case in which $N = 4$, $L_i = 2$ for all i, and $\rho = z_\alpha = 0$. Then the right-hand sides of the inequalities are given in Table 10.1. Note how much larger the bounds are for the decentralized system, especially as we move upstream in the supply chain.

PROBLEMS

10.1 **(Stochastic Price Simulation)** Suppose that the raw materials for a given product are stochastic, as in Section 10.2.4. The price equals $c^L = 3$ with probability 0.8 and equals $c^H = 8$ with probability 0.2. Demands in each period are $N(100, 20^2)$. On-hand inventory at the end of each period incurs a holding cost of $h = 1$ per unit. Unmet demands are backordered with a stockout cost of $p = 20$ per unit.

The firm uses two base-stock levels, S^L and S^H, ordering up to the appropriate level in each period based on the current price. For now, assume $S^L = 200$ and $S^H = 100$.

   a) Simulate this system using spreadsheet software for 100 periods. Build a table like the one in Figure 10.3 listing the time period, starting inventory, demand, price, order size, and any other columns you find useful. Also indicate the total cost in each period, including holding, stockout, and order costs.

   b) Using a spreadsheet-based non-linear optimization package, determine the values of S^L and S^H that minimize the average cost per period for the random sample you have generated. Report the optimal S^L and S^H and the resulting average cost per period. Include the first few rows of your chart in your report.

   c) Calculate $\mathrm{Var}[Q]$ and $\mathrm{Var}[D]$ for your simulation and compare them to verify that the bullwhip effect occurs.

   d) Produce a chart like the one in Figure 10.4 plotting the demands and orders across the time horizon.

10.2 **(Bullwhip Simulation)** In the one-warehouse, multiple-retailer (OWMR) system pictured below, all three retailers, and the warehouse, handle a single product. Demands at the retailers are normally distributed with means and variances as given in the table below, which also lists h, p, and K at each retailer. (As usual, h is the holding cost per item per period, p is the backorder cost per item per period, and K

is the fixed cost per order placed to the warehouse.) Since $K > 0$, it's optimal for the retailers to follow an (s, S) policy rather than a base-stock policy.

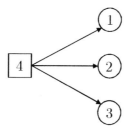

Retailer	μ	σ^2	h	p	K
1	50	8^2	0.6	7	100
2	100	22^2	0.4	8	100
3	40	3^2	0.9	4	100

a) Compute near-optimal values for s and S for each retailer using the power approximation from Section 4.5.4.

b) Simulate this system using a spreadsheet or other software package using the (s, S) values you found in part (a). Simulate at least 1000 periods, with a warm-up interval of 100 periods. Report the standard deviation of the total demands seen by the retailers and the standard deviation of the total demands (retailer orders) seen by the warehouse. Using these values, verify that the bullwhip effect occurs in this system.

c) In a short paragraph, explain why the retailers' (s, S) policies cause the bullwhip effect.

10.3 (Lead-Time Demand under Autocorrelation) For the demand process in Section 10.2.1, prove that D_t^L is normally distributed with mean

$$\mu_t^L = \frac{d}{1-\rho}\left(L - \rho\frac{1-\rho^L}{1-\rho}\right) + D_{t-1}\rho\frac{1-\rho^L}{1-\rho}$$

and standard deviation

$$\sigma_t^L = \frac{\sigma^2}{1-\rho}\left(L - \rho\frac{1-\rho^L}{1-\rho}\right).$$

(Note that σ_t^L is independent of t.)

10.4 (BWE Occurs Even If Demand Parameters Are Known) Suppose that we know d, ρ, and σ in Section 10.2.1. Using the results in Problem 10.3, prove that

$$\frac{\text{Var}[Q]}{\text{Var}[D]} = 1 + \frac{2(1-\rho^{L+1})(\rho-\rho^{L+1})}{1-\rho}.$$

276 THE BULLWHIP EFFECT

(Since this is greater than 1, the BWE occurs even if the parameters are known and therefore no forecasting is required.)

10.5 **(Proving BWE in the Beer Game)** In the "stationary beer game" (Chen and Samroengraja 2000), a serial supply chain faces normally distributed demands at the downstream node, and each stage orders from its supplier in each period. The optimal inventory policy at each stage is a base-stock policy: The size of the order a stage places in a given period is equal to the size of the order received by the stage in that period. If each player followed this policy, there would be no bullwhip effect since the variance of outgoing orders would be the same as that of incoming orders. The beer game is designed to illustrate the irrational behavior of supply chain managers, who tend to over-react to *perceived* trends in demand (even when no actual trend is present) by ordering more than necessary when demands are high and less than necessary when demands are low. In this problem, you will model this over-reaction mathematically and prove that it causes the bullwhip effect.

Consider a retailer who faces demand $D_t \sim N(\mu, \sigma^2)$ in period t. Demands are independent across time periods. The retailer, acting irrationally, over-orders by $\theta \geq 0$ units *for each consecutive period* in which the demand was higher than μ, including the current period. Similarly, it under-orders by θ units for each consecutive period in which the demand was lower than μ, where $\theta \geq 0$ is a constant. That is, although the optimal policy is to set the order size as $Q_t = D_t$, the retailer actually uses

$$Q_t = D_t + \theta X_t^+ - \theta X_t^- ,$$

where X_t^+ is the number of consecutive periods (including t) in which the demand was greater than μ and X_t^- is the number of consecutive periods (including t) in which the demand was less than μ.

a) Prove that $E[Q] = E[D]$ (the retailer's mean order size is equal to the mean demand).

b) Prove that

$$\frac{\text{Var}[Q]}{\text{Var}[D]} \geq 1 + \frac{6\theta^2}{\text{Var}(D)}.$$

Hint 1: What probability distribution describes X_t^+ and X_t^-?
Hint 2: Remember that $\text{Cov}[X, Y] = E[XY] - E[X]E[Y]$.

CHAPTER 11

SUPPLY CHAIN CONTRACTS

11.1 INTRODUCTION

Supply chains are typically composed of multiple players, each with competing goals. For example, the newsvendor wants to pay a small wholesale cost per unit to the supplier, but the supplier wants a large wholesale cost. If each player acts selfishly, the resulting solution is generally suboptimal for the supply chain as a whole—the total profit earned by the supply chain is smaller than if the players could somehow bring their actions in line with one another. (By "selfishly" we don't mean they're behaving meanly or inappropriately—just that each player naturally acts in his or her own best interest, making decisions to maximize his or her own profit.)

Since the mid-1990s, a great deal of research has studied *contracting mechanisms* for achieving supply chain *coordination*—for enticing each player to act in such a way that the total supply chain profit is maximized. The basic idea is that the players agree on a certain contract that specifies a payment, called a *transfer payment*, made from one party to another. The size of the transfer payment can be determined in any number of ways (and identifying these ways are the focus of much of the research). Many are quite intuitive: For example, the retailer might pay a wholesale price to the supplier but receive a credit for unsold merchandise at the end of the period (like the

Fundamentals of Supply Chain Theory, First Edition. Lawrence V. Snyder, Zuo-Jun Max Shen.
© 2011 John Wiley & Sons, Inc. Published 2011 by John Wiley & Sons, Inc.

newsvendor's wholesale price and salvage value). If these mechanisms are designed correctly, then even when each player acts in his or her own best interest, the supply chain profit is maximized.

In this chapter, we return to the newsvendor problem, now considering the newsvendor's supplier as an active player in the game. We will show that under the assumptions studied previously, the newsvendor (whom we'll now refer to as the *retailer*) does not order enough inventory to maximize the total supply chain profit. We will then introduce a few contract types that coordinate the newsvendor model. The material in this chapter originates from Pasternack (1985) and other sources cited below, as well as Cachon (2003), who reviews many of the basic ideas of supply chain coordination. We first review some important concepts from game theory.

11.2   INTRODUCTION TO GAME THEORY

The literature on supply chain coordination draws heavily from game theory. There are many textbooks on game theory, e.g., Osborne (2003); see also the review of game theory as it applies to supply chain analysis by Cachon and Netessine (2004). We will not cover game theory formally here, but it is worth introducing a few terms. A *game* consists of two or more *players* (we will assume exactly two). Each player may choose from a set of *strategies*, and a choice of strategies (one for each player) is called an *outcome*. For each outcome there is a *payoff* to each player.

For example, if there are two players (A and B), each with two strategies (1 and 2), the payoffs might be as given in Table 11.1. Player A's payoff is the first number in the pair, player B's is the second number. If player A chooses strategy 1 and player B chooses strategy 2, the payoff is -4 to player A (a loss) and 2 to player B.

Table 11.1   Payoffs for a sample game.

		Player B	
		1	2
Player A	1	$(1, 1)$	$(-4, 2)$
	2	$(2, -4)$	$(-2, -2)$

Note that there is no randomness in this game. The term "outcome" refers to the deterministic result of choices that the players make, not to the result of some random experiment. In the games we will consider, there is also some randomness that determines the payoffs, in which case the "outcome" represents the expected payoffs to the players.

An outcome is called *Pareto optimal* if there is no other outcome in which both players have higher payoffs, or in which one player has a higher payoff and the other player has the same payoff. For example, in Table 11.1, the outcome in which both players choose strategy 1 is Pareto optimal, since one player can't be made better off without making the other worse off. Pareto optimal outcomes are considered to be "fair" in some sense.

A *Nash equilibrium* is an outcome such that neither player can change strategies unilaterally and improve his or her own payoff. (Nash equilibrium is named after the mathematician and economist John Nash.) If the players act selfishly, the game will move to a Nash equilibrium. There is one Nash equilibrium in the game depicted above: Each player chooses strategy 2. (You should verify that this is the only Nash equilibrium in the game.) However, this outcome is not Pareto optimal, since both players would be better off if they each chose strategy 1.

(The game in Table 11.1 is an example of a *prisoner's dilemma*. In a prisoner's dilemma, the Nash equilibrium is different from the Pareto optimal solution, so the players will always find themselves at an undesirable solution (the Nash equilibrium) even though a mutually better solution (the Pareto optimal solution) is available.)

Now suppose that the players entered into the following simplistic contract: At the end of the game, the players will equally split any profit or loss. The resulting payoff structure is given in Table 11.2.

Table 11.2   Payoffs after implementing a contract.

		Player B	
		1	2
Player A	1	$(1, 1)$	$(-1, -1)$
	2	$(-1, -1)$	$(-2, -2)$

Now the Nash equilibrium is for both players to choose strategy 1 (neither player has any incentive to change strategies), and this strategy is also Pareto optimal. This is the outcome the players would have preferred in the original game, but acting individually they would never have arrived at that outcome. By introducing a simple contract, the players choose the best solution, even when they act in their own interest.

Notice that the contract does not *force* any player to choose a strategy other than the one that maximizes his or her outcome. That is, it does not force the players to choose the outcome $(1, 1)$. It simply re-structures the payoffs so that the players *want* to choose that outcome.

In the supply chain context, we will see that the Nash equilibrium outcome, to which the players would gravitate if acting in their own interest, is generally not Pareto optimal—there are other outcomes that would improve the payoff to both players. The goal of supply chain coordination is to change the structure of the payoffs so that the Nash equilibrium is also Pareto optimal. One important question will be whether, in the resulting Nash equilibrium, both players earn more than they did without the contract. (If not, one party may refuse to enter into the contract.) The goal of supply chain contracts is not to force one player to earn a smaller piece of the pie so that the other player can earn a bigger piece. Rather, it's to make the pie bigger so that both players can get bigger pieces than they had before.

The games presented in Tables 11.1 and 11.2 are called *static games* because the two players choose their strategies simultaneously (though a player may alter his or her strategy in response to the other player's strategy). Supply chain contracts, however, are a different type of game, namely, a *Stackelberg game*, in which one player chooses a strategy first and then the other player chooses one. (Stackelberg games are also known as *leader–follower games*.) The models presented below are based on the newsvendor model, and in these models, the supplier is the leader, setting the parameters of the contract, and the newsvendor is the follower, setting the order quantity.

11.3 NOTATION

As in the classical newsvendor model, we consider a single-period model with stochastic demand. Let D be the demand during the period, with mean μ, pdf f, and cdf F (not necessarily normal). The retail price (i.e., revenue per unit sold) is r per unit. The supplier's production cost is c_s per unit and the retailer's cost is c_r per unit. Note that c_r does *not* get paid to the supplier—it represents the cost of processing, shipping, marketing, etc. at the retailer. It is incurred when the unit is procured, not when it is sold. We assume $c_s + c_r < r$ (otherwise the retailer cannot make any profit).

Unsatisfied demands are lost (since this is a one-period model), incurring a stockout penalty of p_r at the retailer and p_s at the supplier. These costs reflect the loss-of-goodwill that the parties incur; they do not include the lost profit resulting from a lost sale. This is because the profit is already explicitly calculated in this model, so including lost profit in p_r and p_s would double-count this penalty. (In contrast, in earlier chapters, p includes both the lost profit and the loss of goodwill.) For convenience, we let $c = c_s + c_r$ and $p = p_s + p_r$. Each unsold unit at the retailer at the end of the season can be salvaged for a salvage value of v per unit, with $v < c_r$. The retailer's order size is denoted Q.

The notation is summarized in Table 11.3.

Table 11.3 Contracting notation summary.

D	$\sim f, F$
μ	$= E(D)$
r	selling price
c_s, c_r	supplier's, retailer's per-unit cost
c	$= c_s + c_r$
p_s, p_r	supplier's, retailer's loss-of-goodwill cost
p	$= p_s + p_r$
v	salvage value
Q	retailer's order size

11.4 PRELIMINARY ANALYSIS

The following sequence of events occurs in the game:

1. The supplier chooses her[1] contract parameters. (Each contract type has its own parameters.)

2. The retailer chooses his order quantity Q and places his order to the supplier; the order arrives immediately.

3. Demand occurs; as much as possible is satisfied from inventory, and the rest is lost.

4. Costs are assessed and transfer payments are made between the players.

The transfer payment depends on the type of contract, several of which will be explored below. Note that we are assuming the supplier offers the contract to the retailer—that the supplier is the powerful player in the market. This is not necessarily the case, and other models have explored the newsvendor problem when the retailer is the powerful player.

Our first goal is to formulate the supplier's and retailer's expected cost as functions of Q. To that end, let $S(Q)$ be the expected sales as a function of Q:

$$S(Q) = E[\min\{Q, D\}]$$
$$= Q(1 - F(Q)) + \int_0^Q y f(d) dd$$
$$= Q - \int_0^Q F(d) dd$$
$$= Q - \bar{n}(Q), \tag{11.1}$$

where $\bar{n}(Q)$ is the complementary loss function. The third equality follows from (C.31), while the fourth follows from (C.4). Then letting $\bar{F}(Q) = 1 - F(Q)$,

$$S'(Q) = \bar{F}(Q). \tag{11.2}$$

Let $I(Q)$ be the expected inventory on-hand at the end of the period:

$$I(Q) = E[(Q - D)^+] = Q - S(Q). \tag{11.3}$$

Let $L(Q)$ be the expected lost sales:

$$L(Q) = E[(D - Q)^+]$$
$$= E[(D - Q) + (Q - D)^+] \tag{11.4}$$
$$= \mu - Q + I(Q) \tag{11.5}$$
$$= \mu - S(Q). \tag{11.6}$$

---

[1] We'll use the common convention in the contracting literature that the supplier is female and the retailer is male.

(The second equality follows from the fact that, in general, $x = x^+ - x^-$, and $x^- = (-x)^+$.) Finally, let T be the expected transfer payment (whose size is yet to be determined).

The retailer's expected profit function is then

$$
\begin{aligned}
\pi_r(Q) &= rS(Q) + vI(Q) - p_rL(Q) - c_rQ - T \\
&= rS(Q) + v(Q - S(Q)) - p_r(\mu - S(Q)) - c_rQ - T \\
&= (r - v + p_r)S(Q) - (c_r - v)Q - p_r\mu - T. \qquad (11.7)
\end{aligned}
$$

$\pi_r(Q)$ is basically just a newsvendor cost function, written in a very different way—maximizing profit rather than minimizing cost (but the two are mathematically equivalent) and writing the expectations using the functions $S(\cdot)$, $I(\cdot)$, and $L(\cdot)$. The supplier's expected profit function is

$$
\begin{aligned}
\pi_s(Q) &= -c_sQ - p_sL(Q) + T \\
&= -c_sQ - p_s(\mu - S(Q)) + T \\
&= p_sS(Q) - c_sQ - p_s\mu + T. \qquad (11.8)
\end{aligned}
$$

The supply chain's total expected profit function is therefore

$$
\Pi(Q) = \pi_r(Q) + \pi_s(Q) = (r - v + p)S(Q) - (c - v)Q - p\mu. \qquad (11.9)
$$

Let's find the order quantity Q^0 that maximizes the total supply chain profit.

$$
\begin{aligned}
\Pi'(Q^0) &= 0 \\
\iff (r - v + p)S'(Q^0) - (c - v) &= 0 \\
\iff S'(Q^0) = \bar{F}(Q^0) &= \frac{c - v}{r - v + p}. \qquad (11.10)
\end{aligned}
$$

Q^0 is a maximizer, not a minimizer, because

$$
\Pi''(Q) = -(r - v + p)f(Q) < 0,
$$

so Π is concave.

Equation (11.10) agrees with our previous results from the newsvendor model. In particular, if we think of the supply chain as a whole acting as the newsvendor, with per-unit cost c, sales price r, penalty cost p, and salvage value v, then the newsvendor has costs $h' = c - v$ and $p' = r - c + p$, and $h' + p' = r - v + p$. From (4.27), the optimal newsvendor order quantity satisfies

$$
F(Q) = \frac{p'}{h' + p'}
$$

or

$$
\bar{F}(Q) = 1 - \frac{p'}{p' + h'} = \frac{c - v}{r - v + p}.
$$

The question now is, does the retailer choose Q^0 as his order quantity? And, is this also the order quantity that the supplier prefers? That is, if Q_r^* and Q_s^* maximize (11.7) and (11.8) (respectively), then does $Q_r^* = Q_s^* = Q^0$?

The supply chain is considered coordinated if $Q_r^* = Q_s^* = Q^0$. A contract type is said to coordinate the supply chain if there exist contract parameters such that $Q_r^* = Q_s^* = Q^0$ *and* the players each earn positive profit. If the optimal order quantities coincide but one player earns a negative profit, the player's willingness to enter into the contract depends on a number of factors, such as the player's profit under the status quo (which could, after all, be even more negative), the other business relationships the players may jointly have, the players' relative levels of power, and so on. We ignore these rather messy issues and focus below on determining which contract types are guaranteed to have parameters such that the supply chain is coordinated and the players both earn positive profits.

11.5 THE WHOLESALE PRICE CONTRACT

The simplest possible contract is the *wholesale price contract*, in which the retailer pays the supplier a given cost w per unit ordered. This is identical to settings we've discussed previously, in which the retailer pays a per-unit purchase cost that goes to the supplier, except now the purchase cost is the supplier's decision variable. For a given wholesale cost w, the transfer payment is given by

$$T_w(Q, w) = wQ.$$

The subscript w identifies the type of contract, while the arguments specify the two decision variables—order quantity and wholesale cost—one per player.

The retailer's and supplier's expected profits are both functions of w and Q:

$$\pi_r(Q, w) = (r - v + p_r)S(Q) - (c_r - v)Q - p_r\mu - wQ$$
$$= (r - v + p_r)S(Q) - (w + c_r - v)Q - p_r\mu \qquad (11.11)$$
$$\pi_s(Q, w) = p_s S(Q) + (w - c_s)Q - p_s\mu \qquad (11.12)$$

The supply chain is coordinated if there exists a value of w such that $Q_r^* = Q_s^* = Q^0$, where Q_r^*, Q_s^*, and Q^0 are the order quantities that maximize π_r, π_s, and Π, respectively.

It is straightforward to show that π_r and π_s are both concave functions of Q (assuming that w is fixed). Therefore, Q_r^* and Q_s^* satisfy:

$$\left.\frac{\partial \pi_r(Q, w)}{\partial Q}\right|_{Q=Q_r^*} = (r - v + p_r)S'(Q_r^*) - (w + c_r - v) = 0 \qquad (11.13)$$

$$\left.\frac{\partial \pi_s(Q, w)}{\partial Q}\right|_{Q=Q_s^*} = p_s S'(Q_s^*) + (w - c_s) = 0 \qquad (11.14)$$

The next theorem demonstrates that there exists a value of w such that $Q_r^* = Q_s^* = Q^0$. However, for this value of w, the supplier earns a non-positive profit.

Theorem 11.1 $Q_r^* = Q_s^* = Q^0$ *if and only if*

$$w = c_s - \frac{c-v}{r-v+p}p_s. \tag{11.15}$$

Moreover, the supplier earns a non-positive expected profit under this wholesale price.

Proof. Suppose (11.15) holds. Then by (11.13),

$$
\begin{aligned}
S'(Q_r^*) &= \frac{w + c_r - v}{r - v + p_r} \\
&= \frac{\left(c_s - \frac{c-v}{r-v+p}p_s\right) + c_r - v}{r - v + p_r} \\
&= \frac{(c-v)\left(1 - \frac{p_s}{r-v+p}\right)}{r - v + p_r} \\
&= \frac{c-v}{r-v+p} \\
&= S'(Q^0)
\end{aligned}
$$

by (11.10). Since $S'(Q)$ is strictly decreasing and continuous, this implies $Q_r^* = Q^0$. Similarly, by (11.14),

$$
\begin{aligned}
S'(Q_s^*) &= \frac{c_s - w}{p_s} \\
&= \frac{c_s - \left(c_s - \frac{c-v}{r-v+p}p_s\right)}{p_s} \\
&= \frac{c-v}{r-v+p} \\
&= S'(Q^0).
\end{aligned}
$$

Therefore, $Q_r^* = Q_s^* = Q^0$. However, since $v < c_r \leq c < r$ by assumption, $w \leq c_s$. Therefore the supplier earns a non-positive profit. ∎

From (11.14) one can show (see Problem 11.1) that if $w < c_s - p_s$, then π_s is strictly decreasing in Q; if $c_s - p_s < w < c_s$, then π_s is first increasing and then decreasing; and if $w > c_s$, then π_s is strictly increasing. Thus, for sufficiently large w, $Q_s^* = \infty$ since the supplier earns a positive margin on items sold to the retailer, and she pays no penalty for overage at the retailer. For moderate values of $c_s - p_s < w < c_s$, Q_s^* is finite: Although the supplier earns a negative margin on each unit sold to the retailer, she still prefers a non-zero order quantity since small order quantities cause stockouts, for which the supplier incurs a goodwill cost. Her expected profit is still negative, but Q_s^* minimizes the losses. Finally, for small values of w, the supplier's margin is so negative that it more than offsets the goodwill cost, and she sets $Q_s^* = 0$.

The phenomenon evident in Theorem 11.1 is known as *double marginalization* (Spengler 1950): When both players add their own margin (markup) to their costs, the supply chain is not coordinated since the players ignore the total supply chain profit when making their individual decisions. If, on the other hand, the retailer has a positive margin but the supplier has a negative one, the supply chain is coordinated. However, the supplier clearly would not enter into this arrangement, so the wholesale price contract is not considered to be a coordinating one. Nevertheless, there are still several interesting things to say about it.

Now suppose that $w > c_s$, so that the supplier earns positive profit but the supply chain is not coordinated. We first examine the retailer's and supplier's optimization problems and then discuss how close the wholesale price contract comes to coordinating the supply chain.

Theorem 11.2 *Under the wholesale price contract, if $w > c_s$, then $Q_r^* < Q^0$.*

Proof. Omitted; see Problem 11.6.   ∎

Theorem 11.2 says that, assuming the supplier earns a positive profit, the retailer will under-order. This happens because the retailer is absorbing all of the risk of overage, but only part of the risk of underage (since the supplier pays a stockout penalty). Therefore, the retailer orders less than the supplier (and the supply chain as a whole) wants him to. In the contracting mechanisms discussed in later sections, the supplier absorbs some of the risk of overage, thus giving the retailer the flexibility to increase his order quantity. If the contract parameters are set correctly, he'll increase it so that it equals Q^0.

Now let's turn our attention to the supplier's optimization problem. For given w, (11.14) determines the supplier's optimal order quantity. But what if the supplier could choose whatever w she wants? In order to choose w, she must anticipate the Q that the retailer will choose for each value of w. Put another way, the supplier can entice the retailer to choose whatever Q she wishes by selecting the unique wholesale price, call it $w(Q)$, that makes Q optimal for the retailer. In particular,

$$w(Q) = (r - v + p_r)\bar{F}(Q) - (c_r - v) \tag{11.16}$$

(from (11.13)).

Which Q does the supplier want the retailer to choose? The supplier's profit function is now a function of Q and the corresponding $w(Q)$:

$$\pi_s(Q, w(Q)) = p_s S(Q) + (w(Q) - c_s)Q - p_s \mu \tag{11.17}$$

This function is maximized when

$$\frac{\partial \pi_s(Q, w(Q))}{\partial Q} = 0 \tag{11.18}$$

provided that

$$\frac{\partial^2 \pi_s(Q, w(Q))}{\partial Q^2} < 0. \tag{11.19}$$

Well,

$$
\begin{aligned}
\frac{\partial \pi_s(Q, w(Q))}{\partial Q} &= p_s S'(Q) + w(Q) - c_s + w'(Q)Q \\
&= p_s \bar{F}(Q) + (r - v + p_r)\bar{F}(Q) - (c_r - v) - c_s \\
&\quad - (r - v + p_r)f(Q)Q \\
&= (r - v + p_r)\bar{F}(Q)\left(1 + \frac{p_s}{r - v + p_r} - \frac{Qf(Q)}{\bar{F}(Q)}\right) - (c - v)
\end{aligned}
$$

$$(11.20)$$

(11.19) holds if the right-hand side of (11.20) is decreasing in Q. Since $\bar{F}(Q)$ is decreasing, the right-hand side of (11.20) is decreasing if $Qf(Q)/\bar{F}(Q)$ is increasing. This turns out to be an important property in contract analysis, and it has its own name: Demand distributions for which $Qf(Q)/\bar{F}(Q)$ is increasing are called *increasing generalized failure rate* (IGFR) distributions. Many common distributions are IGFR, including normal, exponential, and gamma. In what follows, we will assume that the demand distribution is IGFR. Hence $\pi_s(Q, w(Q))$ is strictly concave, and there is a unique order quantity that maximizes the supplier's profit. (Note that this is the order quantity the supplier would choose if she can also choose w. This is not the same as Q_s^* as defined in (11.14), which is the supplier's optimal quantity for fixed w.) Of course, the supplier does not set this order quantity directly; she sets w to $w(Q_s^*)$ and waits for the retailer to set the order quantity to Q_s^*.

For contracts such as the wholesale price contract that do not coordinate the supply chain, we'd like to know how close they come. This is measured by the *efficiency* of the contract: the proportion of the optimal supply chain profit attained by the Nash equilibrium order quantity, or $\Pi(Q_s^*)/\Pi(Q^0)$. The greater the efficiency, the closer the contract is to achieving coordination. Another important measure is the *supplier's profit share*: the percentage of the total profit captured by the supplier, or $\pi_s(Q_s^*, w(Q_s^*))/\Pi(Q_s^*)$. Both players would like the efficiency to be high, but only the supplier would like the supplier's profit share to be high. Experimental tests using the power distribution show the efficiency to be around 75% and the supplier's profit share to be in the range of 55% to 80% (Cachon 2003).

It is worth noting that the wholesale price contract is considered to be non-coordinating because there is no value of w that (1) makes $Q_r^* = Q_s^* = Q^0$ and (2) guarantees both players positive profits. In contrast, the contract types we discuss in the next sections are considered to be coordinating because there always exist some values of the contract parameters for which both (1) and (2) hold, even though not all parameter values do the trick.

□ **EXAMPLE 11.1**

Matilda's Market sells bagels that are made by Jeffrey's Bakery. Bagels sell for $1. Each bagel that the market buys from the bakery costs the bakery $0.50 to make and costs the market $0.25 in processing costs. Daily demand for bagels is distributed as $N(100, 20^2)$. Unmet demands incur a loss-of-goodwill cost of

$0.20 for each party. Unsold bagels must be thrown out at the end of each day, with no salvage value. Currently, Jeffrey's Bakery charges Matilda's Market a wholesale price of $0.60 per bagel. What is Matilda's Market's optimal order quantity? What is each company's profit, and what is the profit of the supply chain as a whole?

We have $r = 1$, $c_s = 0.5$, $c_r = 0.25$, $p_r = p_s = 0.2$, $v = 0$, and $w = 0.6$. From (11.2) and (11.13), Q_r^* satisfies

$$F(Q_r^*) = 1 - \frac{0.85}{1.2}$$
$$\implies Q_r^* = 89.03.$$

From (11.1), (C.8), and (C.14) one can calculate $S(89.03) = 85.3648$. From (11.11), (11.12), and (11.9),

$$\pi_r(89.03, 0.6) = 1.2S(89.03) - 0.85 \cdot 89.03 - 0.2 \cdot 100 = 6.7627$$
$$\pi_s(89.03, 0.6) = 0.2S(89.03) + 0.1 \cdot 89.03 - 0.2 \cdot 100 = 5.9759$$
$$\Pi(89.03) = 6.7627 + 5.9759 = 12.7386.$$

How does this compare to the optimal total profit? From (11.10),

$$F(Q^0) = 1 - \frac{0.75}{1.4}$$
$$\implies Q^0 = 98.21.$$

We have $S(Q) = 91.0927$, so from (11.9), the total profit is

$$\Pi(Q^0) = 1.4S(98.21) - 0.75 \cdot 98.21 - 0.4 \cdot 100 = 13.8744.$$

Therefore, the total profit under this wholesale price contract is less than the optimal supply chain profit.

Now suppose that Jeffrey's Bakery can choose whichever w it wants. What w will it choose, what Q will Matilda's Market choose as a result, and what will be the resulting profits?

From (11.20), the Q that maximizes Jeffrey's Bakery's profit is the Q that satisfies

$$1.2\bar{F}(Q)\left(1 + \frac{0.2}{1.2} - \frac{Qf(Q)}{\bar{F}(Q)}\right) - 0.75 = 0.$$

The reader can verify that this equation is satisfied (within rounding error) by $Q = 70.23$. Therefore, Jeffery's Bakery will choose

$$w(Q) = 1.2\bar{F}(70.23) - 0.25 = 0.8680$$

and Matilda's Market will choose $Q = 70.23$. Note that $S(70.23) = 69.6283$. The profits will be

$$\pi_r(70.23, 0.8680) = 1.2S(70.23) - 1.1180 \cdot 70.23 - 0.2 \cdot 100 = -14.9652$$

$$\pi_s(70.23, 0.8680) = 0.2 S(70.23) + 0.3680 \cdot 70.23 - 0.2 \cdot 100 = 19.7723$$
$$\Pi(70.23) = -14.9652 + 19.7723 = 4.8072.$$

Jeffrey's Bakery may like this arrangement, but it is clearly bad for Matilda's Market, and it is also suboptimal for the supply chain as a whole.   □

11.6 THE BUYBACK CONTRACT

We now examine a contract type that does coordinate the supply chain. In the *buyback contract* (Pasternack 1985), the supplier charges the retailer w per unit purchased but pays the retailer b for every unit of unsold inventory at the end of the period:

$$T_b(Q, w, b) = wQ - bI(Q) = bS(Q) + (w - b)Q.$$

We assume

$$0 \le b \le r - v + p_r, \tag{11.21}$$

otherwise it is better for the retailer *not* to sell an on-hand item to satisfy a demand (thereby earning $b + v$ but paying p_r than to sell it (earning r). We also assume

$$b \le w + c_r - v, \tag{11.22}$$

otherwise the retailer incurs no overage risk since his revenue for salvaging an item $(b + v)$ is more than what he paid for it $(w + c_r)$.

The name "buyback" is a little misleading, because usually the retailer does not physically return the products, he just receives a credit from the supplier. The supplier is offering to share some of the risk of overage with the retailer in exchange for higher supply chain profits.

Many suppliers offer buyback credits as a way to prevent the unsold goods from being sold at a steep discount. For example, high-fashion clothing makers don't want to see their products on the bargain rack at Marshall's at the end of the season, so they give high-end retailers a credit to prevent them from unloading unsold merchandise to discounters.

Letting $T = T_b(Q, w, b)$ in (11.7), the retailer's profit function becomes

$$\pi_r(Q, w, b) = (r - v + p_r)S(Q) - (c_r - v)Q - p_r\mu - [bS(Q) + (w - b)Q]$$
$$= (r - v + p_r - b)S(Q) - (c_r - v + w - b)Q - p_r\mu. \tag{11.23}$$

The Q that maximizes the retailer's profit satisfies

$$\frac{\partial \pi_r(Q, w, b)}{\partial Q} = (r - v + p_r - b)\bar{F}(Q) - (c_r - v + w - b) = 0$$

$$\iff \bar{F}(Q) = \frac{c_r - v + w - b}{r - v + p_r - b}. \tag{11.24}$$

Now, the supplier can of course choose any values for w and b (subject to (11.21) and (11.22)). However, it turns out that for a given b, the "correct" value of w (i.e., the one that will coordinate the supply chain) is given by

$$w(b) = b + c_s - (c - v)\frac{b + p_s}{r - v + p}. \tag{11.25}$$

(It should not yet be obvious how we get this value of $w(b)$.) Note that $w(b)$ is increasing in b (since $r > c$). Therefore, in exchange for receiving a more generous buyback credit, the retailer must pay a higher wholesale price.

If w and b satisfies (11.21) and (11.25), then they also satisfy (11.22). (See Problem 11.7.) Therefore, we can ignore (11.22) and assume only that the feasible region for b is $[0, r - v + p_r]$.

Theorem 11.3 establishes that, if the parameters are set appropriately, then the optimal order quantities coincide. Moreover, by Theorem 11.4 below, there exists a b such that both parties earn positive profit. Therefore, the buyback contract coordinates the supply chain.

Theorem 11.3 *Under the buyback contract, for any b satisfying (11.21), if $w(b)$ is set according to (11.25), then $Q_r^* = Q_s^* = Q^0$.*

We'll present two proofs of this theorem. The first is more straightforward than the second, but the second is quite elegant and can also be applied in more general settings.

Proof #1. Substituting $w(b)$ into (11.24), we get

$$\bar{F}(Q) = \frac{c_r - v + \left[b + c_s - (c - v)\frac{b + p_s}{r - v + p}\right] - b}{r - v + p_r - b}$$

$$= \frac{(c - v)\left[1 - \frac{b + p_s}{r - v + p}\right]}{r - v + p_r - b}$$

$$= \frac{(c - v)\frac{r - v + p_r - b}{r - v + p}}{r - v + p_r - b}$$

$$= \frac{c - v}{r - v + p}$$

This is the same Q that maximizes the total supply chain expected profit (see (11.10)), so $Q_r^* = Q^0$. Therefore, from the retailer's perspective, the supply chain is coordinated. It remains to show that the supplier also prefers this same Q.

Letting $T = T_b(Q, w, b)$ in (11.8), the supplier's profit function is

$$\pi_s(Q, w, b) = p_s S(Q) - c_s Q - p_s \mu + [bS(Q) + (w - b)Q]$$
$$= (p_s + b)S(Q) - (c_s - w + b)Q - p_s \mu \tag{11.26}$$

The Q that maximizes π_s satisfies

$$\frac{\partial \pi_s(Q, w, b)}{\partial Q} = (p_s + b)\bar{F}(Q) - (c_s - w + b) = 0$$

$$\Longleftrightarrow \bar{F}(Q) = \frac{c_s - w + b}{p_s + b} \tag{11.27}$$

Letting $w = w(b)$ as defined in (11.25), we get

$$\bar{F}(Q) = \frac{c_s - \left[b + c_s - (c - v)\frac{b+p_s}{r-v+p}\right] + b}{p_s + b}$$

$$= \frac{(c - v)\frac{b+p_s}{r-v+p}}{p_s + b}$$

$$= \frac{c - v}{r - v + p}$$

Therefore $Q_s^* = Q^0$. ∎

Before introducing the second proof, we can answer the question of how to determine $w(b)$ (if it wasn't already given by (11.25)): It's the only value of w that makes the conditions $\partial \pi_r / \partial Q = 0$ and $\partial \pi_s / \partial Q = 0$ both reduce to $\bar{F}(Q) = (c - v)/(r - v + p)$. The value of $w(b)$ can be "backed out" from these conditions.

In general, we can use the approach from Proof #1—setting $\partial \pi_r / \partial Q$ and $\partial \pi_s / \partial Q$ to 0 and showing that $Q_r^* = Q_s^* = Q^0$—to prove that a given contracting mechanism coordinates the supply chain. However, there's another elegant way to accomplish this, and this approach is taken by proof #2.

Proof #2. Let

$$\lambda = \frac{r - v + p_r - b}{r - v + p}. \tag{11.28}$$

Then

$$\lambda = 1 - \frac{b + p_s}{r - v + p}$$

$$= \frac{c - v - (c - v)\frac{b+p_s}{r-v+p}}{c - v}$$

$$= \frac{b + c_s - (c - v)\frac{b+p_s}{r-v+p} - b + c_r - v}{c - v}$$

$$= \frac{w(b) - b + c_r - v}{c - v} \tag{11.29}$$

In other words, λ is equal to both fractions (11.28) and (11.29). (This is a result of our definition of $w(b)$.) Since $p_r \le p$ and $b \ge 0$, $\lambda \le 1$. Also, since $b \le r - v + p_r$ (by (11.21)), $\lambda \ge 0$.

From (11.23), the retailer's profit under a buyback contract is

$$
\begin{aligned}
\pi_r(Q, w, b) &= (r - v + p_r - b)S(Q) - (w - b + c_r - v)Q - p_r\mu \\
&= \lambda(r - v + p)S(Q) - \lambda(c - v)Q - p_r\mu \\
&= \lambda\Pi(Q) + \mu(\lambda p - p_r),
\end{aligned} \tag{11.30}
$$

where $\Pi(Q)$ is the total supply chain profit as defined in (11.9). Since $\lambda \geq 0$, the same Q minimizes (11.9) and (11.30), so $Q_r^* = Q^0$. The same argument applies to the supplier since

$$
\pi_s(Q, w, b) = \Pi(Q) - \pi_r(Q, w, b) = (1 - \lambda)\Pi(Q) - \mu(\lambda p - p_r) \tag{11.31}
$$

and $\lambda \leq 1$. ∎

As λ increases, the retailer's profit increases and the supplier's profit decreases, so in a sense λ represents the division of profit between the players. One would like to know whether *any* division is possible—that is, is there some value of λ such that the supplier captures all of the profit and another value such that the retailer captures all of the profit? (Keep in mind that λ is not a parameter of the contract—the supplier does not actually choose λ. But by choosing b, the supplier automatically chooses λ given (11.28).) If so, then there is also a value that gives any desired mix. As the next theorem demonstrates, this is indeed possible.

Theorem 11.4 *If $w(b)$ is set according to (11.25), then the retailer's [supplier's] profit is decreasing [increasing] in $b \in [0, r - v + p_r]$. Moreover, let*

$$
b_1 = r - v + p_r - (r - v + p)\frac{\Pi(Q^0) + \mu p_r}{\Pi(Q^0) + \mu p} \tag{11.32}
$$

$$
b_2 = r - v + p_r - (r - v + p)\frac{\mu p_r}{\Pi(Q^0) + \mu p}. \tag{11.33}
$$

Then $0 < b_1 < b_2 < r - v + p_r$, and:

1. *If $0 \leq b < b_1$, then the supplier earns negative profit (and the retailer earns more than $\Pi(Q^0)$).*

2. *If $b = b_1$, then the retailer earns the entire supply chain profit.*

3. *If $b_1 < b < b_2$, then the profits are shared by the players.*

4. *If $b = b_2$, then the supplier earns the entire supply chain profit.*

5. *If $b_2 < b \leq r - v + p_r$, then the retailer earns negative profit (and the supplier earns more than $\Pi(Q^0)$).*

Proof. We first prove $0 < b_1 < b_2 < r - v + p_r$. The second and third inequalities follow immediately from the fact that $v < r$. To prove $0 < b_1$, first suppose that the demand is deterministic; then the supply chain earns a profit of $\mu(r - c)$ since there is no overage or underage. This provides an upper bound on the maximum possible expected profit under stochastic demand, i.e., $\Pi(Q^0) \leq \mu(r - c)$. Since $v < c_r \leq c$, we have $\Pi(Q^0) < \mu(r - v)$, and therefore

$$\frac{\mu(r-v)+\mu p_r}{\mu(r-v)+\mu p} > \frac{\Pi(Q^0)+\mu p_r}{\Pi(Q^0)+\mu p}.$$

Thus, $b_1 < 0$.

It remains to prove items 1–5. By (11.30) and (11.31), the retailer's profit $\pi_r(Q^0, w(b), b)$ is an increasing function of λ and the supplier's profit $\pi_s(Q^0, w(b), b)$ is a decreasing function of λ. By (11.28), λ is a decreasing function of b. Therefore, the retailer's [supplier's] profit is a decreasing [increasing] function of b. Since the sum of their profits is fixed (to $\Pi(Q^0)$), to prove the theorem it suffices to prove items 2 and 4.

If $b = b_1$, then

$$\lambda = \frac{r - v + p_r - b_1}{r - v + p} = \frac{\Pi(Q^0) + \mu p_r}{\Pi(Q^0) + \mu p} \tag{11.34}$$
$$\implies \Pi(Q^0) = \lambda\Pi(Q^0) + \mu(\lambda p - p_r) = \pi_r(Q^0, w(b), b)$$

by (11.30). Similarly, if $b = b_2$, then

$$\lambda = \frac{\mu p_r}{\Pi(Q^0) + \mu p} \tag{11.35}$$
$$\implies \Pi(Q^0) = (1 - \lambda)\Pi(Q^0) - \mu(\lambda p - p_r) = \pi_s(Q^0, w(b), b)$$

by (11.31). ∎

At first it may seem surprising that the supplier's profit is increasing in b, since b is a payment made to the retailer. However, $w(b)$ is increasing in b, and increases in the buyback credits paid to the retailer are more than offset by increased revenue from the wholesale price.

One consequence of Theorem 11.4 is that, for any non-coordinating contract, there exists b and $w(b)$ such that neither player has a lower profit under the buyback contract, and at least one player has a strictly higher profit. Therefore, the supplier can always choose b and $w(b)$ such that both players prefer the buyback contract to the status quo if the supply chain is not currently coordinated.

Which value of b will she choose? We can't solve this as an optimization problem as we did for the wholesale price contract because the supplier's profit is an increasing function of b. Left to her own devices, she would choose a large b that gives the retailer negative profit. Instead, the choice of b is the result of some sort of negotiation process that reflects the relative power of the two players as well as other factors, which we ignore. The contract types discussed in the following sections are similar in this regard.

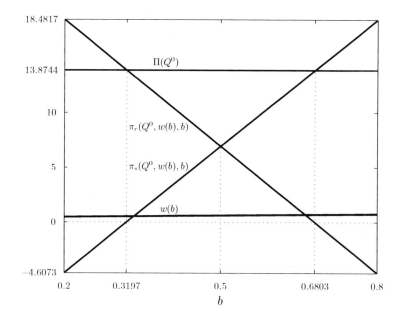

Figure 11.1   Wholesale price and profits as a function of buyback credit.

☐ **EXAMPLE 11.2**

Return to Example 11.1 and suppose that Jeffrey's Bakery offers a buyback contract to Matilda's Market with $b = 0.6$. What w will coordinate the supply chain, and what are the resulting profits?

From (11.25),

$$w(0.6) = 0.6 + 0.5 - 0.75 \cdot \frac{0.6 + 0.2}{1 - 0 + 0.4} = 0.6714.$$

Since the contract coordinates, both players will choose $Q = Q^0 = 98.21$. From (11.23) and (11.26),

$$\pi_r(98.21, 0.6714, 0.6) = 0.6S(98.21) - 0.3214 \cdot 98.21 - 0.2 \cdot 100 = 3.0890$$
$$\pi_s(98.21, 0.6714, 0.6) = 0.8S(98.21) - 0.4286 \cdot 98.21 - 0.2 \cdot 100 = 10.7854.$$

The two profits sum to 13.8744, confirming that the supply chain is coordinated.

Figure 11.1 plots w, $\pi_r(Q^0, w(b), b)$, $\pi_s(Q^0, w(b), b)$, and $\Pi(Q^0)$ as a function of $b \in (0, r - v + p_r)$. Note that when $b = 0.3197$, the retailer (Matilda's Market) earns all of the profit and when $b = 0.6803$, the supplier (Jeffrey's Bakery) earns all of the profit. The reader can confirm that these values equal b_1 and b_2 from Theorem 11.4. The figure therefore confirms the behavior described in the theorem.   ☐

11.7 THE REVENUE SHARING CONTRACT

In the *revenue sharing contract* (Cachon and Lariviere 2005), the supplier charges the retailer a wholesale price of w per unit *and* the retailer gives the supplier a percentage of his revenue. All revenue is shared, including both sales revenue and salvage value. Let ϕ be the fraction of revenue the retailer keeps and $1 - \phi$ the fraction he gives to the supplier. The transfer payment is then

$$
\begin{aligned}
T_r(Q, w, \phi) &= wQ + (1 - \phi)rS(Q) + (1 - \phi)vI(Q) \\
&= (w + (1 - \phi)v)Q + (1 - \phi)(r - v)S(Q).
\end{aligned} \tag{11.36}
$$

Again we magically determine the "correct" value of one contract parameter (w) for a given value of the other (ϕ):

$$
w(\phi) = -c_r + \phi v + (c - v)\frac{\phi(r - v) + p_r}{r - v + p}. \tag{11.37}
$$

If we define $w(\phi)$ in this way, then the supply chain is coordinated. The next theorem demonstrates this; its proof uses a method similar to Proof #2 in Section 11.6, but it could also be proven using a method similar to Proof #1 (see Problem 11.14).

Theorem 11.5 *Under the revenue sharing contract, for any $0 \leq \phi \leq 1$, if $w(\phi)$ is set according to (11.37), then $Q_r^* = Q_s^* = Q^0$, i.e., the supply chain is coordinated.*

Proof. The retailer's profit function is

$$
\begin{aligned}
\pi_r(Q, w, \phi) =&(r - v + p_r)S(Q) - (c_r - v)Q - p_r\mu \\
&- [(w + (1 - \phi)v)Q + (1 - \phi)(r - v)S(Q)] \\
=&(\phi(r - v) + p_r)S(Q) - (w + c_r - \phi v)Q - p_r\mu.
\end{aligned} \tag{11.38}
$$

Let

$$
\lambda = \frac{\phi(r - v) + p_r}{r - v + p} \leq 1; \tag{11.39}
$$

then also (by virtue of the relationship between w and ϕ),

$$
\lambda = \frac{w + c_r - \phi v}{c - v} \geq 0. \tag{11.40}
$$

(Recall that $v < c_r$.) Then

$$
\pi_r(Q, w, \phi) = \lambda\Pi(Q) + \mu(\lambda p - p_r). \tag{11.41}
$$

Since $\lambda \geq 0$, $Q_r^* = Q^0$, and the revenue sharing contract coordinates the supply chain from the retailer's perspective. Since the total supply chain profit is the sum of the retailer's and the supplier's, the supplier's profit is

$$
\pi_s(Q, w, \phi) = \Pi(Q) - \pi_r(Q, w, \phi) = (1 - \lambda)\Pi(Q) - \mu(\lambda p - p_r). \tag{11.42}
$$

Therefore, $Q_s^* = Q^0$ since $\lambda \leq 1$. ∎

The retailer's profit is increasing in λ and the supplier's profit is decreasing in λ. Since λ is increasing in ϕ, the retailer's profit increases and the supplier's profit decreases as the retailer's revenue fraction ϕ increases. One can prove a theorem that is analogous to Theorem 11.4 demonstrating that any allocation of profits is possible under the revenue sharing contract. In particular, the retailer earns the entire profit if

$$\lambda = \frac{\Pi(Q^0) + \mu p_r}{\Pi(Q^0) + \mu p} \tag{11.43}$$

and the supplier earns the entire profit if

$$\lambda = \frac{\mu p_r}{\Pi(Q^0) + \mu p}. \tag{11.44}$$

(Note the similarity to (11.34) and (11.35).)

Revenue sharing and buyback contracts are actually quite similar. For the sake of clarity, denote the wholesale price under the buyback contract and the revenue sharing contract as w_b and w_r, respectively. We can think of a buyback contract as requiring the retailer to pay $w_b - b$ per unit purchased and an additional b per unit sold. (This is equivalent to paying w_b per unit purchased and receiving b per unit unsold.) In a revenue sharing contract, the retailer pays $w_r + (1 - \phi)v$ per unit purchased and $(1 - \phi)(r - v)$ per unit sold. Then a revenue sharing contract with parameters w_r and ϕ is *equivalent* (in the sense that it generates the same profits no matter what the demand is) to a buyback contract if the parameters of the buyback contract satisfy

$$w_b - b = w_r + (1 - \phi)v$$
$$b = (1 - \phi)(r - v),$$

that is,

$$w_b = w_r + (1 - \phi)r \tag{11.45}$$
$$b = (1 - \phi)(r - v). \tag{11.46}$$

However, in more complicated settings (for example, with more than one retailer), the two contracts are not equivalent.

□ **EXAMPLE 11.3**

Return to Example 11.1 and suppose that Jeffrey's Bakery offers a revenue sharing contract to Matilda's Market with $\phi = 0.4$. What w will coordinate the supply chain, and what are the resulting profits?

From (11.37),

$$w(0.4) = -0.25 + (0.75)\frac{0.4(1) + 0.2}{1 + 0.4} = 0.0714.$$

Since the contract coordinates, both players will choose $Q = Q^0 = 98.21$. From (11.38) and (11.42),

$$\pi_r(98.21, 0.0714, 0.4) = 0.6S(98.21) - 0.3214 \cdot 98.21 - 0.2 \cdot 100 = 3.0890$$
$$\pi_s(98.21, 0.0714, 0.4) = \Pi(Q^0) - \pi_r(98.21, 0.0714, 0.4) = 10.7854.$$

These are the same profits as under the buyback contract in Example 11.2. This is to be expected, since the parameters of the two contracts satisfy (11.45)–(11.46).

Other profit allocations are possible, of course. For example, if $\phi = 0.6803$ and $w = 0.2216$, then the retailer earns the entire profit, and if $\phi = 0.3917$ and $w = 0.0284$, the supplier does.   □

11.8 THE QUANTITY FLEXIBILITY CONTRACT

We next introduce the *quantity flexibility contract* (Tsay 1999). The quantity flexibility contract is similar to the buyback contract in that the retailer pays a wholesale price per unit purchased and the supplier reimburses the retailer for unsold goods. The difference is that, in the buyback contract the supplier *partially* reimburses the retailer for *every* unsold item, whereas in the quantity flexibility contract, she *fully* reimburses the retailer for a *portion* of his unsold items.

In particular, the quantity flexibility contract has two parameters, w and δ ($0 \leq \delta \leq 1$). The retailer pays the supplier w per unit ordered, and the supplier pays the retailer $(w + c_r - v) \min\{I, \delta Q\}$, where I is the on-hand inventory at the end of the period. Thus, the supplier agrees to protect the retailer against only a portion of his order: She will reimburse him for his losses on unsold merchandise (which equal $w + c_r - v$ per unit), but only up to a maximum of δQ units.

The quantity flexibility contract coordinates the supply chain from the retailer's end (his optimal order quantity is also the supply chain's optimal order quantity). However, unlike the contracts in Sections 11.6 and 11.7, the quantity flexibility contract only coordinates the supplier's decision for certain values of the parameters.

The transfer payment in the quantity flexibility contract is

$$T_q(Q, w, \delta) = wQ - (w + c_r - v) \left[\int_0^{(1-\delta)Q} \delta Q f(d)\, dd \right.$$

$$\left. + \int_{(1-\delta)Q}^{Q} (Q - d) f(d)\, dd \right] \qquad (11.47)$$

$$= wQ - (w + c_r - v) \int_{(1-\delta)Q}^{Q} F(d)\, dd. \qquad (11.48)$$

(See Problem 11.11).

Let $w(\delta)$ be defined as

$$w(\delta) = \frac{(r - v + p_r)\bar{F}(Q^0)}{\bar{F}(Q^0) + (1 - \delta)F((1 - \delta)Q^0)} - c_r + v. \tag{11.49}$$

Theorem 11.6 *Under the quantity flexibility contract, for any $0 \leq \delta \leq 1$, if $w(\delta)$ is set according to (11.49), then $Q_r^* = Q^0$, i.e., the supply chain is coordinated from the retailer's perspective.*

Proof. The retailer's profit function is

$$\pi_r(Q, w, \delta) = (r - v + p_r)S(Q) - (c_r - v)Q - p_r\mu$$
$$- \left[wQ - (w + c_r - v)\int_{(1-\delta)Q}^{Q} F(d)dd \right]$$
$$= (r - v + p_r)S(Q) - (w + c_r - v)Q - p_r\mu$$
$$+ (w + c_r - v)\int_{(1-\delta)Q}^{Q} F(d)dd. \tag{11.50}$$

In order for Q^0 to maximize $\pi_r(\cdot, w(\delta), \delta)$, it is necessary (but not sufficient) that $\partial \pi_r / \partial Q = 0$ when $Q = Q^0$. (It's not a sufficient condition because we also need to check that the second partial derivative is negative, i.e., that π_r is concave with respect to Q.)

$$\frac{\partial \pi_r(Q, w(\delta), \delta)}{\partial Q} = (r - v + p_r)S'(Q) - (w(\delta) + c_r - v)$$
$$+ (w(\delta) + c_r - v)\left[F(Q) + (1 - \delta)F((1 - \delta)Q)\right]$$

(using (C.18))

$$= (r - v + p_r)\bar{F}(Q)$$
$$- (w(\delta) + c_r - v)[\bar{F}(Q) + (1 - \delta)F((1 - \delta)Q)]. \tag{11.51}$$

When $Q = Q^0$, (11.51) equals 0 by (11.49).

It remains to show that π_r is concave when $w = w(\delta)$, i.e., that its second partial derivative is non-positive.

$$\frac{\partial^2 \pi_r(Q, w(\delta), \delta)}{\partial Q^2} = - (r + p_r - w(\delta) - c_r)f(Q)$$
$$- (w(\delta) + c_r - v)(1 - \delta)^2 f((1 - \delta)Q) \tag{11.52}$$

This is non-positive if

$$v - c_r \leq w(\delta) \leq r + p_r - c_r,$$

which is true for all $0 \leq \delta \leq 1$ because

$$w(0) = (r - v + p_r)\bar{F}(Q^0) + v - c_r \geq v - c_r$$

$$w(1) = r + p_r - c_r$$

and $w(\delta)$ is increasing in δ. Therefore Q^0 maximizes $\pi_r(\cdot, w(\delta), \delta)$, provided that $w(\delta)$ is set according to (11.49).   ∎

We also need to check whether Q^0 is optimal for the supplier; if it is not, the contract does not coordinate the supply chain. The supplier's profit function is

$$\pi_s(Q, w, \delta) = p_s S(Q) + (w - c_s)Q - p_s\mu - (w + c_r - v)\int_{(1-\delta)Q}^{Q} F(d)dd. \quad (11.53)$$

One can show that $\partial\pi_s/\partial Q$ *does* equal 0 when $Q = Q^0$. However, for Q^0 to be a maximizer, the second partial derivative must be non-positive. This derivative is

$$\frac{\partial^2\pi_s(Q, w(\delta), \delta)}{\partial Q^2} = -w(\delta)\left[f(Q) - (1-\delta)^2 f((1-\delta)Q)\right] - p_s f(Q). \quad (11.54)$$

Unfortunately, this expression is not always non-positive. For example, suppose $D \sim N(100, 25^2)$, $r = 10$, $c_r = c_s = 1$, and $p_r = p_s = v = 0$. If $\delta = 0.2$, then (11.54) equals -0.0028 (so Q^0 is a local max) but if $\delta = 0.1$, then (11.54) equals 0.0015 (so Q^0 is a local min).

All of this means that the quantity flexibility contract coordinates the supply chain from the retailer's point of view but not necessarily from the supplier's. In other words, when the retailer places an order of size Q^0, the supplier might wish to deliver an order of a different size Q'. The supplier can certainly not force the retailer to accept a larger order than he placed, so if $Q' > Q^0$ there's nothing the supplier can do about it. But if $Q' < Q^0$, the supplier wants to deliver an order smaller than the order placed by the retailer.

The attitude of the model toward this behavior is called the *compliance regime*. If the supplier is allowed to deliver less than the order size, the regime is called *voluntary compliance*. If the supplier is forced to deliver the entire order (because failing to do so would expose the supplier to a court action or to too much loss of goodwill, for example), it's called *forced compliance*. Since the supplier's optimal decision was also supply chain optimal in the coordinating contracts we've studied so far, the two regimes have been equivalent—the supplier wants to comply, even if she's not forced to do so. In the quantity flexibility contract, the supplier may not voluntarily comply.

Assuming that the supplier complies (either because she is forced to or because the parameters are such that her profit function is concave), the quantity flexibility contract, like the others, can allocate the profits in any way we like. (See Problem 11.13.)

□ **EXAMPLE 11.4**

Return to Example 11.1 and suppose that Jeffrey's Bakery offers a quantity flexibility contract to Matilda's Market with $\delta = 0.15$. What w will coordinate the supply chain, and what are the resulting profits?

First note that

$$\bar{F}(Q^0) = 0.5357$$
$$F((1 - \delta)Q^0) = F(83.4761) = 0.2044$$
$$\int_{(1-\delta)Q^0}^{Q^0} F(d)dd = \bar{n}(Q^0) - \bar{n}((1 - \delta)Q^0) = 4.8193.$$

(The last equality follows from (C.4).) From (11.49),

$$w(0.15) = \frac{1.2 \cdot 0.5357}{0.5357 + 0.85 \cdot 0.2044} - 0.25 = 0.6562.$$

Since the contract coordinates, both players will choose $Q = Q^0 = 98.21$. From (11.50) and (11.53),

$$\pi_r(98.21, 0.6562, 0.15) = 1.2S(98.21) - 0.9062 \cdot 98.21$$
$$- 0.2 \cdot 100 + 0.9062 \cdot 4.8193 = 4.6844$$
$$\pi_s(98.21, 0.6562, 0.15) = 0.2S(98.21) + 0.1562 \cdot 98.21$$
$$- 0.2 \cdot 100 - 0.9062 \cdot 4.8193 = 9.1900$$

If $\phi = 0.0888$ and $w = 0.5450$, then the retailer earns the entire profit, and if $\phi = 0.1827$ and $w = 0.7123$, the supplier does. For all three values of ϕ discussed in this example, $\partial^2 \pi_s / \partial Q^2 < 0$, so Q^0 is a maximum of π_s for all three contracts, as desired. □

PROBLEMS

11.1   (Existence of Q_s^* under Wholesale Price Contract) Prove that, under the wholesale price contract, $\pi_s(Q, w)$ is:

- strictly decreasing in Q if $w < c_s - p_s$
- first increasing and then decreasing in Q if $c_s - p_s < w < c_s$
- strictly increasing in Q if $w > c_s$

11.2   (Wholesale Price Contract for *Breach of Contract*) A new novel, the legal thriller *Breach of Contract*, will begin to be sold at your local bookstore next month. The bookstore must decide how many copies of the book to order, and it cannot re-order again after the initial order. The book will be sold for a certain duration (say, six months), after which all copies will be removed from the shelves and sold to a paper-recycling company as scrap.

Breach of Contract will be sold to consumers for $18.99 per copy. The publisher charges the bookstore a wholesale price of $11.00 per copy. For each copy purchased by the bookstore, the publisher incurs raw-material costs of $3.75, and the bookstore incurs shipping and handling costs of $1.20. (This is not paid to the publisher.)

The total demand for the book during the selling season is expected to be normally distributed with a mean of 1200 and a standard deviation of 340. Unmet demands are lost, incurring loss-of-goodwill costs estimated at $9.00 for the bookstore and $4.00 for the publisher. Unsold books are sold to the recycling company for $0.65 each.

a) What is the bookstore's optimal order quantity?

b) What is the order quantity that maximizes the total expected profit for the supply chain, and what is the optimal total expected profit?

c) What is each company's expected profit, and what is the total expected profit for the supply chain? What is the efficiency of the contract?

d) Suppose the publisher can choose any wholesale price it wishes. What wholesale price will it choose? What order quantity will the bookstore choose as a result? What will be the resulting profits? What will be the efficiency of the contract?

11.3 **(Buyback Contract for *Breach of Contract*)** Consider the supply chain discussed in Problem 11.2. Suppose the publisher offers the bookstore a buyback contract with a buyback credit of $8. (Buyback contracts are common in the publishing industry. However, since it is expensive to ship books, it is common practice for the publisher to require the bookstore to return only the cover of the book, and to destroy the rest of the book (Chopra and Meindl 2001).)

a) What w will coordinate the supply chain, and what will be the resulting profits? What is the supplier's percentage of the profit?

b) What value of b will give the retailer all of the profit? What value will give the supplier all of the profit?

11.4 **(Revenue Sharing Contract for *Breach of Contract*)** Consider the supply chain discussed in Problem 11.2. Suppose the publisher offers the bookstore a revenue sharing contract in which the bookstore keeps 60% of its revenue and gives 40% to the publisher.

a) What w will coordinate the supply chain, and what will be the resulting profits? What is the supplier's percentage of the profit?

b) What value of ϕ will give the retailer all of the profit? What value will give the supplier all of the profit?

11.5 **(Quantity Flexibility Contract for *Breach of Contract*)** Consider the supply chain discussed in Problem 11.2. Suppose the publisher offers the bookstore a quantity flexibility contract with $\delta = 0.4$.

a) What w will coordinate the supply chain, and what will be the resulting profits? What is the supplier's percentage of the profit? Does the supply-chain-optimal order quantity also maximize the publisher's profit function?

b) What value of δ will give the retailer all of the profit? What value will give the supplier all of the profit?

11.6 **(Retailer Under-Orders)** Prove Theorem 11.2.

11.7 (**Redundancy of** (11.22)) Prove that if b and w satisfy (11.21) and (11.25), then they also satisfy (11.22).

11.8 (**Theater Ticket Returns Policies**) A school is planning a class trip for its first-grade students to see a play at a local children's theater. There are 85 students in the first grade. The school will buy tickets in advance for $10 each. On the day of the play, if some children are sick and absent from school, the theater will not allow the unused tickets to be returned or exchanged. Therefore, the school is planning to buy $Q < 85$ tickets. However, if more than Q students show up to school on the day of the play, some of the children will have to stay at school, incurring a child-care cost (paid by the school) of $13 per student. Assume that a given student will be absent from school with probability 0.05, and that absences are statistically independent across students.

   a) What is the optimal number of tickets for the school to purchase? What will be the theater's revenue (ticket sales)?

   Hint: Use the normal approximation to the binomial distribution. You may assume that fractional ticket sales are possible.

   b) Suppose the theater implements a policy under which they will refund the school $6 for each unused ticket. Now what is the optimal number of tickets for the school to purchase? What will be the theater's expected net revenue (ticket sales minus refunds)?

11.9 (**Asymptotic Behavior of Buyback Contract**) Prove that, in a buyback contract, as $b \to 0$ (i.e., as the buyback contract approaches a wholesale price contract), $w(b)$ approaches the w that ensures $Q_r^* = Q_s^* = Q^0$ in the wholesale price contract.

11.10 (**Buyback Parameters Are Valid**) Prove that, for any revenue sharing contract (w_r, ϕ), the equivalent buyback parameters defined in (11.45)–(11.46) satisfy (11.25).

11.11 (**Quantity Flexibility Transfer Payment**) Prove (11.48), taking (11.47) as given. (*Hint*: Use integration by parts.)

11.12 (**First-Order Condition for Quantity Flexibility**) Prove that

$$\left. \frac{\partial \pi_s(Q, w(\delta), \delta)}{\partial Q} \right|_{Q=Q^0} = 0$$

in the quantity flexibility contract. That is, Q^0 is a stationary point for the supplier's profit function.

11.13 (**Profit Allocation under Quantity Flexibility Contract**) Prove that, under the quantity flexibility contract, for any $0 \le \alpha \le 1$, there exists a δ such that the supplier receives exactly α proportion of the total profit; that is, all possible allocations of the profit are possible.

11.14 (**Alternate Proof of Theorem 11.5**) Prove Theorem 11.5 using a method similar to Proof #1 of Theorem 11.3; that is, use the first-order conditions directly to show that $Q_r^* = Q_s^* = Q^0$.

11.15 **(A Simpler Contract?)** A student once made a comment along the lines of, "Why bother with this contracting stuff? If the supply chain profit is not maximized when the retailer orders Q_r^* instead of Q^0, why don't the parties just agree that the retailer will order Q^0 and then they'll split the extra profits somehow?"

In essence, this student has proposed an alternate, potentially simpler, contracting mechanism. Suppose the parties decide to split the profits by bringing the retailer's profit up to the profit he'd earn if he'd ordered Q_r^* instead of Q^0. That is, the supplier agrees to pay the retailer $\pi_r(Q_r^*) - \pi_r(Q^0)$ per period if the retailer orders Q^0. In addition, let's assume there's a wholesale price of w per unit, which is fixed (not a parameter of the contract), and that $w > c_s$.

In other words, the transfer payment T is given by

$$
T = \begin{cases} wQ - (\pi_r(Q_r^*) - \pi_r(Q^0)), & \text{if } Q = Q^0 \\ wQ, & \text{if } Q \neq Q^0, \end{cases}
$$

where π_r is as defined in (11.11).

- **a)** Write the retailer's expected profit function under this simple contract (call it $\pi_r^s(Q)$). You may express $\pi_r^s(Q)$ in terms of $\pi_r(Q)$.
- **b)** Prove that, under this contract, the retailer is indifferent between ordering Q^0 and Q_r^*—both maximize his expected profit.
- **c)** Write the supplier's expected profit function under the new contract (call it $\pi_s^s(Q)$). You may express $\pi_s^s(Q)$ in terms of $\pi_r(Q)$ and $\pi_s(Q)$, where $\pi_s(Q)$ is as defined in (11.12) .
- **d)** Prove that the supplier prefers the retailer to order Q^0 (instead of Q_r^*) if and only if

$$
\pi_s(Q^0) - \pi_s(Q_r^*) > \pi_r(Q_r^*) - \pi_r(Q^0).
$$

  (If the supplier prefers Q_r^*, then the contract fails to coordinate the supply chain, since the supplier wouldn't even propose the contract to begin with.)
- **e)** Perform a numerical study to determine whether the condition given in part (d) seems reasonable. You may assume that the demand is normally distributed. In your report, explain how you performed the study (i.e., what range of values you tested, etc.) and what your conclusions are. Does the supplier seem to prefer Q^0 all of the time? None of the time? Some of the time?

11.16 **(Second Ordering Opportunity)** Consider a supply chain with a single supplier and a single retailer. The retailer has two opportunities to order items from the supplier: once before he knows the actual demand and once after. All demands must be satisfied; therefore, the size of the second order is equal to any shortfall from the first order. However, any demands that are not met after the first order incur a loss-of-goodwill cost p per item since customers will have to wait until the second order is placed before receiving their products.

Demands are random with pdf f, cdf F, and mean μ. Let Q be the size of the first order. The selling price is r per item regardless of when the demand is satisfied.

The supplier charges the retailer a wholesale price of w per item for both the first and second orders. Unsold merchandise at the end of the period may be salvaged for a salvage value of v per unit.

The manufacturer produces to order; that is, she produces exactly the number of units requested by the retailer in each order and does not hold inventory between orders. She incurs a production cost of c_1 for items produced for the first order and c_2 for items produced for the second order. Since the second order typically requires smaller production runs, you can assume $c_1 < c_2$. You can also assume that $v < c_1$ and $c_2 < w$.

The sequence of events in the time period is as follows: The retailer places his first order. The order is delivered immediately. Demand is realized, and all demands that can be met from stock are satisfied; the remaining demands are put on hold until the second order. If any demands are on hold, the second order is placed (for exactly the number of units on hold). The second order arrives immediately, and the on-hold demands are satisfied. If the demand was smaller than the first order, any unsold items are salvaged.

a) Write expressions for the retailer's, supplier's, and supply chain's expected profit as a function of Q, denoted $\pi_r(Q)$, $\pi_s(Q)$, and $\Pi(Q)$, respectively.

    Hint: To check that you have the correct formulas before you use them in the subsequent parts, we'll tell you the following: Assuming that

$$r = 100 \qquad\qquad w = 50$$
$$p = 125 \qquad\qquad c_1 = 25$$
$$v = 20 \qquad\qquad c_2 = 35$$
$$Q = 300$$

and demand is distributed $N(200, 50^2)$, then

$$\pi_r(Q) = 6934.2$$
$$\pi_s(Q) = 7506.4$$
$$\Pi(Q) = 14440.6.$$

b) Prove that the retailer's optimal order quantity is strictly smaller than the supply chain's optimal order quantity. (Therefore the supply chain is not coordinated.)

c) Consider a buyback contract in which the retailer pays the supplier a wholesale price of w (replacing the wholesale price w used in the original model) and the supplier pays the retailer a subsidy of b for every unit of unsold merchandise at the end of the period. Prove that if the wholesale price is given as a function of b by

$$w(b) = b + v + p\frac{c_1 - v}{p + c_2 - c_1},$$

then the supply chain is coordinated. Make sure you verify all relevant necessary and sufficient conditions.

d) In a few sentences, explain why the original supply chain was not coordinated, and why the buyback contract coordinates the supply chain.

CHAPTER 12

AUCTIONS

12.1 INTRODUCTION

Auctions have been around for centuries and the mathematical analysis of auctions dates back decades. But they have enjoyed growing popularity in recent years because the Internet has made efficient implementation of auctions, even complex ones, possible. Consumer auctions like eBay have become household names, but business-to-business (B2B) auctions have grown even more quickly. B2B auctions are mainly procurement auctions in which there is a single buyer and multiple sellers (the reverse of most consumer auctions; in fact, such auctions are called *reverse auctions*). For example, auto manufacturers have set up auctions in which thousands of potential suppliers bid for contracts; the auto company chooses the suppliers with the lowest prices. Clearly, such an undertaking would be virtually impossible without the Internet. We will consider auctions with a single seller and multiple potential buyers.

There are many types of auctions, each with various properties in terms of consumer behavior, efficiency, and so on. Here are just a few of the many types of auctions that have been introduced in the literature and in practice:

- *English*: Perhaps the most familiar type, with each bidder publicly announcing his bid and the price rising until only a single bidder remains. The highest bidder wins and pays his bid.

- *Sealed-bid first price*: Bids are made privately and simultaneously by all bidders. The bidder with the highest bid wins and pays his bid.

- *Sealed-bid second price*: Sometimes known as a *Vickrey* auction, this auction type is like the sealed-bid first price auction except that the winner pays the *second-highest* bid, not his own bid (though the bidder with the highest bid is still the winner). Second price auctions encourage higher bidding since the winning bidder pays a lower price than his own bid.

- *Dutch*: In the Dutch auction, the price starts high and the auctioneer announces successively lower prices. As soon as one bidder accepts the current price, that bidder wins and pays the price, and the auction ends.

In addition to deciding the auction type, the auction designer (who may be the buyer, seller, or a third party like eBay) must decide aspects of the auction structure like how bidders may bid on multiple units (e.g., as a package or individually), what information is available to the bidders (e.g., the bids that have been placed by other bidders), and so on.

. Auctions can be seen as mechanisms for supply chain coordination since they give buyers and sellers an opportunity to negotiate a mutually beneficial agreement. Game-theoretic issues appear in auction analysis, too; for example, players may have an incentive to misrepresent their objectives through misleading bids.

In fact, there are several important properties that are desirable for auctions to have. These desirable properties include:

- *Strategy-proof*: In a strategy-proof auction, truthful bidding is never worse than untruthful bidding, for each buyer and seller. A related, but weaker, concept is *incentive-compatible* which means that truthful bidding is a (Bayesian) Nash equilibrium.

- Ex-post *individually rational*: An auction is *ex-post* individually rational if each buyer and each seller do at least as well if they participate in the auction (under any auction outcome) than if they don't participate.

- Ex-post *budget-balanced*: An auction is *ex-post* budget-balanced if the auctioneer's payoff is non-negative for all possible outcomes; therefore, the auctioneer can hold the auction without an outside subsidy.

- *Optimal or Efficient*: An *optimal* auction implements an allocation that maximizes expected revenue (the sum of the expected payments of the buyers) while an *efficient* auction maximizes social welfare (i.e., achieves the highest possible set of awarded valuations).

Any mechanism must be individually rational and budget balanced to make an auction practical. Moreover, strategy-proofness is desired, since each agent may not know enough information about the other agents to determine his or her optimal strategy. Unfortunately, it is not possible to design an auction mechanism that is efficient, individually rational, incentive compatible, and budget balanced—at least one of these must be sacrificed (Myerson and Satterthwaite 1983).

In Section 12.2, we will analyze a simple English auction and show that the auction itself can be thought of in terms of a linear program and its dual. Then, in Section 12.3 we will discuss a more complicated auction with multiple products and investigate the allocation problem faced by the auctioneer.

12.2 THE ENGLISH AUCTION

In an English auction, there is a set of bidders (also called *agents*), each bidding on a single item. The price begins low and gradually increases. At each price announced by the auctioneer, all bidders announce whether they are still willing to bid on the item at the current price (for example, by raising their hands), and the auction ends when only a single bidder remains. In this section, we analyze such an auction. Our analysis is adapted from Kalagnanam and Parkes (2004).

Let N be the set of agents. Agent $i \in N$ has a valuation v_i that she has assigned to the item: v_i is the maximum she'd be willing to pay for it. Paying v_i is like breaking even, so she'd prefer to pay less. The auctioneer knows v_i for each bidder. His goal is to award the item to the bidder with the highest valuation. (This also maximizes the auctioneer's revenue, assuming he is the seller. However, under this auction the auctioneer will not necessarily receive v_i for the winning bidder.)

In other words, the auctioneer needs to solve the following problem:

$$(\text{IP}) \quad \text{maximize} \quad \sum_{i \in N} v_i x_i \tag{12.1}$$

$$\text{subject to} \quad \sum_{i \in N} x_i \leq 1 \tag{12.2}$$

$$x_i \in \{0, 1\} \qquad \forall i \in N \tag{12.3}$$

where $x_i = 1$ if agent i is awarded the item. The constraint says that at most one agent may be assigned the item. The English auction is one way of solving this problem. Another way is simply to ask each bidder for his or her valuation and to award the item to the bidder with the highest valuation; but bidders may prefer the English auction since it allows them to win the item without paying their maximum valuation.

The following problem is also equivalent to (IP):

$$(\text{LP}) \quad \text{maximize} \quad \sum_{i \in N} v_i x_i \tag{12.4}$$

$$\text{subject to} \quad \sum_{i \in N} x_i + y = 1 \tag{12.5}$$

$$x_i \leq 1 \qquad \forall i \in N \tag{12.6}$$

$$x_i, y \geq 0 \qquad \forall i \in N \qquad (12.7)$$

In this formulation, a new variable y is added that represents the auctioneer not assigning the item to any bidder. Then the constraint can be written as an equality instead of an inequality. Furthermore, in this formulation the integrality restriction has been dropped. We can do this because although problem (IP) is an integer program, it always has an optimal solution in which the x_i are integer. Therefore it is equivalent to its LP relaxation.

Now consider the LP dual of (IP), with p the dual variable for constraint (12.5) and π_i the dual variable for constraint (12.6):

$$(D) \quad \text{minimize} \quad p + \sum_{i \in N} \pi_i \qquad (12.8)$$

$$\text{subject to} \quad \pi_i \geq v_i - p \qquad \forall i \in N \qquad (12.9)$$

$$p \geq 0 \qquad (12.10)$$

$$\pi_i \geq 0 \qquad \forall i \in N \qquad (12.11)$$

Note that p is non-negative (constraint (12.10)) since the coefficient of y in (12.4) is 0, while the non-negativity of π_i (constraints (12.11)) follows from the inequality constraints (12.6).

Suppose p is fixed. The optimal values of π_i are given by $\pi_i = \max\{0, v_i - p\}$. A primal solution x and a dual solution (p, π) are optimal for their respective problems if the complementary slackness conditions hold:

$$p > 0 \implies \sum_i x_i + y = 1 \qquad (CS1)$$

$$\pi_i > 0 \implies x_i = 1 \quad \forall i \in N \qquad (CS2)$$

$$x_i > 0 \implies \pi_i = v_i - p \quad \forall i \in N \qquad (CS3)$$

$$y > 0 \implies p = 0 \qquad (CS4)$$

The dual variables p and π_i have a natural interpretation in the context of the auction: p is the selling price of the item and π_i is the payoff (valuation minus price) to agent i under price p. The complementary slackness conditions are then interpreted as follows:

- If the price is positive, then by CS1 either someone gets it or no one gets it. By CS4, if no one gets it then the price must be 0. So taken together, CS1 and CS4 mean if the price is positive, someone gets the item.

- By CS3, if agent i wins the auction, then the price must equal $v_i - \pi_i$; since $\pi_i \geq 0$ by (12.11), this means the winning agent pays no more than his valuation.

- By CS2, any agent not receiving the item ($x_i = 0$) must have $\pi_i = 0$; this means $v_i \leq p$ by (12.9), i.e., the price is greater than the losing agent's valuation.

Notice that these are exactly the conditions under which the auction ends.

The simplex method is called a *primal algorithm* for solving LPs because it maintains a primal solution at all times and tries to improve it until it finds the optimal solution. Other methods, called *primal-dual algorithms*, maintain both a primal and a dual solution at all times and attempt to move toward optimal solutions by fixing violations in the complementary slackness conditions.

This is exactly the process taken by the English auction! In a sense, the auction is nothing more than a big LP solver in which the actions of the players correspond to steps in the algorithm. In particular, interpret the dual variable p as the current price and the dual variables π_i as the corresponding payoffs for each agent. Interpret the primal variable x_i as indicating whether agent i is the current "provisional" winner of the auction, chosen arbitrarily from among the bidders that are still interested in the item at the current price p. Interpret y as indicating that no bidders are still interested in the item at the current price. Throughout the auction, the primal and dual solutions are both feasible for their respective problems. When the complementary slackness conditions hold, the auction ends, the optimal solutions having been found. Note that in every round, CS1, CS3, and CS4 hold in the auction: If the price is positive, some agent must be the current provisional winner (CS1 and CS4) and the price is less than the value of the provisional winner (CS3). CS2 might not hold since there may be non-winners who still have a positive payoff, that is, whose valuations are less than the current price. The primal-dual approach works by increasing p until CS2 holds.

12.3 COMBINATORIAL AUCTIONS

English auctions involve only a single item for sale. In this section we will discuss auctions in which there are a number of heterogeneous items for sale. In such an auction, bidders may want to bid on combinations of items instead of individual items. For example, suppose you attend an auction of some antique furniture. You might be interested in buying the bed and matching dresser if you could buy them together, but might not be interested in buying only one of them. Or, you might be interested in buying one bed or another, but not both. Valuation, then, is assigned to subsets of items (called *bundles*) rather than to individual items. This makes the auction itself, as well as the auctioneer's allocation problem, considerably more complex. Such auctions are called *combinatorial auctions*. Our analysis of combinatorial auctions is adapted from de Vries and Vohra (2003).

A famous example of a combinatorial auction is the occasional auction of telecommunications spectrum rights held by the United States Federal Communications Commission (FCC). A cell phone carrier, for example, might want to buy one license in each market it's interested in. Bidding for individual licenses misses the point since the value of one license depends on which other licenses the company holds. In the FCC's first auction, in 1994, they allowed bids on individual licenses only (though steps were taken to help bidders obtain bundles they were interested in), thinking it would be too cumbersome to allow bids on bundles. However, in 2003, the FCC held its first auction in which bidders could bid on combinations of licenses.

Another example of a practitioner of combinatorial auctions is JUNAEB, the agency responsible for providing free meals to low-income school children in Chile. Since 1980, the agency has used auctions to select private companies to provide these meals throughout the country. Companies place bids that indicate the geographic region they will serve, the services they will provide, and the price they will charge. Prior to 1997, bids were chosen more or less independently, without considering the interdependencies among the bids. But in 1997, JUNAEB began using combinatorial auctions to allocate bids. Each company can submit multiple bids, for example, covering different combinations of geographical regions. The new auction mechanism saves JUNAEB an estimated US$40 million per year and has also improved the quality of the food, the geographic scope of the assistance program, and the transparency of the entire bidding process (Epstein et al. 2004).

12.3.1 The Combinatorial Auction Problem

Let M be the set of objects being auctioned off, and let N be the set of bidders. For any bundle $S \subseteq M$, let b_{iS} be the bid that agent i has announced he is willing to pay for S. Note that b is different from v since it represents announced bids, not valuations; an agent's bid for a bundle might be less than his valuation. In an auction of any reasonable size, it would be impossible for an agent to specify a bid for all $2^{|M|}$ possible bundles, so you can think of b as a function that takes a bundle suggested by the auctioneer and returns a bid for that bundle. Without loss of generality we can assume $b_{iS} \geq 0$ for all i, S. Let y_{iS} be 1 if agent i is assigned bundle $S \subseteq M$ and 0 otherwise.

The auctioneer's problem is to allocate the bundles to agents in order to maximize her revenue. This problem is known as the *combinatorial auction problem* (CAP) and is formulated as follows:

$$\text{(CAP)} \quad \text{maximize} \quad \sum_{i \in N} \sum_{S \subseteq M} b_{iS} y_{iS} \tag{12.12}$$

$$\text{subject to} \quad \sum_{S \ni j} \sum_{i \in N} y_{iS} \leq 1 \quad \forall j \in M \tag{12.13}$$

$$\sum_{S \subseteq M} y_{iS} \leq 1 \quad \forall i \in N \tag{12.14}$$

$$y_{iS} \in \{0, 1\} \quad \forall i \in N, \forall S \subseteq M \tag{12.15}$$

The objective function maximizes the revenue to the seller. (If the bids are equal to the actual valuations, then this formulation also maximizes the "efficiency" of the auction—assigning bundles to the agents that value them the highest.) Constraints (12.13) ensure that no two bundles assigned to agents contain the same item. (The summation over $S \ni j$ is a summation over all $S \subseteq M$ that contain j.) Constraints (12.14) prevent an agent from receiving more than one bundle. This is necessary to ensure that the auctioneer does not decide to assign bundles S and T to bidder i, instead of $S \cup T$, if $b_{iS} + b_{iT} > b_{i,S \cup T}$. However, we will restrict ourselves to cases in which a bid for a bundle is no smaller than the sum of bids of subsets of the bundle; that is, $b_{i,S\cup T} \geq b_{iS} + b_{iT}$ for all $S, T \subseteq M$. Bid functions for which this property holds are called *superadditive*. If the bid functions are superadditive, then constraints (12.14) are no longer needed since it is always to the seller's advantage to award an agent a single bundle than two separate ones.

We now reformulate (CAP) as an instance of the *set-packing problem* (SPP), in which there is a set M of elements and a collection V of subsets of M with non-negative weights; the objective is to choose the largest-weight collection of subsets such that every element is contained in at most one subset. (The SPP is like the inverse of the set-covering problem, in which we want to choose subsets such that every element is contained in at least one subset. If every element must be contained in exactly one subset, we have the set-partitioning problem.)

Let V be the collection of all subsets of M, and let k be an individual bundle (subset). Define

$$b_k = \max_{i \in N}\{b_{ik}\},$$

that is, b_k is the maximum bid any agent would be willing to pay for bundle k. Let $a_{ik} = 1$ if bundle k contains item i, 0 otherwise. Finally, let $x_k = 1$ if bundle k is selected, 0 otherwise. The problem now reduces to one of partitioning the items into bundles; the actual assignments can be done after the fact based on which agent maximized b_{ik} for each selected bundle k. The CAP can be reformulated as:

$$(\text{SPP}) \quad \text{maximize} \quad \sum_{k \in V} b_k x_k \tag{12.16}$$

$$\text{subject to} \quad \sum_{k \in V} a_{jk} x_k \leq 1 \qquad \forall j \in M \tag{12.17}$$

$$x_k \in \{0,1\} \qquad \forall k \in V \tag{12.18}$$

Constraints (12.17), like constraints (12.13), prohibit the bundles from overlapping. We will focus on this formulation of the CAP in what follows.

12.3.2 Solving the Set-Packing Problem

Unlike the auctioneer's problem in the English auction, the CAP does not naturally have all integer solutions; that is, it is not equivalent to its LP relaxation. Therefore, we can't use LP duality to solve the problem. However, we will use Lagrangian relaxation (which provides a different type of duality) to solve it and show that, like the LP dual, the Lagrangian formulation has a natural interpretation in the auction context.

Let's relax constraints (12.17) in the SPP using Lagrange multipliers λ. The resulting subproblem is

$$(\text{SPP-LR}_\lambda) \quad z_{\text{LR}}(\lambda) = \text{maximize} \quad \sum_{k \in V} b_k x_k + \sum_{j \in M} \lambda_j \left(1 - \sum_{k \in V} a_{jk} x_k\right)$$

$$= \sum_{k \in V} \left(b_k - \sum_{j \in M} \lambda_j a_{jk} \right) x_k + \sum_{j \in M} \lambda_j$$

$$(12.19)$$

$$\text{subject to} \qquad x_k \in \{0, 1\} \qquad \forall k \in V \qquad (12.20)$$

Solving (SPP-LR$_\lambda$) is easy: for each $k \in V$ we set $x_k = 1$ if

$$b_k - \sum_{j \in M} \lambda_j a_{jk} > 0$$

and 0 otherwise. Since (SPP) is a maximization problem, for a given λ, $z_{LR}(\lambda)$ provides an *upper bound* on that of (SPP), and our goal is to find better (i.e., smaller) upper bounds by solving

$$\text{(SPP-LR)} \qquad \min_{\lambda \geq 0} \quad z_{LR}(\lambda).$$

Note that λ is restricted to be non-negative; see Section D.5 in Appendix D. Problem (SPP-LR) is sometimes known as the *Lagrangian dual*, because in many ways it behaves like an LP dual. (SPP-LR) can be solved approximately using subgradient optimization, as we did when using Lagrangian relaxation previously. A solution to (SPP-LR$_\lambda$) can be converted into a feasible solution for (SPP) using some heuristic; this feasible solution then provides a lower bound.

Our interest is not so much in this solution method as in its auction interpretation. The Lagrange multiplier λ_j represents the price on an individual item set by the auctioneer. The agents have already announced their bids for each bundle $k \in V$, the maximum of which is b_k. If $b_k > \sum_{j \in M} a_{jk} \lambda_j$, then, according to the solution to (SPP-LR$_\lambda$), x_k is set to 1—the bundle is temporarily included in the group of bundles to be sold. Presumably, the bundles in that group may overlap (constraints (12.17) may be violated), in which case the auctioneer must adjust the prices λ using subgradient optimization. Prices for items that are included in too many bundles would increase, while prices for items that are in no bundles would decrease.

As in the English auction, feasible solutions to the dual problem represent prices while feasible solutions to the primal problem represent tentative assignments of items to agents. A primal-dual pair is optimal if something akin to the complementary slackness conditions hold:

- If $\lambda_j > 0$, then $\sum_{k \in V} a_{jk} x_k = 1$, i.e., item j is contained in exactly one allocated bundle. Another way of saying this is that if j is not included in any bundle, then it must be a worthless item, so $\lambda_j = 0$.

- If $x_k > 0$, then $\sum_{j \in M} \lambda_j a_{jk} \leq b_k$, i.e., the bundle is worth at least the asking price to some bidder.

12.3.3 Truthful Bidding

In the combinatorial auction described above, the seller allocates bundles to maximize her revenue based on the bids. But there is no guarantee that the bids accurately reflect the bidders' valuations of the items, and bidders may have an incentive to lie. For example, suppose there are three bidders (1, 2, and 3) and two items (A and B). The bidders' valuations of the three possible bundles are given in Table 12.1.

Table 12.1 Valuations that induce non-truthful bidding.

Bidder	Bundle		
	A	B	A,B
1	0	0	100
2	75	75	0
3	40	40	0

The bidders do not need to place bids equal to their valuations. If they *did* bid truthfully, the auctioneer should award A to 2 and B to 3 (or vice-versa), for a revenue of 115. However, if bidder 2 assumes that bidder 3 will continue to bid truthfully, he has an incentive to reduce his bid on A and B, say, to 65. Bidders 2 and 3 still win the auction but bidder 2 pays less. Bidder 3 can reason the same way—but if they both reduce their bids, bidder 1 might win the auction.

If bidders 2 and 3 could collude on their bids, they could ensure that they win the auction, as long as the sum of their bids (for each item) is greater than 100, though this leaves $15 of profit that they need to decide how to share.

Obviously, it is to the auctioneer's advantage if the agents bid honestly. She can't force them to do so, but she can design the auction mechanism so that the bidders' optimal strategy is to bid honestly. This is very similar to the supply chain contracts discussed in Chapter 11: By structuring the payoffs carefully, the mechanism designer motivates the players to behave in a particular way, even when they are acting selfishly. In the case of auctions, however, the auctioneer is trying to manipulate the game so that the agents maximize her own revenue, while in supply chain contracting, the contracts are designed to maximize the common revenue.

12.3.4 The Vickrey-Clarke-Groves Auction

In this section we discuss an auction mechanism in which it is to the agents' benefit to bid honestly. The auction is called the *Vickrey-Clarke-Groves* (VCG) auction, after the researchers who proposed and studied it. The VCG auction is a single-round sealed-bid auction. (If there is only a single item, it is equivalent to a sealed-bid second-price auction.) It works as follows:

1. Agent i reports his valuation v_{iS} for all $S \subseteq M$. There is nothing to prevent the agents from misreporting their valuations, but it turns out to be optimal for them to be honest.

2. The auctioneer solves the following problem:

$$V = \text{maximize} \quad \sum_{i \in N} \sum_{S \subseteq M} v_{iS} y_{iS}$$

$$\text{subject to} \quad \sum_{S \ni j} \sum_{i \in N} y_{iS} \leq 1 \quad \forall j \in M$$

$$\sum_{S \subseteq M} y_{iS} \leq 1 \quad \forall i \in N$$

$$y_{iS} \in \{0,1\} \quad \forall i \in N, \forall S \subseteq M$$

Note that this is just (CAP) with b replaced by v. Let y^* be the optimal solution.

3. The auctioneer solves the following problem for each agent $k \in N$:

$$V^{-k} = \text{maximize} \quad \sum_{i \in N \setminus k} \sum_{S \subseteq M} v_{iS} y_{iS}$$

$$\text{subject to} \quad \sum_{S \ni j} \sum_{i \in N \setminus k} y_{iS} \leq 1 \quad \forall j \in M$$

$$\sum_{S \subseteq M} y_{iS} \leq 1 \quad \forall i \in N \setminus k$$

$$y_{iS} \in \{0,1\} \quad \forall i \in N \setminus k, \forall S \subseteq M$$

This is the allocation problem assuming that player k does not participate in the auction.

4. Bundles are awarded to agents according to y^*. The payment that agent k pays is equal to

$$V^{-k} - \left[V - \sum_{S \subseteq M} v_{kS} y_{kS}^* \right]. \tag{12.21}$$

Note that the VCG auction awards bundles in the same manner as the combinatorial auction in Section 12.3.1, but the payments are different.

Here is the logic behind (12.21). V^{-k} is the "welfare" of the other agents when agent k is excluded from the auction. The term inside the brackets is the welfare of the other agents when agent k participates. So agent k's payment is equal to the difference in the other agents' welfare without him and with him. In other words, agent k reimburses the system for the value that he has taken away by winning his bundle.

Why does agent k have an incentive to tell the truth when he reports v_{kS}? First notice that changing v_{kS} doesn't affect V^{-k} since the V^{-k} auction excludes agent k. Moreover, the term inside the brackets in (12.21) is equal to the optimal objective value of the allocation problem minus agent k's payment. So that term is independent of v_{kS}. Therefore, a winning agent's payment will not change if he under- or over-states his valuation. Finally, if an agent over-states his valuations in the hope of winning a bundle that he wouldn't have won under truthful bidding, then he will pay more for this bundle than his valuation—see Problem 12.4. Therefore, agents have no incentive to mis-represent their valuations when they bid.

If the seller implements the VCG auction, her total revenue will be

$$\sum_{k \in N} V^{-k} - \sum_{k \in N} \left[V - \sum_{S \subseteq M} v_{kS} y_{kS}^* \right] = \sum_{k \in N} \sum_{S \subseteq M} v_{kS} y_{kS}^* + \sum_{k \in N} (V^{-k} - V)$$

$$= V + \sum_{k \in N} (V^{-k} - V).$$

If the number of bidders is large, then V will tend to be very close to V^{-k} since no single agent would have too large an effect on the auction. Therefore, the seller's revenue is close to V, which is the maximum revenue any auction could earn. Implementing a VCG auction for a large number of bidders is very difficult, however (since the CAP is difficult to solve), so they are not common in practice, except for special cases.

☐ **EXAMPLE 12.1**

Suppose first that a single item, called A, is being auctioned off. Three bidders are competing for the item. Their valuations, as reported in Step 1 of the VCG auction, are listed in Table 12.2. The optimal allocation in Step 2 is to award the item to the highest bidder, bidder 2, for a total valuation of $V = 120$. In Step 3, the optimal allocation if bidders 1 or 3 are removed from the auction is still to award the item to bidder 2, with total valuation 120. If bidder 2 is removed, then the item goes to the second-highest bidder, bidder 1, for a valuation of 100. So the V^{-i} values are 120, 100, 120 (respectively). Bidder 2's payment is therefore $V^{-2} - [V - v_{2,A} y_{2,A}^*] = 100 - [120 - 120] = 100$. Note that 100 is also equal to the second-highest bid, confirming that the VCG auction operates as a sealed-bid second price auction in this case.

Table 12.2 Single-item VCG auction: Example.

Bidder (i)	$v_{i,A}$	$v_{i,A} y_{i,A}^*$	V^{-i}	Payment
1	100	0	120	0
2	120	120	100	100
3	10	0	120	0
		$V = 120$		100

Now suppose that two items, A and B, are being auctioned off. The bidders' valuations for these items, and for the bundle consisting of both of them, are given in Table 12.3. The optimal allocation in Step 2 is to award A to bidder 2 and B to bidder 1, for a total valuation of $V = 220$. If bidder 1 is removed from the auction, the optimal allocation is to award A to 2 and B to 3, so

$V^{-1} = 190$. If bidder 2 is removed from the auction, the optimal allocation is to award the bundle AB to bidder 1, so $V^{-2} = 200$. And if bidder 3 is removed, the optimal allocation is unchanged, so $V^{-3} = 220$. Therefore, bidder 1 pays $V^{-1} - [V - \sum_S v_{1S} y_{1S}^*] = 190 - [220 - 100] = 70$ for item A and bidder 2 pays $V^{-2} - [V - \sum_S v_{2S} y_{2S}^*] = 200 - [220 - 120] = 100$ for item B. The total payment is 170.   □

Table 12.3   Two-item VCG auction: Example.

Bidder (i)	$v_{i,A}$	$v_{i,B}$	$v_{i,AB}$	$\sum_S v_{iS} y_{iS}^*$	V^{-i}	Payment
1	100	100	200	100	190	70
2	120	0	0	120	200	100
3	10	70	120	0	220	0
				$V = 220$		170

It is well known that the VCG mechanism is strategy proof, *ex-post* individually rational, and efficient. However, the VCG mechanism is not budget balanced; that is, it is possible that the auctioneer may receive a negative payoff. In a one-sided auction such as the one discussed here (with a single seller and multiple buyers), the budget imbalance arises from the fact that the auctioneer's valuations for the items are not considered in the allocation problem or payment calculation, and therefore the auctioneer could receive payments that fall short of her valuation for the items sold. The same is true for VCG mechanisms in more complicated settings, such as double auctions (with multiple buyers and sellers).

Recently, there has been a focus on using auctions for supply chain procurement and trading in e-marketplaces. The benefits of auctions include lower information, transaction, and participation costs; increased convenience for both sellers and buyers; and, consequently, better market efficiency. While research and practice in operations management has emphasized optimizing the total supply chain, classical auction theory does not consider the operational costs associated with integrating a supply chain, such as logistics and inventory management costs. More recent work attempts to include these costs into the auction design. For example, Chen et al. (2005) consider combinatorial procurement auctions in supply chain settings. They incorporate supply chain costs (e.g., transportation costs in a complex supply chain network) into VCG auctions. Chu and Shen (2006, 2008) propose several double-auction mechanisms for e-marketplaces. Under their proposed double-auction mechanisms, bidding one's true valuation is the optimal strategy for each individual buyer and seller, even when shipping costs and sales taxes are different across various possible transactions. The proposed mechanism also achieves budget balance and asymptotic efficiency (that is, the auction approaches the maximum social welfare as the number of buyers and/or sellers approaches infinity). Furthermore, these results not only hold for an environment in which buyers and sellers exchange identical commodities, but also can be extended to more general environments, such as multiple substitutable commodities and bundles of commodities.

PROBLEMS

12.1 (**Non-Optimality of the English Auction**) Suppose you have decided to sell a valuable collection of baseball paraphernalia. You have identified N potential buyers for the collection. In this problem, you will consider two alternate ways of selling the collection, one involving an auction and one not. You are selling the collection as a whole, not as individual parts.

Each of the N bidders has a valuation v_i for the collection. You do not know the v_i's for each bidder, but you do know that each bidder's valuation is independently and uniformly distributed on $[0, 1]$.

Your first idea involves simply setting a price p and offering the collection for sale at that price. If some bidder wants to buy the item at that price (i.e., if $p < v_i$ for some bidder), he or she buys the item. If there are multiple such bidders, one is chosen randomly. If there are no such bidders, the sale ends unsuccessfully.

- **a)** Let $\gamma(p)$ be the probability that you sell the collection if you set the price to p. Calculate $\gamma(p)$. (Your answer should be in terms of N.)
- **b)** Write your expected revenue as a function of p.
- **c)** Calculate the optimal price p^*, the probability of selling the collection at this price, and the corresponding expected revenue.
- **d)** Show that the optimal revenue is strictly increasing in N.

Next you consider selling the collection using an English auction, in which you start the price at \$0 and gradually increase it until only one bidder remains. Assume that you increase the price continuously (infinitesimally), and that a bidder will not bid if the price equals his or her valuation (only if it's strictly less).

- **e)** Argue that the English auction always results in the winning bidder paying the *second-highest* valuation.
- **f)** The expected value of the second largest of N random variables that are iid $U[0, 1]$ is equal to $(N - 1)/(N + 1)$. Use this fact to show that the expected revenue from the English auction is smaller than that from the non-auction method if $N = 1$ or 2 and is larger if $N \geq 3$. Therefore, the English auction is not optimal from the seller's perspective if $N < 3$.
- **g)** Prove that, in the optimal solution to problem (D) on p. 308, p is equal to the second-highest valuation v_i.
- **h)** Verify the result from part (g) by solving problem (LP) for the data below using an LP solver of your choice. That is, verify that $x_i = 1$ for the bidder with the highest valuation but that p, the dual value for constraint (12.5), equals the second-highest valuation.

Bidder (i)	Valuation (v_i)
1	100
2	120
3	135
4	85
5	90

12.2 **(LP Relaxation of (CAP))** Construct a small example (using as few bidders and items as possible) for which the LP relaxation of (CAP) does not have an integer optimal solution.

12.3 **(VCG Auction for Candy Shipments)** The Truck o' Treats Company, a shipping company that specializes in refrigerated shipments of candy, will send a truck next week from Bethlehem, PA to Chicago, IL, and from there to Berkeley, CA. The current load is insufficient to fill the truck, and the company plans to use a VCG auction to sell the remaining 1000 cubic feet of capacity to a candy company that needs to ship goods along those routes. (The remaining capacity is the same on both legs of the route because the truck will make a delivery in Chicago but pick up an equal volume of goods for shipment to Berkeley.)

Four candy companies each have 1000 cubic feet of candy to ship and are considering bidding for the routes. Horseshoe Candy needs to ship candy from Bethlehem to Chicago and is willing to pay up to $900 for this leg; however, they have no product to ship to Berkeley and do not wish to bid for the second leg. Ares Chocolates, in contrast, has product to ship from Chicago to Berkeley (for which it is willing to pay $1150) but nothing to ship from Bethlehem to Chicago. Valhalla Chocolates has goods to ship to both destinations; it is willing to pay $600 to ship from Bethlehem to Chicago and $1200 to ship from Chicago to Berkeley; however, if they can do both, they are willing to pay $2000 to avoid the hassle of using two separate shipments. Similarly, W&W Candies is willing to pay $800 for the Bethlehem–Chicago leg, $950 for Chicago–Berkeley, and $1900 for both.

What leg(s) will be awarded to each company in the outcome of the VCG auction, and what will each winning bidder pay? What will be the total revenue to Truck o' Treats? Construct a table like Table 12.3 that lists the bids, values of awarded items, V^{-i} values, and payments.

12.4 **(Misrepresenting Valuations in the VCG Auction)** Prove that, in the VCG auction, a bidder does not have an incentive to bid greater than his valuation (in an attempt to win a bundle that he otherwise would not have won). In particular, suppose that bidder k is not awarded a particular bundle $T \subseteq M$ if all bidders state their *true* valuations. Prove that if bidder k over-states his valuation for bundle T to such an extent that he is now awarded bundle T, then the price he pays for bundle T will be greater than or equal to v_{kT}, his true valuation for bundle T.

To keep things simple, you may assume that bidder k does not receive *any* bundle when all bidders state their true valuations, and that when bidder k over-states his valuation for T, the rest of the bundles are awarded to the same bidders that they were awarded to originally; that is, the allocation of bundle T may change, but no other bundles. Furthermore, assume the partitioning of items into bundles does not change.

Hint: First prove the result for a single-item, second-price auction.

12.5 **(Non-Monotonicity of VCG Revenue)** One would expect that the auctioneer's revenue in a VCG auction is non-decreasing in the bids. However, this is not true in general. Consider a two-item auction with three bidders whose bids are given in the table below.

Bidder	Bundle A	B	A,B
1	0	0	100
2	100	100	100
3	100	100	100

a) Show that the optimal allocation assigns item A to bidder 2 and item B to bidder 3, and that the total payment to the auctioneer for this allocation is 0.

b) Show how to reduce some of the bids in the table above so that the auctioneer's revenue becomes strictly positive.

12.6 (Double Auctions) A double auction consists of multiple buyers and multiple sellers. Potential buyers submit their bids and potential sellers simultaneously submit their ask prices to an auctioneer. The auctioneer first eliminates some sellers who ask too much and some buyers who offer too little, and then decides which of the remaining buyers and sellers will transact with each other, and at what price. Transactions incur costs, which may represent costs associated with transportation, quality, lead time, customization, and the buyer–vendor relationship. The transaction costs are assumed to be common knowledge.

Suppose there are multiple commodities to be exchanged in the auction. There is a collection of sellers, each of whom offers for sale a single unit of a single commodity, facing a collection of buyers, each interested in buying a bundle consisting of multiple commodities, but at most one of each. Formulate the problem of maximizing social welfare assuming all agents bid truthfully. Use the following notation:

I	set of buyers
J	set of sellers
C	set of indivisible commodities
f_i	bid price of buyer i for her bundle
g_j	ask price of seller j for his item
q_i	$= (q_i^c)_{c\in C}$, a bundle of goods that buyer i ($i \in I$) wants to procure; $q_i^c = 1$ if buyer i wants to procure one unit commodity c and 0 otherwise
q_j	$= (q_j^c)_{c\in C}$, supply offered by seller j ($j \in J$); $q_j^c = 1$ if seller j supplies one unit commodity c and 0 otherwise
d_{ijc}	transaction cost when buyer i purchases commodity c from seller j

12.7 (Single-Commodity Double Auctions) Consider a simpler version of the double auction in Problem 12.6 in which there is only a single commodity. Assume that when buyer i trades with seller j, transaction cost d_{ij} is incurred.

a) Formulate the single-commodity double auction.

b) Show that the simplified formulation can be solved efficiently.

c) Consider an example with two sellers and three buyers. The transaction cost matrix is given in the table below. The agents have an incentive to truthfully bid their valuations, which are shown in the figure below. Determine which buyer(s) transact with which seller(s) in the efficient allocation. How much should the winning buyers pay? How much should the winning sellers receive?

d_{ij}	1	2
1	4	7
2	6	4
3	9	6

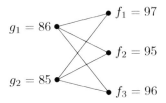

APPENDIX A

MULTIPLE-CHAPTER PROBLEMS

PROBLEMS

A.1 (Inventory Optimization for Deterministic Bass Demands) A new model of wireless router will be introduced shortly. An electronics retail chain expects the aggregate demand for the router at its stores to follow a discrete-time Bass diffusion process (2.27) with parameters $m = 100,000$, $p = 0.01$, and $q = 0.3$. Each time period represents one week. The retail chain holds inventory of the routers at its central warehouse and has an opportunity to place a replenishment order once per week. Each order incurs a fixed cost of $800, and each router held in inventory incurs a holding cost of $0.04 per week. The planning horizon is 52 weeks; any demand after the horizon ends can be ignored. In which weeks should the retailer place orders for routers, and what are the optimal order quantities? What is the total cost?

A.2 (Inventory Optimization for Stochastic Bass Demands) Suppose that the demand for wireless routers in Problem A.1 is now stochastic. The demand in period t is normally distributed with a mean of d_t and a standard deviation of $\sqrt{d_t}$, where d_t is given by the discrete-time Bass model (2.27). Unmet demands are backordered, incurring a stockout cost of $1.25 per router per week. Assume $c = 0$ and $\gamma = 1$. The other cost parameters, and the Bass parameters, are as given in Problem A.1. Although we assumed in Section 4.6.2.2 that the demand process is stationary, an (s, S) policy is still optimal for this problem with non-stationary demands. Determine the optimal parameters, s_t^* and S_t^*, for $t = 1, \dots, 52$.

A.3   (Subscription-Selling Newsvendor) Suppose that, rather than selling individual newspapers, the newsvendor sells *subscriptions* to the newspaper. The subscription is a little unusual and works as follows: There are N customers, and the newsvendor must decide which customers to select. Customers typically request multiple newspapers each day, and customer i's daily demand is $D_i \sim N(\mu_i, \sigma_i^2)$. If customer i is selected, the newsvendor earns a subscription revenue of r_i per day. This revenue is independent of the actual demand.

Just like in the classical newsvendor problem, our newsvendor must decide at the beginning of the day how many newspapers to stock. During the day, random demands are observed from each of the newsvendor's selected customers. At the end of the day, the newsvendor incurs a holding cost of h per unsold newspaper and a stockout cost of p per unmet demand.

Note that the newsvendor must choose his customers, and his order quantity, before demands are observed.

   a) Formulate a mathematical programming model to choose which customers to select in order to maximize the expected profit (revenue minus costs) per day. If you introduce any additional notation, define it clearly.

   Hint: Your model should not need a decision variable that represents the order quantity.

   b) Formulate a polynomial-time algorithm that solves this problem exactly (i.e., not a heuristic). Describe your algorithm step-by-step and explain clearly why it produces the optimal solution every time.

   c) What is the complexity of your algorithm (e.g., $O(N^2)$)?

   d) Suppose $h = 1$ and $p = 18$. The table below lists parameters for four customers. Using your algorithm, determine the optimal set of customers to serve. Report the optimal set of customers and the resulting expected profit.

i	r_i	μ_i	σ_i
1	10	40	8
2	8	20	3
3	3	25	9
4	11	16	3

A.4   (EOQ with Market Selection) Consider a single production stage that manufactures a single item. (We can equivalently view this "production stage" as a retail ordering process that plans orders for a single item.) Let $I = \{1, \dots, n\}$ denote a set of potential markets, indexed by i. Producing the product results in a setup cost K and a variable cost c per item procured. Inventory costs are assessed at a rate of h dollars per unit per year. Market i has a constant and deterministic annual demand rate,

λ_i. We let r_i denote the per-unit revenue from market i less any variable production and (possibly market-specific) delivery costs. Unlike the standard EOQ model, the producer can choose whether or not to satisfy each market's demand. If the producer chooses to supply a certain market, then it must satisfy all of the demand for that market. Rather than minimizing the average annual cost, as in the EOQ model, we maximize the average annual net contribution to profit.

    a) Write an expression for the average annual net contribution to profit and discuss how to solve the corresponding optimization problem. Define any new notation that you introduce.

    b) Suppose that we begin with an n-market problem for which an optimal solution selects markets $1, \ldots, k$, where $k < n$, and then consider the same problem with a single additional new market, $n + 1$. Prove the following proposition: ·

Proposition A.1 *An optimal solution exists for the new $(n+1)$-market problem that selects at least markets $1, \ldots, k$. If this new solution does not select market $n + 1$, then the optimal solution is the same for both the n-market and $(n + 1)$-market problems.*

A.5   (Using Discrete Choice to Forecast Demand) A minor-league baseball stadium has sold 8,000 tickets to tonight's baseball game. The stadium sells three kinds of souvenirs: hats, T-shirts, and puffy hands. Each person who attends the game will buy exactly one souvenir. From historical data, the concession manager at the stadium has developed an estimate, V_{ni}, of the utility that each attendee n derives from each of the souvenirs, for $i = 1, \ldots, 3$. These V_{ni} values are given in the table below.

Souvenir	V_{ni}
Hat	0.48
T-shirt	0.34
Puffy hand	0.21

    a) Assume that the actual utilities U_{ni} differ from the estimated utilities V_{ni} by an additive iid error term that has a standard Gumbel distribution. Using the multinomial logit model, calculate the expected demand for each souvenir.

    b) Let X be a random variable representing the total number of people who buy hats. What is the probability distribution of X? Specify the name and the parameters of the distribution.

    c) The concession manager replenishes the inventory of hats before the game, and any unsold hats after the game incur an opportunity cost of $0.25. Unmet demands for hats incur a stockout cost (including lost profit and loss of goodwill) of $1.75 per hat. How many hats should the manager stock for tonight's game?

       Note: You may solve this problem using the discrete demand distribution you identified in part (b), or you may approximate this distribution with a continuous distribution. If you take the latter approach, justify your approximation carefully.

A.6 (**Base-Stock Policies with Disruptions**) Consider a finite-horizon, periodic-review inventory system with stochastic demand and no fixed cost, for which we proved in Section 4.6.1.2 that a base-stock policy is optimal. There are T periods, the lead time is 0, the demand per period is random with pdf $f(\cdot)$ and cdf $F(\cdot)$, the holding cost is h per item per period, the backorder cost is p per item per period, the per-unit ordering cost is c, and the discount factor is $0 < \gamma \le 1$. If the inventory level is x at the start of period T, we incur a terminal cost of $\theta_{T+1}(x)$, a convex function.

Now suppose that the supplier is unreliable, and that when an order is placed, the supplier delivers it with probability q ($0 < q \le 1$). With probability $1 - q$, the supplier is disrupted—it's as though the order had never been placed, and the firm must wait until the next time period to order again. Evidently, the order placed in the next time period will be larger to make up for the failed order. (This is a special case of the model in Section 6.6.2 in which disruptions follow an iid Bernoulli process.)

  a) Write an expression for $\theta_t(x)$, the expected cost in periods $t, \ldots, T$ if we begin period t with an inventory level equal to x and act optimally in every period. Your expression should be analogous to (4.54) and may use the function $H_t(y)$. If you modify the definition of $H_t(y)$, explain your modifications carefully.

  b) Prove that a base-stock policy is optimal in every period t.
     Note: If you use any results from Section 4.6.1.2 to prove this, argue why these results are still true under your revised cost functions.

  c) Suppose $\theta_{T+1}(x) = -cx$. We know from Section 4.6.1.2 that the same S is optimal in every period if $q = 1$. Do you think the same statement is true if $q < 1$? Explain your answer.

A.7 (**Coordinating the Unreliable Supply Chain**) Consider the newsvendor problem with disruptions discussed in Section 6.6.2. In this problem, you will extend this model to consider the unreliable supplier and the coordination between the two players.

The supplier holds no inventory and has a lead time of 0 when operational. But the supplier is subject to disruptions, and when a disruption occurs, the supplier cannot provide any items. The retailer acts like a newsvendor with deterministic demand of d per period. Excess inventory at the end of the period is held over until the next period at a cost of h_r per unit per period, and unmet demands are backordered, incurring a stockout penalty of p_r per unit per period for the retailer and p_s for the supplier. Let $p \equiv p_r + p_s$.

The supplier's disruption probability is α and its recovery probability is β. The steady-state probability of being in a disruption that has lasted for n periods is π_n, and the cumulative probability of being in a disruption lasting n periods or fewer is $F(n)$, as in (6.26).

Suppose the supplier and retailer have agreed upon a contract that specifies a transfer payment to be made from the retailer to the supplier in an amount based on the current state of the system. From (6.30), the retailer's expected cost can be expressed as a function of its base-stock level S as follows:

$$g_r(S) = h_r \sum_{n=0}^{S/d-1} \pi_n[S - (n+1)d] + p_r \sum_{n=S/d}^{\infty} \pi_n[(n+1)d - S] + T, \quad \text{(A.1)}$$

where T is the expected transfer payment. Similarly, the supplier's expected cost is given by

$$g_s(S) = p_s \sum_{n=S/d}^{\infty} \pi_n[(n+1)d - S] - T \quad \text{(A.2)}$$

and the total supply chain expected cost is given by

$$G(S) = h_r \sum_{n=0}^{S/d-1} \pi_n[S - (n+1)d] + p \sum_{n=S/d}^{\infty} \pi_n[(n+1)d - S]. \quad \text{(A.3)}$$

Let S_r^*, S_s^*, and S^0 be the retailer's, supplier's, and supply chain optimal base-stock level, respectively.

Note that this model is expressed in terms of costs, not profits, and that it assumes backorders, not lost sales; both are changes from the assumptions in Chapter 11.

a) Suppose $T = 0$. Prove that $S_r^* \leq S^0$, and that for some instances, the inequality is strict (in which case the supply chain is not coordinated).

b) In 1 or 2 sentences, explain why the retailer tends to under-order in part (a).

c) Now consider a buyback contract in which the retailer pays the supplier w per unit ordered and the supplier pays the retailer b per unit on-hand at the end of each period. (Note that the items remain on-hand; they are not sent back to the supplier or destroyed. They can, rather, be used to satisfy demand in future periods.) Write expressions for $g_r(S, w, b)$, $g_s(S, w, b)$, and $G(S, w, b)$ under this contract.

d) Write the optimal base-stock levels S_r^*, S_s^*, and S^0 under this contract.

e) Find a value for b in terms of the other problem parameters such that $S_r^* = S^0$.

f) Show that, using the b you found in the previous part, $S_s^* = S^0$. Thus, the supply chain is coordinated.

g) You should have found that b and the optimal S values don't depend on w. Explain in one or two sentences why this makes sense.

A.8   (**A Location–Routing Problem**) Consider a facility location problem in which the customers assigned to each facility are served via a single truck whose route is determined by solving a traveling salesman problem (TSP). The length of the optimal TSP tour through n points located in an area A is often approximated as $k\sqrt{nA}$, where k is a constant. This approximation is called the "square-root rule" (Bearwood et al. 1959).

a) Formulate the problem of locating facilities to minimize the sum of the fixed cost and transportation cost, which is approximated using the square-root rule.

b) Propose an algorithmic method to solve this problem.

A.9   (A Location–Flexibility Design Problem) We wish to locate facilities and decide which facilities will produce which products. Let P be the set of products. Customer demands are stochastic and are described by scenarios; let S be the set of scenarios and let q_s be the probability that scenario $s \in S$ occurs. There is a fixed cost k_{jp} if facility j is configured to produce product $p \in P$. Facility $j \in J$ has a fixed capacity of v_j, and it takes one unit of capacity to produce one unit of product p, for all $p \in P$. Transportation costs are product-specific. We choose facility locations and capabilities (i.e., assignments of products to facilities) before the scenario is observed, and we set the production quantities, shipment quantities, and assignments of customers to facilities after the scenario is observed.

a) Formulate a linear mixed-integer programming model to minimize the expected cost of this system. Define any new notation clearly. Explain the objective function and each of the constraints in words.

b) Sketch an idea for an algorithm to solve this problem.

APPENDIX B

HOW TO WRITE PROOFS: A SHORT GUIDE

B.1 HOW TO PROVE ANYTHING

OK, fine—we can't actually tell you how to prove *everything*. But we can give you some advice that will help you when you try to prove *anything*.

Writing a proof is more art than science. Although there may be a "right" way to prove something (or several right ways), there is still a wide range of styles, formats, and logical implications that follow the same basic argument. (Similarly, you and your friend might write very different essays on "How I Spent My Summer Vacation," even if you did the same things during your vacations.)

Writing a proof is very much like arguing a case in court. (Or at least it's like how it looks on TV.) Like a courtroom argument, a proof should contain a beginning, a middle, and an end.

- The **beginning** tells us what is already known (the assumptions of the theorem), reminds us of important facts that are already in evidence that will be important for the proof, establishes new notation that you will use in the proof, and gives

Fundamentals of Supply Chain Theory, First Edition. Lawrence V. Snyder, Zuo-Jun Max Shen.
© 2011 John Wiley & Sons, Inc. Published 2011 by John Wiley & Sons, Inc.

us a hint of where you're headed and what steps the proof will take. Here are some examples:

> **Courtroom Claim:** Dr. Evil is guilty of stealing pencils from Prof. Plum's desk.
>
> **Courtroom Argument:** Consider the man sitting before you, Dr. Evil. You already know that security camera video from the night of October 6 shows Dr. Evil entering Prof. Plum's office building. Let the security video tape from that night be labeled as "Exhibit A." Today I will convince you, beyond a reasonable doubt, that Dr. Evil stole pencils from Prof. Plum's desk on that night. I will do this by providing physical evidence placing Dr. Evil in Prof. Plum's office and demonstrating that Dr. Evil had, indeed, touched pencils recently.

> **Theorem B.1** *The sum of two convex functions is also convex.*
>
> **Proof:** Consider two convex functions $f(x)$ and $g(x)$. Recall that, by definition, a function $f(x)$ is convex if, for any x and y in its domain and for any $\lambda \in [0, 1]$,
>
> $$f(\lambda x + (1 - \lambda)y) \leq \lambda f(x) + (1 - \lambda)f(y). \qquad \text{(B.1)}$$
>
> Let $h(x) \equiv f(x) + g(x)$, let x and y be in the domain of f and g, and let $\lambda \in [0, 1]$. We will show that $h(x)$ is convex by proving that inequality (B.1) holds.

See how similar their structures are?

- The **middle** provides the evidence that proves the claim. Like evidence in a trial, the steps in your proof must follow logically from one another and must be straightforward to follow.

> **Courtroom Argument:** Exhibit A shows Dr. Evil entering Prof. Plum's office building at 11:37 PM. At approximately 11:45 PM, graduate students saw a dark figure attempting to pick the lock on Prof. Plum's office door. Dr. Evil's fingerprints were found on the door, and in Prof. Plum's office, on the following day (October 7), and since Prof. Plum's office had been steam-cleaned the day before, the fingerprints must have been left on the night of October 6. Moreover, graphite stains on Dr. Evil's shirt match the precise composition of graphite contained in the pencils that Prof. Plum keeps in his desk.

> **Proof:**
>
> $$\begin{aligned} h(\lambda x + (1 - \lambda)y) &= f(\lambda x + (1 - \lambda)y) + g(\lambda x + (1 - \lambda)y) \\ &\leq [\lambda f(x) + (1 - \lambda)f(y)] + [\lambda g(x) + (1 - \lambda)g(y)] \\ &= \lambda[f(x) + g(x)] + (1 - \lambda)[f(y) + g(y)] \\ &= \lambda h(x) + (1 - \lambda)h(y) \end{aligned}$$
>
> The first and last equalities follow from the definition of $h(x)$. The inequality follows from the fact that $f(x)$ and $g(x)$ are convex functions.

Note that, in the proof, we provided justification for the steps that were not immediately obvious but omitted justification for the easy algebraic step. What counts as "easy" or "obvious" is, of course, a subjective matter. In general, a good rule of thumb to use is that, if your fellow students were reading your proof, *they should be able to follow each step without having to look up any facts or write down any additional derivations.*

- The **end** is the arrival point—the claim you are trying to prove.

  > **Courtroom Argument:** Ladies and gentlemen of the jury, the preponderance of evidence demonstrates that Dr. Evil has committed this heinous crime. You have no choice but to find him guilty.

  > **Proof:** Therefore, $h(x)$ is convex.   ■

Just like the lawyer's argument, the proof uses words—not just math—to lead the reader on the path from assumptions to conclusions. Of course, in a legal trial, facts and implications are subject to interpretation—that's why we have judges and juries. In a mathematical proof, however, all facts and logical implications should be incontrovertible.

B.2 TYPES OF THINGS YOU MAY BE ASKED TO PROVE

Here is a (very non-exhaustive) list of the *kinds* of statements you may be asked to prove in this book or at some other point in your proof-writing career:

- $x = y$

  This is the simplest kind of statement (though that does not mean it will require the simplest proof). It simply asks you to prove that two mathematical objects are equal.

  > **Theorem B.2** *Let* $g(Q) = \frac{K\lambda}{Q} + \frac{hQ}{2}$ *and* $Q^* = \sqrt{2K\lambda/h}$. *Then* $g(Q^*) = \sqrt{2K\lambda h}$.

  Notice that in this example, there is a qualifying statement to set up the statement you are asked to prove; this is fairly typical.

- $p \implies q$

  The symbols p and q stand here not for variables but for statements. The symbol $\implies$ is interpreted as "p implies q," and it is the same as saying "if p then q."

  > **Theorem B.3** *If* $0 < r < 1$, *then*

  $$\sum_{n=0}^{\infty} r^n = \frac{1}{1-r}.$$ (B.2)

Here p is "$0 < r < 1$" and q is equation (B.2).

- $p \iff q$

  The symbol $\iff$ means "if and only if" (sometimes abbreviated "iff"). The claim indicates that either both statements are true or both are false. Another description for this kind of statement is that q is a necessary and sufficient condition for p—in order for p to be true, q must be true, and the truth of q is sufficient to ensure the truth of p.

  > **Theorem B.4** *In the newsvendor model under normally distributed demand, the optimal safety stock level, $\sigma \Phi^{-1}\left(\frac{p}{p+h}\right)$, is positive if and only if $p > h$.*

  To prove an iff statement, you must prove both directions of the implication—that is, you must prove that p implies q and that q implies p. Sometimes you can do this all at once using a string of iff implications:

  $$\sigma \Phi^{-1}\left(\frac{p}{p+h}\right) > 0$$
  $$\iff \Phi^{-1}\left(\frac{p}{p+h}\right) > 0$$
  $$\iff \frac{p}{p+h} > \frac{1}{2}$$
  $$\iff p > h$$

  More commonly, though, the proof needs to be divided into two parts. In the first part you prove one implication (e.g., $p \implies q$) and in the second part you prove the reverse implication ($q \implies p$, or its logical equivalent, $\neg p \implies \neg q$).

- $\forall x$ such that [*condition*], [*statement*].

  Here you are asked to prove that for all x that satisfy a certain [*condition*], some [*statement*] is true.

  > **Theorem B.5** *For all x such that $x \geq 1$, $\ln x \geq 0$.*

  To prove a "$\forall x$" claim, you take the [*condition*] as given and prove that the [*statement*] is true. This actually feels a lot like a "$p \implies q$" claim, and in fact they are often logically equivalent.

- $\exists x$ such that [*statement*].

  This time you need to prove that there exists (at least one) x that satisfies the [*statement*]. Sometimes there are qualifying conditions on the type of x that are allowed.

Theorem B.6 *Suppose that* $\lim_{x \to \infty} f(x) = \infty$. *Then for any* x', *there exists an* $x > x'$ *such that* $f(x) > f(x')$.

(In this case there are many x that will do the trick, but you are asked only to prove the existence of one of them.)

- $\neg p$

In other words, you are being asked to *disprove* the statement p.

Theorem B.7 *Let* $f(x)$ *and* $g(x)$ *be convex functions and let* $h(x) \equiv f(x)g(x)$. *Then* $h(x)$ *is not necessarily convex.*

In general it suffices to find a single example for which p is not true. In the example above, you just need to find two convex functions whose product is not convex.

However, if p is of the form "$\exists x$ such that [*statement*]," then to disprove p you must prove that the [*statement*] is false *for all* x. This may be easy or hard. Here's a hard example:

Theorem B.8 *Let* n *be an integer greater than 2. Then there do not exist integers* a, b, *and* c *such that*

$$a^n + b^n = c^n.$$

(This is Fermat's Last Theorem, which went unproved for over 350 years until it was finally proved in 1995.)

B.3   PROOF TECHNIQUES

This section will give you a quick overview of several types of proofs—strategies for proving theorems. (Of course, there are others that this list does not include.) These are tools in your proof-building toolbox. It's your job to figure out which tool(s) to use for each job.

B.3.1   Direct Proof

This is the most common kind of proof—you simply prove the claim directly, through a series of logical implications.

Theorem B.9 *If* $0 < r < 1$, *then*

$$\sum_{n=0}^{\infty} r^n = \frac{1}{1-r}.$$

Proof: Let $0 < r < 1$. Define $A \equiv \sum_{n=0}^{\infty} r^n$. We wish to prove that $A = \frac{1}{1-r}$. Well,

$$A = r^0 + \sum_{n=1}^{\infty} r^n$$

$$= 1 + r \sum_{n=0}^{\infty} r^n$$

$$= 1 + rA.$$

Therefore

$$A = \frac{1}{1-r},$$

as desired.   ∎

B.3.2   Proof by Contradiction

Suppose you are trying to prove that $p \implies q$. In a proof by contradiction, you assume p, as usual, but then you assume that q is *not* true and then prove that a contradiction occurs. In particular, you show that if q is false, then so is p. And since you have assumed that p is true, you have now proven that p is both true and false—an impossibility. Therefore, the assumption of $\neg q$ must have been false—in other words, q must be true.

Theorem B.10 *There are an infinite number of prime numbers.*

Actually, to highlight the structure of a proof by contradiction, let's rewrite the theorem in "$p \implies q$" form, even though it's a little more awkward:

Theorem B.11 (Theorem B.10 Revised) *If N is the number of prime numbers, then $N = \infty$.*

Proof: Suppose (for a contradiction) that N is finite. Let the N primes be denoted $p_1, p_2, \dots, p_N$. Furthermore, let

$$B = \prod_{n=1}^{N} p_n + 1.$$

Now, B is also a prime number: None of the primes $p_1, \dots, p_N$ divides B (each results in a remainder of 1), so by definition, B is prime. Moreover, B is not in $\{p_1, \dots, p_N\}$ since it is larger than each of the p_n. Therefore we have found a new prime, so there must be at least $N + 1$ of them, contradicting our assumption that the number of primes is N. Therefore, there are an infinite number of primes.   ∎

Note the parenthetical phrase "for a contradiction." This is not strictly necessary, but it does help the reader by letting him or her know that the assumption you're about to make is not one that you actually believe—you are making it solely for the purpose of proving a contradiction later.

The *contrapositive* of the statement $p \implies q$ is $\neg q \implies \neg p$, and the two are logically equivalent; therefore, you can prove $p \implies q$ by proving $\neg q \implies \neg p$. This feels a lot like a proof by contradiction—we assume $\neg q$ and prove $\neg p$. The difference is that in a proof by contradiction, we *also assume* p and we use it to derive the contradiction. For example, we used the fact that N is the number of primes to build B, and then we used B to contradict the fact that N is the number of primes. In a proof by contrapositive, we don't need to assume p—we simply assume $\neg q$ and prove $\neg p$.

B.3.3 Proof by Mathematical Induction

Mathematical induction is useful when you need to prove something about all the integers (or all the members of some other countable set). The idea is to prove that if the claim is true for (an arbitrary) n, then it must also be true for $n + 1$. If we can prove this implication, then it holds for any n—that is, the truth of the claim for n implies the claim for $n + 1$, and this in turn implies the claim for $n + 2$, and then for $n + 3$, and so on. Therefore, this general implication (truth for $n \implies$ truth for $n + 1$) is powerful enough to prove that the claim is true for all integers greater than or equal to n. Of course, we also have to get the process started, by proving that the claim is true for $n = 1$.

A proof by induction generally has two parts: In the first (often called the *base case*), we prove that the claim is true for $n = 1$, and in the second (called the *induction step*), we prove that, if the claim holds for n, then it also holds for $n + 1$. In the induction step, we are allowed to assume that the claim holds for n—this is called the *induction hypothesis*.

Theorem B.12 *For all integers $n \geq 1$,*

$$\sum_{i=1}^{n} i = \frac{n(n + 1)}{2}.$$

Proof: By induction on n.
<u>Base Case</u>: If $n = 1$, then

$$\sum_{i=1}^{n} i = 1 = \frac{1(2)}{2}.$$

<u>Induction Step</u>: Suppose the claim holds for n. We need to prove that the claim holds for $n + 1$, i.e., that

$$\sum_{i=1}^{n+1} i = \frac{(n + 1)(n + 2)}{2}.$$

Well,

$$\sum_{i=1}^{n+1} i = \sum_{i=1}^{n} i + (n + 1)$$
$$= \frac{n(n + 1)}{2} + (n + 1) \qquad \text{(by the induction hypothesis)}$$
$$= \frac{n(n + 1) + 2(n + 1)}{2}$$
$$= \frac{(n + 1)(n + 2)}{2},$$

as desired.   ∎

Note the phrase "by induction on n" at the start of the proof. This is not strictly necessary, but it helps the reader by telling him or her how we're going to prove the theorem.

B.3.4   Proof by Cases

In this method, the universe of possibilities is divided into cases and the claim is proved for each case separately. We don't know which case applies—typically, all of the cases are possible. But since we've proved the claim for every case, it doesn't matter which case holds.

Theorem B.13 *Let k be a perfect cube. Then k is either a multiple of 9, or 1 more than a multiple of 9, or 1 less than a multiple of 9.*

Proof: Since k is a perfect cube, there exists an integer n such that $k = n^3$. Every integer is either a multiple of 3, or 1 more than a multiple of 3, or 1 less than a multiple of 3. We will consider three cases:

Case 1: n is a multiple of 3.

Then there exists an integer p such that $n = 3p$. Then $k = n^3 = 9p^3$, so k is a multiple of 9.

Case 2: n is 1 more than a multiple of 3.

Then there exists an integer p such that $n = 3p + 1$. Then $k = n^3 = 27p^3 + 27p^3 + 9p + 1$, which is 1 more than a multiple of 9.

Case 3: n is 1 less than a multiple of 3.

Then there exists an integer p such that $n = 3p - 1$. Then $k = n^3 = 27p^3 - 27p^3 + 9p - 1$, which is 1 less than a multiple of 9.   ∎

B.4   OTHER ADVICE

- *Provide explanations, not just math.* Even though your reader may be a smart mathematician, you should still provide verbal explanations that explain the intuition behind the math whenever the math is a bit complicated. This applies to derivations, but also to definitions.

  For example, suppose you want to say:

  > Let t_i be the order times, let T be the set of order times, let $S = \{t | I(t^-) > 0, t \in T\}$, and let $t_{min} = \operatorname{argmin}_t \{t \in S\}$.

  Then you may wish to help out your reader a bit by also saying:

  > That is, S is the set of order times for which the inventory level (just before ordering) is positive, and t_{min} is the earliest such time.

- *Distinguish between definitional and derivational $=$'s.* The $=$ sign has two meanings: One means "let the left-hand side be defined to equal the right-hand side" and the other means "I have now proved that the left-hand side equals the right-hand side." The first is a definitional equality, the second is a derivational equality. It is important to differentiate between them. The best way to do this is using words: "Let $x = y^2/2$." "Therefore, $s = r - D$." (The difference between these two types of equality is exactly the same as the difference between = and == in C/C++, Java, and other programming languages.)

  For example, consider the following proof fragment:

$$v = r - D$$
$$y = r^2$$
$$D = 2y$$
$$v = \sqrt{y} - 2y$$

  This fragment is confusing. Is v a new symbol that is being defined as $r - D$? Or do we already know that $v = r - D$? Did the first step prove that $y = r^2$? Or do we already know that $y = r^2$? Or is it another new symbol?

  True, a smart reader might be able to figure all this out. But the reader's life would be a lot easer if the proof-writer instead wrote:

  We know that $v = r - D$. Let $y = r^2$. Since $D = 2y$ (by Theorem 4.3), we have
  $$v = r - D = \sqrt{y} - 2y.$$

  This bullet is really a special case of the next.

- *Use complete sentences.* The first example in the previous bullet ($v = r - D$, etc.) becomes a lot easier to read when it's written using complete sentences. If you use sentences, the ambiguities of the $=$ sign are resolved. The same could be said about many other mathematical ambiguities and confusions. Writing in complete sentences—even if your English isn't very good—will instantly make your proofs easier to read.

- *Typeset thoughtfully.* If you are writing your proofs by hand, take care to write them neatly, and think carefully about how the proof will be laid out, including your use of white space. Even better, type your proofs using LATEX or another software package for typesetting mathematical text. Invest the time to learn how to typeset complicated math so that it looks nice and helps convey your meaning. Be considerate of your reader.

  For example, consider the following proof fragment:

$$[(hQ/2) + (K\lambda/Q)]/(hQ^*) = [hQ^2 + 2K\lambda]/(2hQQ^*).$$

The math would be a lot easier to follow if the proof-writer had written the fractions the way they were intended to be written:

$$\frac{\frac{hQ}{2} + \frac{K\lambda}{Q}}{hQ^*} = \frac{hQ^2 + 2K\lambda}{2hQQ^*}.$$

In general, thoughtfully typeset math will make your proof easier to read.

- *Don't stop here.* There are many books and other resources for learning how to write proofs. (See, e.g., Sundstrom (2006), Velleman (2006).) There are also lots of web sites devoted to the topic. Like web sites devoted to any topic, some of these are very good and others are very bad, so be a good critic when you read.

APPENDIX C

HELPFUL FORMULAS

These formulas use the following notation:

$$x^+ = \max\{x, 0\} = x \text{ if } x > 0 \text{ and } 0 \text{ otherwise}$$
$$x^- = |\min\{x, 0\}| = |x| \text{ if } x < 0 \text{ and } 0 \text{ otherwise}$$

(Some authors use $x^- = \min\{x, 0\}$.)

C.1 STANDARDIZING NORMAL RANDOM VARIABLES

Let $X \sim N(\mu, \sigma^2)$ with pdf f and cdf F. Let ϕ and Φ be the pdf and cdf, respectively, of the standard normal distribution.

$$f(x) = \frac{1}{\sigma} \phi \left(\frac{x - \mu}{\sigma} \right) \tag{C.1}$$

$$F(x) = \Phi \left(\frac{x - \mu}{\sigma} \right) \tag{C.2}$$

Fundamentals of Supply Chain Theory, First Edition. Lawrence V. Snyder, Zuo-Jun Max Shen.
© 2011 John Wiley & Sons, Inc. Published 2011 by John Wiley & Sons, Inc.

C.2 LOSS FUNCTIONS

C.2.1 General Distributions

Let X be a continuous, non-negative random variable with pdf f and cdf F. Let $\bar{F}(x) = 1 - F(x)$ be the complementary cdf. The *loss function* and *complementary loss function*[1] are given by

$$n(x) = E[(X - x)^+] = \int_x^\infty (y - x)f(y)dy = \int_x^\infty \bar{F}(y)dy \qquad (C.3)$$

$$\bar{n}(x) = E[(X - x)^-] = \int_0^x (x - y)f(y)dy = \int_0^x F(y)dy \qquad (C.4)$$

(If X can be negative, then the lower limit in (C.4) is replaced by $-\infty$.) The loss function and its complement are related as follows:

$$\bar{n}(x) = x - E[X] + n(x) \qquad (C.5)$$

The derivatives of the loss function and its complement are given by

$$n'(x) = F(x) - 1 \qquad (C.6)$$

$$\bar{n}'(x) = F(x) \qquad (C.7)$$

C.2.2 Standard Normal Distribution

Let $Z \sim N(0, 1)$, with pdf ϕ, cdf Φ, and complementary cdf $\bar{\Phi}$. The *standard normal loss function*, its complement, and their derivatives are given by

$$\mathscr{L}(z) = E[(Z - z)^+] = \int_z^\infty (t - z)\phi(t)dt = \phi(z) - z(1 - \Phi(z)) \qquad (C.8)$$

$$\bar{\mathscr{L}}(z) = E[(Z - z)^-] = \int_{-\infty}^z (z - t)\phi(t)dt = z + \mathscr{L}(z) \qquad (C.9)$$

$$\mathscr{L}'(z) = \Phi(z) - 1 \qquad (C.10)$$

$$\bar{\mathscr{L}}'(z) = \Phi(z) \qquad (C.11)$$

Also:

$$\mathscr{L}(-z) = z + \mathscr{L}(z) = \bar{\mathscr{L}}(z), \qquad (C.12)$$

(The second equation follows from the fact that ϕ is symmetric about 0.)

C.2.3 Non-Standard Normal Distributions

Let $X \sim N(\mu, \sigma^2)$ with pdf f, cdf F, and complementary cdf $\bar{F}$. The *normal loss function* can be computed using the standard normal loss function as follows:

$$n(x) = \int_x^\infty (t - x)f(t)dt = \sigma\mathscr{L}(z) \qquad (C.13)$$

---

[1]The term "complementary loss function" and the notation $\bar{n}(x)$ are our own. They are not standard.

$$\bar{n}(x) = \int_{-\infty}^{x} (x-t)f(t)dt = [z + \mathscr{L}(z)]\sigma \tag{C.14}$$

where $z = (x-\mu)/\sigma$. (In many instances, we assume $\sigma \ll \mu$ so that the probability that $X < 0$ is small; in these cases, we often replace the lower limit of the integral in (C.14) with 0.)

The derivatives of $n(x)$ and $\bar{n}(x)$ are given by (C.6)–(C.7).

C.3 DIFFERENTIATION OF INTEGRALS

C.3.1 Variable of Differentiation Not in Integral Limits

$$\frac{d}{dx} \int_{a}^{b} f(t,x)dt = \int_{a}^{b} \frac{\partial f(t,x)}{\partial x} dt \tag{C.15}$$

C.3.2 Variable of Differentiation in Integral Limits

$$\frac{d}{dx} \int_{a}^{x} f(t)dt = f(x) \tag{C.16}$$

$$\frac{d}{dx} \int_{a}^{g(x)} f(t)dt = f(g(x))g'(x) \tag{C.17}$$

$$\frac{d}{dx} \int_{g_1(x)}^{g_2(x)} f(t)dt = f(g_2(x))g_2'(x) - f(g_1(x))g_1'(x) \tag{C.18}$$

$$\frac{d}{dx} \int_{g_1(x)}^{g_2(x)} f(t,x)dt = \int_{g_1(x)}^{g_2(x)} \frac{\partial f(t,x)}{\partial x} dt + f(g_2(x),x)g_2'(x) - f(g_1(x),x)g_1'(x) \tag{C.19}$$

Equation (C.19) is known as *Leibniz's rule*.

C.4 GEOMETRIC SERIES

If $0 < |r| < 1$, then:

$$\sum_{i=0}^{\infty} r^i = \frac{1}{1-r} \tag{C.20}$$

$$\sum_{i=0}^{k} r^i = \frac{1-r^{k+1}}{1-r} \tag{C.21}$$

$$\sum_{i=k}^{\infty} r^i = \frac{r^k}{1-r} \tag{C.22}$$

$$\sum_{i=1}^{\infty} i r^{i-1} = \frac{1}{(1-r)^2} \tag{C.23}$$

$$\sum_{i=1}^{k} i r^{i-1} = \frac{1-r^k}{(1-r)^2} - \frac{k r^k}{1-r} \tag{C.24}$$

$$\sum_{i=k}^{\infty} i r^{i-1} = \frac{r^{k-1}}{(1-r)^2} + \frac{(k-1)r^{k-1}}{1-r} \tag{C.25}$$

C.5   NORMAL DISTRIBUTIONS IN MICROSOFT EXCEL

Excel has several built-in functions for computing normal distributions. If $X \sim N(\mu, \sigma^2)$ with pdf f and cdf F and $Z \sim N(0,1)$ with pdf ϕ and cdf Φ, then

$$\text{NORMDIST}(x, \mu, \sigma, \texttt{cumulative = FALSE}) \quad = f(x) \tag{C.26}$$
$$\text{NORMDIST}(x, \mu, \sigma, \texttt{cumulative = TRUE}) \quad = F(x) \tag{C.27}$$
$$\text{NORMSDIST}(z) \quad = \Phi(z) \tag{C.28}$$
$$\text{NORMINV}(p, \mu, \sigma) \quad = F^{-1}(p) \tag{C.29}$$
$$\text{NORMSINV}(p) \quad = \Phi^{-1}(p) \tag{C.30}$$

C.6   PARTIAL MEANS

The following formula computes the *partial mean*[2] of a random variable with pdf f and cdf F. (If $b = \infty$, the left-hand side would be the true mean.)

$$\int_0^b x f(x)\,dx = bF(b) - \int_0^b F(x)\,dx = bF(b) - \bar{n}(b) \tag{C.31}$$

A discrete version is also available:

$$\sum_{n=0}^{b} n f(n) = bF(b) - \sum_{n=0}^{b-1} F(n) \tag{C.32}$$

In addition:

$$\int_a^b x f(x)\,dx = bF(b) - \bar{n}(b) - aF(a) + \bar{n}(a) \tag{C.33}$$

---

[2] Again, our term.

APPENDIX D

LAGRANGIAN RELAXATION

D.1 OVERVIEW

Consider an optimization problem of the form

$$(P) \quad \text{minimize} \quad cx \qquad \qquad \text{(D.1)}$$
$$\text{subject to} \quad Ax = b \qquad \qquad \text{(D.2)}$$
$$Dx \le e \qquad \qquad \text{(D.3)}$$
$$x \ge 0 \text{ and binary} \qquad \qquad \text{(D.4)}$$

Here, x is a vector of decision variables, b, c, and e are vectors of coefficients, and A and D are matrices. (It's not necessary that all of the x variables be binary; some or all can be continuous.) Suppose that (P) itself is hard to solve, but that the problem obtained by omitting constraints (D.2) is easier. In this section, we discuss Lagrangian relaxation, a method that is well suited to solve problems like this one. Similar approaches can also be applied to other types of problems, such as nonlinear programming problems.

Fundamentals of Supply Chain Theory, First Edition. Lawrence V. Snyder, Zuo-Jun Max Shen.   **341**
© 2011 John Wiley & Sons, Inc. Published 2011 by John Wiley & Sons, Inc.

There are many sources of additional information about Lagrangian relaxation in journal articles and textbooks; among the most user-friendly treatments are the articles by Fisher (1981, 1985).

The idea behind *Lagrangian relaxation* is to relax (i.e., remove) the hard constraints (D.2) to produce an easier problem. When we remove the constraints, we add a term to the objective function that penalizes solutions for violating the relaxed constraints. This penalty term uses a vector λ of *Lagrange multipliers*, one per constraint, that dictate the magnitude of the penalty. The *Lagrangian subproblem* is then given by

$$(\text{P-LR}_\lambda) \quad \text{minimize} \quad cx + \lambda(b - Ax) \tag{D.5}$$
$$\text{subject to} \quad Dx \le e \tag{D.6}$$
$$x \ge 0 \text{ and binary} \tag{D.7}$$

Problem (P-LR_λ) is easier to solve than problem (P). This, by itself, does not help us very much, because solutions to (P-LR_λ) will typically be infeasible for (P). But it turns out that the optimal solution to (P-LR_λ) provides us with a *lower bound* on the optimal objective value of (P). Feasible solutions to (P) each provide an *upper bound* on the optimal objective value. Such solutions must be found using some other method, typically using a heuristic that is executed once per iteration of the Lagrangian relaxation procedure. When the upper and lower bounds are close (say, within 1%), we know that the feasible solution we have found is close to optimal.

When choosing which constraints to relax, i.e., which constraints to label as "hard," there are three main considerations:

- How easy the relaxed problem is to solve
- How tight the resulting lower bound is
- How many constraints are being relaxed

Choosing which constraints to relax is as much art as science, and often some trial and error is required.

D.2 BOUNDS

Let z^* be the optimal objective value of (P) and let $z_{\text{LR}}(\lambda)$ be the optimal objective value of (P-LR_λ). Let m be the number of rows in A, that is, the number of constraints in (D.2). Then we have the following result:

Theorem D.1 *For any $\lambda \in \mathbb{R}^m$,*

$$z_{\text{LR}}(\lambda) \le z^*.$$

Proof. Let x be a feasible solution for (P). Clearly x is feasible for (P-LR_λ), and it has the same objective value in both problems since the constraint violations all equal 0. Therefore, the optimal objective value for (P-LR$_\lambda$) is no greater than that of (P).   ∎

If (P) has a different structure than given in (D.1)–(D.4)—for example, if it is a maximization problem, or if (D.2) are inequality constraints—then we must make some modifications to Theorem D.1 (and the results that follow); see Section D.5

Since (P) is a minimization problem, we want lower bounds that are as large as possible; these are the most accurate and useful bounds. Different values of λ will give different values of $z_{LR}(\lambda)$, and hence different bounds. We'd like to find λ that gives the largest possible bounds. That is, we want to solve

$$\text{(LR)} \quad \max_\lambda \; z_{LR}(\lambda). \tag{D.8}$$

Suppose for now that we have found the λ^* that solves (LR). (We'll discuss one way to find such λ in Section D.3.) Let $z_{LR} = z_{LR}(\lambda^*)$. How good a bound is z_{LR}? For example, is it better or worse than the bound obtained from the LP relaxation of (P)? The answer turns out to be, "at least as good":

Theorem D.2

$$z_{LP} \le z_{LR},$$

where z_{LP} is the optimal objective value of the LP relaxation of (P) and z_{LR} is the optimal objective value of (LR).

Proof.

$$z_{LR} = \max_\lambda \left\{ \min_x \; cx + \lambda(b - Ax) \,\middle|\, Dx \le e, x \ge 0 \text{ and binary} \right\}$$

$$\ge \max_\lambda \left\{ \min_x \; cx + \lambda(b - Ax) \,\middle|\, Dx \le e, x \ge 0 \right\}$$

(since relaxing integrality can't increase the objective)

$$= \max_\lambda \left\{ \min_x \; (c - \lambda A)x + \lambda b \,\middle|\, Dx \le e, x \ge 0 \right\}$$

$$= \max_\lambda \left\{ \max_\mu \; \mu e + \lambda b \,\middle|\, \mu D \le c - \lambda A, \mu \le 0 \right\}$$

(taking LP dual of what's inside $\{\cdot\}$)

$$= \max_{\lambda,\mu} \left\{ \mu e + \lambda b \,\middle|\, \mu D \le c - \lambda A, \mu \le 0 \right\}$$

$$= \max_{\lambda,\mu} \left\{ \mu e + \lambda b \,\middle|\, \mu D + \lambda A \le c, \mu \le 0 \right\}$$

$$= \min_y \left\{ cy \,\middle|\, Ay = b, Dy \le e, y \ge 0 \right\} \quad \text{(taking LP dual of the entire problem)}$$

$$\tag{D.9}$$

$$= z_{LP}$$

∎

An optimization problem with binary variables is said to have the *integrality property* if its LP relaxation always has optimal solutions that are binary. If the

Lagrangian subproblem has the integrality property for all λ, then the bound from Lagrangian relaxation is exactly equal to the bound from LP relaxation:

Lemma D.1 *If* (P-LR_λ) *has the integrality property for all* λ, *then*

$$z_{\text{LP}} = z_{\text{LR}}.$$

Proof (sketch). The proof follows from the fact that the first two lines of (D.9) hold at equality since removing the integrality restriction does not change the problem. ∎

In a typical Lagrangian relaxation algorithm, we solve (P-LR_λ) for a given λ and then find a solution x that is feasible for (P). This is often done by modifying the solution to (P-LR_λ), converting it somehow from an infeasible solution to a feasible one. We then choose new multipliers λ in the hopes of improving the lower bound. Therefore, each iteration of the procedure consists of (1) solving (P-LR_λ), (2) finding an upper bound, and (3) updating the multipliers. In Section D.3, we discuss one common method for step (3).

To summarize what we have covered so far, at any given iteration of the Lagrangian relaxation procedure, we have

$$z_{\text{LR}}(\lambda) \leq z_{\text{LR}} \leq z^* \leq z(x) \tag{D.10}$$
$$z_{\text{LP}} \leq z_{\text{LR}} \leq z^* \leq z(x), \tag{D.11}$$

where

- $z_{\text{LR}}(\lambda)$ is the objective value of (P-LR_λ) for a particular λ (λ is a feasible solution to (LR))

- z_{LR} is the optimal objective value of (P-LR_λ)

- z_{LP} is the optimal objective value of the LP relaxation of (P)

- $z(x)$ is the objective value of (P) for a particular x (x is a feasible solution to (P))

- z^* is the optimal objective value of (P)

If (P-LR_λ) has the integrality property for all λ, then (D.10)–(D.11) reduce to

$$z_{\text{LR}}(\lambda) \leq z_{\text{LR}} = z_{\text{LP}} \leq z^* \leq z(x,y). \tag{D.12}$$

D.3 SUBGRADIENT OPTIMIZATION

At the end of each iteration of the Lagrangian relaxation procedure, we want to update the Lagrange multipliers to coax the subproblem solution toward feasibility for (P). Let x be the optimal solution to the Lagrangian subproblem for a given λ. Consider a given constraint i and its multiplier λ_i. Should we make λ_i larger or smaller? The answer depends on whether, and how, the constraint is violated. We can write constraint i as

$$\sum_{j=1}^{n} a_{ij}x_j = b_i, \tag{D.13}$$

where n is the number of variables. We are trying to encourage the solution to satisfy this constraint by adding the penalty term

$$\lambda_i \left(b_i - \sum_{j=1}^{n} a_{ij}x_j \right) \tag{D.14}$$

to the objective function. If λ_i is too small, then there's no real penalty for making $\sum_{j=1}^{n} a_{ij}x_j$ small, and it's likely that the left-hand side of (D.13) will be too small. On the other hand, if λ_i is too large, there will be an incentive to make $\sum_{j=1}^{n} a_{ij}x_j$ large, making the term inside the parentheses in (D.14) negative and the overall penalty large and negative. (Remember that (P) is a minimization problem.) By changing λ_i, we can encourage $\sum_{j=1}^{n} a_{ij}x_j$ to be larger or smaller—hopefully equal to b_i—at the next iteration.

So:

- If $\sum_{j=1}^{n} a_{ij}x_j < b_i$, then λ_i is too small; it should be increased.

- If $\sum_{j=1}^{n} a_{ij}x_j > b_i$, then λ_i is too large; it should be decreased.

- If $\sum_{j=1}^{n} a_{ij}x_j = b_i$, then λ_i is just right; it should not be changed.

Now, $z_{\text{LR}}(\lambda)$ is a piecewise-linear concave function of λ. Solving problem (LR) involves maximizing this function. Since it's piecewise-linear (and therefore non-differentiable at some points), we can't just take a derivative with respect to λ. Somehow, though, we want to move from our current value of λ to a better one, over and over, until we're near the maximum of the function.

We will use a common method for updating the Lagrange multipliers called *subgradient optimization*. (Other methods for nonlinear optimization, such as the volume algorithm and bundle methods, have also proved to be very effective for updating Lagrangian multipliers.) In subgradient optimization, each move consists of a step *size* (which is the same for all i) and a step *direction* (which is different for each i).

The step size at iteration t (denoted Δ^t) is computed as follows. Let $\mathcal{L}^t$ be the lower bound found at iteration t (i.e., the value of $z_{\text{LR}}(\lambda)$ for the current value of λ) and let UB be the best upper bound found (i.e., the objective value of the best feasible solution found so far, by any method). Note that while $\mathcal{L}^t$ is the *last* lower bound found, UB is the *best* upper bound found. Then the step size Δ^t is given by

$$\Delta^t = \frac{\alpha^t (\text{UB} - \mathcal{L}^t)}{\sum_{i=1}^{m} \left(b_i - \sum_{j=1}^{n} a_{ij}x_j \right)^2}. \tag{D.15}$$

α^t is a constant that is generally set to 2 at iteration 1 and divided by 2 after a given number (say 20) of consecutive iterations have passed during which the best known lower bound has not improved. The numerator is proportional to the difference between the upper and lower bounds—as we get closer to the maximum of the function, the steps should get smaller. The denominator is simply the sum of the squares of the constraint violations.

The step direction for constraint i is simply given by $b_i - \sum_{j=1}^{n} a_{ij}x_j$ (the violation in the constraint).

To obtain the new multipliers (call them λ^{t+1}) from the old ones (λ^t), we set

$$\lambda_i^{t+1} = \lambda_i^t + \Delta^t \left(b_i - \sum_{j=1}^{n} a_{ij}x_j \right). \tag{D.16}$$

Note that since $\Delta^t > 0$, this update step follows the rules given above:

- If $\sum_{j=1}^{n} a_{ij}x_j < b_i$, then λ_i increases.

- If $\sum_{j=1}^{n} a_{ij}x_j > b_i$, then λ_i decreases.

- If $\sum_{j=1}^{n} a_{ij}x_j = b_i$, then λ_i stays the same.

At the first iteration, λ can be initialized using a variety of ways: For example, set $\lambda_i = 0$ for all i, set it to some random number, or set it according to some other ad-hoc rule.

D.4   STOPPING CRITERIA

The process of solving (P-LR$_\lambda$), finding a feasible solution, and updating λ is continued until some stopping criteria are met. For example, we might stop the procedure when any of the following is true:

- The upper bound and lower bound are within some pre-specified tolerance, say 0.1%

- A certain number of iterations, say 1000, have elapsed

- α^t is smaller than some pre-specified tolerance, say 10^{-6}

D.5   OTHER PROBLEM TYPES

Lagrangian relaxation is a general tool that can be used for any IP. However, some of the rules discussed above change when applied to IPs that have a form other than that given in (D.1)–(D.4).

D.5.1 : Inequality Constraints

The constraints relaxed may be inequality or equality constraints.

- For $\leq$ constraints, λ is restricted to be *non-positive*.

- For $\geq$ constraints, λ is restricted to be *non-negative*.

- For $=$ constraints, λ is unrestricted in sign.

(*Note*: These rules assume the penalty in the objective function is written as

$$\lambda(\text{RHS} - \text{LHS}).$$

If, instead, the right-hand side is subtracted from the left-hand side, these rules are reversed.)

D.5.2 Maximization Problems

If the IP is a maximization problem, then

- The Lagrangian subproblem provides an *upper bound* on the optimal objective value and a feasible solution provides a *lower bound*, so the relationships in (D.10) and (D.11) are reversed:

$$z(x) \leq z^* \leq z_{\text{LR}} \leq z_{\text{LR}}(\lambda) \qquad\qquad (\text{D.17})$$
$$z(x) \leq z^* \leq z_{\text{LR}} \leq z_{\text{LP}}. \qquad\qquad (\text{D.18})$$

- Problem (LR) is of the form

$$\min_{\lambda} \left\{ \begin{array}{l} \max_x \quad \cdots \\ \text{s.t.} \quad \cdots \end{array} \right\}$$

- The $+$ sign in (D.16) becomes a $-$ sign.

- The rules for inequality constraints given in Section D.5.1 are reversed.

D.6 BRANCH AND BOUND

If the Lagrangian procedure stops before the upper and lower bounds are close to each other, there is no guarantee that the solution found is near-optimal. If this happens, we could stop and accept the best feasible solution found without a guarantee of optimality (this treats Lagrangian relaxation as a heuristic), or we could close the optimality gap using branch and bound. The branch and bound process is like the standard process for solving LPs except that (a) lower bounds are obtained by solving the Lagrangian subproblem, not the LP relaxation, and (b) upper bounds are found using the upper-bounding method that is embedded into the Lagrangian procedure, instead of when LP solutions happen to be integer-feasible. At each node of the branch-and-bound tree, a variable is chosen for branching, and that variable is fixed first to 0, then to 1. The mechanics of branching and fathoming are just like those in standard branch and bound.

D.7 ALGORITHM SUMMARY

The Lagrangian relaxation algorithm is summarized below:

Algorithm D.1 (Lagrangian Relaxation)

1. Initialize λ_i for all $i = 1, \ldots, m$.

2. Solve (P-LR$_\lambda$) for the current value of λ.

3. Using the solution to (P-LR$_\lambda$) (or some other method), generate a feasible solution for (P).

4. Update the multipliers using subgradient optimization. If any of the termination criteria is met, go to 5. Otherwise, go to 2.

5. If the (absolute or percentage) gap between the best-known upper and lower bounds is smaller than the desired tolerance, STOP. Otherwise, use branch and bound to close the gap. This algorithm is used at each node of the branch-and-bound tree, with certain variables fixed to 0 or 1.

Bibliography

I. Averbakh and O. Berman. Algorithms for the robust 1-center problem on a tree. *European Journal of Operational Research*, 123(2):292–302, 2000a.

I. Averbakh and O. Berman. Minmax regret median location on a network under uncertainty. *INFORMS Journal on Computing*, 12(2):104–110, 2000b.

S. Axsäter. Simple solution procedures for a class of two-echelon inventory problems. *Operations Research*, 38(1):64–69, 1990.

S. Axsäter. Using the deterministic EOQ formula in stochastic inventory control. *Management Science*, 42(6):830–834, 1996.

B. Aytac and S. Wu. Characterization of demand for short life-cycle technology products. Forthcoming in *Annals of Operations Research*, 2010.

F. Bass. A new product growth model for consumer durables. *Management Science*, 15(5): 215–227, 1969.

F. Bass. Comments on "A new product growth for model consumer durables": The Bass model. *Management Science*, 50(12S):1833–1840, 2004.

J. Bearwood, H. Halton, and J. Hammersley. The shortest path through many points. *Proceedings of the Cambridge Philosophical Society*, 55:299–327, 1959.

S. Beggs, S. Cardell, and J. Hausman. Assessing the potential demand for electric cars. *Journal of Econometrics*, 16:1–19, 1981.

M. Ben-Akiva and S. Lerman. *Discrete Choice Analysis: Theory and Application to Travel Demand*. MIT Press, 1985.

E. Berk and A. Arreola-Risa. Note on "Future supply uncertainty in EOQ models". *Naval Research Logistics*, 41:129–132, 1994.

O. Berman, D. Krass, and M. B. C. Menezes. Facility reliability issues in network p-median problems: Strategic centralization and co-location effects. *Operations Research*, 55(2): 332–350, 2007.

S. Biller, A. Muriel, and Y. Zhang. Impact of price postponement on capacity and flexibility investment decisions. *Production and Operations Management*, 15(2):198–214, 2006.

N. Boudette. Chrysler gains edge by giving new flexibility to its factories. *Wall Street Journal*, April 11 2006.

S. Boyd and L. Vandenberghe. *Convex Optimization*. Cambridge University Press, New York, 2004.

G. P. Cachon. Supply chain coordination with contracts. In A. G. de Kok and S. C. Graves, editors, *Supply Chain Management: Design, Coordination and Operation*, volume 11 of *Handbooks in Operations Research and Management Science*, chapter 6. North-Holland, 2003.

G. P. Cachon and M. A. Lariviere. Supply chain coordination with revenue-sharing contracts: Strengths and limitations. *Management Science*, 51(1):30–44, 2005.

G. P. Cachon and S. Netessine. Game theory in supply chain analysis. In D. Simchi-Levi, S. D. Wu, and Z.-J. M. Shen, editors, *Handbook of Quantitative Supply Chain Analysis: Modeling in the E-Business Era*, chapter 2. Springer, New York, 2004.

L. M. A. Chan, A. Muriel, Z.-J. M. Shen, and D. Simchi-Levi. On the effectiveness of zero-inventory-ordering policies for the economic lot-sizing model with a class of piecewise linear cost structures. *Operations Research*, 50(6):1058–1067, 2002.

B. Chen and C.-S. Lin. Minmax-regret robust 1-median location on a tree. *Networks*, 31(2): 93–103, 1998.

F. Chen and R. Samroengraja. The stationary beer game. *Production and Operations Management*, 9(1):19–30, 2000.

F. Chen and Y. S. Zheng. Lower bounds for multi-echelon stochastic inventory systems. *Management Science*, 40(11):1426–1443, 1994.

F. Chen, Z. Drezner, J. K. Ryan, and D. Simchi-Levi. Quantifying the bullwhip effect in a simple supply chain: The impact of forecasting, lead times, and information. *Management Science*, 46(3):436–443, 2000.

R. R. Chen, R. O. Roundy, R. Q. Zhang, and G. Janakiraman. Efficient auction mechanisms for supply chain procurement. *Management Science*, 51(3):467–482, 2005.

R. Cheung and W. Powell. Models and algorithms for distribution problems with uncertain demands. *Transportation Science*, 30(1):43–59, 1996.

S. Chopra and P. Meindl. *Supply Chain Management: Strategy, Planning and Operation*. Prentice-Hall, Upper Saddle River, NJ, 2001.

M. Chou, G. A. Chua, C. Teo, and H. Zheng. Process flexibility revisited: The graph expander and its applications. Working Paper, NUS Business School, National University of Singapore, Singapore, 2007.

M. Chou, G. Chua, and C. Teo. On range and response: Dimensions of process flexibility. Working Paper, NUS Business School, National University of Singapore, Singapore, 2008a.

M. Chou, C. Teo, and H. Zheng. Process flexibility: Design, evaluation and applications. *Flexible Services and Manufacturing Journal*, 20:59–94, 2008b.

L. Y. Chu and Z.-J. Shen. Agent competition double auction mechanism. *Management Science*, 52:1215–1222, 2006.

L. Y. Chu and Z.-J. Shen. Truthful double auction mechanisms. *Operations Research*, 56: 102–120, 2008.

A. J. Clark and H. Scarf. Optimal policies for a multi-echelon inventory problem. *Management Science*, 6(4):475–490, 1960.

J. L. Cohon. *Multiobjective Programming and Planning*. Academic Press, New York, 1978.

G. Cornuejols, M. L. Fisher, and G. L. Nemhauser. Location of bank accounts to optimize float: An analytic study of exact and approximate algorithms. *Management Science*, 23 (8):789–810, 1977.

Council of Supply Chain Management Professionals (CSCMP). 21st annual state of logistics report: The great freight recession, June 9 2010.

Council of Supply Chain Management Professionals (CSCMP). Supply chain management definitions, 2011. URL http://cscmp.org/aboutcscmp/definitions.asp.

T. Cui, Y. Ouyang, and Z.-J. M. Shen. Reliable facility location design under the risk of disruptions. *Operations Research*, 58(4):998–1011, 2010.

M. S. Daskin. *Network and Discrete Location: Models, Algorithms, and Applications*. Wiley, New York, 1995.

M. S. Daskin, C. R. Coullard, and Z.-J. M. Shen. An inventory-location model: Formulation, solution algorithm and computational results. *Annals of Operations Research*, 110: 83–106, 2002.

S. de Vries and R. V. Vohra. Combinatorial auctions: A survey. *INFORMS Journal on Computing*, 15(3):284–309, 2003.

K. DesMarteau. Leading the way in changing times. *Bobbin*, 41(2):48–54, 1999.

Z. Drezner, editor. *Facility Location: A Survey of Applications and Methods*. Springer-Verlag, New York, 1995.

Z. Drezner and H. W. Hamacher, editors. *Facility Location: Applications and Theory*. Springer-Verlag, New York, 2002.

M. A. Efroymson and T. L. Ray. A branch-bound algorithm for plant location. *Operations Research*, 14(3):361–368, 1966.

R. Ehrhardt. The power approximation for computing (s, S) inventory policies. *Management Science*, 25(8):777–786, 1979.

R. Ehrhardt and C. Mosier. A revision of the power approximation for computing (s, S) policies. *Management Science*, 30(5):618–622, 1984.

G. D. Eppen. Effects of centralization on expected costs in a multi-location newsboy problem. *Management Science*, 25(5):498–501, 1979.

R. Epstein, L. Henríquez, J. Catalán, G. Y. Weintraub, C. Martínez, and F. Espejo. A combinatorial auction improves school meals in Chile: A case of OR in developing countries. *International Transactions in Operational Research*, 11:593–612, 2004.

D. Erlenkotter. A dual-based procedure for uncapacitated facility location. *Operations Research*, 26(6):992–1009, 1978.

A. Federgruen and M. Tzur. A simple forward algorithm to solve general dynamic lot sizing models with n periods in $O(n \log n)$ or $O(n)$ time. *Management Science*, 37(8): 909–925, 1991.

A. Federgruen and Y.-S. Zheng. An efficient algorithm for computing an optimal (r, Q) policy in continuous review stochastic inventory systems. *Operations Research*, 40(4): 808–813, 1992.

A. Federgruen and P. Zipkin. Computational issues in an infinite-horizon, multiechelon inventory model. *Operations Research*, 32(2):818–836, 1984.

M. L. Fisher. The Lagrangian relaxation method for solving integer programming problems. *Management Science*, 27(1):1–18, 1981.

M. L. Fisher. An applications oriented guide to Lagrangian relaxation. *Interfaces*, 15(2): 10–21, 1985.

M. Florian, J. K. Lenstra, and A. H. G. Rinnooy Kan. Deterministic production planning: Algorithms and complexity. *Management Science*, 26(7):669–679, 1980.

J. W. Forrester. Industrial dynamics: A major breakthrough for decision makers. *Harvard Business Review*, 36(4):37–66, 1958.

G. Gallego, O. Özer, and P. H. Zipkin. Bounds, heuristics, and approximations for distribution systems. *Operations Research*, 55(3):503–517, 2007.

L. Garrow. *Discrete Choice Modelling and Air Travel Demand: Theory and Applications.* Ashgane Publishing, 2010.

S. Geary, S. M. Disney, and D. R. Towill. On bullwhip in supply chains—historical review, present practice and expected future impact. *International Journal of Production Economics*, 101(1):2–18, 2006.

A. M. Geoffrion and G. W. Graves. Multicommodity distribution system design by Benders decomposition. *Management Science*, 20(5):822–844, 1974.

S. Graves and B. Tomlin. Process flexibility in supply chains. *Management Science*, 49(7): 907–919, 2003.

S. C. Graves. A multi-echelon inventory model for a repairable item with one-for-one replenishment. *Management Science*, 31(10):1247–1256, 1985.

S. C. Graves. Safety stocks in manufacturing systems. *Journal of Manufacturing and Operations Management*, 1:67–101, 1988.

S. C. Graves and S. P. Willems. Optimizing strategic safety stock placement in supply chains. *Manufacturing and Service Operations Management*, 2(1):68–83, 2000.

S. C. Graves and S. P. Willems. Supply chain design: Safety stock placement and supply chain configuration. In A. G. de Kok and S. C. Graves, editors, *Supply Chain Management: Design, Coordination and Operation*, volume 11 of *Handbooks in Operations Research and Management Science*, chapter 3. North-Holland, Amsterdam, 2003a.

S. C. Graves and S. P. Willems. Erratum: Optimization strategic safety stock placement in supply chains. *Manufacturing and Service Operations Management*, 5(2):176–177, 2003b.

A. Grosfeld Nir and Y. Gerchak. Multiple lotsizing in production to order with random yields: Review of recent advances. *Annals of Operations Research*, 126(1-4):43–69, 2004.

R. Güllü, E. Onol, and N. Erkip. Analysis of a deterministic demand production/inventory system under nonstationary supply uncertainty. *IIE Transactions*, 29:703–709, 1997.

R. Güllü, E. Önol, and N. Erkip. Analysis of an inventory system under supply uncertainty. *International Journal of Production Economics*, 59:377–385, 1999.

R. Hariharan and P. Zipkin. Customer-order information, leadtimes, and inventories. *Management Science*, 41(10):1599–1607, 1995.

F. W. Harris. How many parts to make at once. *Factory: The Magazine of Management*, 10 (2):135, reprinted in *Operations Research* **38**(6), 947–950, 1990, 1913.

A. C. Hax and D. Candea. *Production and Inventory Management*. Prentice-Hall, Englewood Cliffs, NJ, 1984.

J. Henry. BMW says flexible, not lean, is the next big thing in autos. *BNET*, November 24 2009.

Y. T. Herer, M. Tzur, and E. Yücesan. The multi-location transshipment problem. *IIE Transactions*, 38(3):185–200, 2006.

J. L. Heskett and S. Signorelli. Benetton (A). Harvard Business School Case, Sep. 13 1984.

I. Higa, A. M. Feyerherm, and A. L. Machado. Waiting time in an $(S-1, S)$ inventory system. *Operations Research*, 23(4):674–680, 1975.

T. H. Ho, S. Savin, and C. Terwiesch. Managing demand and sales dynamics in new product diffusion under supply constraint. *Management Science*, 48(2):187–206, 2002.

C. C. Holt. Forecasting seasonal and trends by exponentially weighted moving averages. Office of Naval Research Memorandum, No. 52, 1957.

T. Ida and T. Kuroda. Discrete choice model analysis of demand for mobile telephone service in Japan. *Empirical Economics*, 36:65–80, 2009.

K. Inderfurth. Safety stock optimization in multi-stage inventory systems. *International Journal of Production Economics*, 24:103–113, 1991.

W. C. Jordan and S. C. Graves. Principles on the benefits of manufacturing process flexibility. *Management Science*, 41(4):577–594, 1995.

J. Kalagnanam and D. C. Parkes. Auctions, bidding and exchange design. In D. Simchi-Levi, S. D. Wu, and Z.-J. M. Shen, editors, *Handbook of Quantitative Supply Chain Analysis: Modeling in the E-Business Era*, chapter 5. Springer, New York, 2004.

G. E. Kimball. General principles of inventory control. *Journal of Manufacturing and Operations Management*, 1:119–130, 1988.

F. Koppelman. Travel prediction with models of individualistic choice behavior. Technical report, Department of Civil Engineering, MIT, Cambridge, Mass., 1975.

A. A. Kuehn and M. J. Hamburger. A heuristic program for locating warehouses. *Management Science*, 9(4):643–666, 1963.

S. Kunnumkal and H. Topaloglu. A duality-based relaxation and decomposition approach for inventory distribution systems. *Naval Research Logistics*, 55(7):612–631, 2008.

A. A. Kurawarwala and H. Matsuo. Forecasting and inventory management of short life-cycle products. *Operations Research*, 44(1):131–150, 1996.

H. L. Lee. Effective inventory and service management through product and process redesign. *Operations Research*, 44(1):151–159, 1996.

H. L. Lee and C. Billington. Material management in decentralized supply chains. *Operations Research*, 41(5):835–847, 1993.

H. L. Lee, V. Padmanabhan, and S. Whang. Information distortion in a supply chain: The bullwhip effect. *Management Science*, 43(4):546–558, 1997a.

H. L. Lee, V. Padmanabhan, and S. Whang. The bullwhip effect in supply chains. *Sloan Management Review*, 38(3):93–102, 1997b.

H. L. Lee, V. Padmanabhan, and S. Whang. Comments on "Information distortion in a supply chain: The bullwhip effect". *Management Science*, 50(12S):1887–1893, 2004.

S. Li and Z.-J. Shen. Optimal introduction timing for a product line extension with operational cost considerations. Working paper, University of California, Berkeley, 2008.

X. Li and Y. Ouyang. A continuum approximation approach to reliable facility location design under correlated probabilistic disruptions. *Transportation Research–Part B*, 44 (4):535–548, 2010.

G. L. Lilien and A. Rangaswamy. *Marketing Engineering: Computer-Assistend Marketing Analysis and Planning*. Addison-Wesley Educational Publishers, 1998.

G. L. Lilien, A. Rangaswamy, and A. D. Bruyn. *Principles of Marketing Engineering*. Trafford Publishing, 2007.

M. Lim, A. Bassamboo, S. Chopra, and M. S. Daskin. Flexibility and fragility: Supply chain network design with disruption risks. Working paper, Department of Industrial Engineering and Management Sciences, Northwestern University, Evanston, IL, 2009.

K. Linebaugh. Honda's flexible plants provide edge. *Wall Street Journal*, September 23 2008.

T. L. Magnanti, Z.-J. M. Shen, J. Shu, D. Simchi-Levi, and C.-P. Teo. Inventory placement in acyclic supply chain networks. *Operations Research Letters*, 34:228–238, 2006.

V. Mahajan, E. Muller, and F. M. Bass. Diffusion of new products: Empirical generalizations and managerial uses. *Marketing Science*, 14(3S):G79–G88, 1995.

H. Mak and Z.-J. Shen. Stochastic programming approach to process flexibility design. *Flexible Services and Manufacturing Journal*, 21(3):75–91, 2009.

F. E. Maranzana. On the location of supply points to minimize transport costs. *Operational Research Quarterly*, 15(3):261–270, 1964.

P. McCullen and D. Towill. Diagnosis and reduction of bullwhip in supply chains. *Supply Chain Management*, 7(3):164–179, 2002.

D. McCutcheon. Flexible manufacturing: IBM's Bromont semiconductor packaging plant. *Canadian Electronics*, 19(7):26, 2004.

D. L. McFadden. *Conditional Logit Analysis of Qualitative Choice Behavior*. Academic Press, New York, 1974.

D. L. McFadden. Econometric analysis of qualitative response models. In *Handbook of Econometrics*, volume 2. Elsevier Science Publishers BV, 1984.

M. J. Meixell and D. S. Wu. Scenario analysis of demand in a technology market using leading indicators. *IEEE Transactions on Semiconductor Manufacturing*, 14(1):65–75, 2001.

P. B. Mirchandani. Locational decisions on stochastic networks. *Geographical Analysis*, 12 (2):172–183, 1980.

P. B. Mirchandani and R. L. Francis, editors. *Discrete Location Theory*. Wiley-Interscience, New York, 1990.

N. Mladenovic, J. Brimberg, P. Hansen, and J. A. Moreno-Pérez. The p-median problem: A survey of metaheuristic approaches. *European Journal of Operational Research*, 179 (3):927–939, 2007.

J. A. Muckstadt and R. O. Roundy. Analysis of multistage production systems. In S. Graves, A. Rinnooy Kan, and P. Zipkin, editors, *Handbooks in Operations Research and Man-*

agement Science, vol. 4: Logistics of Production and Inventory, chapter 2, pages 59–131. Elsevier, 1993.

R. B. Myerson and M. A. Satterthwaite. Efficient mechanisms for bilateral trading. *Journal of Economic Theory*, 29(2):265–281, 1983.

S. Nahmias. *Production and Operations Analysis*. McGraw-Hill/Irwin, 5th edition, 2005.

M. J. Osborne. *An Introduction to Game Theory*. Oxford University Press, New York, 2003.

O. Özer and H. Xiong. Stock positioning and performance estimation for distribution systems with service constraints. *IIE Transactions*, 40(12):1141–1157, 2008.

M. Parlar and D. Berkin. Future supply uncertainty in EOQ models. *Naval Research Logistics*, 38:107–121, 1991.

B. A. Pasternack. Optimal pricing and return policies for perishable commodities. *Marketing Science*, 4(2):166–176, 1985.

E. Paz-Frankel. Truck driver turnover reaches record level. *Memphis Business Journal*, April 2 2006.

M. Phelan. Ford speeds changeovers in engine production. Knight Ridder Tribune Business News, Washington, Nov. 6 2002.

H. Pirkul and V. Jayaraman. Production, transportation, and distribution planning in a multi-commodity tri-echelon system. *Transportation Science*, 30(4):291–302, 1996.

L. Qi, Z.-J. M. Shen, and L. V. Snyder. The effect of supply disruptions on supply chain design decisions. *Transportation Science*, 44(2):274–289, 2010.

M. Ramming. *Network Knowledge and Route Choice*. PhD thesis, Massachusetts Institute of Technology, 2001.

C. S. ReVelle and R. W. Swain. Central facilities location. *Geographical Analysis*, 2:30–42, 1970.

L. W. Robinson. Optimal and approximate policies in multiperiod, multilocation inventory models with transshipments. *Operations Research*, 38(2):278–295, 1990.

Y. Rong, L. V. Snyder, and Z.-J. M. Shen. Bullwhip and reverse bullwhip effects under the rationing game. Working paper, 2010.

Y. Rong, Z. Atan, and L. V. Snyder. Heuristics for base-stock levels in locally controlled multi-echelon distribution networks with first-come first served policies. Working paper, 2011.

K. Rosling. Optimal inventory policies for assembly systems under random demands. *Operations Research*, 37(4):565–579, 1989.

S. M. Ross. *Stochastic Processes*. Wiley, 2nd edition, 1995.

R. Roundy. 98%-effective integer-ratio lot-sizing for one-warehouse multi-retailer systems. *Management Science*, 31(11):1416–1430, 1985.

P. Rusmevichientong, Z.-J. Shen, and D. B. Shmoys. Dynamic assortment optimization with a multinomial logit choice model and capacity constraint. *Operations Research*, 58(6): 1666–1680, 2010.

J. K. Ryan. *Analysis of inventory models with limited demand information*. Ph.D. dissertation, Northwestern University, Department of Industrial Engineering and Management Sciences, Evanston, IL, 1997.

S. Savin and C. Terwiesch. Optimal product launch times in a duopoly: Balancing life-cycle revenues with product cost. *Operations Research*, 53(1):26–47, 2005.

H. Scarf. The optimality of (s, S) policies in the dynamic inventory problem. In K. Arrow, S. Karlin, and P. Suppes, editors, *Mathematical Methods in the Social Sciences*, chapter 13. Stanford University Press, Stanford, CA, 1960.

G. M. Schmidt and C. T. Druehl. Changes in product attributes and costs as drivers of new product diffusion and substitution. *Production and Operations Management*, 14(3): 272–285, 2005.

A. J. Schmitt, L. V. Snyder, and Z.-J. M. Shen. Centralization versus decentralization: Risk pooling, risk diversification, and supply uncertainty in a one-warehouse multiple-retailer system. Working paper, 2010a.

A. J. Schmitt, L. V. Snyder, and Z.-J. M. Shen. Inventory systems with stochastic demand and supply: Properties and approximations. *European Journal of Operational Research*, 206(2):313–328, 2010b.

D. Serra and V. Marianov. The p-median problem in a changing network: The case of Barcelona. *Location Science*, 6:383–394, 1998.

D. Serra, S. Ratick, and C. ReVelle. The maximum capture problem with uncertainty. *Environment and Planning B*, 23:49–59, 1996.

K. H. Shang and J.-S. Song. Newsvendor bounds and heuristic for optimal policies in serial supply chains. *Management Science*, 49(5):618–638, 2003.

Z.-J. M. Shen, C. R. Coullard, and M. S. Daskin. A joint location-inventory model. *Transportation Science*, 37(1):40–55, 2003.

Z.-J. M. Shen, R. L. Zhan, and J. Zhang. The reliable facility location problem: Formulations, heuristics, and approximation algorithms. Forthcoming in *INFORMS Journal on Computing*, 2010.

C. C. Sherbrooke. METRIC: A multi-echelon technique for recoverable item control. *Operations Research*, 16(1):122–141, 1968.

C. C. Sherbrooke. Waiting time in an $(S - 1, S)$ inventory system: Constant service time case. *Operations Research*, 23(4):819–820, 1975.

J. Shu, C.-P. Teo, and Z.-J. M. Shen. Stochastic transportation-inventory network design problem. *Operations Research*, 53(1):48–60, 2005.

E. A. Silver, D. F. Pyke, and R. Peterson. *Inventory Management and Production Planning and Scheduling*. Wiley, 3rd edition, 1998.

K. F. Simpson, Jr. In-process inventories. *Operations Research*, 6(6):863–873, 1958.

L. V. Snyder. Facility location under uncertainty: A review. *IIE Transactions*, 38(7):537–554, 2006.

L. V. Snyder. A tight approximation for a continuous-review inventory model with supplier disruptions. Working paper, 2009.

L. V. Snyder and M. S. Daskin. Reliability models for facility location: The expected failure cost case. *Transportation Science*, 39(3):400–416, 2005.

L. V. Snyder and M. S. Daskin. Models for reliable supply chain network design. In A. T. Murray and T. H. Grubesic, editors, *Reliability and Vulnerability in Critical Infrastructure: A Quantitative Geographic Perspective*, chapter 13, pages 257–289. Springer, 2007.

L. V. Snyder and Z.-J. M. Shen. Supply and demand uncertainty in multi-echelon supply chains. Working paper, 2006.

L. V. Snyder and B. T. Tomlin. On the value of a threat advisory system for managing supply chain disruptions. Working paper, 2006.

L. V. Snyder, M. P. Scaparra, M. S. Daskin, and R. L. Church. Planning for disruptions in supply chain networks. In M. P. Johnson, B. Norman, and N. Secomandi, editors, *Tutorials in Operations Research*, chapter 9, pages 234–257. INFORMS, 2006.

L. V. Snyder, Z. Atan, P. Peng, Y. Rong, A. Schmitt, and B. Sinsoysal. OR/MS models for supply chain disruptions: A review. Working paper, 2010.

J.-S. Song and P. H. Zipkin. Inventory control with information about supply conditions. *Management Science*, 42(10):1409–1419, 1996.

J. J. Spengler. Vertical integration and antitrust policy. *Journal of Political Economy*, 58(4): 347–352, 1950.

J. D. Sterman. Modeling managerial behavior: Misperceptions of feedback in a dynamic decision making experiment. *Management Science*, 35(3):321–339, 1989.

F. Sultan, J. U. Farley, and D. R. Lehmann. A meta-analysis of applications of diffusion models. *Journal of Marketing Research*, 27(1):70–77, 1990.

T. Sundstrom. *Mathematical Reasoning: Writing and Proof*. Prentice Hall, Upper Saddle River, NJ, 2nd edition, 2006.

J. M. Swaminathan and S. R. Tayur. Managing broader product lines through delayed differentiation using vanilla boxes. *Management Science*, 44(12):S161–S172, 1998.

G. Tagaras. Effects of pooling on the optimization and service levels of two-location inventory systems. *IIE Transactions*, 21:250–257, 1989.

G. Tagaras. Pooling in multi-location periodic inventory distribution systems. *Omega*, 27: 39–59, 1999.

A. C. Tamhane and D. D. Dunlop. *Statistics and Data Analysis: From Elementary to Intermediate*. Prentice Hall, 1999.

M. B. Teitz and P. Bart. Heuristic methods for estimating the generalized vertex median of a weighted graph. *Operations Research*, 16(5):955–961, 1968.

B. T. Tomlin. On the value of mitigation and contingency strategies for managing supply-chaindisruption risks (unabridged version). Working paper, Kenan-Flagler Business School, UNC-Chapel Hill, April 2005.

B. T. Tomlin. On the value of mitigation and contingency strategies for managing supply chain disruption risks. *Management Science*, 52(5):639–657, 2006.

H. Topaloglu. A tighter variant of Jensen's lower bound for stochastic programs and separable approximations to recourse functions. *European Journal of Operational Research*, 199 (2):315–322, 2009.

K. Train. A validation test of a disaggregate mode choice model. *Transportation Research*, 12:167–174, 1978.

K. Train, D. McFadden, and M. Ben-Akiva. The demand for local telephone service: A fully discrete model of residential calling patterns and service choices. *Rand Journal of Economics*, 18(1):109–123, 1987.

K. E. Train. *Discrete Choice Methods with Simulation*. Cambridge University Press, New York, NY, 2nd edition, 2009.

A. A. Tsay. The quantity flexibility contract and supplier-customer incentives. *Management Science*, 45:1339–1358, 1999.

G. L. Vairaktarakis and P. Kouvelis. Incorporation dynamic aspects and uncertainty in 1-median location problems. *Naval Research Logistics*, 46(2):147–168, 1999.

A. J. Vakharia and A. Yenipazarli. Managing supply chain disruptions. *Foundations and Trends in Technology, Information and Operations Management*, 2(4):243–325, 2008.

J. Van Biesebroeck. Complementarities in automobile production. *Journal of Applied Econometrics*, 22(7):1315–1345, 2007.

G. J. van Houtum, K. Inderfurth, and W. Zijm. Materials coordination in stochastic multi-echelon systems. *European Journal of Operational Research*, 95:1–23, 1996.

D. J. Velleman. *How to Prove It: A Structured Approach*. Cambridge University Press, New York, NY, 2nd edition, 2006.

A. Wagelmans, S. V. Hoesel, and A. Kolen. Economic lot sizing: An $O(n \log n)$ algorithm that runs in linear time in the Wagner-Whitin case. *Operations Research*, 40(S1): S145–S156, 1992.

H. M. Wagner and T. M. Whitin. Dynamic version of the economic lot size model. *Management Science*, 5(1):89–96, 1958.

J. R. Weaver and R. L. Church. Computational procedures for location problems on stochastic networks. *Transportation Science*, 17(2):168–180, 1983.

S. Wu, B. Aytac, R. Berger, and C. Armbruster. Managing short life-cycle technology products for Agere systems. *Interfaces*, 36(3):234–247, 2006.

C. A. Yano and H. L. Lee. Lot sizing with random yield: A review. *Operations Research*, 43 (2):311–334, 1995.

W. I. Zangwill. A deterministic multi-period production scheduling model with backlogging. *Management Science*, 13(1):105–119, 1966.

X. Zhang. The impact of forecasting methods on the bullwhip effect. *International Journal of Production Economics*, 88:15–27, 2004.

Y. Zheng. A simple proof for the optimality of (s, S) policies for infinite-horizon inventory problems. *Journal of Applied Probability*, 28:802–810, 1991.

Y.-S. Zheng. On properties of stochastic inventory systems. *Management Science*, 38(1): 87–103, 1992.

Y.-S. Zheng and A. Federgruen. Finding optimal (s, S) policies is about as simple as evaluating a single policy. *Operations Research*, 39(4):654–665, 1991.

P. H. Zipkin. *Foundations of Inventory Management*. Irwin/McGraw-Hill, 2000.

INDEX